Keys to Successful Immigration

THOMAS J. ESPENSHADE
Editor

Keys to Successful Immigration

Implications of the New Jersey Experience

THE URBAN INSTITUTE PRESS
Washington, D.C.

THE URBAN INSTITUTE PRESS
2100 M Street, N.W.
Washington, D.C. 20037

Library of Congress Cataloging in Publication Data

Keys to Successful Immigration: Implications of the New Jersey Experience/
Thomas J. Espenshade, editor.

1. Immigrants—New Jersey.   2. New Jersey—Emigration and immigration.
I. Espenshade, Thomas J.

JV7037.K49   1997   96–49248
325.749—dc21   CIP

ISBN 0-87766-662-8 (paper, alk. paper)
ISBN 0-87766-661-x (cloth, alk. paper)

Urban Institute books are printed on acid-free paper whenever possible.

Printed in the United States of America.

Distributed in North America by:
University Press of America
4720 Boston Way
Lanham, MD 20706

THE URBAN INSTITUTE is a nonprofit policy research and educational organization established in Washington, D.C., in 1968. Its staff investigates the social and economic problems confronting the nation and public and private means to alleviate them. The Institute disseminates significant findings of its research through the publications program of its Press. The goals of the Institute are to sharpen thinking about societal problems and efforts to solve them, improve government decisions and performance, and increase citizen awareness of important policy choices.

Through work that ranges from broad conceptual studies to administrative and technical assistance, Institute researchers contribute to the stock of knowledge available to guide decision making in the public interest.

Conclusions or opinions expressed in Institute publications are those of the authors and do not necessarily reflect the views of staff members, officers or trustees of the Institute, advisory groups, or any organizations that provide financial support to the Institute.

ACKNOWLEDGMENTS

This volume represents the culmination of a project to study the impacts of immigration in New Jersey. The project produced an earlier book, *A Stone's Throw From Ellis Island* (1994), along with numerous journal articles, chapters in books, and papers presented at professional meetings. I am grateful first of all for the financial support provided by the Andrew W. Mellon Foundation and to Stephanie Bell-Rose at the Foundation for her uncommon vision, encouragement, and wise counsel. Herb Abelson and Cynthia Harper at Princeton University's Survey Research Center, and Max Larsen and Jennifer Spielvogel at The Gallup Organization, helped to structure the collection of the public opinion data reported in chapter 4 of this volume. Library, computing, and other administrative core support services were provided by Maryann Belanger, Germán Rodríguez, Kathy Niebo, Wayne Appleton, and Melanie Adams from a Population Research Center Grant from the National Institute of Child Health and Human Development to the Office of Population Research at Princeton University. Numerous individuals in New Jersey State Government, including Pamela Espenshade, Gerald Dowgin, Geraldine Weltman, and Wayne Bockelman, shared their time and expertise with project staff. Helpful feedback on portions of the research was also received from members of the National Research Council's Panel on the Demographic and Economic Impacts of Immigration. Jeffrey Passel, Director of the Urban Institute's Program for Research on Immigration Policy, facilitated the writing of chapter 3. Finally, I am grateful to Molly Ruzicka for her superb editing and to two anonymous referees who provided constructive comments on an earlier draft of the manuscript.

Thomas J. Espenshade
Princeton University
November 1996

TABLE OF CONTENTS

Figures

FOREWORD

The Urban Institute has been studying immigration for almost a decade and a half. In recent years, the Institute's focus has widened to include immigrant integration. Unlike immigration policy, which is a federal responsibility, policies regarding immigrant integration have been left in the hands of states and localities and vary widely by region.

Keys to Successful Immigration: Implications of the New Jersey Experience focuses on the 1980–1990 experience of a high-immigration state whose immigrant population matches the race and ethnic composition of the U.S. population as a whole more closely than any other state.

New Jersey's experience provides evidence of what it takes for a state to manage a relatively smooth transition of its immigrant population into the economic, social, and political mainstream. One important point to emphasize is that the New Jersey economy performed well during the decade of the 1980s, with lower unemployment rates and business failure rates than in the country as a whole. Obviously many factors contribute to the relative success of immigrant integration in a particular area. But it is certainly plausible that the more favorable economic climate helped the economic fortunes of immigrants in New Jersey and also influenced the attitudes of New Jersey natives to entering immigrants. This, in turn, suggests that continuing federal efforts to pursue vigorous long-term macroeconomic growth could contribute substantially to the success of state and local immigrant integration efforts.

As Thomas Espenshade, the volume editor, puts it, "New Jersey's experience with immigration is not necessarily typical of outcomes in other high-immigration states, but it may be replicable on a broader scale. As a new century approaches and as debate over immigration legislation reaches a fever pitch, it is important to analyze, in the fashion of this volume, instances of successful immigration that can serve as examples for other states, the United States as a whole, and possibly other nations as well."

William Gorham
President

Chapter One

NEW JERSEY IN COMPARATIVE PERSPECTIVE

Thomas J. Espenshade

In the closing years of the 20th century, immigration to the United States has acquired a demographic and public policy significance not seen since the early decades of the 1900s. An estimated 23 million foreign-born individuals were living in the United States in 1995, comprising 8.8 percent of the U.S. population (Hansen 1996). The number of such persons is at an all-time high, and the percentage of foreign born is at its greatest level since World War II. From the latter part of the 19th century until about 1920, however, it was commonplace for the proportion of foreign born to range between 13 and 15 percent of the total population (Fix and Passel 1994). Nearly one-quarter of all foreign-born U.S. residents came to the United States between 1990 and 1995, and another 35 percent arrived during the 1980s (Hansen 1996). In all, immigration accounted for 28 percent of U.S. population growth in the five years following 1990 (Hansen and Bachu 1995).

Immigration also promises to be important to the country's future population. The latest U.S. population projections anticipate that, under "middle-series" assumptions for fertility, mortality, and net immigration, the population will grow by 58 percent between 1990 and 2050—from 249 million to 394 million (Day 1996). If net immigration takes a "low" value of 300,000 per year instead of a "middle" value of 820,000 and fertility and mortality are constant at middle values, total population is projected to reach 351 million by 2050—an increase of 41 percent over 1990. Total population size by the year 2050 under the "high" net immigration scenario (1.4 million per year) will be 76 percent above the 1990 level (438 million versus 249 million). The future racial and ethnic composition of the population is also sensitive to immigration levels. Higher immigration produces larger proportions of Latinos and Asians and smaller proportions of non-Hispanic blacks and, especially, non-Hispanic whites.

Owing partly to its magnitude, U.S. immigration has become an increasingly contentious and divisive issue. Public opinion polls that track the proportion of American adults who think the level of immigration to the United States should be reduced show that the prevalence of such responses rose swiftly after 1965, surpassing 60 percent in the early 1980s and again in the mid-1990s (Espenshade and Hempstead 1996). The U.S. Congress passed reforms supported by most Americans to strengthen current efforts at slowing undocumented immigration into the country, but it has enacted more controversial provisions to restrict public benefits for legal immigrants and considered permitting states to deny public education to undocumented immigrant school children (State and Local Coalition on Immigration 1996a, b). Moreover, books with such ominous titles as *The Immigration Time Bomb: The Fragmenting of America* (Lamm and Imhoff 1985), *Peaceful Invasions: Immigration and Changing America* (Bouvier 1991b), *Threatened Peoples, Threatened Borders: World Migration and U.S. Policy* (Teitelbaum and Weiner 1995), and *Alien Nation: Common Sense about America's Immigration Disaster* (Brimelow 1995) are appearing with greater frequency in the immigration literature. All indications suggest that immigration is posing significant challenges to the comfort and certitude of the status quo and that the transition to a new demographic regime in the United States is undergoing a turbulent period.

THE STATE PERSPECTIVE

Immigration is a national issue in the sense that only the federal government is empowered to set immigration policy. Correspondingly, much of what we know about the nature and consequences of U.S. immigration trends comes from studies of the national immigration picture (Kritz 1983; Borjas and Tienda 1985; Greenwood and McDowell 1986; Bean and Tienda 1988; Jensen 1989; Simon 1989; Borjas 1990; Jasso and Rosenzweig 1990; Portes and Rumbaut 1990; Abowd and Freeman 1991; Borjas and Freeman 1992; Briggs 1992; Simon and Alexander 1993; Borjas 1994; Cornelius, Martin, and Hollifield 1994; Fix and Passel 1994; Heer 1996; Isbister 1996).

At the same time, because immigrants are unevenly distributed throughout the United States, the consequences of immigration are channeled toward states and localities where international migrants are concentrated. For example, during 1994 six states (Arizona, California, Florida, New Jersey, New York, and Texas) filed separate suits in federal district courts to recover costs of services to illegal immigrants that states claim they sustained because of the federal government's failure to enforce U.S. immigration policy. And in a dramatic move to rescue their fiscal destinies, voters in California set out to establish their own standards for undocumented migrants' eligibility for public services by approving the ballot initiative known as Proposition 187 by a 3 to 2 margin in November 1994 (Espenshade 1996).

These developments point to the need to examine the implications of U.S. immigration at the subnational level. Information is needed on how immigrants affect the size and composition of state populations, on migrants' labor-market and other institutional impacts, and on immigrants' progress in being incorporated into the mainstream of American life. No single state's experience is necessarily representative of the national situation. However, by taking a case-study approach and systematically examining the consequences of national immigration trends in a variety of high-impact areas, one may expect that a reliable and more textured picture will emerge of the implications of immigration for the entire United States.

Surprisingly little convincing empirical work has focused on these regional impacts. However, one thing is certain; there is bound to be substantial variation in outcomes depending upon where and when one looks. California has for obvious reasons received more attention than any other state (Bouvier 1991a; Bouvier and Martin 1985; Martin and Taylor 1988; McCarthy and Valdez 1986; Muller and Espenshade 1985); but studies of the consequences of immigration, or more generally of population change that take immigration into account, exist also for Texas (Bouvier and Poston 1993; Marshall and Bouvier 1986), Florida (Bouvier and Weller 1992), and New York (Bouvier and Briggs 1988). In addition, cities serving as ports of entry for immigrants have been examined, including Los Angeles (Heer 1990; Light and Bonacich 1988; Waldinger and Bozorgmehr 1996), New York (Foner 1987; Papademetriou and DiMarzio 1986; Waldinger 1986; Winnick 1990), Miami (Grenier and Stepick 1992; Loveless et al. 1996; Portes and Stepick 1993), and Boston (Halter 1995; O'Connor 1995).[1] Nevertheless, these studies have only scratched the surface of a thorough and comprehensive inquiry into how state and local areas are affected by immigration.

WHY NEW JERSEY?

Many people think of California, New York, Florida, and Texas when considering states with large numbers of immigrants. But New Jersey

Table 1.1 NUMBER OF FOREIGN BORN, PROPORTION FOREIGN BORN IN TOTAL
POPULATION, AND DIVERSITY OF FOREIGN-BORN POPULATION: SIX
STATES AND UNITED STATES, 1980 AND 1990

a. Size of Foreign-Born Population (in thousands)

Area	1990		1980	
	Size	Rank	Size	Rank
California	6,459	1	3,580	1
New York	2,852	2	2,389	2
Florida	1,663	3	1,059	3
Texas	1,524	4	856	4
New Jersey	967	5	758	6
Illinois	952	6	824	5
United States	19,767		14,080	

b. Proportion Foreign Born in Total Population

Area	1990		1980	
	Percentage	Rank	Percentage	Rank
California	21.7	1	15.1	1
New York	15.9	2	13.6	2
Florida	12.9	3	10.9	3
New Jersey	12.5	4	10.3	4
Texas	9.0	5	6.0	6
Illinois	8.3	6	7.2	5
United States	7.9		6.2	

is also an important state for immigration. In the 1990 U.S. Census
New Jersey ranked fifth among all major immigration states in the
total number of foreign-born persons, fourth in the proportion of foreign born, and first in the nation in the diversity of its immigrant
population (see table 1.1 for details).[2] Between 1980 and 1990, New
Jersey's immigrant population became more diverse, whereas the distribution of the foreign born in Illinois, California, Texas, and the
entire United States grew more concentrated around one or two nationalities. Individuals who emigrated from Italy were the largest foreign-born group in New Jersey in 1990, accounting for 7.3 percent of
all non-natives, followed by Cuba (6.5 percent), India (5.4 percent),
Germany (4.4 percent), and Colombia (4.2 percent).

By March 1995 the number of foreign-born persons living in the
United States had grown to almost 23 million, while the heterogeneity
of this population continued its 1980–90 slide to a diversity index of
65.5. Mexicans accounted for 29.3 percent of all non-U.S. nationals,

Table 1.1 (continued)

c. Diversity of Foreign-Born Population

	1990		1980	
Area	Score[a]	Rank	Score[a]	Rank
New Jersey	86.2	1	77.8	2
New York	84.8	2	82.5	1
Florida	65.1	3	58.8	4
Illinois	62.0	4	71.8	3
California	54.2	5	57.7	5
Texas	37.0	6	37.8	6
United States	73.6		78.3	

Sources: Lapham (1993a, b).
a. Diversity score is percentage of each area's total foreign-born population including all but the two largest nationalities. For each region, the two largest foreign-born populations and their percentage of all foreign born in 1990 are as follows:

New Jersey—Italy (7.3), Cuba (6.5)
New York—Dominican Republic (8.5), Italy (6.7)
Florida—Cuba (29.9), Haiti (5.0)
Illinois—Mexico (29.6), Poland (8.5)
California—Mexico (38.3), Philippines (7.5)
Texas—Mexico (59.5), Vietnam (3.5)
United States—Mexico (21.7), Philippines (4.6)

For 1980, the corresponding numbers are:
New Jersey—Italy (13.2), Cuba (9.0)
New York—Italy (11.9), Germany (5.7)
Florida—Cuba (34.6), Canada (6.7)
Illinois—Mexico (20.4), Poland (7.8)
California—Mexico (35.7), Philippines (6.6)
Texas—Mexico (58.2), Germany (4.0)
United States—Mexico (15.6), Germany (6.0)

followed by Filipinos at just 5.2 percent (Hansen 1996). In New Jersey the foreign-born population rose above 1 million and represented 13.4 percent of the state's population. New Jersey continued to lead the nation in diversity of new immigrants (U.S. Immigration and Naturalization Service 1996). At the top of the list of individuals who received permanent resident visas in fiscal year (FY) 1995 and who said they intended to reside in New Jersey were immigrants from the Dominican Republic, followed by India, the Philippines, Colombia, and Poland. No one group garnered more than a 10 percent share, however, and the top 10 countries accounted for barely more than one-half (52 percent) of New Jersey's total number of immigrants. By contrast, 21 percent of the FY 1995 legal immigrants in California were from Mexico, and another 14 percent originated in the Philippines. The 10 most prominent countries were responsible for 68 percent of California's total. In Texas, three-quarters of legal immigrants in 1995 came from just 10 countries, and new visas to persons from Mexico alone were 46 percent of the total.

New Jersey is a logical choice for a comprehensive state study of the impact of immigration for other reasons as well. First, it has received remarkably little serious study in the past. The most recent effort is one I coordinated (Espenshade 1994), which is based mainly on 1980 Census data and looks primarily at economic issues such as the impacts of immigrants on the labor-market opportunities of native workers and the costs that immigrants impose on other taxpayers. Second, the racial and ethnic composition of the U.S. population is matched more closely by New Jersey than by any other state (U.S. House of Representatives 1994). Although this does not mean that one can generalize from New Jersey's experience with immigrants, it does confer a special status on the state and suggests that New Jersey is fertile ground for examining the implications of U.S. immigration. Finally, as this volume indicates, New Jersey may be an example of immigrant exceptionalism. The impacts of immigration in New Jersey appear generally less negative and more positive than they do in the country as a whole.

OVERVIEW OF MAJOR FINDINGS

This book is about New Jersey's recent immigration experience—the demographic context for immigration, the impacts that immigrants are having on New Jersey's native population and its institutions, and the processes of immigrants' adaptation to life in a new host society. The volume's contributing authors describe these effects in economic and noneconomic contexts, pointing out similarities and dissimilarities elsewhere in the country. In examining processes of immigrant adjustment, the volume addresses such questions as how immigrants themselves are faring and whether they are being incorporated into American society. Behind these issues lies a broad assimilation/adaptation hypothesis that this volume's authors explore from a variety of perspectives.

The results of this inquiry support the conclusion that immigrants in New Jersey are managing a relatively smooth transition into the economic, social, and political mainstream. New Jersey has not opted for California-style Proposition 187 legislation, nor is there a grass-roots movement in favor of it. There are 21 "English-as-the-official-language" states in the United States, and 9 other states have "official English" legislation pending, but New Jersey is not one of them despite its substantial foreign-born proportion. Governor Christine Todd Whitman gave a cool reception to U.S. congressional proposals that would have permitted states to ban illegal immigrant children from public schools. Finally, New Jerseyans have a more tolerant attitude toward U.S. immigrants than residents of most other states.

This volume also offers clues as to why immigration is apparently more successful in New Jersey than in some other places. These clues revolve around the high level of education and diversity of New Jersey's immigrant population. Foreign-born individuals in New Jersey are better educated and, as already noted, are more heterogeneous than immigrants nationwide. Moreover, illegal immigrants are a relatively insignificant component of New Jersey's overall foreign-born population. This, too, makes a difference in how immigrants are perceived and treated. The remainder of this section provides an overview of significant findings from the individual chapters as well as major themes that the authors develop. Results are described in three parts corresponding to the main sections of the volume: (1) the demographic context to immigration, (2) economic and noneconomic impacts, and (3) the process of immigrant adjustment in New Jersey.

Demographic Context

Bruce Western and Erin Kelly strike several themes in chapter 2. One is diversity. New Jersey's foreign-born population became more diverse between 1980 and 1990. Europeans constituted a majority in 1980 but fell to 38 percent by 1990. Italians and Cubans, who ranked number one and two, respectively, in both 1980 and 1990, were each smaller shares of all foreign individuals at the end of the decade. New Jersey's proportions of European and Asian immigrants converged on the national pattern, but there was a widening gap as far as immigrants from Latin America are concerned. If Mexicans are excluded, New Jersey had larger proportions of Latino migrants than the United States in 1980 and again in 1990, and the gap widened during the decade. But the proportions reverse when Mexican immigrants are included; the United States has a proportionately larger Latin American foreign-born population than New Jersey, and the gap grew during the 1980s. Put differently, the Mexican-origin population in New Jersey is small (less than 2 percent of all foreign born in 1990), whereas more than

20 percent of the U.S. foreign-born population in 1990 was born in Mexico—up from one-sixth in 1980. Western and Kelly refer to the "near absence of Mexican immigrants in New Jersey" and argue that port of entry still seems to be important in explaining the geographic distribution of Mexican nationals in the United States. In contrast to New Jersey, the U.S. foreign-born population is becoming less diverse and is being represented by growing fractions of Mexican immigrants.

New Jersey's immigrant population is also becoming more diverse spatially. Though still concentrated in the northeastern part of the state, the foreign born spread west and south during the 1980s. A similar trend toward decentralization is beginning to emerge among the foreign born nationwide. Between FY 1994 and 1995 the share of new legal immigrants intending to settle in California fell from 26 percent to 23 percent. Declining shares were also noted in other major immigration states such as New York, Texas, and Illinois. On the other hand, significant increases were observed in Florida, along with Michigan, Virginia, and Georgia (U.S. Immigration and Naturalization Service 1996).

A second theme relates to region-specific similarities between New Jersey and the United States. When the foreign born are disaggregated by region of origin (Europe, Asia, Latin America, and other), there are strong similarities between New Jersey and the United States with respect to the proportion naturalized (except for Latinos, where the percentages are higher in New Jersey, owing to a larger Cuban and a smaller Mexican community), period of entry, age at census and, by implication, age at entry to the United States. Along these dimensions, overall differences between New Jersey and the United States are due primarily to differences in the composition of the foreign born by region of origin. For example, New Jersey has higher citizenship proportions among its immigrant population than the United States does because of a relatively larger number of European immigrants who have been in the country for a longer period.

Finally, New Jersey's immigrant population has a generally higher level of educational attainment than immigrants nationwide. In contrast to the patterns described in the previous paragraph, however, the educational advantage of New Jersey's foreign born is maintained among every origin group (Asians, Latinos, and others) except for Europeans. The education gap is particularly striking for the Asian population. Because New Jersey's rising proportion of Asian immigrants has almost reached parity with U.S. proportions and because Europeans are a declining share of the immigrant population in New Jersey and the United States, New Jersey's foreign-born population is likely to enjoy a widening educational advantage over the U.S. foreign born. This trend may be accelerated by the rapidly rising national prominence of Mexican migrants, whose educational backgrounds are frequently inferior to those of other immigrant groups (Vernez and Abrahamse 1996). Partially countering this trend is the fact that inequality in educational attainment across immigrant groups declined between 1980 and 1990, both in New Jersey and throughout the country.

In closing their chapter, Western and Kelly speculate that New Jersey's experience with immigrants may be exceptional and that the state might not be faced with a declining relative quality of immigrants in the Borjas (1995) sense. They postulate that New Jersey's Asian and Latin American immigrant populations may be positively selected and have higher ability or initiative than their counterparts who settle closer to their customary ports of entry.

Rebecca L. Clark and Wendy N. Zimmermann, in chapter 3, present data on New Jersey's undocumented immigrant population. Although New Jersey is one of seven states that together contained 86 percent of an estimated 3.4 million undocumented migrants in the United States in 1992, New Jersey ranked sixth with 116,000 illegal immigrants—just 1.5 percent of the state's total population. Compared with California and the rest of the United States, New Jersey's undocumented aliens are a small fraction of all foreign-born individuals, they represent a geographically diverse population, and they consist mostly of persons who overstayed their visas. The fiscal impacts of New Jersey's illegal aliens are comparatively modest. Whereas New Jersey contained 4 percent of all illegals in the seven-state total, it had a significantly smaller share of the illegals who were incarcerated in state prisons and of undocumented aliens in public schools. At the same time, undocumented immigrants in New Jersey paid nearly 7 percent of the seven-state total of state sales tax, income tax, and state and local property tax. Finally, New Jersey's public policy response to illegal immigration has been more muted than elsewhere. Several new initiatives to reduce the impact of undocumented migrants have been proposed by the New Jersey Legislature, but none has so far been approved. In short, the fact that a disproportionately large fraction of the state's immigrants are legal residents is possibly another key to successful immigration in New Jersey. Illegal immigration is a relatively inconspicuous issue, and it has not aroused the passions of the electorate the way it has in other states.

How do New Jersey residents feel about the presence of immigrants in the state? Some answers are provided by my analysis in chapter 4 of a public opinion poll taken in September 1994. These results are a further indicator that immigration to New Jersey is proceeding smoothly. Fewer than 3 percent of New Jersey adults think the number of immigrants in the state should be increased, slightly more than one-half believe the current number is acceptable, and roughly 40 percent prefer a reduction. However, New Jersey residents have more liberal attitudes about immigration than respondents nationwide, nearly two-thirds of whom think the level of U.S. immigration should be decreased. New Jerseyans who prefer fewer immigrants cite concerns about the number of available jobs, about the state already being overcrowded, as well as fears over higher taxes. Judged in relation to other issues facing the state, immigration is not a pressing cause for concern. It is roughly equivalent in importance to taxes, is less important than crime, but is more salient than jobs.

Many of the individual-level determinants of respondent attitudes appear to have the same effects in New Jersey as they do in national samples. Better-educated, employed, minority (including African American), and foreign-born respondents are more likely to prefer the same or a higher number of immigrants. On the other hand, Catholics, residents of fast-growing counties, and the native-born children of immigrants are more prone to prefer a substantial reduction. The effect of rapid population growth on attitudes advances our understanding of why residents of southern and western states have some of the most restrictionist immigration attitudes (Espenshade and Hempstead 1996). The New Jersey experience suggests that people may not be responding to immigrants per se, but, rather, to excessive population growth that brings more congestion and less open space. Finally, the way New Jersey residents assess the consequences of immigration also affects their attitudes. For instance, perceptions that immigrants compete for jobs and lower the wages of native workers in New Jersey are correlated with a tendency to want fewer immigrants. So, too, are concerns that immigrants are likely to end up on welfare, exert a fiscal burden on other taxpayers, and represent a threat to the primacy of spoken and written English.

Impacts of Immigration

Most previous analyses of the impacts of U.S. immigration have focused on one of two kinds of economic effects. The labor-market impacts of immigrants have received the most attention. How do increased supplies of foreign workers in domestic labor markets affect the earnings and employment opportunities of native workers? A well-established conclusion, based largely on cross-sectional data, is that there are only "modest effects of immigrants on natives' labor market outcomes" (Friedberg and Hunt 1995: 35). Researchers are just beginning to hint at the possibility that some natives are indeed displaced by foreign workers. If these native workers move out of high-immigrant-impact areas to labor markets where their economic prospects are improved, cross-sectional studies may fail to detect negative effects on wages and employment (Filer 1992; Frey 1995; Manson, Espenshade, and Muller 1985; White and Hunter 1993).

A second economic effect concerns the fiscal impacts of immigrants. How much do immigrants pay in taxes to federal, state, and local governments; how large are the benefits immigrants receive in return; and how do these benefits and taxes compare at different levels of government? Using census data, Borjas (1994) found that immigrants were slightly less likely than natives to receive cash welfare benefits in 1970, but that immigrant households were overrepresented among the welfare population by 1990. A larger native-immigrant differential emerges when other noncash programs are included (Borjas and Hilton 1996). Less attention has been paid to estimating immigrants' net fiscal costs. Fix and Passel (1994) have argued that immigrants generate a substantial net surplus for other taxpayers. These effects are not evenly distributed, however, across all levels of government. Immigrant households appear to be a fiscal asset only for the federal government. Revenues and expenditures are more or less offsetting for state governments, and it is typically at the local level where immigrants represent the greatest fiscal burden (Rothman and Espenshade 1992). Chapters in this volume investigate these economic impacts, but they consider a broader variety of social and political implications as well.

In chapter 5, Kristin F. Butcher and Anne Morrison Piehl focus on changes during the 1980s in gaps in wages and employment between seven demographic and skill groups and a reference group of native-born white non-Hispanic male workers. They find no evidence that the fraction of foreign-born workers in state-industry categories is significantly related to these changes and conclude that there are no adverse effects of immigration on the relative wages or employment of the native-born population either in New Jersey or in the country as a whole. These findings for demographic subgroups generally affirm results from previous studies. One notable difference that Butcher and Piehl discover concerns high school dropouts. Nationwide during the 1980s the relative wage gap grew for high school dropouts, but it declined in New Jersey, and the decline was greatest in industries having the highest concentrations of immigrant workers. An individual-level wage analysis corroborates these findings.

Butcher and Piehl also show that changes in the wage distribution in New Jersey in the 1980s did not mirror experience in the rest of the country. The New Jersey distribution became more compressed, whereas there was growing wage inequality throughout the United States. Most New Jersey workers did well compared with their counterparts in other states, but New Jersey's high school dropouts moved up sharply in the U.S. wage distribution. New Jersey's minimum wage was not high in the 1980s and cannot explain why the bottom end of the wage distribution did so well. Butcher and Piehl speculate that a possible reason for the strong economic performance of New Jersey's high school dropouts is related to labor-market complementarities with immigrants. Immigrants in New Jersey have higher skills and higher education, and earn higher wages than dropouts, even though immigrants are low skilled relative to the average native worker. If the authors' reasoning is correct, it suggests in another way that immigrant skill levels are higher in New Jersey than in the remainder of the United States.

In chapter 6, Deborah L. Garvey and I examine the fiscal impacts of immigrant-headed households and compare them against the fiscal effects of households headed by native-born individuals. There are four principal findings. First, the typical New Jersey household, regardless of nativity, uses more services at both the state and local levels than it pays for with taxes. Taxes paid by the corporate sector and monies passed back to the state from the federal government make up the deficit. Second, households headed by immigrants are usually a larger fiscal burden than households with a native-born head. Third, the relatively greater fiscal burden associated with immigrant households is more pronounced for local governments than for the state. And fourth, there is greater diversity within the foreign population when this group is disaggregated by the region of origin of the household head than there is overall between the native and foreign-born population.

These results are generally consistent with other fiscal impact studies showing that the tax and expenditure consequences of immigrants are more negative for localities than for state governments. But this research extends earlier findings and puts them on a firmer footing by comparing immigrants and natives, by examining net fiscal implications, and by basing the estimates on individual household data. Garvey and I also pick up on the themes of diversity and education. A regression analysis shows that nativity turns out not to matter

(except for Latinos) once age, education, marital status, English proficiency, place of residence, and number of children are taken into
account. This suggests that the primary determinants of a household's
fiscal effects are income, family size and composition, and where a
household lives. It also suggests that immigrant households in New
Jersey have more benign fiscal consequences than they otherwise
would if immigrants were not so well educated, a finding partially
anticipated in Clark and Zimmermann's work in chapter 3 on fiscal
impacts of undocumented migrants.

Linguistic diversity among the immigrant population is another
aspect of diversity. It is studied in chapter 7 by Ana María Villegas
and John W. Young in the context of immigrant children who place an
added burden on public schools if they have an inadequate compre-
hension of English. In the early 1990s New Jersey had approximately
60,000 immigrant school-age children who represented a wide variety
of immigrant backgrounds, socioeconomic circumstances, and
mother tongues. Although Spanish is the most common language used
by immigrant school children in New Jersey, limited-English-proficient (LEP) students speak more than 100 different native languages.
Federal and state governments have responded with a patchwork of
programs, including English-as-a-second-language and bilingual education, but there is no coherent or comprehensive immigrant education policy that addresses the holistic needs of immigrant students.
Problems in New Jersey are compounded by the presence of large
numbers of Puerto Rican children who are not immigrants but have
many of the same schooling needs as immigrants, including learning
English and adapting to a new culture. The challenges posed by Villegas and Young imply that education and diversity, positive aspects
of which are discussed in other chapters, can have their downsides if
not dealt with creatively.

In chapter 8, Nancy E. Reichman and Genevieve M. Kenney investigate the determinants of low birthweight for children born to Hispanic women in New Jersey. The effects of prenatal care usage and
the mother's nativity and ethnicity are studied along with other factors. This issue is important because low birthweight has been associated with numerous adverse child development outcomes. Results
for New Jersey parallel national findings in two respects. First, New
Jersey data support a "Mexican paradox"; the children of Mexican
women have higher birthweights than expected given the low social
and economic status of their mothers. In addition, ethnic differentials
within the Latino population are consistent with national patterns.
Puerto Rican women in New Jersey have the least prenatal care and

the highest proportion of low birthweight babies, whereas Cuban women have the most favorable birth outcomes. The absence of a nativity differential in New Jersey is the major exception to the U.S. picture. Nationwide, especially among those of Mexican descent, U.S.-born women are at higher risk of adverse birth outcomes than the foreign born (Rumbaut and Weeks 1996).

The Reichman-Kenney chapter draws attention once again to the role of education, which is significantly related to a greater chance of receiving some prenatal care, of receiving it during the first trimester, and of having heavier babies. The authors' multivariate analysis confirms that, for whites especially, Puerto Rican women have the poorest prenatal care and experience the worst birth outcomes among all Hispanic women. However, non-Hispanic U.S.-born blacks are the most disadvantaged in terms of the likelihood of receiving no prenatal care and of having low birthweight babies. Neither of these groups is foreign born, however, which suggests that immigration is not a cause for concern where birthweight is the issue. This conclusion is reinforced by the fact that the prevalence of low birthweight babies is lower in New Jersey than in the United States as a whole (5.8 percent versus 6.9 percent, respectively, in 1990).

The focus in chapter 9 turns to politics, with Louis DeSipio's analysis of the political impacts and incorporation of New Jersey's Latino immigrant community. This chapter forms a natural bridge between the volume's emphasis on immigrant impacts and the final section on processes of immigrant adaptation. Despite relatively low overall levels of citizenship compared with other immigrant groups in New Jersey, Latinos exhibit a stronger attachment to the United States than Latinos nationwide, as reflected in naturalization rates and other forms of political participation. New Jersey is helped in this regard by the presence of a large Cuban community, most of whose members are legal and have lived in the United States for an extended time with little prospect of returning home. Mexicans, on the other hand, make up a large fraction of the nation's Latino immigrant population. Partly owing to their sojourner, as opposed to settler, behavior and partly to large proportions who have an illegal status, Mexican migrants have typically displayed weaker political allegiances to the United States.

There are avenues for political participation besides voting. Roughly three-quarters of noncitizen Latinos in New Jersey are engaged in some form of U.S. electoral politics (for example, following politics in the news, writing letters to support a political position, and marching in political rallies). These indications suggest that Latino immigrants are not distanced from U.S. politics and that political incorporation is occurring. Finally, DeSipio argues that Latinos can have an impact on electoral politics even as noncitizens. The census counts all immigrants regardless of citizenship, and their numbers influence the design of electoral districts. For example, in New Jersey's 13th congressional district, which includes Hudson County, one-third of whose population is foreign born, noncitizens and the co-ethnic citizen population combined to create a climate enabling the election to Congress in 1992 of a Latino, Robert Menendez.

Processes of Immigrant Adaptation

Because large numbers of new immigrants are admitted for permanent residence in the United States each year, it is important to ask what happens to these individuals after they have entered the country. How well do immigrants subsequently adjust to life in the United States? Are there steps that the host society can take to ease the transition of newcomers and to facilitate the adaptation process? Answering these questions requires greater attention to four issues (Espenshade 1987). First, improved information is needed on the speed of adjustment of different immigrant groups. A comprehensive comparison of disparate immigrant groups' adaptation along economic, social, political, and demographic dimensions is missing. Second, immigrant experiences should be compared in different parts of the United States to determine if immigrant adjustment is a function mainly of immigrants' characteristics and endowments or whether structural characteristics of communities in which immigrants settle play a larger role. Third, historical studies that compare immigrant adaptation at the beginning of the 20th century with contemporary experience are useful to address the perception that many of today's new immigrants are not integrating well. Finally, it is important to begin to identify the facilitators of and barriers to immigrant adaptation and to determine what policy steps may be needed to minimize the obstacles.

Authors of the remaining chapters take a significant step in this direction by examining processes of immigrant adjustment in New Jersey. Issues addressed include fertility patterns among foreign-born women, economic mobility, the move to homeownership, and residential and linguistic segregation. The earlier-mentioned broad assimilation/adaptation hypothesis underlies these issues, where assimilation is used, in Edmonston's (1996: 16) sense, to mean "integration into the social structure on terms of equality." One purpose in reviewing the findings from these remaining chapters is to identify how much evidence New Jersey's experience with immigration provides for the assimilation hypothesis.

Deanna Pagnini, in chapter 10, examines fertility differences between immigrants and natives. She finds that immigrant fertility is about 20 percent higher than fertility among native women. She also finds that time spent living in the United States lowers the fertility of women who immigrated from high-fertility countries, suggesting some evidence for an assimilation story. In particular, place-of-birth effects are important determinants of numbers of children ever born for migrant women who came to the United States as adults. But these effects matter little for women who migrated as children and who have the longest duration of residence in the United States. Further support for an assimilation hypothesis is provided by the fact that acquiring U.S. citizenship and being able to speak English—two independent indicators of political and social incorporation—are correlated with lower fertility among immigrant women who migrated as adults.

At the same time, Pagnini shows that great diversity characterizes the fertility of both foreign- and native-born women when these measures are arrayed by race, ethnicity, and place of birth. This implies that there is not one homogeneous native-born fertility pattern in New Jersey toward which the fertility of immigrant women converges. These findings contrast with some results of analyses based on national samples. Average numbers of children ever born for U.S. women do not differ appreciably between natives and immigrants (Ford 1985), and nativity is not an important predictor of fertility in U.S. samples after other migrant characteristics are controlled (Kahn 1994). On the other hand, national studies usually corroborate results from New Jersey that the fertility of immigrant women becomes more like that of American women and less like that of women in the countries they left behind the longer immigrants reside in the United States (Kahn 1988; Ford 1990).

Chapter 11, by Deborah L. Garvey, tests whether Borjas' (1995) finding of a nationwide decline in the skill mix of immigrants relative to natives also holds in New Jersey. Garvey concludes it does not. Using data from the 1980 and 1990 Censuses to decompose the apparent growth in immigrant earnings observed in a cross section into a within-cohort and an across-cohort component, she shows that one may reject the hypothesis of a secular decline in the so-called quality of immigrants to New Jersey. Evidence suggests that the experience-earnings profiles of immigrants are converging to those of the native born. In brief, New Jersey's immigrants appear to be successfully

assimilating into the local labor market. Most immigrant groups experienced steady within-cohort earnings growth over the decade, a
point observed in chapter 5 by Butcher and Piehl for New Jersey
workers in general. Indeed, estimating this growth from a single cross
section injects little bias. There is even some evidence of a slight
improvement in the skill mix of recent immigrants relative to earlier
cohorts. The New Jersey results for the 1980s contrast sharply with
findings from the rest of the country. For the 1970s, however, New
Jersey and the United States appear more similar; immigrant wage
growth observed in the cross section overstates the wage mobility of
immigrant cohorts. One implication of comparative findings from the
1980s is that studies that rely on national-level data tend to average
over regional variation. Researchers obtain a richer picture from case
studies that expose this variation.

In chapter 12 Nancy McArdle explores the success of New Jersey's
immigrants in achieving homeownership and compares their progress
to natives in New Jersey and to immigrants nationwide. The transition
from renter to owner is viewed as a sign of a more permanent attachment to the United States and as one aspect of assimilation. Roughly
half of all immigrant households in New Jersey and in the United
States are homeowners. Duration of residence in the United States is
strongly related to the probability of homeownership. Data from the
1990 Census suggest that immigrants who arrived prior to 1965 and
Asian migrants who have been in the United States for approximately
20 years have homeownership rates comparable to those of native
whites.

McArdle uses data from successive censuses to track age cohorts
for natives and for immigrants who entered the country during the
1970s. Immigrants, especially Asians but also Latinos, show rapid
growth in tenure proportions and do better than the cross-sectional
data suggest. Although the prevalence of homeownership among Latinos is consistently below Asian levels, immigrants in general in New
Jersey exhibit substantial assimilation into homeownership. For native African Americans the cross section overstates homeownership
progress. Young African Americans today are increasingly likely to be
renters compared with their peers in 1980. Viewed in comparative
perspective, the experience of New Jersey's immigrants in attaining
homeownership is essentially similar to immigrant behaviors elsewhere in the nation.

Most previous research on patterns of residential segregation has
focused on differences among racial and ethnic groups. The work by
Michael J. White and Afaf Omer in chapter 13 is some of the first to

pay attention to the spatial concentration of immigrants. Segregation of the foreign-born population in New Jersey is modest when compared with that for African Americans, Hispanics, and Asians. Only rarely does the index of dissimilarity (D) exceed 30 percent, a figure consistent with the 1980 Census, although both measures are biased down because of the co-residence of immigrant parents and their native-born children. The underlying model that White and Omer test is one of residential assimilation in which new arrivals to an area are geographically clustered, but with the passage of time immigrants adapt, the host society accommodates, and there is greater residential intermingling between the two groups. The analysis provides evidence for this standard model of assimilation. There is a nearly linear inverse association between D measured for immigrant cohorts and duration of residence in the United States. A related vintage model of residential segregation, estimated for the top 25 ethnic groups in New Jersey, offers additional evidence that the degree of spatial concentration is strongly related to period of entry. Two outliers are Puerto Ricans and African Americans, both of whom are more residentially concentrated than their length of time in New Jersey would suggest.

The process of residential assimilation proceeds more slowly than homeownership acquisition. The linear association between D and time of arrival implies a dissimilarity index of approximately zero only for immigrants who came to the United States in the late 19th century. Interpreted differently, the results suggest that complete residential integration does not occur until the second (or, possibly, the third) generation of immigrants. Not only do the results of the chapters on immigrant adaptation provide evidence for an assimilation model, but they also suggest something about the rapidity with which the process occurs. The speed of incorporation depends upon both the immigrant group and the particular dimension of assimilation being investigated. Studies at the national level of English-language acquisition by U.S. immigrants—a process that occurs comparatively quickly—provide additional supporting documentation (Espenshade and Fu forthcoming).

Gillian Stevens and Nancy Garrett take the process of residential segregation one step farther in chapter 14 by considering not only where people live but also what language they speak. Their results offer support for both a linguistic and a residential assimilation model, but the evidence is more circumstantial than in previous chapters. Non-English speakers, especially those with Spanish as their mother tongue, and recent immigrants are concentrated in large non-English neighborhoods in New Jersey. Levels of linguistic segregation are among the highest, however, for new arrivals from Puerto Rico. The analysis suggests that many non-English communities form because of immigration and begin to erode as immigration recedes and migrants move away or shift to English. It also shows that neighborhoods with the largest proportions of recent immigrants or Puerto Rican migrants, non-English speakers whose native tongue is Spanish, and Spanish speakers lacking fluency in English are the most socioeconomically disadvantaged.

Stevens and Garrett's results carry several implications. First, they touch on and help to integrate themes developed in prior chapters, including Garvey and my estimates (chapter 6) showing that fiscal burdens are greatest for immigrants from Latin America, Villegas and Young's analysis in chapter 7 on the diversity of languages in New Jersey, and White and Omer's conclusions in chapter 13 on immigrant patterns of residential segregation. Second, the concentration of non-English speakers and those not fluent in English (especially those having Spanish as a mother tongue) in disadvantaged neighborhoods may limit the progress of migrants and slow their social and economic integration. One particular avenue affects schooling for children. LEP children in greatest need of special help may also be most likely to live in school districts least able to provide it. Third, New Jersey's outcomes may not readily generalize to the rest of the United States because the nature of language communities in other parts of the country may differ from those in New Jersey. Finally, because the data used by Stevens and Garrett do not cross-classify individuals by nativity status and language use, their results sometimes provide an ambiguous message about immigrant assimilation. In other words, some of the socioeconomic disadvantages associated with speaking Spanish may be attributable to New Jersey's Puerto Rican community and not directly to immigrants.

IMPLICATIONS OF THE NEW JERSEY EXPERIENCE

It was argued earlier that no single state's experience with international migration is necessarily representative of the entire United States. Having previewed main findings of the individual chapters, it is relevant to ask whether New Jersey is a mirror for the nation and what lessons the New Jersey experience holds for the rest of the country.

A Mirror for the Nation?

In some respects results from New Jersey parallel those for the United States, but in numerous instances they are different. To summarize the similarities, immigrants appear to have no adverse labor-market impacts on natives; immigrants exert a greater burden on public coffers than natives, especially at the municipal and county levels; great diversity characterizes the varieties of languages spoken by immigrant school children; Puerto Rican women are most disadvantaged and Cubans the most favored among all Latina women in terms of birth outcomes; time in the United States lowers the fertility of immigrant women from high-fertility countries; immigrant levels of residential segregation are low relative to minority racial and ethnic groups; and Asian and Hispanic immigrants make rapid progress toward home-ownership following their arrival in the United States.

Important differences remain, however, between New Jersey and the United States. New Jersey's foreign-born population experienced rapid wage growth during the 1980s, countering national trends of declining relative immigrant quality; greater concentrations of immigrants in local area labor markets had a positive effect on the wages of New Jersey's native-born high school dropouts, suggesting the possibility of labor-market complementarities between the two groups; Latino immigrants in New Jersey exhibited higher rates of citizenship and greater political attachment to the United States than Latinos nationwide; and state-level policies to reduce the presence and impacts of illegal immigrants have been more muted in New Jersey than in other states with a significant undocumented population.

Several factors seem to be responsible for these differences. Immigrants in New Jersey are better educated than immigrants nationwide. The foreign-population is more heterogeneous in terms of countries of origin. For example, in contrast to national trends, Mexicans account for a negligible share of New Jersey's immigrants, and the state's immigrant population is becoming more diverse. Illegal immigration is a relatively unimportant issue in the state. Despite its sizable foreign-born population, New Jersey's undocumented share is below the national average. Finally, income inequality in New Jersey declined during the 1980s, whereas the gap between rich and poor widened throughout the country. In California, the growth in income inequality surpassed national trends (Reed, Haber, and Mameesh 1996). Recent studies by the RAND Corporation suggest that Mexican immigrants' poor educational background and low wages are part of the explanation (Schoeni, McCarthy, and Vernez 1996; Vernez and Abrahamse 1996).

Some of the same causes help to explain why New Jersey attitudes toward immigration are more liberal than those nationwide. Believing that much of immigration is undocumented is an element that creates negative reactions to it (Espenshade and Belanger 1996; Espenshade and Hempstead 1996). The general public's understanding of illegal immigration is formed from televised images on the nightly news of Mexican migrants clandestinely crossing the southern U.S. border. These pictures do not resonate with the experience of most New Jersey residents. New Jersey is far removed from the U.S.–Mexico border, undocumented migrants are a below-average fraction of all New Jersey immigrants, Mexicans represent just 3 percent of all undocumented migrants in New Jersey (versus more than one-half in California and nearly 40 percent nationwide), and the majority of illegal immigrants in the state are of the less-obvious type—that is, people who came legally and then overstayed their visas as opposed to those who entered the country illegally in the first place. It is hardly surprising that just one-third of New Jersey residents believe that most recent immigrants are in the United States illegally, compared with two-thirds of respondents in national polls.

Another reason for New Jersey's relatively more liberal attitudes on immigration could be that the East Coast has a longer immigration tradition than other parts of the country. Where immigration is less of a novelty, it may be considered a smaller disruption to the status quo. In addition, having immigrants in New Jersey who are better educated than their counterparts nationwide may lead people to perceive immigrants as less likely to be a problem and more likely to make a contribution. Finally, the diversity of New Jersey's immigrant population probably helps to create more tolerant attitudes. Diversity makes it difficult to stereotype immigrants. More important, we know from national public opinion data that there is a preferential ordering among immigrants such that Europeans are ranked highest, then those from Asia, and finally migrants from Latin America (Espenshade and Belanger 1996). New Jersey has a disproportionately large fraction of the most favored groups. To the extent that these national sentiments are shared by New Jerseyans, this may help to explain the state's comparatively greater tolerance for immigrants.

A further implication of the New Jersey experience is that American attitudes toward immigration would be more accepting if people were better informed about immigration issues. The majority of U.S. residents feel that most recent immigrants are in the country illegally. But the data suggest otherwise. Evidence from Clark and Zimmermann (chapter 3) indicates that illegals comprise roughly one-sixth of the U.S. foreign-born population. Moreover, more than one-third of U.S. respondents believe that immigrants take jobs away from native workers. But the data do not support this view either. Because the perceptions that most recent immigrants are illegal and that immigrants adversely affect the labor-market opportunities of natives are associated with a stronger preference for fewer immigrants, tolerance toward immigrants would increase and fewer individuals would hold restrictionist attitudes if these views were aligned with reality.

Can the New Jersey Experience Be Replicated?

New Jersey is part of the U.S. experience, but also stands apart from it. Where there are differences, immigrants in New Jersey have generally been more successful than immigrants in the rest of the country. This raises the question of whether the New Jersey experience is replicable in other parts of the United States. The lessons from New Jersey suggest that much will depend on the federal government's response to immigration policy and on its ability to create immigrant streams that are diverse, well educated, and reside legally in the United States.

As noted earlier, the foreign-born population throughout the United States is becoming less diverse, with the proportion of Mexican nationals approaching 30 percent. One way that U.S. immigration policy has sought to create a more heterogeneous foreign population is through the diversity programs of the Immigration Act of 1990 (IMMACT). Under this program, additional visas are made available to residents of countries adversely affected by the 1965 Amendments to the Immigration and Nationality Act (U.S. Immigration and Naturalization Service 1996). Beginning in 1995 with the transition to the permanent diversity program, a total of 55,000 diversity visas were available, with a limit of 3,850 per country. Because nationals from countries with more than 50,000 numerically limited admissions during the preceding five years are precluded from participation, residents of Europe and Africa have been the primary beneficiaries. In FY 1995, permanent U.S. residents admitted under diversity programs totaled more than 47,000, or 6.6 percent of all new lawful entrants. The leading countries of admission included Poland (3,600), Ethiopia (3,100), Nigeria (2,400), Egypt (2,200), and Romania (2,000). Partially as a result of IMMACT's diversity programs, Europe's share among all new legal immigrants rose from 10.4 percent in FY 1985–88 to 17.8 percent in FY 1995, and Africa's total increased from 2.9 percent to 5.9 percent (U.S. Immigration and Naturalization Service 1991, 1996).

IMMACT also attempted to upgrade the educational attainment of new U.S. immigrants by placing greater emphasis on skilled workers. The annual limit on employment-based immigration was raised from 54,000 in 1991 to a minimum of 140,000 beginning in 1992. In addition, IMMACT allocated a higher proportion of these visas to highly skilled immigrants and their family members—more than three-quarters starting in 1992, up from 50 percent in 1991. Many of the skilled-worker visas are going unused, however. Employment-based immigration declined from 123,000 in 1994 to 85,000 in 1995, although there continues to be a backlog for unskilled workers (U.S. Immigration and Naturalization Service 1996). It is worthwhile considering whether education could be made a more explicit criterion for permanent residence and whether this criterion should be extended to include not only employment-based immigration but also family-sponsored migrants. One way to accomplish this aim would be through a point system similar to those now employed in several other countries (Papademetriou and Yale-Loehr 1996). Points could be allotted for years of schooling and other desirable migrant traits, and immigrants could then be selected on the basis of cumulative point totals. Such a system was briefly considered but then rejected by the U.S. Congress in the 1980s.

Ensuring that foreign-born individuals living in the United States are here legally is now being given high priority by the Congress. President Clinton signed a bill at the end of September 1996 that will nearly double the number of border patrol agents and investigators, increase penalties for alien smuggling and document fraud, and establish voluntary pilot programs incorporating new technologies for employers to ensure they are hiring only legal workers (Branigin 1996). Beefing up the border patrol does not address the problem of people who come to the United States legally on temporary visas and then remain after their visas have expired. Such individuals may comprise half of all undocumented migrants (Fix and Passel 1994). Others have suggested that temporary migrants could be required to post a bond of several hundred dollars before an overseas consulate issued their nonimmigrant visas. Aliens who violated the terms of their visas would forfeit the bond to the U.S. government (Harwood 1985). Whether these measures will be effective in curbing the number of undocumented U.S. migrants is unknown, but it is clear that the

American public's willingness to support continued levels of legal immigration depends upon the federal government's ability to bring illegal immigration under control (Espenshade and Belanger 1996).

In addition, although the United States has an explicit immigration policy, it does not have an articulated *immigrant* policy. U.S. immigration policy consists largely of gatekeeping functions of determining who is eligible for entry and who is not. But once immigrants have been admitted for permanent residence, the federal government behaves as though its responsibility to them has ended. The purpose of an immigrant policy is to reduce barriers to immigrant adjustment and to help smooth the transition of new immigrants into U.S. society (Espenshade 1987).

Despite the lack of coordinated efforts, New Jersey's immigrants appear to be assimilating comparatively well. There is evidence that they are adapting along demographic, economic, social, and political dimensions. But perhaps the federal government can and should be doing more. For example, Villegas and Young (chapter 7) call for a comprehensive approach to addressing the multiple barriers immigrant students must overcome—not just language needs but related cultural, psychological, and social barriers that affect the learning process. Moreover, whereas the 1996 enactment of the welfare reform bill puts a premium on legal immigrants becoming citizens to preserve public benefits, there appears to be little in the legislation that reduces obstacles to citizenship. The U.S. Commission on Immigration Reform (1995) has recommended a renewed emphasis on "Americanization" as part of a total package of immigration reforms. Such policies aim to cultivate a shared commitment to enduring American values of liberty, democracy, and equal opportunity. They also encourage naturalization as the path to full civic participation. It would be wholly consistent with the incentives created by enacted welfare reforms if Congress eased the path to citizenship by, for example, reducing the length of the waiting period before legal immigrants are permitted to apply for naturalization (Espenshade 1996).

An unresolved issue concerns the role of New Jersey's economy. How much of New Jersey immigrants' success in economic mobility and other forms of adaptation can be explained not by immigrants' endowments, skills, and other characteristics but by the superior performance of the state's economy compared with the rest of the United States? Could this also partly explain why New Jersey residents appear to have more accepting attitudes toward immigrants than adults nationwide? During the 1970s, New Jersey's economy lagged behind the nation. But beginning in the early 1980s and continuing at least through 1990, both unemployment and business failure rates were lower in the state than in the country as a whole (Dun and Bradstreet, multiple years; New Jersey Department of Labor and Industry, multiple years; U.S. Bureau of the Census, multiple years). We know from Butcher and Piehl (chapter 5) that income inequality diminished in the 1980s in New Jersey, whereas U.S. incomes became more unequal. We also know that people's attitudes toward immigrants are correlated with business cycles, hardening when economic insecurity rises and growing more tolerant when unemployment falls (Espenshade and Hempstead 1996). Whatever role New Jersey's economy played in creating a more positive outlook for immigration in the state, it is clear that economic growth can be an engine for assimilation. Therefore, not only does the New Jersey experience carry implications for U.S. immigration and immigrant policy, but it also places a high priority on continued efforts by the federal government to pursue economic growth with full employment.

Two Futures

Immigrants in New Jersey have received a warmer welcome than they have throughout most of the United States. They have shown signs of strong upward economic mobility during the 1980s, thereby providing a counter-example for claims of a generalized national decline in the relative quality of immigrant cohorts. Immigrant fertility is becoming more like that of native women, and patterns of residential segregation weaken with increased duration of U.S. residence. Latino immigrants are becoming more politically active, and both Asian and Latino immigrants show a relatively rapid trend toward homeownership. Higher densities of immigrants in local labor markets appear to improve the earnings and employment opportunities of high school dropouts. At the same time, New Jersey's policy response to immigration in general, and to illegal immigrants in particular, has been restrained. New Jersey is not an "English-only" state, and its governor is not an outspoken advocate of congressional proposals to permit states to deny public education to illegal immigrant children.

Other parts of the United States are having a different experience with immigration. Numerous states, including some with many immigrants as well as some with few, have English as their official language. Some governors have made a campaign issue out of stopping illegal immigration. Proposition 187 has been given a strong endorsement in California, and its supporters are hoping to pass it elsewhere. New initiatives are underway to make it a crime to sell or rent property to undocumented immigrants. Many of these areas also have a different immigrant profile. The composition of the foreign-born population is more concentrated around one or two nationality groups, immigrants tend to be poorer and less educated, and many migrants are in the United States illegally. In addition, many of these states have recently endured economic hardships greater than those faced by New Jersey.

New Jersey's experience with immigration is not necessarily typical of outcomes in other high-immigration states, but it may be replicable on a broader scale. As a new century approaches and as debate over immigration legislation reaches a fever pitch, it is important to analyze, in the fashion of this volume, instances of successful immigration that can serve as examples for other states, the United States as a whole, and possibly other nations as well.

Notes

Financial support for this research was provided by a grant from the Andrew W. Mellon Foundation. I am grateful to Melanie Adams, Maryann Belanger, Jessica Gurcak, and Emily Niebo for technical and research assistance.

1. This list leaves out numerous studies of the experiences of particular immigrant groups (especially Guatemalans, Brazilians, Salvadorans, Caribbean immigrants, Italians, Soviet and Polish Jews, Chinese, Koreans, and Indonesians) in a given destination (Pittsburgh, San Francisco, Monterey Park [Calif.], Philadelphia, Atlanta, St. Louis, and Washington, D.C., in addition to those cited in the text). Nor does it include the more than two dozen sets of estimates of fiscal impacts of immigrants conducted for selected states, counties, and municipalities. For a review of these fiscal studies, see Rothman and Espenshade (1992) and Vernez and McCarthy (1996).

2. Hawaii has a larger percentage of foreign born than all states except for California— nearly 18 percent in 1995—but the number of foreign born totals just 194,000 (Hansen 1996).

References

Abowd, John M., and Richard B. Freeman, eds. 1991. *Immigration, Trade, and the Labor Market.* Chicago: University of Chicago Press.
Bean, Frank D., and Marta Tienda. 1988. *The Hispanic Population of the United States.* New York: Russell Sage Foundation.

Borjas, George J. 1990. *Friends or Strangers: The Impact of Immigrants on the U.S. Economy.* New York: Basic Books.

_____. 1994. "The Economics of Immigration." *Journal of Economic Literature* 32(4, December): 1667–1717.

_____. 1995. "Assimilation and Changes in Cohort Quality Revisited: What Happened to Immigrant Earnings in the 1980's?" *Journal of Labor Economics* 13(2): 201–45.

Borjas, George J., and Richard B. Freeman, eds. 1992. *Immigration and the Work Force: Economic Consequences for the United States and Source Areas.* Chicago: University of Chicago Press.

Borjas, George J., and Lynette Hilton. 1996. "Immigration and the Welfare State: Immigrant Participation in Means-Tested Entitlement Programs." *Quarterly Journal of Economics* 111(2, May): 575–604.

Borjas, George J., and Marta Tienda, eds. 1985. *Hispanics in the U.S. Economy.* New York: Academic Press.

Bouvier, Leon F. 1991a. *Fifty Million Californians?* Washington, D.C.: Center for Immigration Studies.

_____. 1991b. *Peaceful Invasions: Immigration and Changing America.* Washington, D.C.: Center for Immigration Studies.

Bouvier, Leon F., and Vernon M. Briggs, Jr. 1988. *The Population and Labor Force of New York: 1990 to 2050.* Washington, D.C.: Population Reference Bureau.

Bouvier, Leon F., and Philip Martin. 1985. *Population Change and California's Future.* Washington, D.C.: Population Reference Bureau.

Bouvier, Leon F., and Dudley L. Poston, Jr. 1993. *Thirty Million Texans?* Washington, D.C.: Center for Immigration Studies.

Bouvier, Leon F., and Bob Weller. 1992. *Florida in the 21st Century: The Challenges of Population Growth.* Washington, D.C.: Center for Immigration Studies.

Branigin, William. 1996. "Congress Finishes Major Legislation on Immigration; Focus Is Borders, Not Benefits," *Washington Post,* October 1: A1.

Briggs, Vernon M., Jr. 1992. *Mass Immigration and the National Interest.* Armonk, N.Y.: M. E. Sharpe.

Brimelow, Peter. 1995. *Alien Nation: Common Sense about America's Immigration Disaster.* New York: Random House.

Cornelius, Wayne A., Philip L. Martin, and James F. Hollifield, eds. 1994. *Controlling Immigration: A Global Perspective.* Stanford, Calif.: Stanford University Press.

Day, Jennifer Cheeseman. 1996. "Population Projections of the United States by Age, Sex, Race, and Hispanic Origin: 1995 to 2050." *Current Population Reports.* U.S. Bureau of the Census, Ser. P25-1130. Washington, D.C.: U.S. Government Printing Office.

Dun and Bradstreet. multiple years. *Business Failure Record.* Business Economics Division. New York: Author.

Edmonston, Barry, ed. 1996. *Statistics on U.S. Immigration: An Assessment of Data Needs for Future Research*. Washington, D.C.: National Academy Press.

Espenshade, Thomas J. 1987. "Population Replacement and Immigrant Adaptation: New Issues Facing the West." *Family Planning Perspectives* 19(3, May/June): 115–18.

————. 1996. "Fiscal Impacts of Immigrants and the Shrinking Welfare State." Office of Population Research Working Paper 96-1. Princeton, N.J.: Princeton University.

————. ed. 1994. *A Stone's Throw from Ellis Island: Economic Implications of Immigration to New Jersey*. New York: University Press of America.

Espenshade, Thomas J., and Maryann Belanger. 1996. "U.S. Public Perceptions and Reactions to Mexican Migration." Background paper for Conference on Mexican Migration and U.S. Policy, Center for Strategic and International Studies, Washington, D.C., June 14–15.

Espenshade, Thomas J., and Haishan Fu. "An Analysis of English-Language Proficiency among U.S. Immigrants." *American Sociological Review*, forthcoming.

Espenshade, Thomas J., and Katherine Hempstead. 1996. "Contemporary American Attitudes toward U.S. Immigration." *International Migration Review* 30(2, Summer), 535–70.

Filer, Randall K. 1992. "The Effect of Immigrant Arrivals on Migratory Patterns of Native Workers." In George J. Borjas and Richard B. Freeman, eds., *Immigration and the Work Force: Economic Consequences for the United States and Source Areas* (245–269). Chicago: University of Chicago Press.

Fix, Michael, and Jeffrey S. Passel. 1994. *Immigration and Immigrants: Setting the Record Straight*. Washington, D.C.: Urban Institute.

Foner, Nancy, ed. 1987. *New Immigrants in New York*. New York: Columbia University Press.

Ford, Kathleen. 1985. "Declining Fertility Rates of Immigrants to the United States (with Some Exceptions)." *Sociology and Social Research* 70(1): 68–70.

————. 1990. "Duration of Residence in the United States and the Fertility of U.S. Immigrants." *International Migration Review* 24(1): 34–68.

Frey, William H. 1995. "The New Geography of Population Shifts: Trends toward Balkanization." In *State of the Union—America in the 1990s. Volume II: Social Trends*, edited by Reynolds Farley (271–334). New York: Russell Sage.

Friedberg, Rachel, and Jennifer Hunt. 1995. "The Impact of Immigrants on Host Country Wages, Employment, and Growth." *Journal of Economic Perspectives* 9(2, Spring): 23–44.

Greenwood, Michael J., and J. M. McDowell. 1986. "The Labor Market Consequences of U.S. Immigration: A Survey." *Journal of Economic Literature* 24(4, December): 1738–72.

Grenier, Guillermo J., and Alex Stepick, eds. 1992. *Miami Now! Immigration, Ethnicity, and Social Change*. Gainesville: University Press of Florida.

Halter, Marilyn, ed. 1995. *New Migrants in the Marketplace: Boston's Ethnic Entrepreneurs*. Amherst: University of Massachusetts Press.

Hansen, Kristin A. 1996. "Profile of the Foreign-Born Population in 1995: What the CPS Nativity Data Tell Us." Paper presented at the annual meetings of the Population Association of America, New Orleans, May 9–11.

Hansen, Kristin A., and Amara Bachu. 1995. "The Foreign-Born Population: 1994." *Current Population Reports*. U.S. Bureau of the Census, Ser. P20-486, and accompanying Internet table packages. Washington, D.C.: U.S. Government Printing Office, August.

Harwood, Edwin. 1985. "How Should We Enforce Immigration Law?" In *Clamor at the Gates: The New American Immigration*, edited by Nathan Glazer (73–91). San Francisco: ICS Press.

Heer, David M. 1990. *Undocumented Mexicans in the United States*. Cambridge: Cambridge University Press.

————. 1996. *Immigration in America's Future: Social Science Findings and the Policy Debate*. Boulder, Colo.: Westview Press.

Isbister, John. 1996. *The Immigration Debate: Remaking America*. West Hartford: Kumarian Press.

Jasso, Guillermina, and Mark R. Rosenzweig. 1990. *The New Chosen People: Immigrants in the United States*. New York: Russell Sage Foundation.

Jensen, Leif. 1989. *The New Immigration: Implications for Poverty and Public Assistance Utilization*. Westport, Conn.: Greenwood Press.

Kahn, Joan R. 1988. "Immigrant Selectivity and Fertility Adaptation in the United States." *Social Forces* 67(1): 108–28.

————. 1994. "Immigrant and Native Fertility during the 1980s: Adaptation and Expectations for the Future." *International Migration Review* 28(3): 501–19.

Kritz, Mary M., ed. 1983. *U.S. Immigration and Refugee Policy: Global and Domestic Issues*. Lexington, Mass.: Lexington Books, D.C. Heath Co.

Lamm, Richard D., and Gary Imhoff. 1985. *The Immigration Time Bomb: The Fragmenting of America*. New York: Truman Talley Books/E.P. Dutton.

Lapham, Susan J. 1993a. *The Foreign Born Population in the United States: 1990*. Report CPH-L-98. Washington, D.C.: U.S. Bureau of the Census.

————. 1993b. *1990 Ethnic Profiles for States*. Report CPH-L-136. Washington, D.C.: U.S. Bureau of the Census.

Light, Ivan, and Edna Bonacich. 1988. *Immigrant Entrepreneurs: Koreans in Los Angeles, 1965–1982*. Berkeley: University of California Press.

Loveless, Stephen C., Clifford P. McCue, Raymond B. Surette, and Dorothy Norris-Tirrell. 1996. *Immigration and Its Impact on American Cities*. Westport, Conn.: Praeger.

Manson, Donald M., Thomas J. Espenshade, and Thomas Muller. 1985. "Mexican Immigration to Southern California: Issues of Job Competition and Worker Mobility." *Review of Regional Studies* 15(2, Spring): 21–33.

Marshall, F. Ray, and Leon F. Bouvier. 1986. *Population Change and the Future of Texas*. Washington, D.C.: Population Reference Bureau.

Martin, Philip L., and J. Edward Taylor. 1988. *Harvest of Confusion: SAWs, RAWs, and Farmworkers*. Policy Discussion Paper, Program for Research on Immigration Policy, PRIP-UI-4. Washington, D.C.: Urban Institute.

McCarthy, Kevin F., and R. Burciaga Valdez. 1986. *Current and Future Effects of Mexican Immigration in California*. Santa Monica, Calif.: RAND Corp.

Muller, Thomas, and Thomas J. Espenshade. 1985. *The Fourth Wave: California's Newest Immigrants*. Washington, D.C.: Urban Institute Press.

New Jersey Department of Labor and Industry. multiple years. *New Jersey Economic Indicators*. Trenton, N.J.: Author.

O'Connor, Thomas H. 1995. *The Boston Irish: A Political History*. Boston: Northeastern University Press.

Papademetriou, Demetrios G., and Nicholas DiMarzio. 1986. *Undocumented Aliens in the New York Metropolitan Area: An Exploration into Their Social and Labor Market Incorporation*. Staten Island, N.Y.: Center for Migration Studies.

Papademetriou, Demetrios G., and Stephen Yale-Loehr. 1996. *Balancing Interests: Rethinking U.S. Selection of Skilled Immigrants*. Washington, D.C.: Carnegie Endowment for International Peace.

Portes, Alejandro, and Rubén G. Rumbaut. 1990. *Immigrant America: A Portrait*. Berkeley: University of California Press.

Portes, Alejandro, and Alex Stepick. 1993. *City on the Edge: The Transformation of Miami*. Berkeley: University of California Press.

Reed, Deborah, Melissa Glenn Haber, and Laura Mameesh. 1996. *The Distribution of Income in California*. San Francisco: Public Policy Institute of California.

Rothman, Eric S., and Thomas J. Espenshade. 1992. "Fiscal Impacts of Immigration to the United States." *Population Index* 58(3, Fall): 381–415.

Rumbaut, Rubén G., and John R. Weeks. 1996. "Unraveling a Public Health Enigma: Why Do Immigrants Experience Superior Perinatal Health Outcomes?" *Research in the Sociology of Health Care* 13B: 337–91.

Schoeni, Robert F., Kevin F. McCarthy, and Georges Vernez. 1996. *The Mixed Economic Progress of Immigrants*. Santa Monica, Calif.: RAND Corp.

Simon, Julian. 1989. *The Economic Consequences of Immigration*. Oxford: Basil Blackwell.

Simon, Rita J., and Susan H. Alexander. 1993. *The Ambivalent Welcome: Print Media, Public Opinion, and Immigration*. Westport, Conn.: Praeger.

State and Local Coalition on Immigration. 1996a. "House Approves Illegal Immigration Reform." *Immigrant Policy News . . . (Inside the Beltway)* (Washington, D.C.) 3(2, March 27):1.

————. 1996b. "Senate Passes Illegal Immigration Reform; Restricts Benefits for Legal Immigrants." *Immigrant Policy News . . . (Inside the Beltway)* (Washington, D.C.) 3(3, May 3):1.

Teitelbaum, Michael S., and Myron Weiner, eds. 1995. *Threatened Peoples, Threatened Borders: World Migration and U.S. Policy.* New York: W.W. Norton & Company.

U.S. Bureau of the Census. multiple years. *Statistical Abstract of the United States.* Washington, D.C.: U.S. Government Printing Office.

U.S. Commission on Immigration Reform. 1995. *Legal Immigration: Setting Priorities.* 1995 Executive Summary. Washington, D.C.: Author, June.

U.S. House of Representatives. 1994. "America's Changing Profile." *Hearings Before the Subcommittee on Census and Population of the Committee on Post Office and Civil Service.* 102d Cong., 2d sess. Ser. No. 102-64. Washington, D.C.: U.S. Government Printing Office.

U.S. Immigration and Naturalization Service. 1991. *1990 Statistical Yearbook of the Immigration and Naturalization Service.* Report M-367. Washington, D.C.: U.S. Department of Justice, December.

————. 1996. *Immigration to the United States in Fiscal Year 1995.* Washington, D.C.: U.S. Department of Justice, March.

Vernez, Georges, and Allan Abrahamse. 1996. *How Immigrants Fare in U.S. Education.* Santa Monica, Calif.: RAND Corp.

Vernez, Georges, and Kevin F. McCarthy. 1996. *The Costs of Immigration to Taxpayers: Analytical and Policy Issues.* Santa Monica, Calif.: RAND Corp.

Waldinger, Roger D. 1986. *Through the Eye of the Needle: Immigrants and Enterprise in New York's Garment Trades.* New York: New York University Press.

Waldinger, Roger D., and Mehdi Bozorgmehr, eds. 1996. *Ethnic Los Angeles.* New York: Russell Sage Foundation.

White, Michael J., and Lori M. Hunter. 1993. "The Migratory Response of Native-Born Workers to the Presence of Immigrants in the Labor Market." Working Paper Series 93-08. Providence, R.I.: Brown University, Population Studies and Training Center.

Winnick, Louis. 1990. *New People in Old Neighborhoods: The Role of New Immigrants in Rejuvenating New York's Communities.* New York: Russell Sage Foundation.

Part One

DEMOGRAPHIC CONTEXT

COMPARING DEMOGRAPHIC AND LABOR-MARKET CHARACTERISTICS OF NEW JERSEY AND U.S. FOREIGN BORN

Bruce Western and Erin Kelly

By examining demographic and labor-market characteristics of New Jersey and United States immigrants, this chapter assesses the resemblance of the foreign-born population of New Jersey to the foreign-born population of the United States as a whole. We employ two types of comparisons to make this assessment. First, we contrast characteristics of New Jersey immigrants with U.S. immigrants in general. Second, we analyze data from two time points, 1980 and 1990, to identify recent state and national trends. New Jersey immigration increased extremely quickly during the decade of the 1980s, raising the possibility of local variation from national trends. Taken together, these comparisons from two time points at state and national levels help suggest how studies of New Jersey immigrants might shed light on the condition of immigrants in the country more generally.

Our approach is descriptive for the most part. We begin by comparing the nativity and citizenship of New Jersey immigrants to those of the United States. We then consider age profiles of three main immigrant groups—Asians, Europeans, and Latin Americans. Variation in the age profiles introduces an examination of educational attainment. We show that Asians—among the youngest and most recent immigrants—have the highest educational attainment in New Jersey and nationwide. A simple model of educational transitions shows that the superior educational performance persists, even when age and sex are controlled. These patterns are similar for the 1980 and 1990 data and at the state and national levels of analysis. Finally, we estimate the impact of differential educational attainment on the earnings of different immigrant groups.

Data for this analysis are taken from the 1980 and 1990 Censuses. For 1980 we analyzed the New Jersey 5 percent Public Use Microdata Sample (PUMS) and the U.S. 0.1 percent sample from the Census of Population and Housing, 1980 (U.S. Bureau of the Census [henceforth,

Census Bureau], 1982). The 5 percent PUMS New Jersey sample is also used for 1990. Because there is no summary file for the United States for 1990, we compiled U.S. data from 10 percent subsamples from each of the state 1 percent files (Census Bureau 1992). Since the New Jersey sampling fraction is much larger than that of the United States, the New Jersey samples tend to be larger than the national. In all analyses, immigrants were defined as those born overseas (excluding U.S. territories) not of U.S. parents.

NATIVITY, CITIZENSHIP, AND YEAR OF IMMIGRATION

Patterns of immigration to New Jersey have generally followed national trends, shaped decisively by shifts in eligibility requirements. European immigration dominated in the 130 years from 1820 (when the first national system of recordkeeping was initiated) to 1950. Asian immigration rapidly increased from the early 1970s following enforcement of the 1965 Amendments to the 1952 Immigration and Nationality Act. This legislation expanded the number of visas for the Eastern Hemisphere. Increased Asian immigration was accompanied by sharp rises in Latin American immigration (Pao 1994).

Table 2.1 shows the place of birth for a number of national and regional immigrant groups in New Jersey and the United States in 1980 and 1990. In the earlier year, Europeans were overrepresented in New Jersey compared to the rest of the country, while Asian and Latin Americans were underrepresented. Whereas Europeans—notably those from Germany and Italy—accounted for nearly 60 percent of New Jersey's immigrant population in 1980, only 40 percent of U.S. immigrants were from Europe at this time. On the other hand, about one-third of U.S. immigrants were from Latin America (including Mexico), but only about one-quarter of New Jersey immigrants were Latin American. These differences appear to be related to port of entry, since Mexican immigration is disproportionately drawn to the Southwest.

The foreign-born population grew quickly through the 1980s. Nationwide, the number of immigrants increased by 40 percent, from 14 million in 1980 to nearly 20 million a decade later (Census Bureau 1993). In New Jersey the 28 percent increase in the immigrant population raised the 1980 population from about 760,000 to nearly 970,000 by 1990. This sharp increase in the numbers of foreign born was concentrated in just a few counties in northeastern New Jersey, in

Table 2.1 PERCENTAGE DISTRIBUTION OF FOREIGN BORN IN NEW JERSEY AND
UNITED STATES: 1980 AND 1990

Place of Birth	Year			
	1980 (%)		1990 (%)	
	New Jersey	United States	New Jersey	United States
Canada	2.3	6.3	1.8	4.0
Oceania	0.2	0.6	0.2	0.5
Africa	1.7	1.4	2.6	1.7
Europe	**56.7**	**39.2**	**38.4**	**23.6**
Germany	7.7	6.6	5.0	4.1
Italy	13.9	6.4	7.7	3.0
Other Western Europe	21.2	16.5	16.3	10.7
Eastern Europe	13.9	9.7	9.4	5.8
Latin America	**25.7**	**33.2**	**33.3**	**44.1**
Mexico	0.4	16.7	1.5	23.3
Other Latin America	25.3	16.5	31.8	20.8
Asia	**13.4**	**19.5**	**23.6**	**26.0**
East Asia	4.2	7.2	8.4	9.1
South Asia	7.0	10.4	14.2	16.2
Middle East	2.2	1.9	1.0	0.7
Sample size	35,911	13,142	45,996	17,752

Notes: Samples sizes are unweighted; Latin America includes the Caribbean.

the Newark area. Figure 2.1 shows the distribution of foreign born by county in New Jersey in 1980 and 1990. The immigrant population as a percentage of the total population grew fastest in Middlesex and Somerset counties. Immigrants were most strongly represented in Hudson County where, by 1990, they accounted for almost one-third of the total population (Census Bureau 1983, 1994).

The nativity profile of immigrants had changed dramatically by 1990. In New Jersey and nationwide, European representation in the immigrant population had shrunk by about one-third. The proportion of Latin American immigrants had increased by about one-third to over 30 percent of the total immigrant population in New Jersey and about 44 percent in the United States (table 2.1). The Asian immigrant population has grown even faster. Although Asians comprised only 13 percent of all New Jersey immigrants in 1980, they accounted for around one-quarter of all foreign born by 1990. Thus, Asian immigration in New Jersey had accelerated to approach the national distribution by the end of the decade (table 2.1). Perhaps as a consequence of

Figure 2.1. FOREIGN BORN AS PERCENTAGE OF TOTAL POPULATION, NEW
JERSEY COUNTIES: 1980 AND 1990

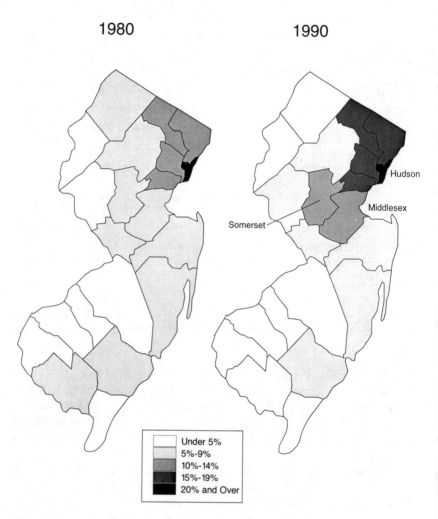

Source: Census Bureau (1983, 1994).

the family reunification policy, it seems that port of entry became less
important for the nativity profile of New Jersey immigrants through
the 1980s. The clear exception to this trend is the near absence of
Mexican immigrants in New Jersey, despite their accounting for more
than one-fifth of all foreign born in the country as a whole.

Figure 2.2 provides a more detailed picture of countries of origin. The figure plots countries of origin for New Jersey and United States as a proportion of all foreign born. Countries falling on the dashed 45-degree line in the figure are represented in equal proportions in the state and the nation. The striking feature of this plot is the massive underrepresentation of Mexicans among New Jersey's foreign born. This underrepresentation increases with growing Mexican immigration to the Southwest United States from 1980 to 1990. From New Jersey's perspective, the Italian and Cuban communities are particularly large, although the overrepresentation of these two groups decreases from 1980 to 1990, illustrating New Jersey's convergence on the U.S. pattern.

Some sense of the assimilation of New Jersey and U.S. immigrants is given in table 2.2, which shows the rate of naturalization among different nativity groups. In both 1980 and 1990, the national and state-level figures look very similar. European immigrants are about twice as likely to become citizens as Asians or Latin Americans. The propensity for Asians to become citizens increases over time. The major difference between the state and national figures is the relatively high probability of naturalization among New Jersey Latin Americans. This may in part be due to the relative underrepresentation of Mexicans and the overrepresentation of Cubans among the New Jersey foreign born. It seems likely that Cubans seek citizenship more frequently than Mexicans because their chances of repatriation are small. Perhaps their political organization also provides large benefits to the politically active.

Changes in the nativity profile during the decade of the 1980s and patterns of citizenship seem systematically related to successive waves of immigration, first from Europe and later from Latin America and Asia. Table 2.3 reports information about the timing of immigration from each of the three regions. Here, the New Jersey figures are almost identical to those from the country as a whole. Whereas almost half of all Europeans immigrated before 1960, only a handful of Asian and Latin American immigrants had arrived by that time. In contrast, at least 50 percent of Latin Americans and Asians arrived in the decade from 1980 to 1990. Only about one-fifth of all European immigrants are counted among these recent arrivals.

AGE AND EDUCATION

Conforming to the timing of the different waves of immigration from each of the three major regions, each immigrant group has a distinc-

Figure 2.2 PERCENTAGE OF FOREIGN BORN BY COUNTRY OF ORIGIN FOR NEW JERSEY AND U.S. RESIDENTS: 1980 AND 1990

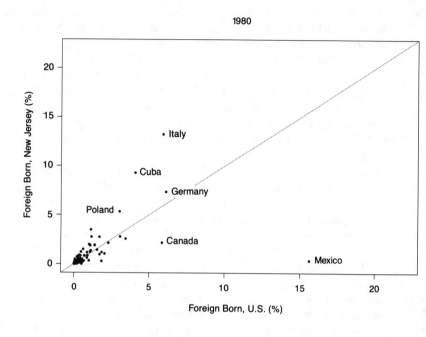

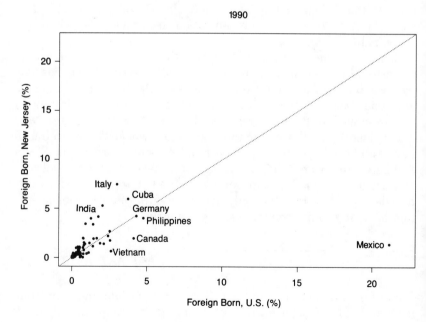

Table 2.2 PERCENTAGE OF NATURALIZED CITIZENS AMONG DIFFERENT
NATIVITY GROUPS, U.S. FOREIGN BORN: 1980 AND 1990

	Year			
	1980 (%)		1990 (%)	
Nativity	New Jersey	United States	New Jersey	United States
Asian	32	34	42	41
European	73	74	68	65
Latin American	34	29	35	27
Other	61	59	46	44
All foreign born	58	51	50	41

Table 2.3 PERCENTAGE DISTRIBUTION OF NATIVITY GROUPS BY YEAR OF
IMMIGRATION, U.S. FOREIGN BORN: 1990

	Nativity (%)			
Year of Immigration	Asian	European	Latin American	Other
New Jersey Immigrants				
Before 1960	4	48	4	18
1960–69	10	18	19	13
1970–79	31	16	26	26
1980–84	23	7	22	20
1985–90	33	10	29	24
Total	100	99	100	101
United States Immigrants				
Before 1960	5	49	7	29
1960–69	9	18	15	15
1970–79	30	14	28	19
1980–84	25	7	22	15
1985–90	30	13	28	22
Total	99	100	100	100

tive age profile. The age distribution of Asians, Europeans, and Latin
Americans in New Jersey and the United States is shown for 1980 in
figure 2.3. The age distribution for Asians at both state and national
levels has a mode in the mid- to late 30s and a long positive tail. The
age distribution for European immigrants, on the other hand, has no
clear peak, with a range of modal values between 40 and 70. This
reflects the sustained impact of European immigration in the period

Figure 2.3 AGE DISTRIBUTIONS FOR NEW JERSEY AND U. S. IMMIGRANTS from ASIA, EUROPE, AND LATIN AMERICA: 1980.

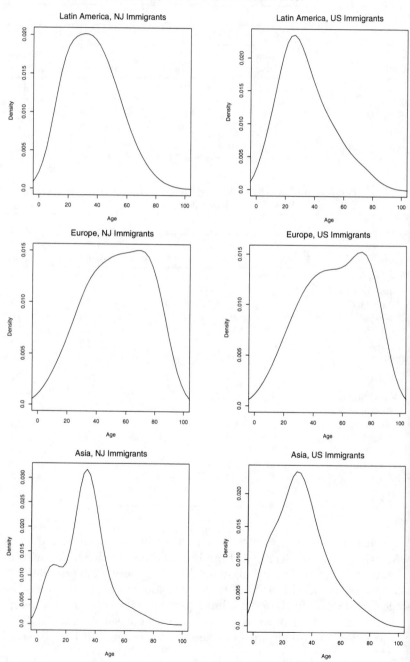

since World War I. Again, both state and national distributions show strong similarities. The European age distribution can be contrasted with the Latin American. For Latin Americans, the modal value is in the mid- to late 20s, reflecting the most recent wave of immigration.

Ten years later, in 1990, the age distributions still look fairly similar (figure 2.4). The European age distributions now have a more regular shape, reflecting both the mortality of the older European immigrants and the decline in European immigration among the young. Compared to the 1980 data, there are strong similarities in the age distributions for New Jersey and the United States. In short, although there may be differences in nativity at the state and national levels, the timing of immigration and age at immigration for different groups seem similar regardless of destination within the United States. Regression analysis not reported here provides additional evidence that the foreign born immigrate in their late 20s, on average, regardless of nativity.

The age distribution of different immigrant groups is reflected in educational attainment (table 2.4). The oldest group, Europeans, has lower educational attainment than Asians and Latin Americans in both 1980 and 1990. Consistent with other research, the striking feature of the statistics on educational attainment is the high rate of college attendance among the Asian foreign born (Jasso and Rosenzweig 1990: 64–65). In both 1980 and 1990, nearly three-quarters of all adult Asian immigrants in New Jersey had attended college. Asian immigrants throughout the country had significantly lower, but still very high, rates of college attendance in both census years. The main difference between national and state figures is the high level of educational attainment of the New Jersey immigrant population. Latin American immigrants from New Jersey are thus less likely to have dropped out of high school and are more likely to attend college than the national average. This may reflect the nativity mix of Latin American immigrants—perhaps the high representation of Cubans—in the New Jersey Latin American population.

To investigate how strongly educational differences are patterned by the age profile of different immigrant groups, we estimated a simple model of educational transitions (e.g., Mare 1980) that calculated both the probability of high school graduation and the probability of college attendance given high school graduation. In estimating differences across immigrant groups, we controlled for the effects of age and sex. In these regressions, nativity was dummy coded, with Asians forming the omitted category.

Figure 2.4 AGE DISTRIBUTIONS FOR NEW JERSEY AND U.S. IMMIGRANTS from ASIA, EUROPE, AND LATIN AMERICA: 1990.

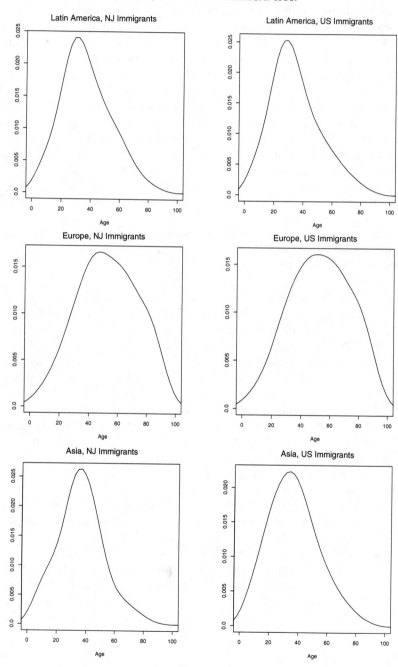

Table 2.4 PERCENTAGE DISTRIBUTION OF EDUCATIONAL ATTAINMENT OF
FOREIGN BORN OVER 30 YEARS OF AGE, NEW JERSEY AND
UNITED STATES: 1980 AND 1990

Education	Place of Birth (%)			
	Asia	Europe	Latin America	Other
New Jersey, 1980				
Less than high school	14	57	50	43
Completed high school	13	25	27	26
Attended college	73	18	23	31
Sample frequency	2,344	17,323	5,434	2,677
United States, 1980				
Less than high school	28	51	60	42
Completed high school	19	25	20	28
Attended college	53	24	20	30
Sample frequency	1,166	4,343	2,168	1,424
New Jersey, 1990				
Less than high school	15	46	45	29
Completed high school	14	25	25	22
Attended college	71	29	30	49
Sample frequency	7,047	15,084	9,217	2,709
United States, 1990				
Less than high school	26	38	61	34
Completed high school	18	25	16	22
Attended college	56	37	24	43
Sample frequency	2,817	3,544	4,161	1,260

Logistic regression coefficients reported in table 2.5 show that in
1980, even when age is controlled, strong differences in educational
attainment still persist among Asians, Europeans, and Latin Americans. These estimates show that European immigrants to New Jersey
are less than a quarter as likely as Asian immigrants to graduate from
high school. Latin Americans are even less likely to report high school
graduation. In 1980, the educational gap between Asian and other
immigrants was smaller in the country as a whole, but remained large
nonetheless. As we move up the ladder of educational attainment,
differences between Asians and other immigrants become even more
pronounced. Both European and Latin American immigrants in New
Jersey are about 20 percent as likely to attend college as their Asian
counterparts. The growing educational gap at the college level between Asians and Europeans can also be found in the U.S. data.
National estimates indicate that Europeans in 1980 were only about

Table 2.5 LOGISTIC REGRESSION ANALYSIS SHOWING PLACE-OF-BIRTH EFFECTS ON SCHOOL TRANSITIONS, CONTROLLING FOR AGE AND SEX, U.S. FOREIGN BORN OVER 30 YEARS OF AGE: 1980 AND 1990

	Year							
	1980				1990			
	New Jersey		United States		New Jersey		United States	
Independent Variables	High School	Some College	High School	Some College	High School	Some College	High School	Some College
European	.239	.164	.658	.444	.336	.285	.869	.598
	(22.92)	(26.49)	(5.42)	(8.64)	(28.24)	(29.39)	(2.40)	(7.23)
Latin American	.186	.165	.247	.375	.215	.238	.216	.453
	(25.61)	(24.52)	(17.10)	(9.23)	(38.42)	(31.81)	(27.94)	(10.80)
Other	.350	.249	.799	.487	.536	.483	.868	.706
	(14.43)	(16.93)	(2.52)	(6.60)	(11.16)	(11.86)	(1.85)	(3.77)
Age	.959	.981	.958	.978	.959	.980	.965	.975
	(48.43)	(14.61)	(28.64)	(10.07)	(50.72)	(17.79)	(25.33)	(13.13)
Female	.838	.514	.898	.495	.848	.594	.935	.595
	(6.77)	(18.24)	(2.36)	(11.34)	(6.80)	(17.17)	(1.66)	(9.68)
Intercept	43.267	17.890	21.649	10.596	45.403	16.207	16.42	13.831
	(51.82)	(33.44)	(29.90)	(18.15)	(70.81)	(43.44)	(33.23)	(23.97)
Deviance Change	4,402	1,818	1,287	405	5,436	466	1,617	449
Sample Size	27,778		9,101		34,057		11,782	

Notes: Cell entries are odds multipliers (exponentiated logistic regression coefficients). Absolute t-ratios in parentheses. The deviance change compares the reported model to the null model, with all predictors omitted.

half as likely as Asians to report some college education, while Latin Americans attend college only about a third as often as Asians.

The story of educational attainment in 1990 is similar to that in the 1980s. Asians continued to outperform all others, the gap between Asians and others being larger in New Jersey than in the United States (table 2.5). Estimates indicate that, controlling for age and sex, Asians in New Jersey were about four times more likely than Europeans and Latin Americans to report some college attendance. The U.S. data show that Europeans and Latin Americans in 1990 were only about half as likely as Asians to report college attendance. Interestingly, the nativity effects estimated with the 1990 data are generally smaller than the estimates from 1980. This indicates that differences in educational attainment by nativity declined through the 1980s. Considering the increase in college attendance over the last decade, growing equality in the distribution of education can be attributed to a rising general level. Thus, European and Latin Americans are catching up to the very high educational attainment of Asians. This trend can be seen in New Jersey and nationwide.

THE LABOR MARKET

To see how these differences in educational attainment are reflected in the labor market, we conducted a simple analysis of earnings for men and women, distinguishing earnings differentials among the three immigrant groups. Annual median earnings of adult full-time and part-time wage and salary earners for the different immigrant groups are reported in table 2.6. Surprisingly, perhaps, Asian immigrants in New Jersey report relatively high earnings compared to both their foreign-born non-Asian counterparts and Asian immigrants in other parts of the country. This may be partly owing to the very high educational attainment of Asians from New Jersey. Between 1980 and 1990, earnings inequality between Asian and European immigrants remained stable. This was particularly true at the national level. On the other hand, Latin Americans did increasingly worse compared to other nativity groups through the 1980s. The wage gap between Latin American and European men increased at both state and national levels between 1980 and 1990, but by more at the national level than in New Jersey. Nationally in 1990, Latin Americans were only earning half as much as Europeans. Similar trends, but with generally less

Table 2.6 MEDIAN ANNUAL EARNINGS FOR ASIAN, EUROPEAN, AND LATIN
AMERICAN FOREIGN BORN, NEW JERSEY AND UNITED STATES: 1980
AND 1990 (IN 1996 DOLLARS)

Place of Birth	New Jersey		United States	
	Men	Women	Men	Women
Earnings in 1980				
Asia	19,005	10,005	14,655	8,005
Europe	17,845	7,655	17,800	8,005
Latin America	12,005	7,005	10,585	7,005
Other	16,125	8,005	15,005	8,005
Earnings in 1990				
Asia	32,290	16,560	24,000	15,600
Europe	34,000	16,560	30,000	16,000
Latin America	20,000	14,000	15,000	11,000
Other	26,000	18,000	22,300	15,300

wage dispersion, can be found for women. In this case, state and
national trends show a stronger resemblance.

To see differences in earnings among different immigrant groups
controlling for education and other demographic and job characteristics, we estimated a number of regression models where the log of
wage or salary income is written as a linear function of nativity, and
variables that capture the effects of human capital and job characteristics. These variables are described in table 2.7.

First, examining the earnings equation in table 2.8 for 1980, among
New Jersey men, strong age effects work to the advantage of European
immigrants. These are offset to some degree by large education effects
which reward the superior educational attainment of Asian immigrants. When both these variables are controlled, however, the estimates show that Europeans earn slightly higher wages than Asians
and much larger wages than Latin Americans. European men earn
about 5 percent more than Asians, and Asian men earn about 15
percent more than Latin Americans. Earnings differentials for women
show a different pattern, as Asians earn about 7 or 8 percent more
than both Latin American and European immigrant women.

The story is a little different in the national data in 1980. As in New
Jersey, European men enjoy a substantial wage advantage over their
Asian counterparts. The national estimate of the earnings gap between Europeans and Asians of more than 10 percent is nearly twice
as large as the New Jersey estimate (table 2.8). However, national estimates show that the earnings of Asian and Latin American men are
similar once demographics and job characteristics are controlled for.

Table 2.7 DESCRIPTIONS OF VARIABLES USED IN REGRESSION ANALYSIS OF
EARNINGS, NEW JERSEY AND UNITED STATES: MEN AND WOMEN,
1980 AND 1990

Dependent Variable

Earnings   Total annual wage or salary income.

Independent Variables

Nativity   A four-category variable distinguishing Asians, Europeans, Latin
Americans, and others. This is coded as three dummy variables,
with Asians the omitted category.

Cohort   Immigration cohort coded as three categories for those immigrating within 10 years of the census year, those immigrating
between 10 and 20 years of the census, and those immigrating
more than 20 years before the census. The most recent cohort is
in the omitted category.

English skills   A dichotomous English-proficiency variable distinguishing those
who speak English "well" or "very well" from those who do not.

Age   Age of respondent in years. A quadratic term is included in the
regression to account for nonlinearities in the age effect. Only
respondents ages 21 to 65 were included for analysis.

Education   A three-category variable distinguishing those who have not
completed high school, high school graduates, and those with
some college education. This was coded as two dummy variables
with high school graduates in the omitted category.

Industry   A four-category variable distinguishing workers in (1) mining
and agriculture, (2) manufacturing, transport, and utilities,
(3) wholesale and retail sales, and (4) service industries. This
is coded as three dummy variables, with manufacturing industry workers the omitted category.

Occupation   A three-category variable distinguishing upper-white-collar
occupations (managerial and professional occupations), lower-
white-collar (technical, sales, and service occupations), and
manual occupations. Manual workers form the omitted category.

Part-time   A dummy variable indicating respondents working less than 30
hours a week.

As a result, the earnings gap of around 10 percent between European
and Latin American men is smaller nationwide than in New Jersey,
where Europeans earn about one-quarter more than Latin Americans.
In short, there appear to be strong differences among the three immigrant groups in earnings in New Jersey, whereas in the nation as a
whole only one clear line of earnings inequality emerges—between
Europeans and the rest.

For women, the 1980 national patterns are broadly similar to those
from New Jersey (table 2.8). In contrast to the men, Asian women are
the wage leaders, earning greater than 10 percent more than all other
immigrants. This wage gap is about twice as large as that found in

Table 2.8 REGRESSIONS ON LOG EARNINGS, MEN AND WOMEN, NEW JERSEY
AND UNITED STATES: 1980 (ABSOLUTE T-RATIOS IN PARENTHESES)

Predictors	New Jersey		United States	
	Men	Women	Men	Women
Intercept	7.380	8.043	7.302	8.360
	(66.67)	(62.19)	(37.40)	(38.32)
Nativity				
Europe	.053	−.067	.105	−.115
	(1.89)	(1.99)	(2.09)	(2.25)
Latin America	−.148	−.078	−.054	−.109
	(5.15)	(2.36)	(1.10)	(2.16)
Other	−.051	−.078	−.057	−.124
	(1.56)	(1.91)	(1.03)	(2.07)
Human Capital				
Immigrated in 1960s	.159	.096	.229	.176
	(7.95)	(4.03)	(5.94)	(4.05)
Immigrated in 1950s or before	.187	.093	.256	.099
	(7.77)	(3.08)	(5.68)	(1.92)
English skills	.237	.170	.192	.236
	(10.09)	(6.10)	(4.44)	(4.48)
Age	.010	.034	.099	.026
	(18.54)	(5.50)	(10.33)	(2.40)
Age^2	−.001	−.003	−.001	−.000
	(16.56)	(4.04)	(9.41)	(1.80)
Less than high school	−.124	−.010	−.121	−.176
	(5.72)	(3.82)	(2.72)	(3.70)
College	.116	.131	.093	.075
	(5.23)	(5.04)	(2.11)	(1.69)
Job Characteristics				
Mining, agriculture	−.019	.104	−.108	−.167
	(.61)	(.89)	(2.19)	(1.40)
Sales	−.160	−.291	−.142	−.318
	(7.00)	(8.85)	(3.10)	(5.34)
Service	−.141	−.160	−.177	−.199
	(6.70)	(5.72)	(4.38)	(3.78)
Lower white collar	−.037	.156	−.083	.096
	(1.66)	(5.20)	(1.98)	(1.67)
Upper white collar	.381	.557	.390	.537
	(15.72)	(14.21)	(8.31)	(7.50)
Part-time	−.461	−.679	−.635	−.698
	(13.97)	(27.30)	(10.34)	(15.92)
R^2	.24	.22	.24	.22
Sample size	9,057	10,124	3,005	2,261

New Jersey. Similar to New Jersey, however, differences in earnings between European and Latin American women are small.

By 1990, the earnings gap between European and Asian men had widened both in New Jersey and in the United States as a whole (table 2.9). Europeans were earning between 15 and 20 percent more than Asians and Latin Americans at the state and national levels. Earnings inequality between Latin American and Asian men in New Jersey also persisted into the 1990s. Here, the results suggest that the New Jersey and U.S. patterns are converging where the increasing wage inequality separates Europeans from Asians, and Asians from Latin Americans. Among women, only small differences remain between the earnings of Asians and Europeans. On the other hand, Asian women continue to earn upwards of 10 percent more than their Latin American counterparts. As in 1980, national-level wage disparity between Latin American women and other immigrant women in 1990 was larger than in New Jersey.

CONCLUSION

Two broad conclusions can be drawn from this review of the demographic and labor force characteristics of New Jersey and U.S. immigrants. First, there are strong differences in nativity between New Jersey and the United States. At the beginning of the 1980s, Europeans were overrepresented by about 50 percent and Asians were underrepresented by about 25 percent in New Jersey compared to the nation as a whole; these differences narrowed in the course of the decade. The distribution of Latin American immigrants by country of origin is even more striking. The Mexican community of New Jersey is very small, while representing about 20 percent of all foreign born nationwide. Despite these differences in nativity, the year of immigration and citizenship statistics for the different nativity groups are virtually identical at state and national levels.

Second, demographic and labor force characteristics of New Jersey immigrants are broadly similar to those of their counterparts in the rest of the country. The age distribution of Asians, Europeans, and Latin Americans shares the same distinctive shape at both levels of analysis, reflecting successive waves of immigration first from Europe, then from Asia, and finally from the Americas. The age differences are related to, but do not exhaustively explain, differences in educational attainment. At both state and national levels, Asian immigrants

Table 2.9 REGRESSIONS ON LOG EARNINGS, MEN AND WOMEN, NEW JERSEY AND UNITED STATES: 1990 (ABSOLUTE T-RATIOS IN PARENTHESES)

Predictors	New Jersey		United States	
	Men	Women	Men	Women
Intercept	8.059	8.658	7.921	8.340
	(93.98)	(85.50)	(53.77)	(47.55)
Nativity				
Europe	.112	−.056	.166	−.039
	(6.09)	(2.54)	(4.52)	(.97)
Latin America	−.115	−.095	−.098	−.150
	(6.43)	(4.60)	(3.09)	(4.32)
Other	−.047	−.044	−.036	−.034
	(1.92)	(1.48)	(.84)	(.69)
Human Capital				
Immigrated in 1970s	.186	.178	.220	.186
	(11.79)	(9.32)	(7.98)	(5.45)
Immigrated in 1960s or before	.294	.199	.355	.187
	(16.39)	(9.28)	(10.94)	(4.76)
English skills	.197	.158	.189	.217
	(10.78)	(7.02)	(6.28)	(5.41)
Age	.085	.041	.085	.049
	(10.61)	(8.46)	(11.61)	(5.77)
Age^2	−.001	−.004	−.001	−.001
	(18.19)	(7.89)	(10.22)	(4.84)
Less than high school	−.093	−.074	−.149	−.095
	(5.00)	(3.37)	(4.38)	(2.37)
College	.163	.182	.169	.213
	(9.20)	(9.43)	(4.97)	(5.86)
Job Characteristics				
Mining, agriculture	.013	.041	−.133	−.271
	(.59)	(.62)	(3.84)	(3.09)
Sales	−.124	−.240	−.144	−.257
	(6.94)	(10.15)	(4.30)	(5.60)
Service	−.080	−.141	−.159	−.166
	(4.87)	(6.84)	(5.15)	(4.08)
Lower white collar	.034	.128	−.001	.104
	(1.97)	(5.37)	(.04)	(2.32)
Upper white collar	.443	.564	.449	.463
	(23.50)	(19.70)	(12.53)	(8.62)
Part-time	−.570	−.775	−.563	−.847
	(21.76)	(38.45)	(14.00)	(23.68)
R^2	.31	.28	.34	.30
Sample size	13,312	10,124	4,697	3,481

show substantially higher educational attainment, even while controlling for age. The educational performance of New Jersey Asians is particularly strong, with chances of college attendance greater than 70 percent compared to the national average for Asians of around 55 percent. Despite the superior educational performance of Asians, European men enjoy a wage advantage of around 10 to 15 percent, both in New Jersey and the United States as a whole, once a variety of human capital and industry variables are controlled for. This wage gap has increased substantially in the decade between 1980 and 1990. Among women, large but stable differences in earnings can be found between Latin Americans and other immigrant groups.

Although patterns and trends in the distribution of education and earnings are similar at state and national levels, New Jersey immigrants are generally more educated and better paid. In particular, New Jersey Latin Americans show superior educational attainment compared to the national average. If, as some researchers suggest, immigrant quality in the country as a whole has relatively declined in the last two decades, New Jersey may prove to be exceptional (Borjas 1995). Furthermore, Asians from New Jersey do slightly better than Asian immigrants in the United States more generally. Educational attainment in relation to Europeans and Latin Americans is superior, and the earnings gap between Europeans and Asians in New Jersey is smaller than the national average. These differences may result from selection effects. Many Asian immigrants settle close to their port of entry in the western states. Those travelling to the East Coast, perhaps in search of educational and job opportunities, may have higher ability or initiative. Further investigation of this issue could involve more detailed analyses of differences in the performance of Asian immigrants on the East and West Coasts.

Note

The authors gratefully acknowledge the comments of Thomas J. Espenshade and participants at the "Conference on Impacts of Immigration to New Jersey," at Princeton University, Princeton, N.J., May 18–19, 1995.

References

Borjas, George J. 1995. "Assimilation Changes in Cohort Quality Revisited: What Happened to Immigrant Earnings in the 1980s?" *Journal of Labor Economics* 13:201–45.

Census Bureau. *See* U.S. Bureau of the Census.

Jasso, Guillermina, and Mark R. Rosenzweig. 1990. *The New Chosen People: Immigrants in the United States.* New York: Russell Sage Foundation.

Mare, Robert D. 1980. "Social Background and High School Continuation Decisions." *Journal of American Statistical Association* 75:295–305.

Pao, Mary K. 1994. "Historical Perspectives on Immigration to New Jersey." In *A Stone's Throw from Ellis Island: Economic Implications of Immigration to New Jersey*, edited by Thomas J. Espenshade (1–44). Lanham, Md.: University Press of America.

U.S. Bureau of the Census. 1982. *Census of Population and Housing, 1980: Public Use Microdata Samples, U.S.* [machine-readable data files]. Washington, D.C.: Author.

————. 1983. *1980 Census of Population, Chapter C, General Social and Economic Characteristics.* Part 32, New Jersey. Washington, D.C.: Author.

————. 1992. *Census of Population and Housing, 1990: Public Use Microdata Samples, U.S.* [machine-readable data files]. Washington, D.C.: Author.

————. 1993. *Statistical Abstract of the United States, 1993.* Washington, D.C.: Author.

U.S. Bureau of the Census, Ethnic and Hispanic Branch, Population Division. 1994. *1990 Age, Nativity, and Citizenship for the United States, States and Counties.* Washington, D.C.: Author.

Chapter Three

UNDOCUMENTED IMMIGRANTS IN NEW JERSEY: NUMBERS, IMPACTS, AND POLICIES

Rebecca L. Clark and Wendy N. Zimmermann

Much of the recent debate over immigration has focused on a relatively small share of the total immigrant population—those living in the United States illegally. This debate has centered not only on proposals for keeping illegal or undocumented immigrants[1] out of the country but also on the impacts of such immigrants on state and local governments.

In the mid-1980s, Congress passed the first major legislation dealing with illegal immigration, the Immigration Reform and Control Act of 1986 (IRCA). IRCA's premise was that undocumented aliens were drawn to the United States by the availability of jobs and welfare (most research suggested that jobs were the stronger attraction). The legislation was aimed at sharply reducing the number of undocumented aliens living in the United States through two major new strategies. The first strategy was to legalize two large segments of the nation's undocumented alien population: those who had been U.S. residents since January 1, 1982, and those who had worked in agriculture for 90 or more days between May 1, 1985, and May 1, 1986. Through IRCA's legalization programs, approximately 2.7 million formerly undocumented aliens became legal U.S. residents.

The second strategy was to reduce the future flow of undocumented aliens by making the United States a destination that was both less attractive and more difficult to reach. Although it was already illegal for undocumented aliens to work in the United States, in an attempt to make it harder for them to find jobs, IRCA for the first time imposed employer sanctions—civil and criminal penalties on employers who knowingly hired undocumented workers.[2] To discourage undocumented aliens from settling in the United States in order to receive welfare, IRCA also required states to verify the immigration status of applicants for the primary welfare, housing, and educational assistance programs.[3] In addition, IRCA significantly increased the resources devoted to controlling the U.S. border.

Only 10 years after passage of this landmark legislation, illegal immigration is yet again the focus of fierce public debate and the subject of recently passed legislation. Three major factors account for this renewed interest.

First, despite IRCA measures designed to reduce the flow of undocumented aliens, the number of undocumented aliens in this country is increasing. Specifically, because of the wide availability of fraudulent documents and weak enforcement, the employer sanctions provision of IRCA has proved ineffective (Fix 1991). After passage of IRCA, the number of undocumented aliens in the United States dropped, but analysts suggested that this was primarily because of the legalization of a large portion of the nation's undocumented population, and not because of a significant reduction in the number of undocumented aliens entering the United States (Passel, Bean, and Edmonston 1990; Woodrow and Passel 1990). By fall 1996, the number of undocumented aliens in the United States may have nearly reached pre-IRCA levels (Warren 1995).[4]

Second, economic downturns in many parts of the country, including New Jersey, have led to concerns that undocumented aliens may be displacing American workers and, through their use of government services, draining state and local coffers. California, home to more than 40 percent of the nation's undocumented population, was especially hard hit by the economic recession of the early 1990s. California's Governor Pete Wilson's outspokenness about the negative impact of undocumented aliens during his gubernatorial and presidential campaigns helped keep the issue of illegal immigration on the national agenda.

Finally, a series of 1993 incidents involving illegal immigrants helped keep the spotlight focused on illegal immigration. First, when the *Golden Venture*, a boat holding hundreds of illegal immigrants traveling from China, ran aground off the coast of New York, the desperate circumstances of many would-be undocumented immigrants were brought to light. Second, the nomination of Zoë Baird for attorney general failed because she had hired an undocumented alien as a nanny for her children and paid no Social Security taxes for her. Third, terrorists, some of whom were undocumented immigrants, bombed the New York World Trade Center. This bombing also highlighted the issue of visa overstay and its contribution to the size of the illegal immigrant population (Espenshade 1995).

The nation's undocumented population is highly concentrated, with 86 percent in only seven states: California, New York, Texas, Florida, Illinois, New Jersey, and Arizona (Warren 1995). As a result of this concentration, the impact of undocumented immigration is felt disproportionately by only a few states. New Jersey presents an interesting case study of how a state has responded to this impact. As in the other states, New Jersey policymakers have taken steps to reduce and ameliorate the effect of undocumented aliens on state finances. New Jersey is one of six states that have sued the federal government—unsuccessfully—for some of the costs associated with undocumented aliens. And the state legislature is now considering several bills designed to restrict undocumented immigrants' access to jobs and benefits.

Yet New Jersey differs from most of the other six states in significant ways. For one thing, undocumented aliens in New Jersey constitute a relatively small share of the state's total and foreign-born populations. Partly as a result of this, the estimated costs of providing major state and local services to undocumented aliens are relatively low. New Jersey's undocumented population—like that of its immediate neighbor, New York—contains a substantially smaller share from Mexico and a substantially larger share from Europe than the undocumented population in the United States as a whole. Perhaps because of such differences, the public and political responses to undocumented aliens in New Jersey have been less strident than elsewhere.

This chapter covers three broad topics. First, we describe the demographic characteristics of undocumented aliens in New Jersey and compare them with those of undocumented aliens elsewhere in the United States. Second, we discuss some of the fiscal impacts of undocumented aliens. Specifically, we assess two major costs to state and local areas attributable to undocumented aliens, public primary and secondary education and incarceration in state prisons, as well as—a much less discussed topic—the tax contributions undocumented aliens make. Third, we discuss federal and state public policies aimed at reducing the size and impact of the undocumented population.

DEMOGRAPHIC SETTING

How many undocumented immigrants live in New Jersey? According to official Immigration and Naturalization Service (INS) estimates, in

October 1992 there were approximately 116,000 such individuals, and, by October 1996, there would be approximately 152,000 (Warren 1995). Before discussing the characteristics of these undocumented aliens, it is useful to briefly explain how this and other analytically based estimates of the undocumented aliens were derived.[5]

Estimating the Numbers

Estimating the size of a population that is in the country illegally is a challenge. In the 1970s, this challenge was typically met by speculation rather than empirical analysis, leading to a wide range of estimates.[6] In 1976, for instance, INS Commissioner Leonard J. Chapman informed a congressional subcommittee that in 1975 there were between 4 million and 12 million undocumented immigrants in the United States. A few months later, Chapman informed a press group that in 1976 there were between 6 million and 8 million undocumented aliens in the United States. In a report commissioned by the INS, Lesko Associates asserted that in 1975 there were 8.2 million undocumented aliens in the country. This assessment was based on a survey of unnamed experts' estimates. In 1978, Chapman's successor, Leonard Castillo, informed another congressional subcommittee that there were between 3 million and 6 million undocumented aliens in the United States. (For reviews of early estimates of the size of the undocumented population, see Siegel, Passel, and Robinson 1980; Hill 1985; and Edmonston, Passel, and Bean 1990).

In the 1980s, speculation was replaced by a series of demographic analyses that applied both standard and innovative techniques to large bodies of official data. These techniques yielded estimates of the illegal population considerably smaller than the guesstimates of the 1970s. Three pieces of work are particularly noteworthy in this context: Warren and Passel (1987), Woodrow and Passel (1990), and Warren (1995). Estimates from these studies are shown in figure 3.1.

The estimates by Warren and Passel (1987) and Woodrow and Passel (1990) are similar in scope—they include only undocumented aliens who were included in large-scale data collections by the U.S. Bureau of the Census—as well as in technique—they are based on "residual methodology." The foreign born are identified in the Census Bureau data, but their legal status cannot be ascertained. Using INS and the Office of Refugee Resettlement counts of the number of naturalized citizens, legal permanent residents, refugees, and other legally resident aliens, the researchers estimated the number of legally resident immigrants, which they subtracted from the total number of foreign

Figure 3.1. ESTIMATES OF UNDOCUMENTED ALIENS IN UNITED STATES: 1980–92

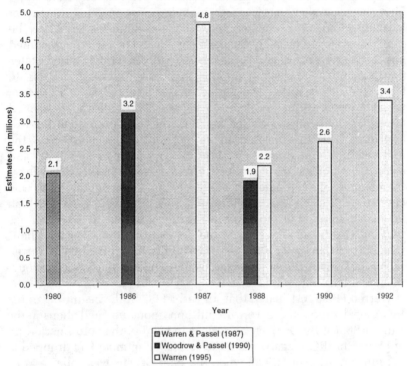

born in the Census Bureau data. The remainder, or residual, is the estimated number of undocumented immigrants.

Applying this technique to the 1980 Census, Warren and Passel (1987) estimated that it included approximately 2.1 million undocumented aliens. Woodrow and Passel (1990) applied the same technique to the Current Population Surveys (CPSs) of June 1986 (the year IRCA was enacted) and of June 1988 (after IRCA was implemented).[7] They concluded that the 1986 and 1988 CPSs included approximately 3.2 and 1.9 million undocumented aliens, respectively. They furthermore concluded that this decline reflected the widespread legalization of formerly undocumented aliens under IRCA, but that IRCA had not cut off the flow of new undocumented aliens to the United States.

Warren's (1995) estimates of the undocumented population for 1987 through 1992 improved on previous estimates in two important ways. First, he expanded the scope to include undocumented aliens not located by Census Bureau enumerators. Second, for 1982 and later, he directly estimated overstays, a major component of the undocumented population. Overstays are aliens who lawfully enter the United States (for example, as tourists, temporary visitors, or workers), but fail to leave when their authorized period of stay has expired. This group, which Warren estimates constitutes about half of all undocumented aliens who entered in or after 1982, can be tracked through the INS I-94 form. This form has an arrival portion that is collected by the INS from nonimmigrant aliens when they enter the United States and a departure portion that is collected from these aliens when they leave the country.[8] To estimate the number of undocumented aliens who entered the United States before 1982, Warren (1995) assumed that, for each country of origin, only two-thirds of those eligible to legalize under IRCA did so. To estimate the number of undocumented aliens who surreptitiously crossed the U.S. border in or after 1982, Warren relied on Census Bureau data, adjusted to take into account undocumented aliens not enumerated.

Warren (1995) estimated that, in early 1987, at the beginning of the IRCA legalization, there were 4.8 million undocumented aliens in the United States. By October 1988, near the end of the cutoff period for applying for IRCA legalization, the estimated number had dropped to 2.2 million. By April 1990, when the 1990 Census was collected, the estimated number had increased to 2.6 million. By October 1992, Warren estimated that there were 3.4 million undocumented aliens in the United States. As can be seen from figure 3.1, Warren's 1987 estimates were considerably larger than the estimate for 1986 by Woodrow and Passel (1990). Warren's estimate for 1988, however, is rather similar to Woodrow and Passel's estimate for the same year.

In addition to estimating the stock of undocumented immigrants at points in time, these researchers also estimated the net inflows of undocumented aliens. Woodrow and Passel (1990: 53, table 2.6; 56–57) estimated that between 1979 and 1988, the net annual increase was between 176,000 and 246,000. Warren (1995: 13; 31, table 3) estimated that between 1988 and 1992, the net annual increase was just under 300,000. Warren cautioned that his estimates are not strictly comparable to Woodrow and Passel's estimates because the earlier estimates are based on Census Bureau data, which exclude a significant portion of the undocumented population (Warren 1995: 14, A16–A17).

Estimates of the number of undocumented aliens in New Jersey are available for 1980 and 1992. In a companion paper to Warren and Passel (1987), Passel and Woodrow (1984) estimated that the 1980 Census included 37,000 undocumented aliens residing in New Jersey. Warren, who assumed that, for each country of origin, the geographic distribution of undocumented aliens in 1992 was the same as the distribution for IRCA amnesty applicants, estimated that there were 116,000 undocumented aliens residing in New Jersey in 1992. Again, these estimates are not strictly comparable because Passel and Woodrow's estimates only include undocumented aliens who appear in the 1980 Census, whereas Warren's estimates include all undocumented aliens.

Warren's (1995) estimates of the size, countries of origin, and geographic distribution of the undocumented population in 1992 are now the official estimates of the INS. The description of New Jersey's undocumented population that follows is based on Warren's point estimates. It should be kept in mind that these estimates have fairly large standard errors.

Undocumented Aliens in New Jersey

Size and Net Annual Increase of Undocumented Population

In October 1992, New Jersey contained approximately 116,000 undocumented aliens, making it the state with the sixth largest undocumented population (Warren 1995). The INS estimates that, in October 1992, there were 3.4 million undocumented aliens in the United States (see table 3.1). Overall, undocumented aliens constitute 1.4 percent of the U.S. population. In New Jersey, the share is slightly higher, 1.5 percent. As noted, these aliens are concentrated in a handful of states: California (42.7 percent), New York (13.3 percent), Texas (10.6 percent), Florida (9.5 percent), Illinois (5.2 percent), New Jersey (3.4 percent), and Arizona (1.7 percent).

Between 1988 and 1992, the average net annual increase in the number of undocumented aliens in the United States was 299,000. For New Jersey during this period, the net annual increase was approximately 9,000. Given its share of the nation's undocumented population, 3.4 percent, New Jersey's share of the net annual increase in undocumented aliens is relatively small, only 3.0 percent. Nonetheless, according to Warren's (1995) estimates, by 1992, the number of undocumented aliens in New Jersey equaled or slightly surpassed the number of undocumented aliens in the state before passage of IRCA (Warren 1995: figure 6).

Table 3.1 UNDOCUMENTED ALIENS IN THE UNITED STATES: 1992 (POPULATION IN 1,000s)

State	Number of Undocumented Aliens	Percentage of Total Undocumented Aliens	Percentage of Undocumented Aliens in Seven States	Percentage of 1992 Total Population	Net Annual Increase, 1988–92	Undocumented Aliens as Percentage of Foreign-born Population
Total United States	3,379	100		1.4	299	16.0
New Jersey	**116**	**3.4**	**4.0**	**1.5**	**9**	**11.3**
California	1,441	42.7	49.4	4.8	125	20.3
New York	449	13.3	15.4	2.5	41	15.6
Texas	357	10.6	12.2	2.1	32	21.5
Florida	322	9.5	11.0	2.4	34	17.2
Illinois	176	5.2	6.0	1.5	12	17.3
Arizona	57	1.7	2.0	1.5	5	17.5
All other	460	13.6		0.3	41	8.7

Sources: Warren (1995), U.S. Bureau of the Census (1990b: 15, table 3; 1992; 1994).
Note: See text for details.

Undocumented aliens constitute a smaller share of all immigrants in New Jersey than they do in the United States overall. We estimated the size of the total foreign-born population in 1992 by averaging data from the 1990 Census and the 1994 March CPS. We found that, for the entire United States, 16.0 percent of the foreign born were undocumented aliens, compared with 11.3 percent for New Jersey (table 3.1).[9]

COUNTRY OF ORIGIN

Table 3.2 and figures 3.2 through 3.5 show how the country of origin of New Jersey's undocumented population (figure 3.2) compares with the undocumented population in New York (figure 3.3) (the only other state in the Northeast with a large undocumented population and the state most like New Jersey in terms of the composition of its undocumented population); in California (figure 3.4) (the state with the largest undocumented population); and in the United States overall (figure 3.5). (For data cited in the paragraphs following, refer to the table and figures just cited.) New Jersey and New York differ from the United States overall and from California in three major ways.

First, New Jersey and New York contain a much smaller percentage of undocumented aliens from Mexico and El Salvador. For the nation as a whole, the two countries contribute nearly half of all undocumented aliens—Mexico (39 percent) and El Salvador (10 percent). In California, Mexico and El Salvador are even more dominant, contributing 55 percent and 14 percent, respectively. In contrast, Mexicans constitute only 3 percent and 2 percent in New Jersey and New York, and Salvadorans only 4 percent in both states. The small contributions of Mexico and El Salvador translate into a much lower percentage of undocumented aliens from North America in New Jersey and New York (26 percent and 39 percent) than in California and in the United States as a whole (81 percent and 71 percent). New York contains a higher proportion of undocumented aliens from North America than New Jersey because it has a larger share of undocumented aliens from the Caribbean islands. Furthermore, no country dominates the undocumented population in New Jersey the way Mexico dominates the undocumented population in California. In New Jersey, only one country—Portugal—contributes more than 10 percent of the undocumented population.

Second, New Jersey and New York contain a much larger share of undocumented immigrants from Europe. European countries contribute 34 percent of New Jersey's and 21 percent of New York's undocumented population, compared with 3 percent of California's and 9 percent of undocumented aliens in the United States overall. Most of

Table 3.2 MAJOR SOURCES OF UNDOCUMENTED ALIENS: NEW JERSEY, NEW YORK, CALIFORNIA, AND UNITED STATES

Area or country	New Jersey	New York	California	United States
Number (1,000s)	**116**	**449**	**1,441**	**3,379**
All (%)	**100**	**100**	**100**	**100**
Europe (%)	**34**	**21**	**3**	**9**
Portugal (%)	12	1	0	1
Poland (%)	8	5	0	3
Italy (%)	7	6	1	2
Yugoslavia (%)	3	2	0	1
Other Europe (%)	4	7	2	3
North America (%)	**26**	**39**	**81**	**71**
El Salvador (%)	4	4	14	10
Haiti (%)	4	4	0	3
Mexico (%)	3	2	55	39
Canada (%)	2	2	2	3
Guatemala (%)	2	1	6	4
Honduras (%)	2	2	2	2
Bahamas (%)	1	1	0	2
Nicaragua (%)	1	1	2	2
Other North America (%)	8	22	1	7
South America (%)	**17**	**13**	**2**	**5**
Colombia (%)	7	4	0	2
Ecuador (%)	5	5	0	1
Peru (%)	3	1	0	1
Other South America (%)	3	3	0	1
Asia (%)	**14**	**17**	**9**	**9**
Philippines (%)	5	2	4	3
Other Asia (%)	9	16	4	6
Africa (%)	**7**	**6**	**1**	**3**
Egypt (%)	3	1	0	0
Other Africa (%)	4	5	1	3
Oceania (%)	**0**	**0**	**1**	**0**
Stateless/Unknown (%)	**3**	**4**	**4**	**4**

Source: Warren (1995).
Note: Countries of origin are shown individually if they are one of the top 12 contributors for either New Jersey or United States overall.

New Jersey's European undocumented population is from three countries: Portugal (12 percent of the New Jersey total), Poland (8 percent), and Italy (7 percent). These three countries, along with Ireland, also dominate the European-born undocumented population in the United States overall.

Third, New Jersey and New York contain larger shares of undocumented aliens from South America. South Americans constitute 17 percent of New Jersey's and 13 percent of New York's undocumented

Figure 3.2. MAJOR SOURCES OF UNDOCUMENTED ALIENS: NEW JERSEY, 1992

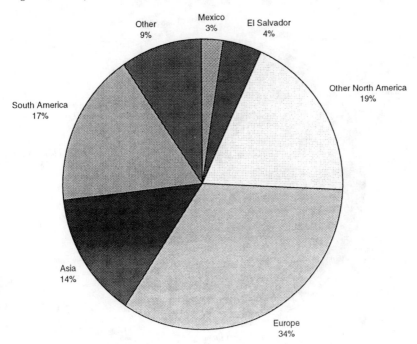

Note: Figures may not add to 100 due to rounding.

populations compared with only 2 percent of California's and 5 percent of the United States' overall. Nearly all of New Jersey's undocumented aliens from South America are from three countries: Colombia (7 percent of the New Jersey total), Ecuador (5 percent), and Peru (3 percent). These countries also dominate the South American-born undocumented population in the United States overall.

Undocumented aliens from two countries, Portugal and Egypt, are concentrated in New Jersey. Whereas New Jersey contains only 3 percent of the country's undocumented aliens, it contains 45 percent of undocumented aliens from Portugal and 25 percent of undocumented aliens from Egypt. New Jersey also contains large shares of the nation's undocumented aliens from Yugoslavia (16 percent), Peru (14 percent), Colombia (14 percent), Ecuador (13 percent), Jordan (13 percent), Italy (13 percent), Ghana (11 percent), Cuba (11 percent), and Poland (10 percent).

Figure 3.3. MAJOR SOURCES OF UNDOCUMENTED ALIENS: NEW YORK, 1992

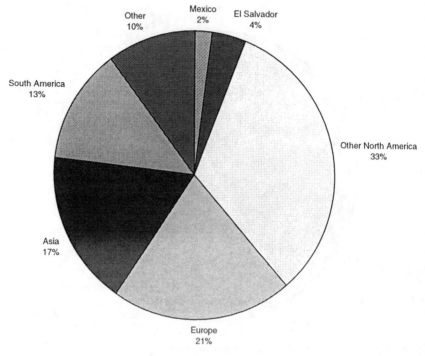

Note: Figures may not add to 100 due to rounding.

The differences between undocumented aliens in New Jersey and undocumented aliens in the United States overall are similar to those reported by Western and Kelly (chapter 2, this volume) for all foreign-born individuals in the 1990 Census. Although Western and Kelly used somewhat different country-of-birth groupings, they also found that, compared with foreign-born individuals in the United States overall, the foreign born in New Jersey are less likely to be from Mexico, but more likely to be from elsewhere in Latin America.[10] The foreign born in New Jersey are also more likely to be from Europe than the foreign born in the United States overall. Nonetheless, among those in New Jersey, there are a few differences in country of origin for undocumented aliens and the foreign born in the 1990 Census. Compared with the foreign-born individuals in the 1990 Census, un-documented aliens are less likely to be from Asia (14 percent versus 24 percent) and more likely to be from Latin American countries other

Figure 3.4. MAJOR SOURCES OF UNDOCUMENTED ALIENS: CALIFORNIA, 1992

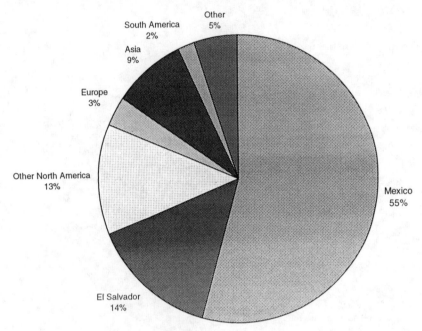

Note: Figures may not add to 100 due to rounding.

than Mexico (39 percent versus 32 percent). (These data are from table 3.2 and from table 2.1 [chapter 2].)

METHOD OF ENTRY

How did undocumented aliens in New Jersey enter the United States? A widespread misconception is that most undocumented aliens entered the United States by illicitly crossing the border with Mexico. But, as noted, slightly more than half of all undocumented aliens residing in the United States in 1992 are actually people who stayed after their authorized period of entry had expired. Although the INS estimates the percentage of undocumented aliens who entered the United States illegally (called "EWIs," for entered without inspection) by country of origin, it does not make this type of estimate for states. By examining data on undocumented aliens from New Jersey's major contributing countries, however, we can make reasonable inferences about how the state's undocumented aliens entered the country.

Figure 3.5. MAJOR SOURCES OF UNDOCUMENTED ALIENS: UNITED STATES, 1992

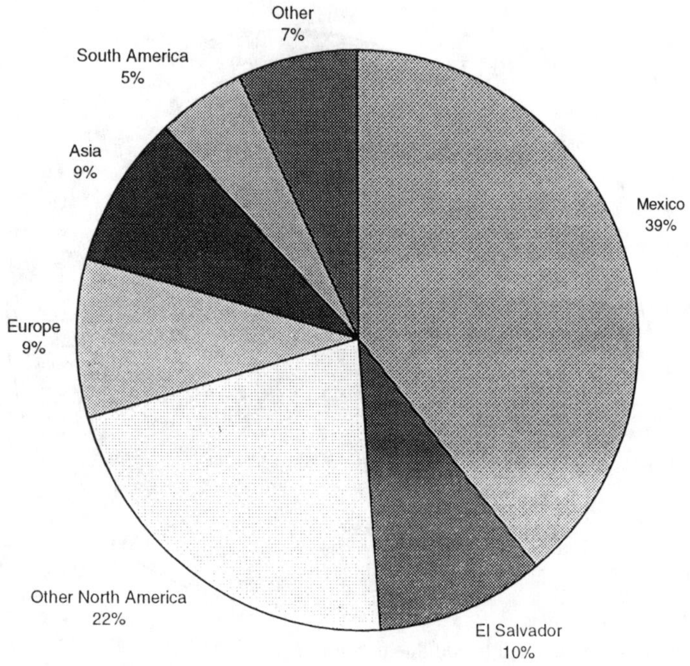

Note: Figures may not add to 100 due to rounding.

Using Warren's country-of-birth-specific estimates of the number of overstays and EWIs for the United States overall for 1988–92, we calculated the percentage of all undocumented aliens who were overstays for the top 23 countries contributing undocumented aliens to New Jersey (Warren 1995: 29, table 2).[11] Together, undocumented aliens from these countries constitute 82 percent of New Jersey's undocumented alien population. For each of these country-of-origin groups, we assumed that the percentage of undocumented aliens who were overstays was the same for New Jersey as for the United States as a whole. According to the calculations, 84 percent of New Jersey's undocumented aliens are overstays, compared with 53 percent for the United States as a whole.

FISCAL IMPACTS

Much of the recent public antipathy toward undocumented aliens arises from the perception that undocumented aliens have a negative impact on the states and local areas they reside in—that is, they use more in government services than they contribute to government coffers. However, public perceptions of the types of services for which undocumented aliens are currently eligible are often inaccurate. In August 1996 undocumented immigrants were barred from receiving services under virtually all federal, state, and local programs. Even before that, under federal law, undocumented aliens were barred from receiving what most people consider welfare—Aid to Families with Dependent Children (AFDC), Supplemental Security Income (SSI), and Food Stamps. They were also ineligible for most other federal, state, and local public benefits, including Medicaid (except for emergency conditions, including childbirth), legal services, job training, unemployment compensation, and postsecondary student financial aid. They were, and continue to be, eligible for only limited services such as emergency care under Medicaid and short-term emergency relief.

State officials have expressed particular concern about the costs of providing three types of services to undocumented aliens: public primary and secondary education, incarceration in state prisons, and Medicaid for emergency conditions (including costs associated with childbirth). In 1994, governors of seven states with large numbers of undocumented aliens met with Leon Panetta, then director of the Office of Management and Budget (OMB), and other federal officials to discuss the impact of undocumented aliens on their states, in general, and the costs of providing these three services, in particular. In response, the Urban Institute was asked by the U.S. Department of Justice to estimate the costs of providing these three services and to assess estimates produced by the seven states, to estimate the number of undocumented aliens in each of these states and to assess other researchers' estimates, and to estimate how much undocumented aliens contributed in selected state taxes in these states. In addition, The Urban Institute was asked to develop methods of estimating costs of undocumented aliens using standard methodologies and readily available data sources that the states, and others, could use to estimate these costs in the future.

This chapter reports New Jersey estimates for the three major budget categories included in The Urban Institute study: public primary and secondary education, incarceration, and state taxes.[12] The other states for which estimates were made are California, New York, Texas, Florida, Illinois, and Arizona. Because of data limitations, we were unable to produce estimates of the costs of providing emergency Medicaid to undocumented aliens.[13] All cost estimates were based on average (mean) costs; that is, total costs divided by total users. Because we only made estimates for a limited number of services used and taxes paid, these estimates cannot be used to calculate the net costs of undocumented aliens.[14]

Public Expenditures

UNDOCUMENTED ALIENS IN STATE PRISONS

We calculated the number of illegal aliens incarcerated in state prisons using data the states provided on all individuals they identified as foreign born among those incarcerated in March 1994. These individuals were matched to INS databases. From individuals who could not be matched to these databases, we selected a representative random sample. The legal status of these sample members was determined by matching them by hand to INS databases or by matching them to paper files in INS district offices. As a last resort, INS staff interviewed prisoners and verified the information they received. (For more details, see Clark and Bjerke 1994: 35–60.)

New Jersey has a disproportionately small share of illegal aliens in state prisons (see table 3.3). New Jersey contained 4.0 percent of the undocumented aliens in the seven states, but, according to our estimates, it contained only 1.3 percent of illegal aliens incarcerated in state prisons in the seven states, that is, 285 out of 21,395. We estimated that the total cost of incarcerating illegal aliens in state prisons in the seven states was $474.2 million. Despite its relatively high per prisoner costs—$23,095 compared with the mean cost of $18,226 for the seven states—New Jersey's estimated expenditures on illegal aliens in state prisoners, $6.6 million, is disproportionately low, accounting for only 1.4 percent of the seven-state total (U.S. Department of Justice 1992).

UNDOCUMENTED ALIENS IN PUBLIC SCHOOLS

The number of undocumented children in public schools cannot be directly counted. We therefore used demographic techniques to indirectly estimate the number of undocumented aliens in public schools. The total number of such aliens was estimated by multiplying together three factors: (1) the INS official estimate of the number of undocumented aliens in each state (Warren 1994); (2) a census-based estimate of the percentage of the undocumented alien population ages 5–19;[15] and (3) a census-based estimate of the percentage of school-age undocumented aliens who were enrolled in public school. The census-based estimates were constructed using data on immigrants from the same

Table 3.3 COSTS OF INCARCERATING ILLEGAL ALIENS: 1994

State	Illegal Alien Prisoners	Per Inmate Costs ($)	Total Cost ($Millions)	State Estimate as Percentage of Seven-State Total			
				Number of Prisoners	Total Cost	Undocumented Alien Population	
Total, Seven states	21,395	$18,226[a]	$474.2	100	100	100	100
New Jersey	**285**	**23,095**	**6.6**	**1.3**	**1.4**	**4.0**	
California	15,109	24,336	367.7	70.6	77.5	49.4	
New York	2,158	20,827	44.9	10.1	9.5	15.4	
Texas	1,594	14,489	23.1	7.5	4.9	12.2	
Florida	951	15,508	14.7	4.4	3.1	11.0	
Illinois	348	17,826	6.2	1.6	1.3	6.0	
Arizona	950	11,502	10.9	4.4	2.3	2.0	

Source: Clark and Bjerke (1994).
a. Average (mean) for seven states, unweighted.

countries of origin as the undocumented aliens in each state. (For more details, see Clark 1994a: 61–106.) The total costs were estimated by multiplying the estimated number of undocumented aliens in public school by the state and local share of average (mean) per student costs (National Center for Education Statistics 1994: 39, table 35; 1993: 152, table 157).[16]

New Jersey has a disproportionately small share of undocumented aliens in public primary and secondary schools (see table 3.4). New Jersey contained 4.0 percent of the undocumented aliens in the seven states, but only 2.5 percent of the undocumented aliens in public schools, 16,343 out of 643,692. This relatively small share is primarily due to the relatively low percentage of undocumented aliens in New Jersey of school age (18.0 percent compared with the seven-state unweighted average of 25.5 percent; see Clark 1994a, for details).

Although New Jersey has a small share of undocumented aliens in public schools compared to the six other states, the costs of educating these students—approximately $146.2 million—is somewhat high. New Jersey contains 4.0 percent of the undocumented aliens in these seven states but accounts for 4.7 percent of all public school expenditures on undocumented aliens in these states. New Jersey's outlays are high because the state and local public school expenditures per pupil are extremely high—$8,949 compared with an unweighted average of $5,371 for all seven states. Nonetheless, compared to undocumented aliens' share of the New Jersey population, these public school expenditures are not out of line: undocumented aliens account for 1.6 percent of New Jersey's population and 1.4 percent of New Jersey's public school expenditures.

TAXES PAID

For the Urban Institute report to OMB (Clark et al. 1994), three types of 1992 taxes were estimated: state sales tax, state income tax, and state and local property taxes.[17] The results therefore do not include *total* tax contributions by undocumented aliens. In New Jersey, these taxes constitute 47 percent of general revenues from state and local sources. As with public education, there is no way to directly estimate undocumented aliens' contribution to tax coffers. To develop these tax estimates, Urban Institute researchers developed proxy populations using Warren's (1995) state-specific estimates of the undocumented population combined with 1990 Census data (see Passel 1994 for details). The tax estimates were derived from calculations from a report by the Los Angeles County Internal Services Division (LAC-ISD 1992) generalized to the seven states. It was assumed that com-

Table 3.4 NUMBERS OF UNDOCUMENTED ALIENS ENROLLED IN PUBLIC SCHOOL AND ASSOCIATED COSTS: ACADEMIC YEAR 1993–1994

State	Number of Enrolled Undocumented Aliens	Per Student Costs ($)	Total Cost ($Millions)	State Estimate as Percentage of Seven-State Total			Estimates for Undocumented Aliens as Percentage of 1993 State Total	
				Number of Students	Total Cost	Undocumented Alien Population	Expenditures	Population
Total	643,692	5,371[a]	3,091.5	100.0	100.0	100.0		
New Jersey	16,343	8,949	146.2	2.5	4.7	4.0	1.4	1.6
California	309,686	4,199	1,300.3	48.1	42.1	49.4	5.8	5.0
New York	87,702	7,227	633.8	13.6	20.5	15.4	3.2	2.7
Texas	93,992	4,461	419.3	14.6	13.6	12.2	2.6	2.2
Florida	97,251	4,363	103.2	15.1	13.7	11.0	4.8	2.6
Illinois	23,652	4,774	112.9	3.7	3.7	6.0	1.2	1.6
Arizona	15,066	3,626	54.6	2.3	1.8	2.0	2.2	1.6

Source: Clark (1994a).

a. Average (mean) for seven states, unweighted.

Note: Estimates of undocumented aliens as percentage of state population are for 1993, not 1992, as in other tables.

pliance with sales tax was high because it is, of course, mandatory and easy to collect. It was also assumed that tax compliance for property tax was high. For owners, nonpayment of property tax can lead to the government imposing punitive assessments and, eventually, seizing one's property. For renters—who, it was assumed, indirectly paid roughly half of the property tax through their rent—nonpayment of rent could lead to eviction. For income tax, compliance is clearly more of an issue. In the LAC-ISD (1992) report, it was assumed that undocumented aliens' compliance rate was 56 percent for income tax. Since our income tax estimates were based on the LAC-ISD estimates, the low compliance rate is built in.

Overall, for these three taxes, an estimated $1.9 billion was collected from undocumented aliens in the seven states. For all seven states, undocumented aliens' contribution in taxes is less than their proportion in the state population. In New Jersey, undocumented aliens constitute 1.5 percent of the state population and paid 0.9 percent of the total collected for the three taxes—$130 million. Because undocumented aliens are clustered in low-wage jobs, their relatively low tax contribution is not surprising (see table 3.5).

Undocumented aliens in New Jersey pay an estimated $65 million in sales tax. As in most of the other states, undocumented aliens pay more in sales tax than in the other two types of taxes. The amount paid in sales tax is also roughly proportional to the undocumented alien share of the population, 1.6 percent compared with 1.5 percent. This is because the sales tax is the most regressive of the three taxes estimated.

Of the three taxes estimated, undocumented aliens in New Jersey make the smallest contribution through state income tax, paying about $6 million. Compared to their share of the state population, 1.5 percent, their share of state income tax is extremely low, 0.1 percent, probably owing to the low incomes of undocumented aliens and the low levels of tax compliance used in the original ISD estimates.

Undocumented aliens contribute $59 million in state and local property taxes, roughly 10 times more than they do in state income taxes. Again, the contribution is disproportionately low, accounting for about 1.0 percent of the total, but is clearly not as disproportionately low as the income tax payments (table 3.5).

New Jersey collects a disproportionately large share of taxes paid by undocumented aliens in the seven states. The state contains 4.0 percent of the undocumented aliens, yet receives 6.9 percent of taxes paid by undocumented aliens in the seven states. New York, with 15.4 percent of the undocumented aliens and 22.4 percent of the taxes paid

Table 3.5 ESTIMATED TAXES PAID BY UNDOCUMENTED ALIENS: 1992 (TAXES IN $MILLIONS)

State	Taxes Paid by Undocumented Aliens				Estimates for Undocumented Aliens as Percentage of State Total					Estimates for Undocumented Aliens as Percentage of Seven-State Total	
	Total, Three Taxes	Sales Tax	State Income Tax	State and Local Property Tax	Total, Three Taxes	Sales Tax	State Income Tax	State and Local Property Tax	Population	Total Taxes	Population
Total	1,886	1,069	92	724	1.3	2.2	0.2	1.5	2.8	100	100.0
New Jersey	**130**	**65**	**6**	**59**	**0.9**	**1.6**	**0.1**	**1.0**	**1.5**	**6.9**	**4.0**
California	732	467	46	219	1.7	3.1	0.3	2.0	4.8	38.8	49.4
New York	422	155	34	233	1.2	2.6	0.2	1.8	2.5	22.4	15.4
Texas	202	121	—	81	1.2	1.4	—	1.0	2.1	10.7	12.2
Florida	277	181	—	96	1.8	2.1	—	1.4	2.4	14.7	11.0
Illinois	94	62	6	26	0.8	1.5	0.1	0.9	1.5	5.0	6.0
Arizona	29	18	1	10	0.6	0.9	0.1	0.6	1.5	1.5	2.0

Source: Passel (1994: table 6.2).
Note: Property taxes for California, Illinois, and New Jersey are for 1991.

by undocumented aliens in the seven states, also receives a dispro-portionately large share of these taxes. In contrast, California, which contains 49.4 percent of the undocumented aliens in the seven states, receives only 38.8 percent of undocumented aliens' taxes.

POLICY ON UNDOCUMENTED IMMIGRATION

Several states with large numbers of immigrants have taken steps to limit both the size and economic impacts of their undocumented population. These actions have mirrored—and in some instances spurred—recent federal efforts to improve control of illegal immigra-tion, to reduce costs by restricting access to public services, and to increase federal reimbursement to states and localities for costs at-tributable to undocumented immigrants. Efforts by New Jersey and other states reflect the changing role states are playing in both setting and implementing immigration policy.

Federal Policy

When IRCA passed in 1986, the number of illegal immigrants in the United States was large and growing. As a result, concerns were rising about their use of public services and their impacts on the labor market and the public coffers. The same conditions held true in 1996, when the U.S. Congress passed the most comprehensive reform of illegal immigration policy since IRCA, the Illegal Immigration Reform and Immigrant Responsibility Act of 1996. About one month before the passage of the immigration law, Congress passed the Personal Responsibility and Work Opportunity Reconciliation Act of 1996, which overhauls the nation's welfare system and restricts the access of both illegal and legal immigrants to public services. The illegal immigration reform law strengthens efforts to reduce illegal immigra-tion by improving border controls—including doubling the size of the border patrol—increasing penalties for document fraud and alien smuggling, increasing numbers of workplace inspectors, and testing a verification system through which employers would be able to verify the immigration status of new employees. It also restricts judicial review for illegal immigrants, making it easier to exclude illegal immigrants at ports of entry and to deport those already in the United States.

Even before the passage of this legislation, the INS had taken nu-merous steps to reduce the growing flow of illegal immigration. Between fiscal years 1993 and 1995, a time when most federal agencies' budgets were shrinking, the INS budget increased by 72 percent. The lion's share of this budget increase was directed at strengthening border control by improving technology and equipment and increasing staff at the borders. Although the INS nearly doubled the number of employer sanctions investigators between fiscal years 1993 and 1996, total resources devoted to border control still far outweigh those aimed at interior enforcement. In addition, the INS is implementing its third, and largest yet, employment verification pilot, under which employers verify with the INS the documents presented by noncitizen job applicants.[18]

Although the new immigration legislation does increase the number of workplace inspectors, it does not impose greater penalties on employers and continues to focus far more resources at the border than at the workplace.[19] If future enforcement efforts continue to focus primarily on controlling the border, these efforts will have little effect on the undocumented population of New Jersey, which appears to be composed predominantly of overstays who entered legally. Improvements in interior enforcement, such as significantly strengthening work site enforcement and tracking overstays, are more likely to affect the size of the illegal immigrant population in states such as New Jersey.

State Initiatives and Changing Roles

Although the federal government has authority over setting and enforcing immigration policy, many of the impacts of immigration are felt at the state and local levels. Some states have responded by taking steps to restrict illegal immigration to their state and reduce its costs. New Jersey and other states have attempted, for example, to curb illegal immigrants' access to public services and have sought federal reimbursement for state costs of services to illegal immigrants. Prior to passage of the immigration and welfare laws, some of these efforts had been limited by court rulings affirming the federal government's sole authority to regulate immigration.[20] The immigration and welfare laws, however, give states new authority to control illegal immigration and to restrict all immigrants' access to a wide range of public benefits.[21]

ACCESS TO SERVICES AND IMMIGRATION CONTROL

California is the state most actively fighting illegal immigration. Its primary vehicle has been Proposition 187, a ballot initiative approved in 1994 that bars illegal immigrants from public services such as elementary, secondary, and higher education, social services, and health care. The initiative also criminalizes the manufacturing, sale, and use of fraudulent documents and requires state officials, including teachers and health care workers, to report information about immigration status to the INS. In November 1995, a federal district judge struck down many of the major provisions of Proposition 187, holding that they are preempted by federal law. She also held that Supreme Court precedent in *Plyler v. Doe* (457 US 202 [1982]) precludes the state from depriving illegal immigrant children of elementary and secondary school education. She did rule, however, that certain provisions, such as denying access to state-funded higher education and social services, may be lawful. The only provisions that have been put into effect as of this writing are those relating to fraudulent documents. Although no other state has yet passed a law like Proposition 187, efforts to do so are underway in Arizona and Florida. California's Proposition 187 not only provided an example for other states to follow, it also introduced many of the restrictions on illegal immigrant eligibility for benefits that later appeared in both the welfare and immigration laws.

While the new welfare law (and similar provisions in the new immigration law) gives states broad flexibility in determining legal immigrants' eligibility for public benefits, it takes away states' authority to set eligibility rules for illegal immigrants.[22] The new laws require states and localities to bar "not qualified aliens" including illegal immigrants from nearly all of their public benefit programs and from publicly funded grants, contracts, loans, and professional and commercial licenses. This requirement runs counter to recent congressional efforts to reduce federal mandates and increase the states' authority to administer social welfare programs. The legislation requires states to bar certain immigrants from receiving benefits, even if a state judges that such a bar would have a negative fiscal impact—for example, because the administrative costs of checking immigration status are high or the long-term consequences of denying services such as preventive health care are costly. If states choose to provide services to undocumented immigrants, they must pass a new law to do so.

The new immigration legislation also gives states new authority to enforce the immigration laws. It provides that state and local employers can perform the function of an immigration officer by, for example, apprehending and detaining aliens in the United States, as long as they have entered into a written agreement with the federal government and have adequate training.

INTERGOVERNMENTAL COST SHARING

Over the last several years, states have brought the issue of intergovernmental cost sharing, or cost shifting, to the forefront of the immigration debate. In so doing, they have succeeded in persuading the federal government to offset some of the state and local costs of undocumented immigration. The new immigration legislation authorizes further reimbursement for some of these costs.

Two factors strengthen state arguments that they bear a burden from illegal immigration. First, as mentioned, undocumented immigrants are concentrated in a handful of states—the undocumented population is even more concentrated than the immigrant population as a whole—meaning that their impacts and costs are also highly concentrated. Second, although the federal government receives most of the taxes paid by illegal immigrants, the states and localities pay for most of the services provided to them (Rothman and Espenshade 1992).

In response to the inequitable distribution of costs, California, Florida, New York, Arizona, Texas, and New Jersey sued the federal government for reimbursement of the costs of providing services to illegal immigrants. These suits rested primarily on the grounds that the federal government had failed to enforce its immigration policy. All the suits demanded reimbursement for incarceration, and several demanded education, health care, and social services costs.

The New Jersey lawsuit requested reimbursement for the costs of incarcerating approximately 500 illegal aliens and for educating approximately 16,343 undocumented alien students. The state sued for reimbursement of $50.5 million for fiscal year 1993—$13 million for housing illegal aliens and $37.5 million for the costs of building a medium security prison.[23] The OMB study (Clark et al. 1994), however, found that, in March 1994, there were only 285 illegal aliens in New Jersey state prisons, costing an estimated $6.6 million. New Jersey also sued for $162 million in education costs—using a cost figure slightly higher than that reported by the OMB studies and the same number of undocumented students used in the study.

Federal district judges have dismissed all of the states' lawsuits. Florida's appeal failed and, in May 1996, the Supreme Court ended the suit by refusing to hear the case. In July 1996, the U.S. Court of Appeals upheld the lower court's decision to dismiss New Jersey's case. The other state suits have either failed or are pending in the appeals court. In dismissing the suits, the judges have generally found that the claims involve a political, not a judicial, question because they would require the courts to evaluate the adequacy of the content and execution of the government's immigration system.

Although the lawsuits have failed thus far in the judicial system, they have had modest success as a political strategy. Following the filing of the lawsuits, Congress authorized $1.8 billion over six years in grants to states to help pay for the costs of incarcerating illegal immigrants.[24] Under the State Criminal Alien Assistance Program (SCAAP), New Jersey has so far received $2.8 million of the $130 million total distributed for fiscal year 1995. These funds, however, represent only about 16 percent of each state's total costs in that year, which the U.S. Department of Justice (1996) estimates were $17.6 million in New Jersey.

The immigration bill recently signed into law also authorizes further reimbursement for emergency medical services to illegal immigrants though no funds were appropriated for such reimbursement. Under current law, states and localities are reimbursed under Medicaid for approximately half of emergency medical costs.

NEW JERSEY INITIATIVES

Recent state restrictions on illegal immigrants' eligibility for benefits, and several bills introduced in the New Jersey legislature, reflect the desire of some legislators to toughen policies against illegal immigrants. For the most part, these restrictive, or exclusionary, proposals mirror actions already taken by the federal government or changes made under the recently enacted federal immigration bill. For example, two bills are pending in the state that would bar from entering into public contracts employers who have been federally sanctioned for hiring unauthorized workers.[25] These bills are similar to, but extend further than, the presidential executive order signed in February 1996.[26] The executive order requires that federal agency officials consider barring companies that have been fined for knowingly hiring unauthorized workers from receiving federal contracts for one year. In New Jersey, public entities would be *required* to bar sanctioned employers from contracts for *three* years. A third bill would require public entities to include in all contracts a provision that the contract will be terminated if the employer is sanctioned for employing unauthorized aliens in connection with that contract.[27]

Another set of bills resembles congressional efforts to restrict illegal immigrants' access to a wide variety of services, contracts, and licenses. Proposed legislation in New Jersey would restrict unauthorized immigrants from receiving a state contract, loan, tax deferral or reduction, grant, subsidy, loan guarantee, or license. This legislation would impose the same restrictions on employers who did not verify the employment eligibility of their employees.[28]

Another New Jersey proposal would restrict illegal immigrants' eligibility for workers' compensation.[29] Legislative debate, however, revealed that if illegal immigrants were ineligible for workers' compensation, they could file personal injury lawsuits, potentially costing employers even more. Ironically, workers' compensation was originally designed to substitute for such lawsuits.

Prior to the requirement to do so under welfare reform, the state restricted illegal immigrants' access to welfare. Previously, New Jersey allowed illegal immigrants to use its two principal cash assistance programs. In 1993, illegal immigrants were barred from receiving General Assistance, a program for poor single adults, and, in 1995, they were barred from receiving benefits from a state-funded cash assistance program for two-parent families ineligible for the federal and state-funded AFDC program.[30]

As on the federal level, New Jersey's current and proposed actions aimed at illegal aliens were spurred in large part by slow economic growth and a few highly publicized incidents that sparked legislators' interest. The restrictions on public contracts, for example, stemmed from a raid on the state house, where illegal immigrants were found working for a janitorial service.[31]

Despite these restrictions, New Jersey has not taken the kinds of draconian steps proposed by other states, such as California. It is significant, for example, that there are no serious efforts in New Jersey to pass a measure like Proposition 187. And unlike California, which has moved to bar undocumented immigrants from state-funded prenatal care, New Jersey, as of this writing, has made no such efforts to quickly implement the federal law. Further, although 21 states have made English their official language, New Jersey has not (Aleman, Bruno, and Dale 1996). On the other hand, New Jersey has not taken a particularly welcoming, or inclusive, approach to illegal immigrants. Although New Jersey's leadership has not spoken out against illegal immigration like California's Governor Pete Wilson, it has not supported the rights of legal and illegal immigrants as has New York City's Mayor Rudolph Giuliani (Schmitt 1996).

CONCLUSION

As has occurred in other states with sizable undocumented populations, politicians in New Jersey have attempted to lessen the fiscal impacts of undocumented aliens and discourage them from settling in the state by restricting their access to jobs, services, and benefits. These initiatives reflect a new state activism in the setting of immigration policy. Nonetheless, New Jersey's efforts have been relatively mild compared with those of other states.

The demographic and fiscal analyses presented in this chapter provide some possible explanations for why New Jersey has taken a less restrictive or less exclusionary approach to illegal immigration. First, undocumented aliens constitute a smaller share of the state population than in most of the other states with large undocumented populations. For example, in 1992, undocumented aliens constituted an estimated 1.5 percent of the population of New Jersey, but 4.8 percent of the population of California—the state that has passed the most restrictive measures against undocumented aliens. Second, New Jersey's undocumented population is more diverse than that of other states, with a larger share of Europeans and relatively fewer Mexicans and Salvadorans. This diversity makes the undocumented population similar to the rest of the state's population and perhaps less visible. Further, since the majority of New Jersey's undocumented population is composed of immigrants who enter legally and stay after their authorized period has expired, a smaller share is represented by the more highly publicized illegal border crossers.

In addition, the fiscal impacts of undocumented aliens in New Jersey are small relative to the impacts of other states with large undocumented populations. Whereas the state contains 4 percent of the undocumented aliens in the seven states, it has only 1.4 percent of the incarceration costs associated with illegal aliens, and it receives 6.9 percent of the seven-state total for sales tax, state income tax, and state and local property taxes collected from undocumented aliens. Whether public education costs in New Jersey are relatively high or low depends on the measure. New Jersey's share of public education costs attributable to undocumented aliens in the seven states is somewhat high: New Jersey contains 4.0 percent of the undocumented aliens in the seven states, but accounts for 4.7 percent of public education expenditures on undocumented aliens in the seven states. But New Jersey is one of only two states (Illinois being the other) where the share of public education costs attributable to undocumented aliens was lower than their share of the total population: undocumented aliens constituted 1.6 percent of New Jersey's population in 1993, but accounted for only 1.4 percent of public education expenditures.

Despite these relatively moderate impacts, New Jersey residents, like those in other states, would prefer that fewer illegal immigrants settle there. Whether New Jersey succeeds in reducing the size of its growing undocumented population by restricting access to jobs and services remains to be seen. By focusing attention on the impacts of undocumented immigration, however, New Jersey and other states have succeeded in obtaining greater federal reimbursement for the costs of undocumented immigrants and in contributing to the passage of major immigration policy reform.

Notes

This chapter was funded in part by the Ford Foundation through The Urban Institute's Program for Research on Immigration Policy. The views expressed are the authors' and do not necessarily reflect those of other staff members or trustees of The Urban Institute, or any organization financially suporting The Urban Institute.

1. Throughout this chapter, we use the terms "illegal immigrant," "undocumented immigrant," "illegal alien," and "undocumented alien" interchangeably. We refer to incarcerated undocumented aliens as illegal aliens to conform to federal statute (IRCA 1986, Section 501).

2. Out of concern that employers might respond to these sanctions by requesting additional documents from, or simply not hiring, job applicants who appeared to be foreign-born, IRCA included an antidiscrimination provision. For more information on IRCA, see Bean, Vernez, and Keely (1989) and Fix (1991).

3. IRCA established the Systematic Alien Verification for Entitlements (SAVE) program, through which states were mandated to verify the status of applicants for certain assistance programs. See Zimmermann (1994).

4. According to Warren (1995), when the IRCA legalization process began in early 1987, there were approximately 4,774,000 undocumented aliens in the United States. By October 1992, there were approximately 3,379,000 undocumented aliens. The estimated net annual increase between 1988 and 1992 was 299,000. If this level of increase has continued, by October 1996, there should be approximately 4,575,000 undocumented aliens in the United States.

5. This discussion includes only undocumented aliens who have settled in the United States. This is presumably the group with the greatest impact. We consider neither "sojourners"—"persons who enter the United States for a specific purpose, usually to seek employment, and who return to their home countries after a brief stay"—nor "commuters"—persons who "cross the border into the United States on a daily or weekly basis, working in the United States but residing across the border" (Edmonston et al. 1990: 22–23).

6. This discussion of speculative estimates of the number of undocumented aliens in the United States is summarized from Edmonston et al. (1990: 15–19).

7. Every month, the Census Bureau surveys approximately 57,000 households to measure the employment and demographic characteristics of the noninstitutionalized population of the United States (Census Bureau 1990a). This survey, the CPS, occasionally also includes supplements with questions on a variety of topics. The June 1988 CPS

included a special supplement with information on country of birth, citizenship, year of immigration, and country of birth of parents.

8. The Nonimmigrant Information System (NIIS), which tracks information from the I-94 forms, is incomplete because the departure portion of the I-94 is not always collected and data are sometimes entered incorrectly. Warren devised a method of correcting for this system error using data on countries with very low rates of overstay.

9. To the extent that undocumented aliens are omitted from the census and the CPS, this method will overestimate the percentage of the foreign born who are undocumented aliens. (For instance, Warren [1995] argued that the June 1988 CPS undercounts undocumented aliens from Mexico who arrived between 1982 and 1986 by 38 percent.) However, unless census/CPS coverage of undocumented aliens is significantly worse in New Jersey than in the nation as a whole, we can still conclude that New Jersey's foreign-born population contains a smaller share of undocumented aliens than the United States overall.

10. Latin America comprises all of North and South America except the United States and Canada.

11. We calculated the number of overstays by subtracting the number of undocumented aliens who adjusted their status, departed, or died during 1988–92 from the gross number of overstays for this period. This method may overestimate the number of overstays for the 1988–92 period because some of the undocumented aliens who adjusted their status or departed may have entered before 1988.

12. This discussion is drawn from chapters 1, 3, 4, and 6 of Clark et al. (1994).

13. Readers interested in a discussion of state estimates of Medicaid costs attributable to undocumented aliens are referred to Zimmermann (1994: 107–30).

14. On average, for fiscal year 1994, these seven states spent 17.3 percent of their total state budgets on public primary and secondary education, 8.2 percent on the state portion of Medicaid, and 2.7 percent on correctional institutions (Census Bureau 1996 and Urban Institute 1996).

15. We used 5–19 as the school age range, rather than the more traditional 5–17, because according to 1990 Census data, 23 percent of individuals ages 18–19 without a high school diploma are enrolled in public school.

16. At the request of the OMB, we used mean costs to estimate the costs of providing public education for undocumented alien students. However, on average, undocumented aliens probably cost more to educate than other students. Because undocumented aliens are less likely to speak English fluently and are more likely to come from poor families, they are more likely to need bilingual education and free or reduced-price lunches (Clark 1994b).

17. For New Jersey, California, and Illinois, property taxes were estimated for 1991.

18. In an earlier verification pilot involving employers in Santa Ana, Calif., approximately 26 percent of about 11,500 inquiries could not be verified as authorized to work. Of the unverified cases, 30 (1 percent) were later determined to be work authorized (*Immigration Advisor* 1996).

19. The immigration law did authorize 300 additional investigators of visa overstayers for fiscal year 1997, but no funds were appropriated to pay for those positions.

20. See, for example, *Plyler v. Doe* (457 US 202 [1982]) and *Graham v. Richardson* (403 US 67 [1971]).

21. Despite the passage of the new legislation, states may still face lawsuits if they choose to impose new restrictions since it is not clear that the federal government can delegate this authority.

22. Prior to this legislation, states had authority to determine the eligibility rules for certain state and local assistance programs for illegal immigrants, but states could not restrict the access of legal immigrants to state and locally funded assistance.

23. *State of New Jersey v. United States of America,* Civil Action No. 3-94-03471 (U.S.D.C., NJ, 1994).

24. IRCA included a provision authorizing reimbursement to states for the costs of incarcerating illegal immigrants, but funds were not appropriated until after passage of the 1994 crime bill.

25. See New Jersey Assembly Bill No. 2002, introduced May 13, 1996; Senate Bill No. 1134, introduced May 9, 1996.

26. Executive Order 12989, signed February 13, 1996.

27. New Jersey Assembly Bill No. 2003, introduced May 13, 1996.

28. New Jersey Senate Bill No. 207, introduced January 11, 1996; Assembly Bill No. 1690, introduced March 4, 1996.

29. New Jersey Senate Bill No. 212, approved by the Senate on February 26, 1996.

30. For more information on state approaches to providing services to immigrants, see Zimmermann and Fix (1994).

31. The company employing the workers had apparently checked their documents and had even conducted background checks with the state police, which suggests that the unauthorized workers had fraudulent documents that were not detected by the employers. This employer would not be subject to the proposed New Jersey bar, since sanctions are only imposed on employers who "knowingly" hire unauthorized workers.

References

Aleman, Steven R., Andorra Bruno, and Charles V. Dale. 1996. *English as the Official Language of the United States: An Overview.* Washington, D.C.: Congressional Research Service, May.

Bean, Frank, Georges Vernez, and Charles Keely. 1989. *Opening and Closing the Doors: Evaluating Immigration Reform and Control.* Washington, D.C.: Urban Institute Press.

Census Bureau. *See* U.S. Bureau of the Census.

Clark, Rebecca L. 1994a. "Costs of Providing Primary and Secondary Education to Undocumented Aliens in Seven States." In *Fiscal Impacts of Undocumented Aliens: Selected Estimates for Seven States,* by Rebecca L. Clark, Jeffrey S. Passel, Wendy N. Zimmermann, and Michael E. Fix. Report sponsored by Office of Management and Budget and U.S. Department of Justice. Washington, D.C.: Urban Institute.

————. 1994b. "The Costs of Providing Public Assistance and Education to Immigrants." *Program for Research on Immigration Policy Discussion Paper,* PRIP-UI-34. Washington, D.C.: Urban Institute. Also presented at the 1994 Joint Statistical Meetings, August 13–18, Toronto, Ontario; and at the 1994 Annual Meeting of the Population Association of America, May 4–7, Miami.

Clark, Rebecca L., and John Bjerke. 1994. "Costs of Incarcerating Illegal Aliens in Seven States." In *Fiscal Impacts of Undocumented Aliens: Selected Estimates for Seven States,* by Rebecca L. Clark, Jeffrey S. Passel, Wendy N. Zimmermann, and Michael E. Fix. Report sponsored by Office of Management and Budget and U.S. Department of Justice. Washington, D.C.: Urban Institute.

Clark, Rebecca L., Jeffrey S. Passel, Wendy N. Zimmermann, and Michael E. Fix. 1994. *Fiscal Impacts of Undocumented Aliens: Selected Estimates for Seven States.* Report sponsored by Office of Management and Budget and U.S. Department of Justice. Washington, D.C.: Urban Institute.

Edmonston, Barry, Jeffrey S. Passel, and Frank D. Bean. 1990. "Perceptions and Estimates of Undocumented Migration to the United States." In *Undocumented Migration to the United States: IRCA and the Experience of the 1980s,* edited by Frank D. Bean, Barry Edmonston, and Jeffrey S. Passel. Santa Monica, Calif., and Washington, D.C.: RAND Corp. and Urban Institute.

Espenshade, Thomas J. 1995. "Unauthorized Immigration to the United States," *Annual Review of Sociology* 21: 195–216.

Fix, Michael. 1991. *The Paper Curtain: Employer Sanctions' Implementation, Impact, and Reform.* Washington, D.C.: Urban Institute Press.

Fix, Michael, Jeffrey Passel, with Maria Enchautegui, Wendy Zimmermann. 1993. "Immigration and Immigrants: Setting the Record Straight." Washington, D.C.: Urban Institute.

Hill, Kenneth. 1985. "Illegal Aliens: An Assessment." In *Immigration Statistics: A Story of Neglect,* edited by David B. Levine, Kenneth Hill, and Robert Warren. Washington, D.C.: National Academy Press.

Immigration Advisor. 1996. Vol. 2, Issue 1 (July). LRP Publications, Horsham, Pa.

LAC-ISD. *See* Los Angeles County Internal Services Division.

Los Angeles County Internal Services Division. 1992. *Impact of Undocumented Persons and Other Immigrants on Costs, Revenues and Services in Los Angeles County: A Report Prepared for Los Angeles County Board of Supervisors.* Los Angeles: Author.

National Center for Education Statistics. 1993. *Digest of Education Statistics, 1993.* U.S. Department of Education, Office of Educational Research and Improvement. Washington, D.C.: U.S. Government Printing Office.

———. 1994. *Digest of Education Statistics, 1994.* U.S. Department of Education, Office of Educational Research and Improvement. Washington, D.C.: U.S. Government Printing Office.

Passel, Jeffrey S. 1994. "Estimated Tax Contributions of Undocumented Immigrants in Seven States." In *Fiscal Impacts of Undocumented*

Aliens: Selected Estimates for Seven States, by Rebecca L. Clark, Jeffrey S. Passel, Wendy N. Zimmermann, and Michael E. Fix. Report sponsored by Office of Management and Budget and U.S. Department of Justice. Washington, D.C.: Urban Institute.

Passel, Jeffrey S., Frank D. Bean, and Barry Edmonston. 1990. "Undocumented Migration Since IRCA: An Overall Assessment." In *Undocumented Migration to the United States: IRCA and the Experience of the 1980s,* edited by Frank D. Bean, Barry Edmonston, and Jeffrey S. Passel. Santa Monica, Calif., and Washington, D.C.: RAND Corp. and Urban Institute Press.

Passel, Jeffrey S., and Karen A. Woodrow. 1984. "Geographic Distribution of Undocumented Immigrants: Estimates of Undocumented Aliens Counted in the 1980 Census by State." *International Migration Review* XVIII(3): 642–71.

Rothman, Eric S., and Thomas J. Espenshade. 1992. "Fiscal Impacts of Immigration to the United States." *Population Index* 58(3): 381–415.

Schmitt, Eric. 1996. "NYC Mayor Criticizes GOP and Dole on Immigration." *New York Times.* June 7.

Siegel, J. S., J. S. Passel, and J. G. Robinson. 1980. "Preliminary Review of Existing Studies of the Number of Illegal Residents in the United States." Report to the U.S. Select Commission on Immigration and Refugee Policy. Washington, D.C.: U.S. Bureau of the Census. Reprinted 1981 in *U.S. Immigration Policy and the National Interest: The Staff Report of the Select Commission on Immigration and Refugee Policy.* Washington, D.C.: U.S. Government Printing Office.

The Urban Institute. 1996. *Health Policy Center Database.* State Medicaid expenditures based on Health Care Financing Administration forms 64 and 2082. Washington, D.C.: Author.

U.S. Bureau of the Census. 1990a. *Current Population Survey, March 1990 Tape Technical Documentation.* Washington, D.C.: U.S. Bureau of the Census, Data User Services Division, Data Access and Use Staff.

————. 1990b. *Projections of the Population of States, by Age, Sex, and Race: 1989 to 2010. Current Population Reports,* Ser. P-25, No. 1053. Washington, D.C.: U.S. Government Printing Office.

————. 1992. *Census of Population and Housing, 1990: Public Use Microdata Samples, U.S.* Machine-readable data files. Washington, D.C.: Author.

————. 1994. *Current Population Survey, March 1994.* Machine-readable data files. Washington, D.C.: Author.

————. 1996. *Annual Survey of Government Finances, 1994 (Preliminary).* E-mail from Donna Hirsh, U.S. Bureau of the Census. Washington, D.C., July 8.

U.S. Department of Justice. 1996. "New Justice Department Grants to Reimburse States that Jail Criminal Illegal Aliens." Press release, January 31. Washington, D.C.: Author.

U.S. Department of Justice, Bureau of Justice Statistics. 1992. *Census of State and Federal Correctional Facilities, 1990.* Washington, D.C.: U.S. Government Printing Office.

Warren, Robert. 1995. "Estimates of the Undocumented Immigrant Population Residing in the United States, by Country of Origin and State of Residence: October 1992." Paper presented at the annual meetings of the Population Association of America, San Francisco, April.

Warren, Robert, and Jeffrey S. Passel. 1987. "A Count of the Uncountable: Estimates of Undocumented Aliens Counted in the 1980 United States Census." *Demography* 24(3): 375–93.

Woodrow, Karen A., and Jeffrey S. Passel. 1990. "Post-IRCA Undocumented Immigration to the United States: An Assessment Based on the June 1988 CPS." In *Undocumented Migration to the United States: IRCA and the Experience of the 1980s,* edited by Frank D. Bean, Barry Edmonston, and Jeffrey S. Passel. Santa Monica, Calif., and Washington, D.C.: RAND Corp. and Urban Institute.

Zimmermann, Wendy N. 1994. "Costs of Providing Emergency Services under Medicaid to Undocumented Aliens." In *Fiscal Impacts of Undocumented Aliens: Selected Estimates for Seven States,* by Rebecca L. Clark, Jeffrey S. Passel, Wendy N. Zimmermann, and Michael E. Fix. Report sponsored by Office of Management and Budget and U.S. Department of Justice. Washington, D.C.: Urban Institute.

Zimmermann, Wendy N., and Michael Fix. 1994. "Immigrant Policy in the States: A Wavering Welcome." In *Immigration and Ethnicity: The Integration of America's Newest Arrivals,* edited by Barry Edmonston and Jeffrey S. Passel, Washington, D.C.: Urban Institute Press.

Chapter Four

TAKING THE PULSE OF PUBLIC OPINION TOWARD IMMIGRANTS

Thomas J. Espenshade

As noted in preceding chapters, data from the Current Population Survey show that the proportion of foreign-born U.S. residents reached 8.8 percent in March 1995, up from 7.9 percent in 1990, and nearly double the 1970 figure of 4.8 percent (Hansen 1996; U.S. Bureau of the Census 1995). Persons born outside the United States now comprise the largest fraction of the U.S. population since World War II. Of the 23 million foreign-born U.S. residents, nearly one-quarter have arrived here since 1990. Roughly one-third live in California, but other states having large numbers of immigrants include New York (with 3 million), Texas (2.1 million), Florida (2 million), and New Jersey (1.1 million).

Legislative agendas at the federal and state levels mirror these demographic shifts and associated concerns with rising immigration and its impacts. Most of the new initiatives (1) seek reimbursement from the federal government for services that states and local areas are required to provide to undocumented migrants, (2) aim to establish English as the official language in public discourse, (3) hope to limit access to welfare and other social services not only by illegal immigrants but also by certain categories of legal permanent resident aliens, or (4) otherwise attempt to reduce the flow of undocumented immigrants into the country (Federation for American Immigration Reform 1995; State and Local Coalition on Immigration 1995a, b). Measures similar to California's Proposition 187 are gaining momentum in other states (Ayres 1994; Sherwood 1994); some private groups are attempting to limit immigration visas for skilled workers (Bradsher 1995); and in advance of its 1997 final report, the U.S. Commission on Immigration Reform has released preliminary recommendations to curb the number of undocumented and legal immigrants coming into the United States (U.S. Commission on Immigration Reform 1994, 1995).

Despite the growing demographic and legislative impacts of immigration, we know surprisingly little about Americans' attitudes toward immigrants and immigration. What we do know is based largely on national public opinion samples (Simon and Alexander 1993), which tend to show that tolerance is highly correlated with the state of the U.S. economy (Espenshade and Hempstead 1996). Attitudes toward immigrants tend to be more positive when unemployment rates are low, but when unemployment rises, more people say that the level of immigration to the United States should be reduced.

Relatively little attention has been paid to public opinion at the state level. California has collected the most data (Muller and Espenshade 1985), but much of it has gone unexamined in any systematic way. Data from national polls suggest that Californians' attitudes do not differ appreciably from opinions of residents in other states in the West, South, or North Central regions once controls are introduced for other respondent characteristics. Residents in the Northeast, and especially those in New England, appear to have the most liberal attitudes toward immigrants. This finding stands up even after controlling for whether individual respondents think of themselves as politically liberal, moderate, or conservative (Espenshade and Hempstead 1996).

With more than 1 million foreign-born residents, New Jersey is an important immigration state. Approximately 13.4 percent of all New Jerseyans have been born outside the United States or Puerto Rico (Hansen 1996). Yet seldom have public opinion surveys been conducted exclusively within the state to assess residents' opinions about immigrants. We do not know, for example, how similar New Jersey is to the rest of the United States, whether the perceptions of New Jersey's residents concerning the labor market and other impacts of immigration are substantially correct, how population subgroups differ from each other with respect to immigrant attitudes, or the underlying determinants of broader attitudes toward the appropriate number of immigrants in the state.

This chapter reports findings from a public opinion survey designed to measure New Jersey residents' attitudes about immigrants and their perceived impacts. The major focus is on responses to a survey question about the preferred number of foreign-born persons in the state. Following a discussion of the sample and resulting data, survey results are presented, organized into two parts: first, an exploratory analysis that situates the importance of immigration in relation to other issues facing the state and begins to examine people's opinions about the appropriate level of New Jersey immigration; and, second, a regression analysis of factors affecting public opinion toward immigrants. A summary section concludes the chapter.

DATA

The survey sample consisted of 1,201 adult New Jersey residents who were interviewed in English in a telephone survey conducted by the Gallup Poll Organization during the first two weeks of September 1994. Households were contacted by random-digit dialing methods to provide representation of both listed and unlisted (including not-yet-listed) numbers. Within each household, one respondent was selected by choosing the adult (age 21 or older) with the most recent birthday. Gallup's five-call design, used to preserve the representativeness of the sample, resulted in an overall response rate of 63 percent. The questionnaire obtained information about the number of adults and the number of separate telephone lines into the household. Data were weighted using the ratio of adults to telephone lines to ensure that each adult had equal probability of being contacted. Gallup also compared the age, gender, and educational characteristics of the weighted sample of interviewed adults with the adult population of New Jersey as determined by the Current Population Survey. Poststratification weighting was used to obtain a sample that matches the adult New Jersey population.

Two types of questions were asked during the interview, which usually lasted about 15 minutes. The first part of the survey elicited information about respondents' attitudes, including their attitudes about problems facing the United States and New Jersey, feelings about an appropriate level of immigration into New Jersey, and perceptions of the characteristics and impacts of immigrants in such contexts as the labor market, dependency on social services, and use of the English language. The second half of the questionnaire asked about respondents' demographic and socioeconomic characteristics. Resulting measures pertain to age, sex, marital status, and religion, and to a variety of indicators for place of residence, political views, socioeconomic status, ethnicity, and nativity.

EXPLORATORY ANALYSIS

This section presents information on the importance of immigration in relation to other issues facing New Jersey residents. It also begins to consider factors associated with respondents' preferences for the number of immigrants in the state.

Salience of Immigration Issues

Early in the interview, prior to questions about immigration, respondents were asked whether they thought crime, taxes, and jobs were serious problems in New Jersey. Weighted responses, derived from the full sample of 1,201 individuals, are shown in table 4.1. Based on the proportion of respondents believing that any issue is a "big problem," it appears that New Jersey residents are most concerned with crime, followed by taxes, and then jobs. No question required respondents to construe immigration as a problem. Rather, people were subsequently asked, "Thinking of all the issues facing New Jersey today, how important an issue is immigration from other countries?" Roughly 55 percent of those sampled believed that immigration is "very important," another 27 percent felt it is "somewhat important," and 18 percent considered it either "not too important" or "not at all important." These responses suggest that issues surrounding immigration are roughly comparable in importance to those related to taxes if "issue" is interpreted as meaning "problem." Immigration is considered somewhat less important than crime, but definitely more important than a lack of jobs. The salience of immigration issues in New Jersey runs counter to a suggestion by Harwood (1986) that the public's attitude toward immigration is both inconsistent and lacking in intensity. To support his view, Harwood cited a 1984 Gallup survey in which illegal immigration ranked along with protecting the environment and well behind the significance that respondents attached to unemployment, inflation, or the threat of nuclear war as "very important problems."

Table 4.1. SERIOUSNESS OF THREE PROBLEMS FACING NEW JERSEY (WEIGHTED PERCENTAGE DISTRIBUTION. N = 1.201)

Response	Crime	Taxes	Jobs
Big problem	70.1	58.1	43.5
Somewhat of a problem	26.3	31.7	42.6
Not a problem	2.1	8.4	10.5
Don't know	1.2	1.5	3.0
Refused	0.3	0.3	0.5
Total	100.0	100.0	100.0

Preferred Number of Immigrants

Respondents were presented several general questions about immigration, including whether today's new immigrants would be welcomed if they moved into their neighborhood and whether most of the recent immigrants to New Jersey have a positive or negative effect on the state. The broadest of such questions, and the one with most relevance to immigration policy, was an item querying respondents' views on the appropriate number of immigrants in New Jersey. In particular, each sampled individual was asked, "Would you like to see the number of immigrants in New Jersey increased, kept at the present level, or decreased?"

Responses to this question are shown in table 4.2. Fewer than 3 percent of New Jersey adults want the number of immigrants in the state to increase. Slightly more than half feel that the current number is about right, and nearly 40 percent say that the number is too high and should be reduced. Whether or not these views can be interpreted as anti-immigrant sentiment, residents of New Jersey exhibit greater tolerance for immigrants than people in the rest of the United States. For example, in a 1993 nationwide CBS News/New York Times poll, more than 60 percent of adults expressed a preference for lowered levels of immigration (Espenshade and Hempstead 1996).

Table 4.2 also cross-tabulates views about the desired number of immigrants by whether respondents consider immigration to be an important issue. People who believe that immigration to New Jersey is a "very important" issue are the most likely to feel that the number of immigrants already in the state should be lowered. As the perceived seriousness of immigration declines, so also does the proportion of respondents who feel the number of immigrants should be reduced.

Table 4.2. DESIRED NUMBER OF IMMIGRANTS IN NEW JERSEY BY IMPORTANCE OF IMMIGRATION ISSUE (WEIGHTED PERCENTAGE DISTRIBUTION, N = 1,201)

Desired Number of Immigrants in New Jersey	Importance of Immigration Issues Facing State				
	Very Important	Somewhat Important	Not too Important	Not at All Important	Total[a]
More	3.1	1.7	4.6	3.2	2.9
Keep at present level	42.6	62.4	71.5	42.3	51.4
Fewer	51.3	26.8	15.7	45.8	39.6
Don't know	2.2	6.1	5.4	6.0	4.3
Refused	0.8	3.0	2.9	2.7	1.8
Total	100.0	100.0	100.0	100.0	1,201

a. Includes 0.8 percent of respondents who said "don't know" or who refused to answer.

Among adults who think that immigration is "not too important" an issue, just 15.7 percent want fewer immigrants, whereas 71.5 percent judge the present number to be satisfactory. The category of persons thinking that immigration is "not at all important" represents an aberration, but only a small fraction of New Jersey adults (5.3 percent) fall into this group. Based on these data, it seems reasonable to conclude that when respondents hear "issue" in the context of immigration, they think "problem." And the more serious a problem people believe immigration is, the more likely they are to want fewer immigrants.

We also examined respondents' preferences for the number of New Jersey immigrants by whether survey participants themselves were born outside the United States. Not surprisingly, foreign-born individuals express the greatest liking for other immigrants. Only 21 percent of foreign-born New Jersey adults say the number of immigrants in the state should be decreased, whereas one-half prefer keeping the current number, and 11 percent think the number should be raised. At the other extreme, slightly more than half of all second-generation migrants—that is, native-born individuals who have at least one foreign-born parent—feel that the number of immigrants should be reduced, and just 2 percent believe the number should be raised. Native-born respondents having two native-born parents express views that are between those of first- and second-generation immigrants. Because these individuals comprise roughly 70 percent of the total sample, their attitudes are very similar to all adults in New Jersey. Among these so-called third (or higher-order) generation immigrants, 38 percent prefer a reduction in the foreign-born population, 54 percent believe the current number is appropriate, and just 2 percent would like the number raised.

To begin to uncover what lies behind respondents' beliefs that immigration is a problem, individuals who said that the number of immigrants should be reduced were asked open-ended questions about why they felt this way. The most important reason related to fears that there are not enough jobs to go around and that immigrants take jobs away from native workers. Almost 40 percent of adults who prefer fewer immigrants cited this factor. Other important reasons relate to concerns that New Jersey is already overcrowded and does not need more people (expressed by 17 percent of respondents wanting fewer immigrants), that immigrants place a welfare, social service, and educational burden on the state, causing taxes to rise (12 percent), and that New Jersey already has enough problems and needs to take care of its own people first (7 percent). Smaller proportions of respondents mentioned that many immigrants are in the United States illegally, that many who come are without proper skills or education, and that new immigrants are unwilling to learn English.

More than half (55 percent) of second-generation immigrants responded that fear of job competition was their primary reason for wanting fewer immigrants. Concerns that immigrants were partly responsible for the rise in criminal activity were also important among second-generation immigrants; more than half of those who wanted fewer immigrants gave as an additional reason a belief that immigrants contribute to the crime problem. These findings suggest that second-generation immigrants feel more vulnerable to the threat of immigration than do foreign-born persons or individuals with deeper roots in the United States.

If respondents said they preferred a reduction in the number of New Jersey's immigrants, they were asked whether the number should be decreased "a lot" or "a little." Nearly three-fourths expressed the opinion that immigration should be decreased "a lot." Economic reasons were more likely to be given by people who want a substantial reduction in the number of immigrants. Roughly 60 percent cited as their prime consideration the belief that immigrants took jobs away from native workers, lowered the general wage level, caused taxes to go up, or otherwise had an adverse impact on the economy. Only 15 percent of these respondents cited overcrowding as a consideration. Among adults who preferred just "a little" reduction in the number of immigrants, economic considerations were mentioned by approximately 50 percent of adults, whereas environmental/overcrowding issues were cited by nearly one-quarter of individuals.

REGRESSION ANALYSIS

The response variable (NUMBER) in this study's regression analysis is constructed from answers to two questions. Each sample individual was asked whether he or she would like to see the number of immigrants in New Jersey increase, stay the same, or decrease. Those who said decrease (increase) were then asked, "Is this decrease (increase) a lot or a little?" As noted earlier, fewer than 3 percent of New Jersey's adult population prefer an increase in the foreign-born presence in the state. Consequently, the response variable consists of four categories: persons who would like to see the number of immigrants in the state (1) increase, (2) stay the same, (3) decrease a little, or (4) decrease a lot. Some people in the sample responded in ways that precluded their being assigned to one of these categories. These individuals typically said they did not know how they felt, or they refused to answer the question. There were 86 such individuals out of a total sample of 1,201 adults, and they were excluded from the regression analysis. Table 4.3 shows the distribution of the remaining 1,115 cases into four ordinal response categories. Most adults in New Jersey seem satisfied with the current number of immigrants. However, among those who are not, individuals who prefer a substantial reduction in immigrants outnumber the total in the two remaining categories.

Methods

Because of the ordinal nature of the response variable, individual response categories are coded as: decrease a lot = 1, decrease a little = 2, kept the same = 3, and increase = 4. With this scheme, a positive (negative) regression coefficient means that an increase in the value of a given predictor variable will lower (raise) the likelihood of people preferring smaller numbers of immigrants. We fit our weighted regression models using ordered-logit (or proportional odds) regression techniques (McCullagh 1980; McKelvey and Zavoina 1975). With these methods, a regression coefficient of, say, 0.2 may be interpreted as meaning that a one-unit increase in the corresponding explanatory variable is expected to be associated with a $[\exp\{-0.2\} - 1] \times 100$, or an 18 percent reduction in the odds of falling into or below any given response category. Negative regression coefficients increase the odds of being in a particular response category or a lower one. We also refit some of our models with ordered-probit regression methods, which are also appropriate given the nature of the dependent variable. These models appear to fit the data less well

Table 4.3. DISTRIBUTION OF RESPONSE VARIABLE (NUMBER) INTO RESPONSE CATEGORIES (UNWEIGHTED, N = 1,115)

Response Category	Frequency	Percentage
Increase	39	3.5
Stay the same	613	55.0
Decrease a little	131	11.7
Decrease a lot	332	29.8
Total	1,115	100.0

than ordered-logit methods do. In addition, regression coefficients derived from ordered-probit approaches are not as easily interpreted.

Role of Respondent Characteristics

A potential source of variation in individual responses to the NUMBER question is the fact that respondents differ from each other with respect to demographic and other socioeconomic characteristics. The influence of sample persons' characteristics is shown in figure 4.1 where the size of individual regression coefficients is given by the length of the horizontal bars extending to either side of the "zero" line. This model includes such basic demographic determinants as age, marital status, and religion, but it also incorporates the effects of individuals' place of residence, political views, socioeconomic status, and ethnicity. This specification was chosen after some preliminary work to identify potentially significant explanatory variables in simpler pair-wise comparisons.

Age is a significant predictor of immigrant attitudes. Older respondents are more likely to want fewer immigrants. But once people reach retirement age, their attitudes no longer appear to differ much from those of persons under age 30 (who comprise the reference group). These results are generally consistent with an analysis of southern Californians' attitudes toward undocumented immigrants (Espenshade and Calhoun 1993), but they are at odds with findings by Hoskin and Mishler (1983), who discovered no clear relationship with age in their U.S. data. The apparent influence of age is open to interpretation. Because the shape of the age effect parallels the change of income over the life cycle, it could be that the negative effect of age corresponds to concerns with the labor-market impacts of immigrants. These concerns are likely to grow as individuals reach their peak income-earning years and then subside once they are no longer in the labor force. It could also be that age is partially correlated with conservative propensities, as suggested by Lipset and colleagues (1954). Another possible explanation is that, in relation to immigration, older people sense a greater amount of social change in comparison to when they were young; these departures from the status quo might also be expected to engender anxiety.[1]

This analysis is the first to examine the regression effect of marital status, and we found that married individuals have significantly more tolerant attitudes toward immigrants than unmarried persons. The reason for this differential is unclear, but it may relate to perceived

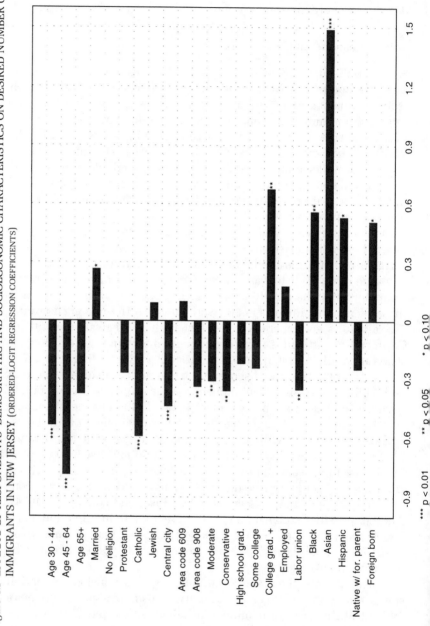

Figure 4.1 EFFECTS OF RESPONDENTS' DEMOGRAPHIC AND SOCIOECONOMIC CHARACTERISTICS ON DESIRED NUMBER OF IMMIGRANTS IN NEW JERSEY (ORDERED-LOGIT REGRESSION COEFFICIENTS)

*** $p < 0.01$ ** $p < 0.05$ * $p < 0.10$

labor-market impacts of immigrants. Married respondents typically have a spouse who can contribute or already is contributing to household income, thereby spreading the risks and reducing a family's vulnerability to a job loss in comparison to risks faced by a single earner.

Nor has the influence of religion been studied previously. Our results suggest that Catholics have more negative feelings toward immigrants than other religious groups, including those with no religious preference. This result is surprising in light of the strong support for liberal immigration policies articulated by the Catholic Church in the United States (Simcox 1993, 1995), but other polls suggest that the majority of the Catholic laity do not agree with its pro-immigration positions (Beck 1993). This finding is at least consistent with the division that exists between the church's members and the teachings of the Vatican on other matters such as the practice of birth control (Westoff and Bumpass 1973).

What influence does place of residence have on immigrant attitudes? The existing literature identifies two contrasting sources of effects. The contact hypothesis suggests that greater contact with immigrants fosters familiarity and understanding and therefore more sympathetic attitudes (Amir 1969, 1976; Kinder and Mendelberg 1995; Rothbart and John 1993; Stephan 1985). Other work supports an alternative group conflict hypothesis whereby intergroup contact intensities conflict (Kinder and Mendelberg 1995; Van den Berghe 1967). Work by Espenshade and Calhoun (1993) suggests that recent contact with an undocumented migrant is associated with a greater sense that illegal immigration is a serious problem, but it has no relation to whether undocumented migrants are believed to have an unfavorable effect on California.

Figure 4.1 contains two indicators of residential location. Central-city residents show significantly more intolerance for immigrants than suburban dwellers. This, together with the fact that New Jersey's foreign-born population is disproportionately located in central cities, suggests that greater contact with immigrants fosters more negative opinions about them, which is consistent with the group conflict hypothesis. This study also had information on respondents' telephone area codes. Area code 201, which is the reference group in figure 4.1, includes Bergen, Essex, Hudson, and Passaic counties in the northeastern part of New Jersey, where most of the state's immigrant population is concentrated. The belt of counties surrounding the 201 area code includes Warren, Hunterdon, Somerset, Middlesex, Union, Monmouth, and Ocean and comprises most of the 908 area code. Residents in the west central and southern part of New Jersey occupy area code 609. It is apparent that individuals from the 908 area code are significantly less inclined to favor more immigrants than are other New Jersey adults.[2]

When the county intercensal population growth rate from 1980 to 1990 is included in the model, the effect of area code disappears, which suggests that residents in the rapidly growing counties display the most negative immigrant attitudes. Not surprisingly, counties in the 908 area code are some of the fastest growing in New Jersey. There are two possible reasons why local area population growth might influence feelings toward immigrants. First, long-time residents of these counties might simply object to the overcrowding, added congestion, and disappearance of open space that come with rapid growth. Some of the open-ended answers to survey questions, in fact, provide support for this view. Long-time residents may not object to immigrants qua immigrants, but simply because immigration adds one more element to general population growth. Second, some of the newcomers to rapid-growth counties may be refugees from central-city environments who bring with them anti-immigrant feelings spawned in urban settings (Frey 1995). Whatever the underlying cause, there is a clear association in the data between immigrant sentiment and region of residence, with local area population growth rates playing an important intervening role.[3]

An individual's political identification is also associated with his or her attitudes toward immigrants. Moderates are significantly less tolerant than liberals (the omitted category), and conservatives have the most negative views. These results are consistent with findings that politically conservative respondents in California and in three southern states expressed more negative attitudes toward Indo-Chinese migrants than did their liberal counterparts (Starr and Roberts 1982), but the results contradict research by Day (1990: 5), who concluded that immigration "is not an issue that divides people easily along partisan or ideological lines."

College graduates are more likely to express a preference for the same or higher numbers of immigrants than adults who have not completed a college degree. Among those with less education, however, there seems to be little difference in the way immigrant numbers are viewed. These results are generally consistent with those reported by Espenshade and Calhoun (1993) and by Espenshade and Hempstead (1996). Other studies have also found evidence that negative attitudes toward immigrants decrease with more education (Day 1989,

1990; Hoskin and Mishler 1983; Moore 1986; Starr and Roberts 1982; Tarrance et al. 1989a, b). Just how one should interpret the influence of education is a subject of controversy. One view is the education-as-liberation hypothesis, by which an advanced formal education confers a more enlightened perspective that is less susceptible to appeals to intergroup negativism (McCloskey and Brill 1983; Sniderman, Brody, and Kuklinski 1984). An alternative perspective is that education produces a more sophisticated cognitive style that is able to resist simplistic, categorical, or value-laden questions, whereas persons with less education are likely to succumb because the available response categories seem close enough to their views (Jackman and Senter 1980). Finally, Jackman and Muha (1984) argue that advanced education simply allows individuals to construct more sophisticated ideologies to protect dominant group interests. However one chooses to interpret education-attitudes linkages, available theories usually predict that persons with more education will also have more liberal views about the consequences of immigration.

As noted earlier, one of the most prevalent beliefs about immigrants is that they take jobs away from native workers, increase unemployment, and reduce wages and working conditions in selected low-wage occupations (Espenshade and Calhoun 1993). Typically, poorer native workers have the greatest anxieties that these consequences will materialize (Simon 1987). Linkages between socioeconomic status and attitudes toward immigrants are often explained by a labor-market competition hypothesis, according to which people with higher incomes, more education, and higher-status occupations will be more optimistic about the implications of immigration. Employed persons may experience greater economic security than unemployed individuals or those out of the labor force and, by implication, may be less likely to express a preference for fewer immigrants. In contrast, to the extent that union members are drawn disproportionately from the lower end of the skills distribution, either being a union member or living in a household that contains a union member might be expected to be associated with less tolerance for immigrants. The employment status and labor union membership variables in figure 4.1 are generally consistent with these expectations. Being employed is positively associated with the preferred number of immigrants, but the effect is insignificant. Labor union affiliation is significantly correlated with wanting fewer immigrants in New Jersey. (Members of labor unions in southern California were also substantially more likely to believe that the influx of undocumented migrants into the region had an unfavorable effect on the state [Espenshade and Calhoun 1993]). As previously noted, the influence of education is also consistent with the labor-market competition hypothesis.

Nonwhites and blacks, in particular, may hold more restrictionist immigration views for fear of job competition from migrants (Cain and Kiewiet 1986; Harwood 1985; Simon 1985). Briggs (1995), for example, has argued that the urban black labor force has been adversely affected by the resurgence of mass immigration into cities of the North and West. In a 1983 survey conducted for the Federation for American Immigration Reform, 82 percent of blacks believed that illegal immigrants take jobs away from native workers, compared with 58 percent of Hispanic Americans (Harwood 1986; see also Jackson 1995; Sullivan 1995). And in a 1989 Texas survey, blacks showed more concern about the effects of undocumented migration than Hispanics (Tarrance et al. 1989a). At the same time, however, blacks may feel a sense of solidarity with other people of color, and perhaps this sentiment also extends to current immigrants, many of whom are nonwhite (Tanton 1995).

A feeling of solidarity with immigrants might also shape the attitudes of Hispanics and Asians, because most of the recent legal and undocumented migrants to the United States come from either Latin America or Asia (Fix and Passel 1994). It may not be surprising, therefore, that Hispanics display more pro-immigrant views than non-Hispanics (Cain and Kiewiet 1986; Day 1989; Harwood 1983, 1985; Miller, Polinard, and Wrinkle 1984). This relation is sometimes also explained by a cultural affinity hypothesis (Espenshade and Calhoun 1993). Cultural and ethnic ties to recent immigrants promote pro-immigrant attitudes and appeals for more liberal immigration policies (Day 1989, 1990). The results in figure 4.1 generally support the cultural affinity/ethnic solidarity hypothesis. They show that blacks, Asians, and Hispanics are all significantly more likely than non-Hispanic whites in New Jersey to prefer the same or a higher number of immigrants. The Asian effect is especially large and significant. These results, including those for blacks, are consistent with minority-group effects found by Espenshade and Hempstead (1996) in a nationwide opinion survey.

Foreign-born individuals and their children might more readily identify with other immigrants than do people whose ancestors have been in the United States for several generations. This expectation is supported by Day (1990), who found in an analysis of a 1986 poll that first- and second-generation immigrants typically have more pro-immigrant sentiments and are more likely to support relaxing U.S.

immigration policy. Moreover, Hispanic immigrants in California are more optimistic than native-born Hispanics about the fiscal contributions of undocumented migrants, are less restrictive in their views about U.S. immigration policy, and are less concerned that illegal workers are taking jobs away from Americans (Day 1989). For instance, the proportion of Hispanics agreeing that undocumented migrants take jobs away from American workers is least for Hispanic immigrants (9 percent) and then rises monotonically with generational status to 27 percent for the fourth generation. Our New Jersey results only partially agree with these earlier findings. Foreign-born adults are significantly more likely than native-born individuals with two native-born parents to believe that immigration should be kept the same or increased. On the other hand, the native-born children of immigrants are the most likely group to express a preference for fewer immigrants. As noted earlier, fears associated with job competition appear to weigh heavily among this group's concerns.

Overall, the model shown in figure 4.1 fits the data well. The model has a pseudo-R^2 = .077 and a significant chi-squared test statistic of 180.07 on 23 degrees of freedom, which allows one to reject the hypothesis that the true model coefficients are jointly equal to zero. The study also fit an expanded model to the data that includes all the predictors in figure 4.1 together with a respondent's sex, income, and party affiliation (Republican, Democrat, or Independent), whether he or she lives in one of the six counties in northeastern New Jersey that contain the largest number of immigrants, whether he or she owns or operates a business, and whether he or she is politically active as evidenced by registering to vote, voting in the 1993 gubernatorial election, volunteering to work for political candidates, or often contacting elected officials. A likelihood-ratio chi-squared test (with a test statistic of 6.17 on 11 degrees of freedom) failed to reject the hypothesis that the true coefficients of the newly included variables are jointly zero. I therefore concluded that the larger model does not improve significantly on the fit of the model in figure 4.1.

Role of Respondent Attitudes

Particular views that respondents hold, either about the consequences of immigration or about issues that at first may appear unrelated to immigration, are a second potential source of variation in answers to the NUMBER question. The influence of these attitudinal variables is shown in figure 4.2. Six groups of attitudinal dimensions are represented, including New Jersey adults' beliefs about problems facing the

Figure 4.2 GROSS AND NET EFFECTS OF RESPONDENTS' ATTITUDES ON DESIRED NUMBER OF IMMIGRANTS IN NEW JERSEY
(ORDERED-LOGIT REGRESSION COEFFICIENTS)

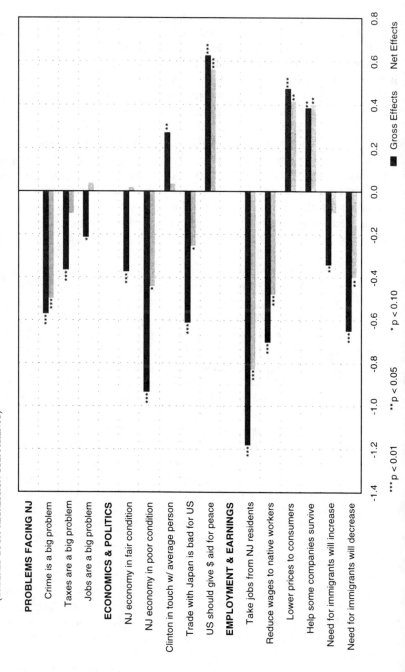

Figure 4.2 (continued)

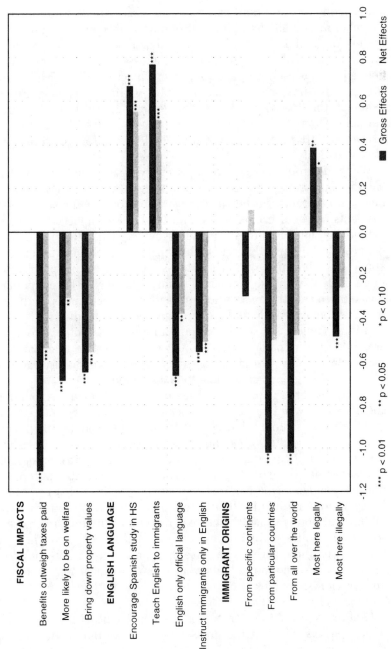

state, economic, and political issues not closely tied to immigration; the labor market and fiscal impacts of immigrants; matters concerning the use of English in schools and in public discourse; and the origins and legal status of recent immigrants. Figure 4.2 shows two regression coefficients for each predictor variable. The gross effect results from fitting only those explanatory variables within a given group (for example, the "problems facing New Jersey" group) to the response variable. The net impact of each covariate is derived from fitting an ordered-logit regression model to all predictors in figure 4.2 simultaneously.

When the problems facing New Jersey are considered by themselves, each is significantly and negatively associated with the desired number of immigrants. Earlier it was seen in table 4.1 that New Jersey residents consider crime, taxes, and jobs to be important problems facing the state. Figure 4.2 contains evidence that immigrants are believed to be partially responsible for these problems, because respondents who think that crime, taxes, or jobs are a big problem are more likely to want the number of immigrants in New Jersey reduced. Based on the relative magnitudes of regression coefficients, it appears that New Jersey residents link immigrants most readily with crime and increasingly less so to taxes and to jobs. When other predictors are added to the model in figure 4.2, only the crime dimension remains statistically significant, perhaps because explanatory variables in subsequent groups also relate to taxes and jobs.

Recent research using nationwide opinion poll data has found associations between respondents' desired level of U.S. immigration and their views about the health of the nation's economy, their sense of social and political alienation, and the degree to which their economic and political orientations can be characterized as either isolationist or universalistic (Espenshade and Hempstead 1996). In particular, respondents who feel that the economy is in robust health and likely to grow rapidly in the future are more tolerant of higher levels of immigration; residents who feel marginalized from mainstream social and political institutions are inclined toward lower levels of U.S. immigration, perhaps because they blame immigrants for part of their problems; and individuals whose views are most consistent with an isolationist outlook prefer fewer immigrants than people with a more global perspective.

Results from the New Jersey poll are consistent with these nationwide findings. Each of the gross effects under the economics and politics heading in figure 4.2 is statistically significant and has the expected sign. Residents who believe that New Jersey's economy is in either fair or poor condition want fewer immigrants than people who believe the economy is in excellent or good circumstances. And the lower one's assessment of the current economic situation is, the more negative are one's attitudes about the appropriate number of immigrants in the state. Figure 4.2 includes only one measure of political alienation—whether President Bill Clinton has kept in touch with what average people think. Those who believe he has (that is, the less-alienated respondents) are more likely to prefer the same or a higher number of immigrants.

Figure 4.2 includes two measures of isolationist sentiment, one dealing with economic issues and the other with foreign relations. Individuals who believe that trading with Japan—both buying and selling products—is bad for the U.S. economy are significantly less likely to want the same or a higher number of immigrants in New Jersey. Respondents who think that the United States has a responsibility to give financial help to military peacekeeping efforts around the world—an indicator of a global outlook—are more likely to prefer the same or even a higher number of New Jersey immigrants. The net effects of predictors in this category are generally smaller than the gross effects, but their signs and levels of significance nevertheless support the suggestion that attitudes that on the surface appear to have little in common with immigration do in fact tap underlying dimensions that are tied to how one perceives immigrants.

The next category in figure 4.2 pertains to presumed effects of immigrants on the employment and earnings opportunities of native workers. Some of these attitudes relate to immigrants' labor-market impacts, whereas others are indicators of a broader range of concerns that fit into a cost-benefit evaluation of the consequences of immigration to New Jersey. According to this perspective, respondents who feel that immigrants are likely to have favorable economic repercussions are also likely to be more supportive of generous immigrant allotments. The results in figure 4.2 strongly support these expectations. Respondents in the sample are more likely to prefer reduced levels of immigration if they believe that immigrants take jobs away from other New Jersey residents and lower the wages paid to native workers in occupations with an immigrant presence. The effect of perceived job competition is especially strong and consistent with my earlier observation that worry about an insufficient number of jobs is the principal reason New Jersey residents give for wanting fewer immigrants. Similar results have been found by Espenshade and Hempstead (1996). On the other hand, believing that paying lower wages to immigrants results in lower prices to consumers or that some companies depend on immigrant workers to stay in business is associated with more tolerant attitudes.

Respondents who feel that the future need for immigrant workers in New Jersey will either increase or decrease are significantly more likely to prefer fewer immigrants than residents who foresee no change. The symmetry of responses is interesting. Wanting fewer immigrants is understandable if the foreign-born component of the workforce is likely to decline. Why respondents also prefer fewer immigrants when they believe that the demand for this group of workers will grow is less clear. Perhaps some people feel that these jobs should go to native workers instead. This paradox disappears when net effects of these predictors are considered; the effect of thinking the need for immigrant workers will increase is no longer significant. Net influences of the remaining attitudinal predictors remain strong, however, and maintain their expected directions.

Fiscal considerations surrounding immigration to New Jersey refer to taxes that immigrants pay and social benefits they receive, as well as to tax and expenditure implications for the native population. The results in figure 4.2 suggest that New Jersey adults' perceptions of immigrants' fiscal impacts are significant predictors of attitudes about the desirable size of the state's foreign-born population. Respondents who believe that immigrants receive more in education, health, and other state benefits than they pay for with their taxes are more likely to prefer a reduction in the number of immigrants. Preferences for a smaller foreign-born population are also associated with feelings that immigrants are more likely than other New Jersey residents to end up on welfare and that immigrants bring down property values in neighborhoods where they are concentrated. The net influence of these predictors remains significant even when all other attitudinal measures are included in the model. These findings are consistent with other research. Americans are less likely to prefer a decrease in the level of U.S. immigration when they believe that most new immigrants do not end up on welfare (Espenshade and Hempstead 1996). Southern California residents are significantly more likely to feel that undocumented migrants constitute a serious problem when they think that these individuals are more likely than natives to receive welfare benefits or that illegal immigrants imply a greater fiscal burden for other taxpayers (Espenshade and Calhoun 1993).

In contrast to approaches that stress tangible costs and benefits of immigration, the symbolic politics model of attitude formation emphasizes attachments to enduring values as sources of public opinion (Sears and Citrin 1985; Sears and Huddy 1987; Sears et al. 1980).

Citrin, Reingold, and Green (1990) have extended the symbolic politics model to include attitudes toward cultural minorities. They found that the primary symbols of being an American are "speaking and writing English" and "treating people of all races and backgrounds equally" (or what some have called egalitarianism). For example, in describing a series of successful state-level initiatives to promote English as the official language, they noted:

> When voters were presented with the opportunity to translate attitudes into action, there was no doubt that in America, as elsewhere, language is a powerful symbol of national identity among most social and political groups. Symbolic challenges to the status of English and to the status of the dominant culture in general inevitably arouse hostility among the majority. (p. 1149)

The symbolic politics model predicts that respondents who are most concerned about possible future threats to the English language from non-English speakers will have the strongest anti-immigrant views. On the other hand, one may hypothesize that the staunchest advocates of egalitarian principles will be least likely to view immigrants in negative terms.

The results in figure 4.2 pertaining to language issues provide additional support for this theory. Sample individuals were asked whether, given all the changes in the mix of people in New Jersey, they thought it a good idea to encourage students to take Spanish in high school. They were also asked whether the public schools should be expected to provide classes to teach English to immigrant school children who do not speak English. Responding in the affirmative to these questions is an indication of support for egalitarian norms that are part of a liberal conception of civic identity (Citrin et al. 1990). Affirmative responses are also significantly associated with a greater likelihood of preferring the same or larger numbers of immigrants.

Twenty-one states in the United States have passed legislation making English their official state language (State and Local Coalition on Immigration 1995b). Although New Jersey is not among them, survey participants who believe that English is the only language that should be used on government forms and public signs are significantly more inclined than others to prefer a reduction in the number of immigrants in the state. So, too, are New Jersey residents who feel that the public schools should use English-only classes to instruct immigrant school children who do not speak English. These findings are consistent with what Citrin et al. (1990) have called a more restrictive or ethnocentric version of American nationality, and they support the current study's hypothesis that individuals most concerned about possible threats to the English language are most likely to prefer fewer immigrants in New Jersey. It is noteworthy that the net effects of the English-language variables remain strong when other attitudinal measures are added to the model. The analysis by Espenshade and Calhoun (1993) of attitudes toward undocumented migrants in southern California provides additional support for a language-oriented symbolic politics model.

The last set of issues in figure 4.2 pertains to immigrant origins— where New Jersey's immigrants come from and whether they are here legally. A preliminary analysis suggested that recent migrants who come from Latin America or Asia are viewed no less favorably than European immigrants.[4] But if respondents had any opinion at all about where immigrants originate, they were more likely to have negative views concerning the desirable number of immigrants than individuals who gave "don't know" as an answer. Residents who named a particular country as the source of most new immigrants to New Jersey or who said that immigrants come from all over were most inclined to prefer fewer immigrants. These effects disappear once other attitudinal dimensions are introduced. Sample participants were also asked whether they thought that most of the recent immigrants to New Jersey were in the state legally or illegally. Figure 4.2 suggests that attitudes about the appropriate number of immigrants in New Jersey are considerably more lenient when residents believe that most immigrants are here legally. The net effects of legal status are substantially weaker, however, than the gross effects. Perceptions of migrants' legal status also influence how respondents nationwide feel about whether the level of U.S. immigration should be reduced (Espenshade and Belanger 1996; Espenshade and Hempstead 1996).

The net-effects model that contains all the attitudinal predictors in figure 4.2 fits the data well. It has a pseudo-$R^2 = .181$ and a significant chi-squared test statistic of 421.97 on 26 degrees of freedom. Using a likelihood-ratio comparison to test this model against a null model with no explanatory variables, one may reject the hypothesis that the effects of the complete set of attitudinal predictors are jointly zero.

Comparisons among Models

To this point, I have considered two separate models. One model demonstrates the importance of respondents' demographic and socio-economic characteristics as determinants of attitudes toward immigrants, and the other model shows the strong influence associated with attitudes that respondents hold about a variety of issues. Do the conclusions about the relevance of these two sets of factors hold up when their effects are considered simultaneously? To address this question, I estimated a combined model containing all the predictor variables from figures 4.1 and 4.2. The log-likelihood statistics and degrees of freedom associated with the individual and combined models are shown in table 4.4. When the characteristics variables are added to a model containing the attitudinal predictors, the joint effects of the newly included variables are significant at the 0.001 level (the chi-squared statistic for a likelihood-ratio test is 73.6 on 23 degrees of freedom). Similarly, when the combined model is compared with the characteristics model, the added effects of the attitudinal measures are also significant at 0.001 (chi-squared statistic equals 315.5 on 26 degrees of freedom). Therefore, both sets of factors contribute to a better understanding of New Jersey residents' attitudes about the desired number of immigrants in the state.

It should be stressed that the strength and direction of the net effects in figures 4.1 and 4.2 are maintained in a combined model. Perceptions that immigrants have negative labor-market and fiscal impacts or that they pose a threat to the primacy of the English language are associated with preferences for fewer immigrants. Respondents who are older or Catholic, or who live in rapidly growing counties, have significantly stronger anti-immigrant attitudes, whereas residents who are married or from an Asian background continue to have more tolerant attitudes.

CONCLUSIONS

New Jersey's adult population was polled in September 1994 about its attitudes concerning the number of foreign-born individuals in the

Table 4.4. LOG-LIKELIHOOD STATISTICS AND DEGREES OF FREEDOM FOR COMPARING THREE MODELS

Model		Log Likelihood	Degrees of Freedom
C:	Characteristics model, includes all predictors in figure 4.1	−1074.62	23
A:	Attitudes model, includes all predictors in figure 4.2	−953.68	26
C + A:	Combined model, contains all predictors in figures 4.1 and 4.2	−916.87	49

state. Approximately one-half of those interviewed believed that the current number of immigrants was satisfactory, and another 40 percent thought this number should be reduced. Only a small fraction (less than 5 percent) felt the number needed to be increased. This chapter has explored the determinants of these attitudes. Foremost in the minds of those who want fewer immigrants is anxiety about the sufficiency of jobs for everyone. Concerns about higher taxes and overcrowding are also prominent. A regression analysis demonstrates that respondents' demographic and socioeconomic characteristics are closely linked to how they feel about immigrants. Older, less-educated, central-city, and Catholic residents are more likely to want fewer immigrants, whereas married individuals and members of minority groups are more tolerant. A separate analysis of survey participants' attitudes about a variety of narrower immigration issues shows that New Jersey residents are least tolerant when immigrants are believed to affect adversely the labor-market opportunities of native workers, to represent a drain on the welfare and social service system, and to undermine the primacy of the use of English both for instructional purposes in schools and in public discourse. The importance of respondents' perceptions about the impacts of immigrants on the state cannot be explained away by the demographic makeup of sample individuals. A combined analysis of the joint influence of respondents' beliefs and characteristics shows that both are significant predictors of attitudes about the appropriate number of immigrants in New Jersey.

Notes

I would like to thank Herb Abelson, Maryann Belanger, Stephanie Bell-Rose, Pamela Espenshade, Cynthia Harper, Katherine Hempstead, Max Larsen, and Jennifer Spielvogel for their help in designing and pretesting the survey instrument, as well as Melanie Adams, Wayne Appleton, Nicholas DiMarzio, George Mitchels, and J. R. Venza for useful comments on the analysis. I am also grateful to Melanie Adams and Amy Worlton for preparing the figures and tables and to Jennifer Alexander for bibliographic assistance. Financial support was provided by a grant from the Andrew W. Mellon Foundation.

1. An alternative interpretation is offered by the generational/persistence model of attitude formation. According to this view, developed by Sears (1981, 1983) and supported by recent research by Alwin, Cohen, and Newcomb (1991) on the stability and change of sociopolitical attitudes among Bennington College graduates in the 1930s and 1940s, young people are highly impressionable and vulnerable to new ideas. This stage is then followed by a long period of increasing persistence and stability in atti-

tudes over the remainder of the life course. This interpretation of age effects in cross-sectional data suggests that age differences are less a reflection of life-course changes than of intercohort variation.

2. Within the 908 area code, residents of Warren, Somerset, and Ocean counties have significantly more negative attitudes.

3. This last finding may help to explain why in national samples residents in the slower-growing northeastern part of the United States have the most favorable attitudes toward immigrants, all else constant (Espenshade and Hempstead 1996).

4. On the other hand, a clear ranking emerges in national poll data, with European immigrants the most preferred, followed by Asian immigrants, and, lastly, migrants from Latin America (Espenshade and Belanger 1996).

References

Alwin, Duane F., Ronald L. Cohen, and Theodore M. Newcomb. 1991. *Political Attitudes over the Life Span: The Bennington Women after Fifty Years*. Madison: University of Wisconsin Press.

Amir, Yehuda. 1969. "Contact Hypothesis in Ethnic Relations." *Psychological Bulletin* 71(5): 319–42.

_____. 1976. "The Role of Intergroup Contact in Change of Prejudice and Ethnic Relations." *Towards the Elimination of Racism*, edited by Phyllis A. Katz (245–308). New York: Pergamon Press.

Ayres, B. Drummond, Jr. 1994. "Anti-Alien Sentiment Spreading in Wake of California's Measure." *New York Times*, December 4: 1.

Beck, Roy. 1993. "Religions and the Environment: Commitment High until U.S. Population Issues Raised." *Social Contract* 3(2, Winter): 76–89.

Bradsher, Keith. 1995. "Skilled Workers Watch Their Jobs Migrate Overseas." *New York Times*, August 28: A1.

Briggs, Vernon M., Jr. 1995. "Immigration Policy Sends Blacks Back to the South." *Social Contract* 5(4, Summer): 270–71.

Cain, Bruce, and Roderick Kiewiet. 1986. "California's Coming Minority Majority." *Public Opinion* 9(February/March): 50–52.

Citrin, Jack, Beth Reingold, and Donald P. Green. 1990. "American Identity and the Politics of Ethnic Change." *Journal of Politics* 52(4, November): 1124–54.

Day, Christine L. 1989. "U.S. Hispanics and Immigration Reform." Paper presented at the annual meeting of the Midwest Political Science Association, Chicago, April 13–15.

_____. 1990. "Ethnocentrism, Economic Competition, and Attitudes toward U.S. Immigration Policy." Paper presented at the annual meeting of the Midwest Political Science Association, Chicago, April 5–7.

Espenshade, Thomas J., and Maryann Belanger. 1996. "U.S. Public Perceptions and Reactions to Mexican Migration." Paper presented at the "Conference on Mexican Migration and U.S. Policy," Center for Strategic and International Studies, Washington, DC, June 14–15.

Espenshade, Thomas J., and Charles A. Calhoun. 1993. "An Analysis of Public Opinion toward Undocumented Immigration." *Population Research and Policy Review* 12: 189–224.

Espenshade, Thomas J., and Katherine Hempstead. 1996. "Contemporary American Attitudes toward U.S. Immigration." *International Migration Review* 30(2, Summer): 535–70.

Federation for American Immigration Reform. 1995. "House Immigration Reform Bill Moves on Fast Track through House Subcommittee." *FAIR Immigration Report* (Washington, DC) 15(8, August).

Fix, Michael, and Jeffrey S. Passel. 1994. *Immigration and Immigrants: Setting the Record Straight.* Washington, DC: Urban Institute.

Frey, William H. 1995. "Immigration and Internal Migration 'Flight' from U.S. Metropolitan Areas: Toward a New Demographic Balkanisation." *Urban Studies* 32(4/5): 733–57.

Hansen, Kristin A. 1996. "Profile of the Foreign-born Population in 1995: What the CPS Nativity Data Tell Us." Paper presented at the annual meeting of the Population Association of America, New Orleans, May 9–11.

Harwood, Edwin. 1983. "Alienation: American Attitudes toward Immigration." *Public Opinion* 6(June/July): 49–51.

———. 1985. "How Should We Enforce Immigration Law?" In *Clamor at the Gates,* edited by Nathan Glazer (73–91). San Francisco: Institute for Contemporary Studies.

———. 1986. "American Public Opinion and U.S. Immigration Policy." In *Immigration and American Public Policy,* edited by Rita J. Simon (201–12). Vol. 487, *The Annals of the American Academy of Political and Social Science.* Beverly Hills, Calif.: Sage Publications, September.

Hoskin, Marilyn, and William Mishler. 1983. "Public Opinion toward New Migrants: A Comparative Analysis." *International Migration* 21(4): 440–62.

Jackman, Mary R., and Michael J. Muha. 1984. "Education and Intergroup Attitudes: Moral Enlightenment, Superficial Democratic Commitment, or Ideological Refinement?" *American Sociological Review* 49: 751–69.

Jackman, Mary R., and Mary Scheuer Senter. 1980. "Images of Social Groups: Categorical or Qualified?" *Public Opinion Quarterly* 44: 341–61.

Jackson, Jacquelyne Johnson. 1995. "Competition between Blacks and Immigrants." *Social Contract* 5(4, Summer): 247–54.

Kinder, Donald R., and Tali Mendelberg. 1995. "Cracks in American Apartheid: The Political Impact of Prejudice among Desegregated Whites." *Journal of Politics* 57(May): 402–24.

Lipset, Seymour M., Paul F. Lazarsfeld, Allan H. Barton, and Juan Linz. 1954. "The Psychology of Voting: An Analysis of Political Behavior." In *Handbook of Social Psychology*, vol. 2, edited by Gardner Lindzey (1124–75). Cambridge, U.K.: Cambridge University Press.

McClosky, Herbert, and Alida Brill. 1983. *Dimensions of Tolerance*. New York: Russell Sage Foundation.

McCullagh, Peter. 1980. "Regression Models for Ordinal Data." *Journal of the Royal Statistical Society* 42(2): 109–42.

McKelvey, Richard D., and William Zavoina. 1975. "A Statistical Model for the Analysis of Ordinal Level Dependent Variables." *Journal of Mathematical Sociology* 4: 103–20.

Miller, Lawrence W., Jerry L. Polinard, and Robert D. Wrinkle. 1984. "Attitudes toward Undocumented Workers: The Mexican American Perspective." *Social Science Quarterly* 65(June): 482–94.

Moore, Stephen. 1986. "Social Scientists' Views on Immigrants and U.S. Immigration Policy: A Postscript." In *Immigration and American Public Policy*, edited by Rita J. Simon (213–17). Vol. 487, *The Annals of the American Academy of Political and Social Science*. Beverly Hills, Calif.: Sage Publications.

Muller, Thomas, and Thomas J. Espenshade. 1985. *The Fourth Wave: California's Newest Immigrants*. Washington, DC: Urban Institute Press.

Rothbart, Myron, and Oliver P. John. 1993. "Intergroup Relations and Stereotype Change: A Social-Cognitive Analysis and Some Longitudinal Findings." In *Prejudice, Politics, and the American Dilemma*, edited by Paul M. Sniderman, Philip E. Tetlock, and Edward G. Carmines (32–59). Stanford, Calif.: Stanford University Press.

Sears, David O. 1981. "Life-Stage Effects on Attitude Change, Especially among the Elderly." In *Aging: Social Change*, edited by Sara B. Kiesler, James N. Morgan, and Valerie K. Oppenheimer. New York: Academic Press.

———. 1983. "On the Persistence of Early Political Predispositions: The Roles of Attitude Object and Life Stage." In *Review of Personality and Social Psychology*, vol. 4, edited by Ladd Wheeler (79–116). Beverly Hills, Calif.: Sage Publications.

Sears, David O., and Jack Citrin. 1985. *Tax Revolt*, 2nd ed. Cambridge, Mass.: Harvard University Press.

Sears, David O., and Leonie Huddy. 1987. "Bilingual Education: Symbolic Meaning and Support among Non-Hispanics." Paper presented at the annual meeting of the American Psychological Association, New York, September 1.

Sears, David O., Tom R. Tyler, Richard R. Lau, and Harris M. Allen. 1980. "Self-Interest vs. Symbolic Politics in Policy Attitudes and Presidential Voting." *American Political Science Review* 74: 670–84.

Sherwood, Ben. 1994. "California Leads the Way, Alas." *New York Times*, Op-Ed, November 27: 11.

Simcox, David. 1993. "The Catholic Hierarchy and Immigration: Boundless Compassion, Limited Responsibility." *Social Contract* 3(2, Winter): 90–95.

————. 1995. "The Catholic Church's War on Borders." *Social Contract* 5(3, Spring): 167–71.

Simon, Rita J. 1985. *Public Opinion and the Immigrant: Print Media Coverage, 1880–1980.* Lexington, Mass.: Lexington Books, D.C. Heath & Co.

————. 1987. "Immigration and American Attitudes." *Public Opinion* 10 (July/August): 47–50.

Simon, Rita J., and Susan H. Alexander. 1993. *The Ambivalent Welcome: Print Media, Public Opinion, and Immigration.* Westport, Conn.: Praeger.

Sniderman, Paul M., Richard A. Brody, and James H. Kuklinski. 1984. "Policy Reasoning and Political Values: The Problem of Racial Equality." *American Journal of Political Science* 28: 75–94.

Starr, Paul D., and Alden E. Roberts. 1982. "Attitudes toward New Americans: Perceptions of Indo-Chinese in Nine Cities." *Research in Race and Ethnic Relations* 3: 165–86.

State and Local Coalition on Immigration. 1995a. "Immigration Legislation Introduced in the 104th Congress." *Immigrant Policy News: Inside the Beltway,* 2 (2, February 28): 3.

————. 1995b. "Two More States Pass Official English Laws." *Immigrant Policy News: The State-Local Report,* 2 (1, May 12): 1.

Stephan, Walter G. 1985. "Intergroup Relations." In *Handbook of Social Psychology,* vol. 2, 3rd ed., edited by Gardner Lindzey and Elliot Aronson (599–658). New York: Random House.

Sullivan, John. 1995. "Immigration and African Americans." *Social Contract* 5(4, Summer): 259–61.

Tanton, John. 1995. "Back to the Back of the Bus?" *Social Contract* 5(4, Summer): 239.

Tarrance and Associates. 1989a. *Research Report: California Immigration Survey.* Houston: Author, April.

————. 1989b. *Research Report: Texas Immigration and Border Security Study.* Houston: Author, May.

U.S. Bureau of the Census. 1995. "The Foreign-Born Population: 1994." *Current Population Reports,* P20-486. Washington, DC: U.S. Government Printing Office, August.

U.S. Commission on Immigration Reform. 1994. *U.S. Immigration Policy: Restoring Credibility.* A Report to Congress. 1994 Executive Summary. Washington, DC: Author, September.

————. 1995. *Legal Immigration: Setting Priorities.* 1995 Executive Summary. Washington, DC: Author, June.

Van den Berghe, Pierre L. 1967. *Race and Racism: A Comparative Perspective.* New York: John Wiley & Sons.

Westoff, Charles F., and Larry L. Bumpass. 1973. "The Revolution in Birth Control Practices of U.S. Roman Catholics." *Science* 179: 41–44.

Part Two

ECONOMIC, SOCIAL, AND POLITICAL IMPACTS

Chapter Five

IMMIGRATION AND THE WAGES AND EMPLOYMENT OF U.S.-BORN WORKERS IN NEW JERSEY

Kristin F. Butcher and Anne Morrison Piehl

Historically, the most contentious issue in the debate surrounding immigration has been the effect of immigrants on the wages and employment of native-born citizens. During the 1980s, this issue took on particular urgency as low-skilled workers experienced a decline in their real wages. At the same time, the decade witnessed the largest inflow of immigrants since the 1900s, many of them low skilled. Policymakers and researchers seeking the cause of the decline in real wages of low-skilled natives are thus focusing on the possibility that immigrants have increased the relative supply of low-skilled workers and driven down wages of low-skilled native-born workers.

Although past research has provided little evidence to support adverse wage and employment effects of immigration (e.g., Altonji and Card 1991; Borjas 1990: chapter 5; Butcher and Card 1991; Espenshade 1992), the question continues to arise for several reasons. The effect of immigration on wages and employment depends on many factors: the skills of the native born and immigrants in a particular labor market, the production technology in a given labor market, and demand conditions affecting the local labor market. All of these factors may differ over time and across geographic areas. As a result, previous work on the effect of immigration on the wages of natives may not apply today. Furthermore, what is true in the aggregate may not apply to the experience of a particular region.

This chapter focuses on the impact of immigration on the changes in wages and employment of individuals born in the United States and living in New Jersey from 1980 to 1990. Little economic research on the topic of immigration and labor-market outcomes of natives has focused on a specific geographic area. New Jersey is an interesting state to study, since it is a high-immigration state with a diverse industrial and demographic base. By concentrating on New Jersey, we may find answers that deviate from previous research. If not, we may convince researchers that results from the nation apply to smaller geographic units of analysis and also convince policymakers that the findings are relevant to their constituencies.

We examine the effects of immigration on the New Jersey labor market on several levels. First, we analyze the changes in wage gaps between various groups of workers from 1980 to 1990. We do this for two reasons. One reason is that some people are concerned that immigration may exacerbate wage gaps for particular demographic and/or skill groups. The second reason is that we need an anchor for the two cross sections in order to compare the performance of people at different points in the wage distribution. The mean wage for each group provides a good proxy for one point in the wage distribution. By looking at how a number of groups fared over the decade (e.g., black women, white women, and high school dropouts), we can map changes in the overall native-born wage distribution. This analysis concentrates on the relationship between changes in the wage gap for various groups (relative to a comparison group) and the degree to which particular industries in particular states use immigrant labor.

If wages do not adjust downward because of rigidities in the labor market, then immigrant competition may not push wages down but, instead, result in decreased employment for native-born workers. We address this question in our second level of analysis by looking at employment-population ratios by state. Finally, we return to the impact of immigration on wages by analyzing individual data to more fully control the effect of worker characteristics in explaining wages. This third approach analyzes the wage levels of New Jersey residents by focusing on the effect of the fraction foreign born in a worker's industry.

We found no evidence of adverse effects of immigration on the wages or employment of the native born in New Jersey or in the United States as a whole. However, New Jersey's experience does differ from that of the nation in several important respects. For instance, New Jersey residents experienced less growth in inequality over the 1980s than the country as a whole. Moreover, high school dropouts in New Jersey in industries with a high fraction foreign-born workers experienced relatively high wage growth. This was not the case in the United States overall.

This chapter is organized into four sections. The first section describes the data and the New Jersey labor market. The second section discusses the impact of immigration on changes in wage gaps and employment gaps for natives. The third section investigates the effect of working in an immigrant-intensive industry on the wages of workers in New Jersey. Concluding comments are contained in the fourth section.

DATA AND DESCRIPTIVE STATISTICS

The data we use are from the 5 percent Public Use Microdata Samples of the United States Censuses for 1980 and 1990.[1] Since we were interested in labor market outcomes, we included only those individuals between the ages of 16 and 64. We excluded all those who were born in United States outlying areas (e.g., Puerto Ricans) as well as those born abroad of U.S. parents. These groups are not immigrants, and yet grouping them with the native born also seems inappropriate.

As noted by Western and Kelly (chapter 2, this volume), the population of foreign born in New Jersey and in the United States as a whole increased during the 1980s. Although the United States and New Jersey show similar patterns, there are some notable differences. For example, immigrants from Western Europe account for a much larger fraction of the foreign born in New Jersey than in the United States in general. In addition, Mexico, which was responsible for one-fifth to one-quarter of the foreign born in the United States, sends very few immigrants to New Jersey. Relative to the rest of the country, immigrants in New Jersey are more likely to be white, less likely to be Asian, and less likely to be Hispanic. Although immigrants in New Jersey are better educated than the rest of the immigrant population in the United States, immigrants in New Jersey have substantially lower education levels than the average native-born New Jersey resident. Thus, if immigrants compete with natives for jobs, this competition will fall disproportionately on those natives with few skills.

Indeed, one reason for the current concern over immigration is that the burden of increased competition from immigrants may harm some groups of U.S. workers more than others. As has been shown by many researchers (e.g., Juhn, Murphy, and Pierce 1993), the income distribution in the United States was marked by increasing inequality over the 1980s. Not only did low-skilled workers do poorly relative to those with more skills, they experienced a drop in their real wages. For example, the wage gap between black and white male workers, after narrowing during the 1960s and 1970s, began to increase again during the 1980s (Card and Krueger 1992; Levy and Murnane 1992).

This chapter analyzes whether immigration has affected the relative wages of various groups of workers, and whether New Jersey's experience has differed from that of the United States in general. Table 5.1 shows what has happened to the log weekly wages[2] of various groups of workers in New Jersey vis-à-vis the rest of the United States. The eight groups we focus on are black males and females, Hispanic males and females, white non-Hispanic males and females, high school dropouts, and college graduates. Table 5.1 shows where the mean log weekly wage of each of these groups of New Jersey native-born workers fits into the overall distribution of weekly wages in New Jersey and the United States in 1980 and 1990.

On the whole, New Jersey workers fared much better over the decade than did United States workers (table 5.1). The average wage for all workers in New Jersey went from the median of the United States distribution in 1980 to the 58th percentile in 1990. Groups that did very poorly over the 1980s in the United States did much better in New Jersey. For example, high school dropouts in New Jersey actually improved their relative position in New Jersey slightly, while moving up a full 14 percentile points in the United States distribution. This shows that New Jersey workers were doing well compared to the rest of the country, and also that New Jersey did not experience the same increase in inequality that characterized the nation.[3] The three New Jersey groups that fell in their relative positions in the state's wage distribution are white non-Hispanic males, black males, and Hispanic males. All groups of female workers in New Jersey moved up in the

Table 5.1 NEW JERSEY MEAN LOG WEEKLY WAGE AS PERCENTILE OF OVERALL WAGE DISTRIBUTIONS IN NEW JERSEY AND UNITED STATES, BY DEMOGRAPHIC GROUP: 1980 AND 1990

	New Jersey 1980	New Jersey 1990	U.S. 1980	U.S. 1990
Immigrants	0.41	0.43	0.45	0.54
Native born:				
All	0.46	0.48	0.50	0.58
Black males	0.52	0.44	0.55	0.55
Black females	0.29	0.35	0.32	0.47
Hispanic males	0.52	0.45	0.56	0.57
Hispanic females	0.26	0.29	0.29	0.40
White males	0.62	0.59	0.68	0.69
White females	0.28	0.38	0.31	0.49
High school dropouts	0.27	0.31	0.30	0.44
College graduates	0.73	0.68	0.76	0.76

Notes: Data are from a sample of 1980 and 1990 Censuses (5 percent Public Use Microdata Sample [PUMS]). Mean wages for New Jersey are calculated from employed individuals ages 16–64 (sample sizes: 890 in 1980 and 1,142 in 1990).

wage distributions in the state and the country as a whole (cf. Blau and Kahn 1994). The first row of table 5.1 reveals that although immigrants in New Jersey do not earn as much as native-born workers, they do not fall far short.

Although table 5.1 shows that workers in New Jersey in general, and low-skilled groups in particular, did well when compared to the rest of the United States, some groups fared better than others. Was the relatively weak performance of black and Hispanic males in New Jersey, or the relatively strong performance of women in New Jersey, in any way related to immigration? The answer depends to some extent on the scope for complementarity between these groups of workers and immigrants in New Jersey. Table 5.2 presents evidence regarding which groups of native-born workers tend to overlap with immigrants. One might expect that native-born workers who are in the same industry as immigrants would be among the first to feel any labor-market effects of immigration.

Table 5.2 presents information on the 1980 distribution of immigrant and native-born workers by industry in New Jersey. Each worker is classified into one of 18 industry categories based on his or her three-digit SIC code in the United States Census.[4] The bottom row of table 5.2 shows the percentage of all workers who belong to each of the demographic groups. Thus, a group is overrepresented in a particular industry if the group comprises a higher percentage of that industry's work force than of the employed population overall. The second column shows the fraction immigrant in each of these industries. Immigrants are overrepresented in several manufacturing industries: food and tobacco; textile mill, paper and leather; apparel and finished textiles; chemicals and petroleum; and durables manufacturing. Black female workers are also overrepresented in apparel and finished textiles, indicating that there may be some scope for competition between black women workers and immigrants. On the other hand, the first column of the table reveals that the apparel and finished textiles industry only employs 1.2 percent of workers overall, indicating that this potential competition is not affecting a very large number of native-born workers.

The last two columns of table 5.2 show the industrial distribution of high school dropouts and college graduates. Public concern tends to focus on the potential for low-skilled immigrants to affect the job opportunities of low-skilled natives; yet two of the major employers of high school dropouts—construction and retail trade—are not industries with heavy concentrations of immigrants. Interestingly, one of the industries in which both immigrants and high school dropouts

Table 5.2 NEW JERSEY 1980 INDUSTRY EMPLOYMENT PROFILE, BY DEMOGRAPHIC GROUP

Industry	Industry Share of Total Employment	Immigrant	Fraction of Industry's Employment							
			Black Male	Black Female	Hispanic Male	Hispanic Female	White Male	White Female	H.S. Dropout	College Grad
Construction	0.051	0.100	0.050	0.008	0.006	<0.001	0.709	0.125	0.378	0.042
Food and tobacco manufacturing	0.007	0.436	0.182	0.060	0.014	<0.001	0.302	<0.001	0.134	0.006
Textile mill, paper, leather manufacturing	0.026	0.202	0.066	0.050	0.004	0.009	0.332	0.332	0.126	0.116
Apparel and finished textiles manufacturing	0.012	0.851	<0.001	0.104	0.010	0.029	<0.001	<0.001	0.059	<0.001
Chemicals and petroleum manufacturing	0.074	0.138	0.064	0.041	0.002	0.002	0.577	0.173	0.203	0.187
Durables manufacturing	0.135	0.152	0.073	0.041	0.005	0.002	0.503	0.220	0.189	0.164
Transportation	0.072	0.090	0.088	0.035	0.019	0.007	0.468	0.292	0.129	0.189
Wholesale trade: durables	0.027	0.111	0.064	0.016	0.005	0.010	0.556	0.238	0.017	0.079
Wholesale trade: nondurables	0.029	0.086	0.073	0.029	0.009	<0.001	0.582	0.218	0.154	0.147
Retail trade	0.150	0.093	0.026	0.040	0.005	0.006	0.422	0.408	0.329	0.045
Finance, insurance, and real estate	0.051	0.113	0.041	0.049	<0.001	0.011	0.328	0.451	0.027	0.218
Business and repair services	0.057	0.091	0.030	0.045	0.004	0.003	0.525	0.300	0.167	0.151
Personal services	0.032	0.092	0.026	0.146	<0.001	0.004	0.066	0.662	0.336	<0.001
Professional services	0.210	0.079	0.026	0.073	0.004	0.005	0.211	0.601	0.100	0.350
Public administration	0.066	0.044	0.038	0.077	0.006	0.004	0.635	0.190	0.034	0.175
Fraction of all workers		0.115	0.050	0.053	0.006	0.005	0.414	0.354	0.177	0.172

Notes: These data are from a sample of the 1980 U.S. Census (5 percent PUMS) for New Jersey. Cells are estimates of the actual distribution of employment. Data are only for employed individuals ages 16–64 (sample size: 890).

are overrepresented—chemicals and petroleum manufacturing—also employs a high fraction of college graduates.[5]

Table 5.2 shows that certain groups of native-born workers and immigrants are overrepresented in some industries. To the extent that labor markets are segmented along state and industry lines, we would expect the native-born workers in labor markets that more heavily employ immigrants to experience the greatest impact of immigration. The next section investigates this hypothesis.

CHANGES IN WAGE GAPS

Since economic growth in the 1980s accrued mostly to those with high skills and because minorities in the United States are disproportionately low skilled, the 1980s resulted in increasing wage gaps between African American and white non-Hispanic natives, for example. To test the hypothesis that immigrants adversely affect labor-market outcomes of native-born workers, we first looked at changes in various wage gaps over the decade. If immigration leads to poor wage growth, the adverse effects should be concentrated on those with the lowest skill levels.

To evaluate the experiences of various demographic groups over the decade, we measured wage changes for each of seven groups against the wage changes of white non-Hispanic male native-born workers, by industry. We used a comparison group as a benchmark because it allowed us to adjust for inflation without worrying about the appropriate price deflator for a particular geographic region. We were also thus able to control for industry-level demand conditions that might shift the wages of everyone employed in a particular industry. This is particularly important since the fraction immigrant in an industry might be a function of these demand conditions if, for example, immigrants are overrepresented in growing industries.

Using data for native-born workers only, we constructed average weekly wages for each industry within each state using data from the 1980 and 1990 Censuses. A separate mean weekly wage was calculated for each of the demographic groups of interest in each of the two census years. Each measure was defined, therefore, for 918 state-industry cells.[6] We used these state-industry averages for each group to construct wage gaps between each of the disaggregated demographic groups and white non-Hispanic male workers in each year. We then used these wage gaps to construct changes in wage gaps from 1980 to

1990. For example, to define the change in the white non-Hispanic male to black male wage gap, we first subtracted the average log weekly wage among black male workers in a particular state-industry cell from the average log weekly wage among white non-Hispanic male workers in that cell. The change in the gap was then the difference between the gap in 1990 and the gap in 1980. A positive number indicates the wage gap grew between 1980 and 1990.

To analyze the correlation between the changes in these wage gaps and immigration, we constructed the fraction of the state-industry cell that is composed of immigrants. We used the fraction immigrant in the industry in 1980 to represent the "immigrant intensity" of the industry. The question we addressed was whether inequality among native-born workers in heavily immigrant industries increased relative to the inequality growth in other industries.

One might think that the change in the fraction immigrant over the decade in a particular state-industry cell is the relevant effect for changes in wages. However, we found that the immigrant-intensive-industries tended to stay immigrant intensive and vice versa. The fraction immigrant at the beginning of the period seems a better way to characterize which industries contain the greatest overlap between native-born and immigrant workers.

There are two ways to interpret the results of this analytic approach. The first is to focus on the wage gaps and implied inequality among the groups analyzed. Here, a finding that the white male to black female wage gap increased over the 1980s in industries with a large fraction immigrant could be interpreted as immigrants having a great deal of overlap with black women. The second interpretation is to take the group means as representing various points along the overall wage distribution. Since we report comparisons for seven demographic and skill classifications, together they map out the impact of immigrant intensity for people who fall at different points along the distribution. From this perspective, changes in the white male to black female gap are seen as representative of the experience of the worker at the 29th percentile at the beginning of the period. The mean wages of the three groups of women and the high school dropouts proxy for the lower end of the wage distribution; black and Hispanic males proxy for the middle of the distribution, and college graduates proxy for the high end of the distribution.

Table 5.3 presents regression results where the dependent variables are the changes in wage gaps previously described. The explanatory variables are the fraction immigrant in the state-industry cell in 1980, a dummy variable equal to one if the observation is from New Jersey,

Table 5.3 ESTIMATED EFFECTS OF FRACTION IMMIGRANT IN INDUSTRY-STATE
CELLS ON CHANGES IN LOG WEEKLY WAGE GAPS BETWEEN WHITE
MALE NATIVE-BORN WORKERS AND OTHER DEMOGRAPHIC GROUPS
(NATIVE BORN ONLY) (HUBER-CORRECTED STANDARD ERRORS)

	Mean of Dependent Variable	(1)	(2)	(3)	(4)	(5)
Black Male Gap	−0.019					
(n = 234)	(0.034)					
Fraction immigrant, 1980		0.476		0.532	0.425	0.155
		(0.540)		(0.548)	(0.569)	(0.667)
New Jersey			−0.028	0.133	0.148	0.133
			(0.075)	(0.124)	(0.141)	(0.142)
NJ × fraction immigrant, 1980				−1.479*	−1.545*	−1.293
				(0.709)	(0.760)	(0.913)
Other industry controls		No	No	No	Yes	No
Industry dummies		No	No	No	No	Yes
R-square		0.0070	0.0002	0.0095	0.0181	0.1072
Black Female Gap	−0.058					
(n = 226)	(0.035)					
Fraction immigrant, 1980		−0.571		−0.637	−0.792	−0.394
		(0.657)		(0.682)	(0.673)	(0.534)
New Jersey			0.040	−0.111	−0.081	−0.104
			(0.071)	(0.119)	(0.121)	(0.125)
NJ × fraction immigrant, 1980				1.422	1.378	1.384
				(0.832)	(0.820)	(0.785)
Other industry controls		No	No	No	Yes	No
Industry dummies		No	No	No	No	Yes
R-square		0.0089	0.0003	0.0115	0.0193	0.1405
Hispanic Male Gap	−0.010					
(n = 240)	(0.034)					
Fraction immigrant, 1980		0.165		0.222	0.174	0.012
		(0.436)		(0.438)	(0.462)	(0.541)
New Jersey			−0.109	0.030	0.032	−0.034
			(0.163)	(0.279)	(0.289)	(0.289)
NJ × fraction immigrant, 1980				−1.209	−1.119	−0.546
				(1.653)	(1.685)	(1.828)
Other industry controls		No	No	No	Yes	No
Industry dummies		No	No	No	No	Yes
R-square		0.0007	0.0019	0.0040	0.0099	0.0419

(continued)

and an interaction term between New Jersey and the fraction immigrant in the industry. In some regressions we also controlled for the education levels of workers in the industry: the fraction with a high school degree, the fraction with some college, the fraction with a college degree and above. To control for industry-level unobservables,

Table 5.3 ESTIMATED EFFECTS OF FRACTION IMMIGRANT IN INDUSTRY-STATE CELLS ON CHANGES IN LOG WEEKLY WAGE GAPS BETWEEN WHITE MALE NATIVE-BORN WORKERS AND OTHER DEMOGRAPHIC GROUPS (NATIVE BORN ONLY) (HUBER-CORRECTED STANDARD ERRORS) (continued)

	Mean of Dependent Variable	(1)	(2)	(3)	(4)	(5)
Hispanic Female Gap (n = 228)	− 0.089* (0.033)					
Fraction immigrant, 1980		0.461 (0.355)		0.449 (0.361)	0.369 (0.423)	− 0.010 (0.458)
New Jersey			0.164 (0.141)	0.128 (0.238)	0.124 (0.249)	0.045 (0.292)
NJ × fraction immigrant, 1980				0.291 (2.740)	0.458 (2.779)	1.180 (2.790)
Other industry controls		No	No	No	Yes	No
Industry dummies		No	No	No	No	Yes
R-square		0.0064	0.0044	0.0105	0.0171	0.1141
White Non-Hispanic Female Gap (n = 237)	− 0.090* (0.030)					
Fraction immigrant, 1980		0.345 (0.509)		0.399 (0.502)	0.274 (0.495)	− 0.033 (0.504)
New Jersey			− 0.080 (0.110)	0.500 (0.331)	0.519 (0.336)	0.349 (0.322)
NJ × fraction immigrant, 1980				− 5.550 (3.379)	− 5.505 (3.441)	− 3.785 (2.938)
Other industry controls		No	No	No	Yes	No
Industry dummies		No	No	No	No	Yes
R-square		0.0043	0.0015	0.0149	0.0230	0.1589
High School Dropout Gap (n = 253)	0.057* (0.028)					
Fraction immigrant, 1980		0.540 (0.438)		0.769* (0.363)	0.611 (0.388)	0.633 (0.431)
New Jersey			− 0.301* (0.135)	0.348* (0.166)	0.370* (0.171)	0.385* (0.170)
NJ × fraction immigrant, 1980				− 5.658* (1.242)	− 5.606* (1.257)	− 5.991* (1.148)
Other industry controls		No	No	No	Yes	No
Industry dummies		No	No	No	No	Yes
R-square		0.0121	0.0227	0.0785	0.0885	0.1908

(continued)

in some specifications we included industry fixed effects. This means that the effect of the fraction immigrant is identified by variation in the fraction immigrant across states. To the extent that labor markets are more segmented along state lines than along industry lines, one might expect the variation in the fraction immigrant in these speci-

Table 5.3 ESTIMATED EFFECTS OF FRACTION IMMIGRANT IN INDUSTRY-STATE CELLS ON CHANGES IN LOG WEEKLY WAGE GAPS BETWEEN WHITE MALE NATIVE-BORN WORKERS AND OTHER DEMOGRAPHIC GROUPS (NATIVE BORN ONLY) (HUBER-CORRECTED STANDARD ERRORS) (continued)

	Mean of Dependent Variable	(1)	(2)	(3)	(4)	(5)
College Graduate	−0.034					
Gap (n = 242)	(0.037)					
Fraction immigrant,		0.364		0.334	0.277	−0.439
1980		(0.998)		(1.043)	(1.002)	(0.603)
New Jersey			0.201	0.191	0.193	0.027
			(0.104)	(0.181)	(0.181)	(0.170)
NJ × fraction				0.016	0.079	1.580
immigrant, 1980				(1.464)	(1.431)	(1.394)
Other industry controls		No	No	No	Yes	No
Industry dummies		No	No	No	No	Yes
R-square		0.0036	0.0066	0.0096	0.0140	0.1259

Notes: Dependent variables are changes in relative wage gaps, where white non-Hispanic native-born males are taken as the comparison group. Data are constructed from 1980 and 1990 U.S. Censuses (5 percent PUMS). "Other industry controls" are fraction of workers with a high school degree, fraction with some college, and fraction with a college degree. A constant is included in each regression. Asterisk indicates estimate is statistically significantly different from zero at the 5 percent level.

fications more likely to be exogenous. This is the fifth specification in table 5.3.[7]

The first set of regressions in table 5.3 presents results for changes in the wage gap between native-born white non-Hispanic male workers and native-born black male workers. Regression (1) shows that the fraction immigrant in an industry had no significant relationship with the change in this gap. Regression (2) shows that the change in this gap was no different in New Jersey than in other states in the United States. However, the results in columns (3) and (4) suggest that within New Jersey, the wage gap shrank in industries that had higher concentrations of immigrant workers. This effect falls to insignificance when industry-level control variables are added. This indicates that the particular mix of industries in New Jersey was driving the divergence between New Jersey and the nation in columns (3) and (4). Hence, relative black male weekly wages are affected by the industrial mix but do not appear to be affected by the fraction immigrant in the industry, either in New Jersey or in other states.

Although there are some cases where the wage gap changed significantly over the decade, we did not find any evidence to support the idea that immigration was significantly related to these changes.[8] The exception to this is the results for the high school dropout wage gap, as shown in the bottom panel of the first page of table 5.3. Overall, the relative wage gap grew for high school dropouts, which is consistent with competition between immigrants and low-skilled native labor. However, columns (3) through (5) show that the relationship between the wage gap and the fraction immigrant in industries is, at best, weakly statistically significant. Surprisingly, in New Jersey the wage gap between white male native-born workers and workers with less than a high school degree was *negatively* related to the fraction immigrant in the industry. This is a dramatic, strongly significant, and robust result, and suggests that high school dropouts in New Jersey did particularly well in industries where they overlap with immigrants to a large degree.

Under the assumption that these state-industry cells represent distinct labor markets, a larger fraction immigrant in an industry represents a shift in the labor supply curve of (mostly) low-skilled workers to that industry. Although there is a fair degree of segregation between these industries, the assumption that industries form distinct labor markets is quite extreme. If it is easy for workers to move between different industries within a state, then it is possible that the fraction immigrant in an industry would show up as having little effect on relative wage changes. If this is the case, then state-level relative wage changes would be a more appropriate unit of analysis. To investigate this, we ran regressions similar to the preceding ones using state-level changes in wage gaps (results not reported, available upon request). Whereas we found that the changes in wage gaps in New Jersey were significantly different from those in other states (especially for female workers), we again found no evidence that immigrants contributed to increasing wage gaps between white non-Hispanic male workers and the seven demographic groups considered.[9]

One reason we did not see a negative effect on changes in wage gaps for these groups of workers may be that wages are downwardly rigid. If this is the case, then we would expect to see a relative decrease in employment among these groups. We turn to this issue in the next set of results.

Table 5.4 presents the effect of immigration on native-born workers' employment. The specifications are analogous to the wage-gap analysis. First, we defined the employment-population ratio for each group in all 50 states and the District of Columbia. We then defined the employment gap as the employment-population ratio of white non-Hispanic male native-born workers minus the employment-

Table 5.4 ESTIMATED EFFECTS OF FRACTION IMMIGRANT IN THE STATE ON
CHANGES IN RELATIVE EMPLOYMENT-POPULATION RATIOS
BETWEEN WHITE MALE NATIVE-BORN INDIVIDUALS AND OTHER
DEMOGRAPHIC GROUPS (NATIVE BORN ONLY)
(HUBER-CORRECTED STANDARD ERRORS)

	Mean of Dependent Variable	(1)	(2)	(3)	(4)
Black Male Gap (n = 47)	0.011 (0.016)				
Fraction immigrant, 1980		−0.074 (0.251)		−0.045 (0.254)	−0.453 (0.399)
New Jersey			−0.055* (0.017)	−0.053* (0.019)	−0.015 (0.030)
Other state controls		No	No	No	Yes
R-square		0.0008	0.0053	0.0056	0.1104
Black Female Gap (n = 46)	−0.085* (0.016)				
Fraction immigrant, 1980		0.042 (0.261)		0.007 (0.273)	0.105 (0.364)
New Jersey			0.066* (0.017)	0.065* (0.020)	0.043 (0.030)
Other state controls		No	No	No	Yes
R-square		0.0003	0.0099	0.0099	0.0371
Hispanic Male Gap (n = 49)	−0.016 (0.017)				
Fraction immigrant, 1980		0.334 (0.341)		0.324 (0.347)	0.021 (0.341)
New Jersey			0.034 (0.018)	0.018 (0.021)	0.036 (0.027)
Other state controls		No	No	No	Yes
R-square		0.0154	0.0018	0.0159	0.1996
Hispanic Female Gap (n = 51)	−0.106* (0.017)				
Fraction immigrant, 1980		0.321 (0.276)		0.331 (0.278)	0.355 (0.337)
New Jersey			−0.003 (0.017)	−0.019 (0.016)	−0.046 (0.028)
Other state controls		No	No	No	Yes
R-square		0.0143	<0.0001	0.0149	0.1437
White Non-Hispanic Female Gap (n = 51)	−0.113* (0.014)				
Fraction immigrant, 1980		0.067 (0.232)		0.025 (0.231)	0.051 (0.324)
New Jersey			0.078* (0.014)	0.077* (0.017)	0.078* (0.025)
Other state controls		No	No	No	Yes
R-square		0.0009	0.0146	0.0147	0.0328

(continued)

Table 5.4 ESTIMATED EFFECTS OF FRACTION IMMIGRANT IN THE STATE ON
CHANGES IN RELATIVE EMPLOYMENT-POPULATION RATIOS
BETWEEN WHITE MALE NATIVE-BORN INDIVIDUALS AND OTHER
DEMOGRAPHIC GROUPS (NATIVE BORN ONLY)
(HUBER-CORRECTED STANDARD ERRORS) (*continued*)

	Mean of Dependent Variable	(1)	(2)	(3)	(4)
High School	−0.001				
Dropout Gap ($n = 51$)	(0.011)				
Fraction immigrant,		−0.065		−0.058	0.106
1980		(0.219)		(0.225)	(0.289)
New Jersey			−0.015	−0.013	−0.035
			(0.012)	(0.016)	(0.022)
Other state controls		No	No	No	Yes
R-square		0.0013	0.0009	0.0019	0.0663
College Graduate	−0.047*				
Gap ($n = 51$)	(0.013)				
Fraction immigrant,		0.236		0.234	0.319
1980		(0.205)		(0.209)	(0.248)
New Jersey			0.014	0.003	−0.015
			(0.013)	(0.016)	(0.021)
Other state controls		No	No	No	Yes
R-square		0.0138	0.0006	0.0138	0.0411

Notes: Dependent variables are changes in relative employment population ratios, where white non-Hispanic native-born males are taken as the comparison group. Data are constructed from 1980 and 1990 U.S. Censuses (5 percent PUMS). "Other state controls" are fraction of workers with a high school degree, fraction with some college, and fraction with a college degree. A constant is included in each regression. Asterisk indicates estimate is statistically significantly different from zero at the 5 percent level.

population ratio for each of the seven demographic groups. The change in the gap is the gap in 1990 minus the gap in 1980. We investigated the change in the employment gap as a function of the fraction of New Jersey's population that was foreign born in 1980. The fraction immigrant in 1980 is not significantly related to the employment gaps for any of the demographic groups. However, New Jersey does appear to be statistically significantly different from the rest of the country. The employment gap for black male workers in New Jersey decreased more than in other areas of the country. This effect falls to insignificance when state-level education variables are added, implying that the effect in New Jersey is a result of differences in the relative education levels of black and white male workers. The employment gap for black and white female workers widened more in New Jersey than elsewhere. However, this is because women in New Jersey had higher employment-population ratios in 1980 than women in the rest of the country. Thus, the positive effect in New Jersey comes from women in the rest of the country "catching up," rather than from falling employment among women in New Jersey.

Taken together, the results in tables 5.3 and 5.4 provide no evidence of adverse effects of immigration on the relative wages and employment of native-born workers. The evidence does suggest that workers in New Jersey, especially low-skilled workers, fared well during the 1980s compared to the rest of the country. High school dropouts did particularly well in heavily immigrant industries in New Jersey. The next section carries the analysis one step further by looking at the wages of individuals in New Jersey.

INDIVIDUAL WAGES

The regressions presented so far are relatively parsimonious. If there are omitted characteristics of the workers that are correlated with the fraction immigrant in an industry and affect the worker's wage, then these effects will be manifested through the coefficient on the immigration variable. This section investigates whether there is an effect of the fraction immigrant on a worker's wage, and whether that effect changes when the worker's own characteristics are held constant.

Table 5.5 presents the results for individual native-born workers in New Jersey. The dependent variable is the individual-level log weekly wage. Since we did not have panel data, we could not investigate changes in wages for individuals between 1980 and 1990. Instead, we pooled the data for the two years. In each specification, we included a dummy variable for 1990 to control for changes in the nominal wage level over the decade. We also included a variable representing the fraction of workers in an industry who were foreign born. The first column in the table shows that there is no significant effect of fraction immigrant in an industry on workers' wages. When race and education controls are added to the regression, in column (2), the coefficient on fraction immigrant becomes positive and moderately significant.

The specification in column (2) of table 5.5 forces the effect of fraction immigrant to be the same for all groups of workers. As discussed earlier, there are reasons to believe that immigrants might affect various groups differently, depending on the substitutability between immigrant and native-born labor. Therefore, in column (3), we interacted the fraction immigrant with dummy variables repre-

Table 5.5 ESTIMATED EFFECT OF FRACTION IMMIGRANT IN WORKER'S
INDUSTRY ON WAGES OF NATIVE BORN IN NEW JERSEY
(HUBER-CORRECTED STANDARD ERRORS)

	(1)	(2)	(3)
1990	0.760*	0.637*	0.627*
	(0.058)	(0.048)	(0.053)
Fraction immigrant, by industry	0.612	1.208*	−0.463
	(0.641)	(0.588)	(1.147)
High school dropout		−0.204*	−0.621*
		(0.080)	(0.213)
College graduate		0.338*	0.427
		(0.071)	(0.317)
Black male		−0.012	0.097
		(0.077)	(0.173)
Black female		−0.207*	−0.311
		(0.074)	(0.173)
Hispanic male		0.187*	0.272
		(0.076)	(0.163)
Hispanic female		−0.075	0.110
		(0.075)	(0.160)
White female		0.084	−0.228
		(0.149)	(0.273)
Asian male		0.259	0.404
		(0.135)	(0.227)
Asian female		−0.039	−0.098
		(0.138)	(0.352)
Other race male		0.157	−0.031
		(0.086)	(0.233)
Other race female		−0.262	−0.188
		(0.159)	(0.272)

(continued)

senting various demographic groups. The coefficients suggest that the
sign of this effect differs across the various demographic groups; however, only the interaction between high school dropouts and the fraction immigrant is significant. This coefficient is positive, which
means that native-born high school dropouts in New Jersey who are
in industries with heavy concentrations of immigrants earn more than
other high school dropouts. This result corroborates the evidence in
table 5.3 that the wage gap between high school dropouts and white
non-Hispanic male workers narrowed in New Jersey in those industries with a high fraction of workers who are foreign born.

The results for individual-level wages in New Jersey contrast with
those for the United States. When the regressions in table 5.5 were
run for the nation, the effect of the fraction immigrant on the wages
of high school dropouts was negative and statistically significant until

Table 5.5 ESTIMATED EFFECT OF FRACTION IMMIGRANT IN WORKER'S
INDUSTRY ON WAGES OF NATIVE BORN IN NEW JERSEY
(HUBER-CORRECTED STANDARD ERRORS) (*continued*)

	(1)	(2)	(3)
Industry Fraction Immigrant Interactions			
Black male			−0.660
			(1.022)
Black female			0.892
			(1.035)
Hispanic male			−0.311
			(0.947)
Hispanic female			−1.127
			(0.954)
White female			2.082
			(1.402)
Asian male			−0.047
			(1.204)
Asian female			0.709
			(2.020)
Other race male			1.505
			(1.505)
Other race female			−0.232
			(1.245)
High school dropout			2.877*
			(1.377)
College graduate			−0.702
			(2.279)
R-square	0.0482	0.3127	0.3191

Notes: Data are from a stratified sample of the 5 percent PUMS of the 1980 and 1990 U.S. Censuses. These regressions are weighted to reflect sampling. A constant, age, and age squared were included in each specification. Only employed people are included in these regressions. Sample size: 2,032. Asterisk indicates estimate is statistically significantly different from zero at the 5 percent level.

we controlled for industry effects, when the effect became statistically insignificant. This is the same relationship we found in table 5.3, where the industrial mix was important in explaining differential wage growth. In addition, the individual-level results for the nation as a whole revealed no statistically significant effects of the fraction immigrant for any of the other demographic groups.

The differences between the results for New Jersey and the United States as a whole affirm our earlier conclusion that changes in the wage distribution in New Jersey during the 1980s did not mirror the experience of the rest of the United States.

This chapter's analysis of immigration yields no evidence of adverse wage or employment effects for seven demographic and skill groups, even with a rich set of controls for worker characteristics, in New Jersey or the United States overall. However, there were differences between New Jersey and the rest of the nation. In particular, over the 1980s, the wage distribution in New Jersey became more compressed, whereas the rest of the nation experienced growing inequality. For example, high school dropouts in New Jersey moved up dramatically in the United States wage distribution.

The one robust effect of immigration on wages is for New Jersey high school dropouts. Surprisingly, these workers performed well in industries characterized by a high fraction immigrant. Why might immigration be associated with strong economic performance of high school dropouts in New Jersey? One possible explanation, a high minimum wage shoring up the bottom of the wage distribution, is easily dismissed: New Jersey's minimum wage did not exceed the federal minimum wage for the period studied here. There are four other potential explanations. First, there may be complementarity between immigrants and low-skilled workers. The usual story tells of complementarity between high-skilled native-born workers and low-skilled immigrants. In New Jersey, whereas immigrants are low skilled relative to the average native-born worker, they have higher skills than high school dropouts. (The mean wage among immigrants is 10 to 15 percentile points above the mean wage among high school dropouts.) Thus, immigrants may complement the low-skilled labor of native-born high school dropouts. Second, there may have been a demand shock in New Jersey, beneficial to low-skilled labor, to industries that happen to employ large concentrations of immigrants. In this case, a relationship between immigration and the performance of high school dropouts in New Jersey could not be interpreted as causal. A third possible explanation is that the fraction immigrant in an industry is not exogenous. If native-born workers leave industries as immigrants arrive, and those leaving are disproportionately low skilled conditional upon other characteristics, then the coefficient on fraction immigrant will be biased upward. A final possible explanation is that the availability of a pool of low-skilled immigrants allows industries that employ low-skilled people to stay in business rather than moving to locations with lower labor costs. This has a spillover effect onto low-skilled native-born residents. New Jersey is a state in which this is particularly likely to occur, since its native-born residents have relatively high skills.

Notes

We thank Thomas Espenshade and participants at the "Conference on Impacts of Immigration to New Jersey," at Princeton University, Princeton, N.J., May 18–19, 1995, for useful comments on this research.

1. We selected a stratified sample of individuals from the censuses. All of the numbers reported here have been weighted to reflect our sampling scheme.

2. We calculated the log weekly wage from census data on total wages and salary and number of weeks worked. Only employed workers are included in these calculations. We trimmed outliers from the log weekly wages in both 1980 and 1990.

3. A higher minimum wage in New Jersey does not explain this, since the state minimum wage was less than or equal to the federal level from 1979 to 1989.

4. The groupings follow the broad census groups fairly closely. The exact industry classifications are available from the authors upon request. Only 15 of the 18 industry categories were represented in sufficient numbers in New Jersey in 1980 to be included.

5. The 1990 distributions are similar. It is worth noting, however, that there was dramatic growth in the fraction immigrant in the nondurables wholesale trade industry.

6. That is, 51 states (including the District of Columbia) multiplied times 18 industries. Some of the cells were quite small. Any cell with less than 50 observations in either year was omitted from the subsequent analysis.

7. Throughout the tables, we report Huber-corrected standard errors that are robust to arbitrary forms of heteroskedasticity. In addition, since the number of observations used to create the state-industry cell averages differs markedly, we give more weight to those cells with more individuals. All regressions are weighted by the square root of the average cell size in 1980 and 1990.

8. In results not reported in the tables, we examined several different ways to capture the immigrant intensity of a particular state-industry cell. One might think that the total fraction of workers who are immigrants is too aggregate a measure. To address this question, we calculated the fraction "recent" immigrant (arrived within five years) in an industry. We also calculated the fraction immigrant with less than a high school degree. The effect of these immigration variables was not significantly different from the effect of the fraction immigrant overall.

9. To the extent that low-skilled native-born workers move away from geographic areas with heavy immigrant concentrations, the state-level analysis will also be biased toward finding no effect of immigration on wages of the native born. Some researchers have found positive correlations between inflows of immigrants and inflows of natives (Butcher and Card 1991), and other research has found offsetting flows (Filer 1992; Imai and White 1994).

References

Altonji, Joseph, and David Card. 1991. "Immigration and the Labor Market Outcomes of Less-Skilled Natives." *Immigration, Trade, and the Labor Market*, edited by John Abowd and Richard Freeman (201–34). Chicago: University of Chicago Press.

Blau, Francine, and Lawrence Kahn. 1994. "Rising Wage Inequality and the U.S. Gender Gap." *American Economic Review* 84 (2, May): 23–33.

Borjas, George. 1990. *Friends or Strangers: The Impact of Immigrants on the U.S. Economy*. New York: Basic Books.

Butcher, Kristin F., and David Card. 1991. "Immigration and Wages: Evidence from the 1980's." *American Economic Review* (2, May): 292–96.

Card, David, and Alan Krueger. 1992. "School Quality and Black–White Relative Earnings: A Direct Assessment." *Quarterly Journal of Economics* 107 (February): 151–200.

Espenshade, Thomas J. 1992. "Immigrants, Puerto Ricans, and the Earnings of Native Black Males." Princeton, N.J.: Princeton University, Office of Population Research. Photocopy.

Filer, Randall K. 1992. "The Effect of Immigrant Arrivals on Migratory Patterns of Native Workers." In *Immigration and the Workforce*, edited by George Borjas and Richard Freeman (245–71). Chicago: University of Chicago Press.

Imai, Yoshie, and Michael White. 1994. "The Impact of U.S. Immigration upon Internal Migration." *Population and Environment* 15 (3, January): 189–211.

Juhn, Chinhui, Kevin M. Murphy, and Brooks Pierce. 1993. "Wage Inequality and the Rise in Returns to Skill." *Journal of Political Economy* 101(3): 410–42.

Levy, Frank, and Richard Murnane. 1992. "U.S. Earnings Levels and Earnings Inequality: A Review of Recent Trends and Proposed Explanations." *Journal of Economic Literature* 30(3): 1333–81.

U.S. Bureau of the Census. 1982. *Census of Population and Housing, 1980: Public Use Microdata Samples, U.S.* Machine readable data files. Washington, D.C.: Author.

———. 1992. *Census of Population and Housing, 1990: Public Use Microdata Samples, U.S.* Machine readable data files. Washington, D.C.: Author.

Chapter Six

STATE AND LOCAL FISCAL IMPACTS OF NEW JERSEY'S IMMIGRANT AND NATIVE HOUSEHOLDS

Deborah L. Garvey and Thomas J. Espenshade

Studies of the economic impacts of immigration on receiving countries have focused primarily on the labor-market consequences of immigrants. For example, how are the wages and employment opportunities of native-born Americans affected by the growing presence of foreign workers in local area labor markets? Much of the available research has concentrated on identifying potential adverse impacts for native minority workers (including women, blacks, and Latinos) and quantifying the change in either native workers' wages or their employment prospects (Abowd and Freeman 1991; Borjas 1994; Borjas and Freeman 1992). Considerably less effort has been expended by economists to estimate the fiscal impacts of immigrants or to evaluate how these effects compare with the governmental benefits received and taxes paid by the native-born population. Indeed, these issues are barely mentioned in two recent reviews by Friedberg and Hunt (1995, 1996).

Examining the impacts of immigrants from a budgetary perspective involves estimating their revenue contributions to federal, state, and local governments, as well as the benefits they receive from each level of government in return, and then determining the degree to which the two amounts differ at each jurisdictional level. If revenues provided by a household exceed government expenditures on that household, the household is considered to be a net fiscal asset, or a gain, to other taxpayers. If, on the other hand, fiscal costs exceed the revenues generated by a household, then the household is a net fiscal burden, or drain, on remaining taxpayers (Rothman and Espenshade 1992). Fiscal costs include transfer payments from means-tested entitlement programs, expenditures on elementary and secondary school education, and a range of government services that are provided to all residents regardless of age or need (for example, trash collection, public roads, and police and fire protection). Fiscal revenues include an assortment of tax payments, fees and licenses, and voluntary contributions made to governments by households. In recent years, knowledge of the fiscal impacts of immigrant households has taken on added policy significance as numerous states have sued the federal government for the costs of services they are required by law to provide to resident illegal immigrants (Clark et al. 1994; U.S. General Accounting Office 1994, 1995).[1]

Some studies of immigrants' fiscal impacts have been conducted by university researchers, but most have been prepared by analysts working for state or local governments.[2] Census data suggest that immigrants were slightly less likely than native-born Americans in 1970 to receive cash welfare payments (e.g., Aid to Families with Dependent Children [AFDC] and Supplemental Security Income [SSI]), but that by 1990 immigrant households were overrepresented among the welfare population (Borjas 1994). In 1990 the fraction of immigrant households receiving welfare was 9.1 percent, versus 7.4 percent among native households. Tracking immigrant cohorts reveals that immigrants "assimilate into welfare" the longer they are in the United States. Using data from the 1984, 1985, 1990, and 1991 panels of the Survey of Income and Program Participation, Borjas and Hilton (1996) found little difference between natives and immigrants in the probability of receiving cash welfare benefits, but a larger differential emerges when both cash and noncash means-tested programs are analyzed. For example, the fraction of immigrant households that receive some kind of public assistance is 21 percent, compared with 14 percent among natives.

Part of the increase in the fraction of immigrant households receiving welfare is explained by growth in the refugee population. When refugees are excluded, Fix and Passel (1994) found that working-age migrants are less likely to receive welfare than their native-born counterparts, a conclusion consistent with Borjas' (1994) observation that households from Cambodia or Laos had a welfare participation rate in 1990 of almost 50 percent. Immigrants' legal status also matters in other ways. Current illegal immigrants pay less in taxes than former undocumented migrants who received amnesty under the terms of the 1986 Immigration Reform and Control Act (IRCA), who in turn pay less than permanent resident aliens. Members of the native-born population pay the highest taxes, but the authors of these findings point out that the differentials reflect differences in average income rather than anything intrinsic to immigration status (Vernez and McCarthy 1995).

There is only limited evidence bearing on the question of immigrants' net fiscal implications. Fix and Passel (1994) concluded that immigrant households on average are substantial fiscal benefits to other U.S. taxpayers when all levels of government are considered simultaneously. But these effects are not uniformly distributed. Only at the federal level do immigrants appear to contribute more than they receive (Vernez and McCarthy 1995). Revenues and expenditures associated with immigrants appear to be more or less offsetting for state governments, whereas it is typically at the level of local governments where the fiscal impacts of immigrants are most negative (Rothman and Espenshade 1992). Evidence from the 1980 Census for New Jersey suggests that both immigrant and native families are fiscal burdens for local governments, and that the negative impact is greater for immigrants (Espenshade and King 1994).

Existing studies usually exhibit some combination of three methodological problems. First, they look selectively at particular expenditure or revenue items associated with immigrants, which means that it is impossible to draw conclusions about immigrants' net fiscal impacts.[3] Second, only one previous study (Espenshade and King 1994) makes use of available micro-level information about the demographic and economic circumstances of individual immigrant households that can be obtained routinely from decennial census data. Instead, researchers commonly employ a "top-down," or average cost, strategy that amounts to allocating a simple pro rata share of government expenditures or revenues to each household. This approach ignores potentially important sources of household-level variation.[4] For instance, Clark et al. (1994) assumed the same per capita school expenditure for all students in a given state, even though these expenditures vary substantially by school district. Incorporating place of residence into estimates of elementary and secondary school expenditures could make a significant difference in the results. Third, researchers often emphasize the fiscal impacts of the immigrant population and ignore taxes paid and benefits received by native households. This approach may cast immigrants in a prejudicial light by overlooking the fact that both immigrants and natives can be fiscal drains on state and local government budgets (Espenshade and King 1994). Results for immigrants should be interpreted in the context of natives' impacts.

In addition, one challenge for all fiscal impact studies is to cast the analysis in the context of a general equilibrium economic framework (Isbister 1996). In contrast to simpler budgetary accounting approaches, general equilibrium models examine the lifetime interactions of natives and immigrants in the economy as workers, consumers, entrepreneurs, taxpayers, and recipients of government services. For example, educating immigrant children or providing them with sufficient health care to make learning possible may impose high short-run fiscal costs on local governments. However, as productive adults, these individuals are also potential net benefits to local governments as wage earners and as payers of sales and property taxes. Even in the short run, government expenditures flow as wages to teachers, health care workers, and other suppliers of goods or services to immigrant children. Moreover, if immigrants depress wage rates and reduce the employment opportunities of native workers, then there is an interaction between immigrants and the fiscal impacts of natives that is typically ignored in available research.

This chapter examines the fiscal impacts of immigrants from a micro perspective, utilizing household-level information on New Jersey's population from the 1990 Census. A comprehensive view is taken of state and local government revenues from and expenditures on the resident, noninstitutional population, which means that we are able to evaluate the net fiscal implications associated with immigrant families. Finally, we compare the budgetary consequences of households headed by native-born versus foreign-born individuals. Our results suggest that the typical New Jersey household, whether native or foreign born, uses more state and local government services than it pays for with taxes. Among nonelderly household heads, the negative fiscal impact of immigrant households exceeds that of native households by 46 percent at the state level and by 60 percent for county and municipal governments. In general, however, there is greater diversity within the foreign-born population, when stratified by region of origin, than there is between natives and immigrants.

CONCEPTUAL AND OTHER ISSUES

Attempts to estimate the fiscal impacts of immigrants encounter a variety of conceptual, methodological, and data issues. We do not claim to have resolved these issues definitively. Rather, this section describes the most critical ones as the basis for a subsequent discussion of the choices and assumptions we made in producing estimates for New Jersey.

Unit of Analysis

One issue involves the appropriate unit of analysis—whether it should be an individual, a family, or a household. There are reasons to prefer a household definition. First, many local government services such as fire and police protection are provided to households, and numerous taxes (such as property taxes) are paid by households. Second, a household comes closer to approximating a functioning socioeconomic unit of mutual exchange and support than a family. Using the "family" in the Census Bureau's sense of two or more individuals who are living together and who are related by blood, marriage, or adoption may be unnecessarily limiting for budgetary accounting purposes. Third, in most instances it makes little practical difference whether a family or household definition is used. In 1990, roughly 89 percent of the noninstitutional population in New Jersey lived in family households, approximately 8 percent lived alone, and just 3 percent lived in households with unrelated persons.

Households are usually labeled "immigrant" or "native" according to the householder's place of birth. But this practice encounters difficulty whenever some household members are foreign born and others are native born (Vernez and McCarthy 1995). Immigrant-headed households may contain native-born children, and native-born householders may have a foreign-born spouse.

Marginal versus Average Cost

Some services that governments provide have the characteristic of being pure or nearly pure public goods in the sense that consumption by one additional individual or household does not necessarily diminish the consumption of everyone else. National defense is the classic example at the federal level. Parks and other recreational facilities are illustrations of near-pure public goods at the state and local levels. How should these expenditures be allocated to households? Some analysts argue that the appropriate cost to assign to an immigrant household for a public good is zero, because the marginal cost of servicing an additional household is negligible. There are two problems with this approach, however. One is the arbitrary manner of identifying the "last" household or households to benefit from the expenditure. A related difficulty pertains to threshold effects—that is, to assigning discrete jumps in marginal cost to particular households when population growth creates the need, for example, for a new school, road, or firehouse.

An alternative perspective is that costs should be averaged over the general population if they cannot be earmarked to a well-defined subset of beneficiaries. This approach avoids the invidious comparisons inherent in marginal cost assignments, while recognizing that each household privately consumes a small portion of near-pure public goods. The issue is perhaps less important at the state level, because many services provided by the state arise from means-tested transfer programs in which recipient households are readily identifiable. At the county and municipal levels, however, a larger fraction of expenditures is not directly attributable to individual households. Net of education expenditures that benefit a student population, most of the goods provided by New Jersey's local governments are relatively public in nature (for example, parks and recreation, public health departments, public libraries, and judicial and legislative functions).

Top-Down versus Bottom-Up

Two general and competing methodologies for assigning governmental expenditures and revenues are the top-down and bottom-up strategies—also known as macro and micro procedures, respectively. In the top-down approach one begins with a global sum, derived from governmental balance sheets, and then devises rules to distribute that total among beneficiary or taxpayer households. An alternative procedure, the bottom-up approach, builds up to the aggregate total by inspecting the benefits received and the taxes paid by each household in the population and then cumulating results. In principle, both methods should give the same or nearly the same answer, not only in the aggregate but also in the distribution of benefits and costs across households.[5] In practice, however, a macro (top-down) approach minimizes variation across households, because analysts frequently assign each household a prorated share of total tax revenue and public expenditure on goods and services. This approach will be inappropriate whenever the goods or services in question are not public goods or if households exhibit substantial variation by demographic or socioeconomic characteristics. Most studies of immigrants' fiscal impacts have used a macro perspective (Rothman and Espenshade 1992). Recent exceptions include work by Borjas (1994) and by Espenshade and King (1994).

Immigrants' Legal Status

Another practical difficulty is the common inability to distinguish among immigrants by their legal status. Decennial census data and the monthly Current Population Survey (since January 1994) contain questions on place of birth, year of immigration, and citizenship status for the foreign-born population. Roughly two-thirds of New Jersey's foreign-born household heads are naturalized U.S. citizens, but it is impossible to tell with census data whether noncitizen householders are permanent legal residents, temporary residents, refugees, or illegal migrants. Previous studies have suggested that different categories of immigrants have differential patterns of benefit receipt and tax payments (Fix and Passel 1994; Rothman and Espenshade 1992; Vernez and McCarthy 1995, 1996). This problem is attenuated in studies that use a micro-level approach to calculate household benefit receipts and tax payments, because differences in average benefits received and taxes paid are permitted to fall out of the estimation and are not imposed by arbitrary rules that assign expenditures and revenues to households. Simply prorating government expenditures and revenues across households blurs the distinctions between native- and foreign-born populations and between naturalized citizens and resident aliens.

The ability to distinguish the legal status of immigrants is also relevant to policy. We have mentioned the state lawsuits against the federal government to recover costs of services for undocumented aliens. In addition, the heretofore largely unimportant difference between naturalized citizens and permanent resident aliens has acquired new salience since passage of welfare reform this past August (the Personal Responsibility and Work Opportunity Act of 1996). The law restricts eligibility of current lawful permanent residents for major federal means-tested entitlement programs, and places a 5-year ban on benefit receipt for new lawful permanent residents, with some exceptions (Espenshade 1996; State and Local Coalition on Immigration 1996).

Who Benefits and Who Pays?

There are also questions regarding the proper attribution of tax revenues received by state and local governments. First, the problem of tax incidence—that is, who really bears the burden of a given tax levy—has been largely ignored in the demographic literature. However, tax incidence has generated considerable research in public finance (Fullerton and Rodgers 1993; Metcalf 1993; Pechman 1985). Previous studies of the fiscal impacts of immigrants have assumed that the statutory payer of a tax bears the full incidence. Second, similar incidence questions arise on the benefits side. Who are the beneficiaries of local public school expenditures? The proximate beneficiaries of public education expenditures are the students, but an important rationale for public funding of elementary and secondary schooling is that society as a whole is better off in the long run with a more educated population. Third, the household sector is not the sole beneficiary of state and local government expenditures. The corporate sector benefits when, for example, an improved transportation or communication system permits a company to function more efficiently, or when a more educated work force makes a business more productive. The fourth question concerns the proper allocation of the costs of capital construction projects. Unlike a government's current expenditures on goods and services that are consumed in a single period, capital investments (for example, roads, schools, water treatment plants) generate a stream of services over time. For these items, it is not obvious how to identify the population of beneficiaries. Should it be the residents of a jurisdiction when construction is completed? Should it include residents when the debt is retired? What about future residents who will enjoy the benefits years after the initial capital outlays have been obligated? These could include as-yet-unborn children and future in-migrants from other states or localities.

DATA

Numerous data sets from federal, state, and local sources were combined to produce the estimates described in this study. The principal source of information is the 5 percent Public Use Microdata Sample (PUMS) for New Jersey from the 1990 Census of Population and Housing conducted by the U.S. Bureau of the Census. This file contains detailed information on the demographic and socioeconomic characteristics (as of April 1, 1990) of approximately 145,000 randomly selected New Jersey households. We excluded from our analysis residents of institutional and noninstitutional group quarters, who constituted less than 2 percent of New Jersey's total population. Income data for household members pertain to the 1989 calendar year.

Census data were extensively supplemented with state and local government budget information. The major source of additional information at the state level was the *State of New Jersey Budget: Fiscal Year 1991–1992* (State of New Jersey 1991). This document contains actual state program expenditures during the 1990 fiscal year (ending June 30, 1990) as well as explanations of program participation parameters and eligibility criteria. When these data were inadequate to identify the relevant beneficiary populations, we obtained additional information and program data from individual departments in the executive branch of state government and from independent research organizations. For example, information about municipal aid distributions came from *State Aid Programs for Municipalities, 1989 and 1990* (Forsberg 1995). Data on the state's share of school district expenditures were derived from the *1990 New Jersey Legislative District Data Book* (Rutgers 1990). The principal supplementary sources of information at the local level were detailed municipal and county budget and tax data found in the *Fifty-Second Annual Report of the Division of Local Government Services, 1989* (State of New Jersey 1990b). Clarifications of definitions for revenue and expenditure categories were frequently provided by representatives of the respective state and local agencies. A full listing of all data sources used is contained in Garvey and Espenshade (1996).

A demographic profile of our study population is shown in table 6.1. It was constructed by multiplying unweighted PUMS data by 20. There were almost 3 million households in New Jersey in 1990. More than 85 percent of these are headed by someone born in the United States. Among foreign-born households, those headed by individuals born in Europe or Canada are the most numerous and comprise nearly one-half of the foreign-born total. Immigrant households are significantly larger than native households, although there is considerable diversity within the foreign population. Households with a head from Europe or Canada are somewhat smaller than the typical native household, whereas households headed by nonnatives from other regions of the world have significantly more members.

There are also striking differences in age composition. The relative concentrations of children versus the elderly suggest that immigrant households are, on average, substantially younger than native households (see table 6.1). Once again, however, there are sharp contrasts within the foreign population. Households headed by migrants from Europe or Canada are markedly older than their counterparts from other regions and have fewer minor children. On the other hand, households headed by Asian immigrants are the youngest on average, have the fewest elderly, and the most children. Differences in the average age of household heads confirm these conclusions. In short, the picture that emerges reflects a relatively large proportion of foreign households, nearly half of which are headed by European immigrants. These migrants tended to come to the United States earlier in the 20th century and now head households that are both smaller and older than

Table 6.1 DEMOGRAPHIC PROFILE OF NEW JERSEY HOUSEHOLDS: 1990

| Characteristic (mean) | Total | Native Born | Foreign Born | Foreign-Born Households by Region of Origin | | | |
				Europe/ Canada	Asia	Latin America	Other
Number of households	2,897,560	2,505,400	392,160	182,460	77,100	111,200	21,400
Persons in household	2.74	2.68	3.10*	2.62*	3.59*	3.51*	3.16*
Children <18 years of age in household[a]	0.66	0.63	0.81*	0.52*	1.14*	1.02*	0.99*
School-age children in household[a]	0.43	0.41	0.54*	0.38*	0.76*	0.65*	0.59*
In public school	0.34	0.33	0.42*	0.30*	0.60*	0.49*	0.45*
LEP children <18 years of age in household[b]	0.03	0.01	0.11*	0.04*	0.19*	0.18*	0.10*
LEP children in bilingual education[c]	0.02	<0.01	0.08*	0.03*	0.13*	0.12*	0.07*
Persons 65+ in household	0.36	0.36	0.35	0.56*	0.15*	0.19*	0.19*
Age of household head	50.03	50.03	50.01	57.74*	42.06*	43.98*	44.06*
Percentage of households with male head	68.36%	67.45	74.14*	70.53*	85.40*	71.80*	76.54*

Note: Asterisk (*) indicates native- and foreign-born means are significantly different at 5 percent level.

a. School-age children are defined as ages 6 to 17, inclusive.

b. LEP, limited-English-proficient. LEP children are defined as those who speak a language other than English at home and who speak English "well," "not well," or "not at all," as opposed to "very well."

c. Defined as LEP children ages 6 to 17, inclusive, who are enrolled in public elementary and secondary schools.

the average. Immigrants from Asia and Latin America predominate among more recent migrant cohorts, and they are now heads of households that are larger and more youthful than even native households.

The average number of children under age 18 who are enrolled in public school is significantly greater for immigrant households, with the exception of those from Canada and Europe (see table 6.1). These differentials reflect differences in the number of minor children, not in the propensity of immigrant families to use public education services. Conditional on having school-age children, immigrant-headed households are no more likely to enroll their children in public school than native-headed households. Because local governments spend a large proportion of their budgets on public schools, these demographic differences across households have important fiscal consequences. Just slightly more than one-quarter (26 percent) of the average number of minor children in foreign-born households are themselves foreign born (0.21 out of 0.81) (calculations not shown in table 6.1). This proportion ranges between 15 percent in households headed by persons born in Europe or Canada to 32 percent in Asian-headed households. Of the 0.21 average number of foreign-born children in the typical foreign household, 84 percent are 6 to 17 years old. And of these, nearly 80 percent are enrolled in public elementary or secondary school. As we see in table 6.1, approximately 80 percent of native-born school-age children are also enrolled in public elementary or secondary school (0.33/0.41). In other words, foreign- and native-born children have similar school attendance patterns, regardless of the nativity status of the native children's parents. Finally, there is remarkable uniformity in public school enrollment rates among foreign-born children when households are stratified by region of origin.

Socioeconomic variations by household type are shown in table 6.2. Immigrant households from outside Europe and Canada have significantly above-average numbers of earners when compared with natives. This is partly a reflection of their greater size and youthfulness. Not only are households headed by Latin American immigrants significantly poorer than native households, but they are also more likely to receive public assistance income than any other group of households. European and Asian immigrants are less likely to rely on public assistance than natives. On average, foreign-born households in 1989 had incomes that were about 6 percent below those for natives. However, income differences within the immigrant population are significantly greater than they are between natives and foreigners. Mean household income for Asian migrants, for example, is 56 percent higher than the average income for Latin American immigrants.

Table 6.2 SOCIOECONOMIC PROFILE OF NEW JERSEY HOUSEHOLDS: 1990

Characteristic	Total	Native Born	Foreign Born	Foreign-Born Households by Region of Origin			
				Europe/ Canada	Asia	Latin America	Other
Mean number of wage earners in household	1.39	1.37	1.51*	1.22*	1.76*	1.78*	1.54*
Percentage of households receiving public assistance income[a]	5.31%	5.24	5.79*	4.19*	4.46*	9.37*	5.70
Percentage of households receiving SSI	1.66%	1.62	1.91	2.07*	0.96*	2.45*	1.21
Percentage of households receiving AFDC	2.58%	2.57	2.63	1.01*	3.04	4.93*	2.99
Mean public assistance income of recipient households, 1989	$4,428	4,459	4,250	4,502	4,163	4,135	3,905
Median public assistance income of recipient households, 1989	$3,900	3,926	3,775	3,870	3,600	3,864	3,612
Mean household income, 1989	$50,684	51,085	48,122*	46,886*	62,836*	40,279*	46,404*
Mean per capita household income,[b] 1989	$20,946	21,477	17,557*	19,335*	19,941*	13,144*	16,747*
Median household income, 1989	$41,929	42,110	39,000	37,200	54,180	34,000	37,000

Note: Asterisk (*) indicates native- and foreign-born means are significantly different at 5 percent level.
a. Public assistance income includes General Assistance (GA), Supplemental Security Income (SSI), and Aid to Families with Dependent Children (AFDC).
b. Found by calculating per capita income for each household and averaging over all households in the category.

A simple measure of relative economic well-being may be obtained by calculating per capita income for each household and averaging across all households in a category. For the total population, per capita household income equals more than $20,900 (see table 6.2). It is approximately $21,500 for natives versus $17,600 for immigrants. But among foreign-born households, this measure ranges between $13,100 for Latinos to nearly $20,000 for households from Europe, Canada, and Asia. It is apparent that Latin American migrants are typically among the poorest of all immigrant households in New Jersey. As discussed later in the chapter, this finding, too, has implications for fiscal impacts.

METHODOLOGY

We concentrated our analysis on the household sector comprising the resident, noninstitutional population in New Jersey, using the individual household as our principal unit of analysis. The central problem was then one of attributing to households the expenditures made and the revenues received by state and local governments during fiscal year (FY) 1989–90. To construct our estimates of fiscal impacts, we adopted a micro-analytic perspective and examined each of the 145,000 households on the New Jersey PUMS file for 1990. We made four calculations for each household based on its demographic and socioeconomic makeup: (1) taxes paid to state government; (2) taxes paid to county and municipal governments; (3) benefits received from state government; and (4) benefits received from county and municipal governments. Each of these calculations was further disaggregated to reflect the composition of taxes paid and benefits received. These estimates were then appended to each household's record.

New Jersey's state budget for FY 1990 totaled $12.15 billion. Current expenditures constituted $11.47 billion of this total. We excluded from consideration capital construction costs and the value of state bond redemptions, because it was impossible to identify unambiguously the set of beneficiary households. Moreover, approximately $1.1 billion from current state expenditures was spent on goods and services not directly consumed by households. Roughly half of these costs were attributable to corrections and incarceration, while the remaining amounts were spent on the institutionalized population with physical and/or mental disabilities. We also excluded these expenditures on behalf of institutionalized populations, since we focused the analysis on the household sector. This left $10.38 billion in state expenditures to allocate to households.

We made simplifying assumptions about tax incidence that reflect the general consensus in the literature (Metcalf 1993; Pechman 1985; Rothman and Espenshade 1992). We assumed, for example, that the personal income tax was borne by the household paying the tax and that the sales and use tax was borne by consumers in proportion to their expected total expenditures. Purchasers of goods on which excise taxes are levied were presumed to bear the tax, and owners of personal business property and homeowners bore the burden of taxes assessed on these properties. Owners of residential rental properties, however, were assumed to pass local property taxes on to tenants. Equivalent assumptions were made about the incidence of public benefits; the proximate beneficiary was assumed to be the ultimate one. So, for example, we postulated that the benefits of public school expenditures lodged in households with school-age children who were enrolled in public schools and that there were no spillovers to the general population. Likewise, we neglected the possibility that government transfer payments or public expenditures on goods and services generated jobs and additional tax revenues when injected back into the economy. These multiplier effects could be accounted for in a general equilibrium model, but we do not consider them here.

Our study adopts a cross-sectional approach as a first step and implicitly ignores life-cycle costs and benefits of immigrants and natives. To our knowledge, no fiscal impact analysis has been conducted with an explicit time dimension. Single-period accounting frameworks, while providing a useful guide to annual balance-sheet impacts of immigrant and native households, cannot distinguish between cohort and aging effects. They cannot furnish evidence on how patterns of benefit receipt and tax payments vary with immigrant tenure in the United States, nor do they yield information on differential net fiscal impacts across immigrant cohorts. On the other hand, our household-level estimates would permit separating cohort and age effects if we applied the same methodology to two consecutive censuses.[6]

Another potential limitation of this study is our assumption that, apart from capital costs and institution-related expenditures, all governments' expenditures represent exclusive benefits to the household sector. But households are only one source of state revenues.[7] Corporations also pay taxes; the most important of these in New Jersey are the corporation income tax, real estate taxes on commercial property, and fees and profits taxes on banks and insurance companies operating in the state. Neglecting corporate sector taxes causes us to underestimate state revenues by at least 25 percent. The potential revenue understatement for local property taxes is perhaps greater and varies across municipalities by the proportion of valued property owned by businesses. To anticipate some of our later findings, these omissions help to explain why both native- and immigrant-headed households are net fiscal drains at the state and local levels. They also suggest the use of caution in interpreting the results. Readers should perhaps view the fiscal impact estimates in relative instead of absolute terms; that is, estimates for natives can be compared with immigrants at each level of government.

Illustrative Examples

Three different estimation strategies were used to produce our estimates of fiscal impacts. First, government expenditures on pure or near-pure public goods and on those where it was otherwise difficult to identify an appropriate subset of beneficiaries were allocated to households on an *average* cost or prorated share basis. For state expenditures, the proration pertains to all households in New Jersey. For county and municipal expenditures, the relevant geographic unit is the Census Bureau's Public Use Microdata Area (PUMA), which is the smallest area that is identifiable with PUMS data. A PUMA is typically smaller than a county; New Jersey has 21 counties and 56 PUMAs. Populous counties usually have several PUMAs, with socioeconomically and geographically similar municipalities grouped together.[8] All households within a given PUMA were assumed to benefit equally from public goods expenditures made by local governments. Differences in local fiscal impacts between native and immigrant households may arise after aggregation to the state level to the extent these populations exhibit dissimilar spatial distributions across New Jersey communities. State expenditures that are distributed using an average cost approach include general state services/state aid and municipal aid. At the local level, general county expenditures and general municipal expenditures are apportioned in the same fashion.

Second, numerous revenue and expenditure components were allocated using an average cost or benefit formula applied to the relevant population of "eligibles" (e.g., individuals, households, or automobiles). Wherever possible, we simulated public benefits to households, as well as taxes paid, by applying a knowledge of program rules and eligibility requirements to each household's income and demographic profile. The following aggregate expenditures were assigned using this methodology: administrative expenditures on elementary and secondary school education (both the state and local shares); higher education, including community colleges; Medicaid; general administrative expenses on AFDC, SSI, and General Assistance (GA); Pharmaceutical Assistance to the Aged and Disabled (PAAD); employment and training; programs for the aged, disabled, and veterans; property tax reimbursement; farm programs and agricultural extension services; Department of Motor Vehicle (DMV) administrative expenses; and gas and utility credits. Some revenue items were also estimated this way, including taxes on automobiles and gasoline, alcohol and tobacco, inheritances and estates, and business personal property.

Third, a micro-analytic approach was taken to build up estimates from the individual household level whenever the required information was included on the PUMS household record or when enough relevant data exist to approximate the benefit or tax payment with reasonable confidence. Items that are measured this way include AFDC benefits (from state and local government), per pupil expenditure on public elementary and secondary education, income taxes, state sales taxes, realty transfer taxes, property taxes, and utility taxes.

Of the nearly $10.4 billion in current state expenditures that could reasonably be associated with households, we were able to assign nearly 70 percent on the basis of actual or probable use—that is, using either the second or third methodological approach just mentioned. The remaining 30 percent were for general state services. These comprised a number of general activities, including public safety and criminal justice; community development and environmental management; economic planning; transportation; and government administrative services (for example, legislature or governmental review). Government legislative and administrative functions accounted for nearly 40 percent of this total. These general costs were prorated among households. With the exception of education, most locally provided goods cannot be assigned to households on an actual-use basis. Most of these costs are truly general expenditures on indivisible public goods, and we allocated them using an average cost calculation. At the county level these items include general government expenditures, public safety, and public health.

Rather than provide a detailed explanation of how we estimated each revenue and expenditure item allocable to households, we give three examples (readers interested in a complete methodological description may consult Garvey and Espenshade 1996). The examples have been chosen to illustrate the three estimation strategies just described, to include both revenue and expenditure items, and to relate both to state and local governments. They also correspond to items that are significant in dollar terms and/or that exhibit substantial variation across households of different types.

GENERAL STATE SERVICES/STATE AID

Expenditures on state-provided services and state aid programs that are not otherwise allocable to individual households are assigned on a per-household average-use basis. Total general expenditures are equal to the sum of expenditures on law enforcement, military activities, and the judiciary; general physical and mental health services; cultural and intellectual development services and supplemental education and training programs; community development and management of natural resources and recreational areas; economic planning and regulation, and general social services programs; transportation programs, local and state highway facilities and public transport; government direction, management, and control functions; and special government services. We took one-twentieth of reported state total general expenditures and divided that figure by the number of New Jersey households (both institutional and noninstitutional) in the 5 percent PUMS data for 1990. The resulting quotient of $1,119 was allocated equally to all New Jersey households, under the assumption of average use by all households.

LOCAL ELEMENTARY AND SECONDARY SCHOOL EXPENDITURES

In New Jersey, a locality's share of the overall school district budget varies by the resources available to the district.[9] In general, the level of state funding varies inversely with property wealth in the school district. Average per pupil expenditure for each PUMA was found by taking a weighted average of per pupil expenditure within each school district in the PUMA, using as weights the average daily enrollment figures supplied by school districts. The same weights are applied to local school district data to compute a PUMA-wide average share of public schooling costs borne by localities (as opposed to the state). The product of the PUMA's average per pupil expenditure and the fraction of this expenditure for which localities are responsible gives a dollar figure for each PUMA's local elementary and secondary school costs per pupil. This dollar figure is then allocated to every child who, according to 1990 Census data, lives in the PUMA, is 6–17 years old, and attends public school. The more school-age children a household contains, the higher is its utilization of publicly funded school services.[10]

Property taxes are the most important taxes paid by households to local governments. To estimate property tax payments, we used actual property taxes paid by homeowners and imputed property taxes paid by renters. Householders who own their own dwellings were asked to report on their 1990 Census questionnaire the amount of property tax they paid in 1989. Property taxes paid by such households are reported as ranges in the PUMS data, and we took the midpoint of the category as a point estimate. For homeowners who were in the highest category with no upper bound on property tax paid and for those who did not report paying real estate taxes, we used the estimated market value of the residence (also asked on the census form) and multiplied the response by the population-weighted equalized property tax rate for the PUMA where the dwelling is located.[11]

To estimate property taxes paid by renters, we assumed that taxes are capitalized in the value of the rental property (Yinger 1982) and that property taxes are passed on to renters by owners. If we conceptualize rent as payment for a stream of housing services, property taxes paid are equal to annual contract rent (defined as 12 times the monthly contract rent as reported on the census form) multiplied by $(t/(t + i))$, where t is the local equalized property tax rate and i is a discount rate, assumed for our purposes to be the average 30-year mortgage rate over the 1985–95 period, or 8 percent.[12] Details of the formula derivation may be found in Garvey and Espenshade (1996).[13]

RESULTS

We present our results in terms of averages per household after stratifying households by type. Households are grouped according to characteristics of the household head, including age and sex, nativity status (that is, whether foreign or native born), and region of birth for immigrants. Using decennial census data, we were unable to identify legal administrative status among noncitizen immigrant households.

State Estimates

The main results at the state level are displayed in table 6.3. The table's first panel shows state expenditures on households in FY 1989–90. General state services and state aid along with costs for public elementary and secondary school education are the largest items in dollar terms. General state services are the same for all households because they are prorated using average cost principles. There are sharp differences in education expenditures according to the age of the householder, because there are relatively few school-age children in households headed by senior citizens.

Total estimated state expenditures are summed across the bottom row of the first panel of table 6.3. They show that the state spent an average of approximately $3,700 on each household with a head under age 65 and more than $2,300 on elderly households. This age difference is preserved among different types of households and primarily reflects the gap in educational expenditures between younger and older households. In general, immigrants are more costly to the state than natives. Immigrant households with younger heads received roughly $400 more in benefits than natives in 1989–90. Among older households, the immigrant advantage was closer to $200.

Differentials between immigrants and natives are small, however, in comparison with the variation in state expenditures among the foreign-born population. European households commanded relatively fewer state expenditures, whereas Asian, Latin American, and other immigrants received state benefits well in excess of the foreign-born average. Latin American households are especially costly to the state. They received public benefits that were almost $900, or 25 percent, greater than amounts going to the typical younger New Jersey household (see table 6.3). Elderly Latino households had more than an $1,800, or nearly 80 percent, advantage. Higher-than-usual expenditures on education, and especially on Medicaid and welfare, explain most of the Latin American differential. As shown in table 6.2, Latin American migrants' greater reliance on Medicaid and welfare is related to their poverty status. Education, including higher education, and Medicaid costs help to explain the relatively higher amounts spent on Asian immigrants. Both education and Medicaid were comparatively less important for immigrants from Europe and Canada. Fewer school-age children largely accounts for lower educational expenditures on European and Canadian households.

Revenues that the state received from New Jersey households are shown in the lower panel of table 6.3. The most important of these are income taxes, followed by sales and then automobile and gasoline taxes. Younger households paid a larger average amount in total taxes in FY 1989–90 than senior households (roughly $2,400 versus $1,100), principally because labor force participation rates and income levels are higher for younger persons. Differences between immigrants and

Table 6.3 AVERAGE STATE EXPENDITURES, REVENUES, AND NET FISCAL IMPACT PER HOUSEHOLD, BY AGE AND NATIVITY STATUS OF HEAD: FY 1989–90 (IN DOLLARS)

| State Expenditures[a] | Total ($) | | Native Born ($) | | Foreign Born ($) | | Foreign-Born Households by Region of Origin ($) | | | | | | | |
| | | | | | | | Europe/Canada | | Asia | | Latin America | | Other | |
	<65	65+	<65	65+	<65	65+	<65	65+	<65	65+	<65	65+	<65	65+
General state services/state aid	1,119	1,119	1,119	1,119	1,119	1,119	1,119	1,119	1,119	1,119	1,119	1,119	1,119	1,119
Elementary and secondary education	1,523	124	1,489	127	1,733	101	1,466	46	1,808	295	1,971	416	1,767	78
Higher education	382	74	365	70	490	103	410	88	622	200	481	180	504	90
Medicaid	289	410	288	394	297	521	180	365	245	733	468	1,453	291	723
AFDC/GA/SSI	79	70	79	67	78	86	42	57	66	138	125	255	88	113
PAAD	14	143	13	138	19	176	17	167	21	166	21	243	16	174
Municipal aid programs	84	85	76	82	137	107	87	86	80	110	229	239	163	134
Employment and training programs	25	15	26	15	20	12	27	10	10	26	19	19	18	16
Programs for aged, veterans, and disabled	25	91	27	94	10	72	15	76	6	69	7	49	7	70
Property tax reimbursement	101	124	102	125	94	119	106	123	90	107	85	91	88	110
Other allocable expenditures	52	70	52	69	48	74	52	72	48	76	45	89	41	77
Total	3,693	2,324	3,636	2,300	4,044	2,489	3,520	2,208	4,115	3,037	4,569	4,153	4,102	2,705

Table 6.3 AVERAGE STATE EXPENDITURES, REVENUES, AND NET FISCAL IMPACT PER HOUSEHOLD, BY AGE AND NATIVITY STATUS OF HEAD, FY 1989–90 (IN DOLLARS) (continued)

| | | | | | | | | Foreign-Born Households by Region of Origin ($) | | | | | | |
| | Total ($) | | Native Born ($) | | Foreign Born ($) | | Europe/Canada | | Asia | | Latin America | | Other | |
State Revenues	<65	65+	<65	65+	<65	65+	<65	65+	<65	65+	<65	65+	<65	65+
Income tax	1,375	411	1,389	410	1,291	417	1,419	396	1,620	792	934	417	1,145	517
Sales tax	504	317	508	319	484	301	512	296	549	403	412	296	449	323
Auto/fuels tax	249	156	252	159	227	133	261	133	244	183	185	114	198	141
Alcohol/tobacco tax	121	102	119	101	134	105	129	99	137	143	139	128	123	105
Inheritance tax	68	74	74	75	29	68	46	73	14	42	22	48	17	59
Business property tax	6	3	5	3	7	3	8	3	8	4	5	2	5	4
Realty transfer tax	41	7	40	7	48	9	45	8	77	35	28	6	51	18
Total	2,364	1,070	2,387	1,075	2,220	1,036	2,419	1,008	2,648	1,602	1,725	1,011	1,988	1,166
Net fiscal impact	−1,329	−1,254[b]	−1,249	−1,225	−1,824[c]	−1,453[b,d]	−1,101	−1,199	−1,467[e]	−1,435	−2,844[e]	−3,142[f]	−2,114[e]	−1,539

a. See text for explanation of expenditure and revenue categories. Net fiscal impact equals revenues minus expenditures.

b. Under age 65 and age 65+ mean deficits are significantly different at 5 percent level.

c. Native- and foreign-born mean deficits differ significantly for household heads under 65.

d. Native- and foreign-born mean deficits differ significantly for household heads 65 and older.

e. Foreign-born household heads under 65 from Europe and Canada have significantly smaller mean deficits than their counterparts from other regions.

f. Foreign-born household heads 65 and older from Europe and Canada have significantly smaller mean deficits that those from Latin America.

natives are once again small; total taxes paid by immigrant households averaged no more than 4–7 percent less than natives' tax contributions to the state. However, there is substantial diversity within the immigrant community. Compared to the statewide average for younger households, for example, total tax payments ranged between 12 percent above average for younger households headed by Asian immigrants to 27 percent below the statewide average for younger Latin American households. Much of the gap between younger Asians and Latinos is explained by differences in income taxes, which in turn reflect underlying differences in household income, as described in table 6.2.

Households' net fiscal impacts are shown in the last row of table 6.3. They are calculated by subtracting estimated per household state expenditures from state revenues. Our estimates suggest that every household type was a net burden on state government in FY 1989–90, receiving more in state services than they paid for with state taxes. The typical budgetary deficit amounted to approximately $1,300 for each household in New Jersey. Some readers may wonder how this result is possible when the state's budget must balance every year. It arises because we have neglected other sources of revenue from corporations and the federal government that flow into the state's treasury and also because we have attributed as benefits to households some state expenditures that benefit the corporate sector.

There is a small difference in the general population between younger and older households' fiscal effects. Significantly larger gaps emerge between immigrants and natives. Among younger households, the fiscal burden associated with immigrants is $575, or 46 percent greater than for natives (table 6.3). Elderly foreign households generate a smaller discrepancy ($228), but one that is nevertheless 19 percent higher than the comparable figure for natives. Disparities in fiscal impacts are greater among immigrant groups than between immigrant and native-born households. European and Asian immigrant families engender fiscal consequences that are not much different from those of all families. On the other hand, immigrants from Latin America and from other places are least likely to be paying their way. The estimated net fiscal deficit for Latinos is well over twice as large as it is for the typical household in the state, and younger migrant families from other countries impose a fiscal burden 60 percent greater than all younger families combined. These results are consistent with findings from earlier studies (Espenshade and King 1994).[14]

We used regression analysis to test whether differences in fiscal impacts result from something intrinsic to nativity status or simply reflect differences in socioeconomic and demographic characteristics between immigrants and natives. After controlling for age, education, marital status, English proficiency, place of residence and number of children, we found that the difference in net fiscal impacts associated with nativity status was not statistically significant.[15] Our results suggest that it is not the fact of being foreign born per se, but, rather, the different configuration of immigrants' household characteristics that influences their net fiscal impacts on state government. Latin American and other immigrants, who are younger and have more children (and therefore incur greater state costs for elementary and secondary schooling), exert a larger fiscal imposition than their native-born counterparts. Asian immigrants also have large families, but their disproportionate use of state education benefits is largely offset by higher incomes and tax payments.

The household-level net fiscal deficits are cumulated up to the state level and shown separately for male- and female-headed households in table 6.4. The household sector ran a combined $3.8 billion deficit in FY 1989–90. Immigrant households contributed $683 million to this total. Even though immigrants comprised 13.5 percent of all New Jersey households, they accounted for 18 percent of the aggregate budget gap. Latino households were just 3.8 percent of all households in the state, but they contributed 8.4 percent of the aggregate deficit. Within the foreign-born population, Latinos constituted 28 percent of all households, whereas they accounted for nearly half (47 percent) of the fiscal deficit attributable to migrants. The average net fiscal deficit associated with female-headed households was significantly larger than its male counterpart. The relative gap between the sexes is especially pronounced for younger households. This finding is hardly surprising. Women earn less than men on average and usually have custody of children that result from nonmarital births and parental divorces, making female-headed households eligible for AFDC and Medicaid.

Local Estimates

Table 6.5 contains estimates of local government expenditures on households and of household-level taxes that flow back to counties and municipalities. General county and municipal expenditures consist of such items as general government, judiciary, public safety, public works, health and welfare (excluding expenses for county welfare boards and for welfare/public assistance), recreation and conservation, nonschool education (for example, public libraries), public em-

Table 6.4 NET FISCAL IMPACT OF HOUSEHOLDS ON STATE OF NEW JERSEY, BY AGE, SEX, AND NATIVITY STATUS OF HOUSEHOLD HEAD: FY 1989–90 (IN DOLLARS)

Net Fiscal Impact	Total N.J. Households ($)		Native Born ($)		Foreign Born ($)		Foreign-Born Households by Region of Origin ($)							
							Europe/Canada		Asia		Latin America		Other	
	<65	65+	<65	65+	<65	65+	<65	65+	<65	65+	<65	65+	<65	65+
All Households														
State total (millions)	−2,943	−856	−2,384	−732	−559	−124	−124	−83	−108	−5	−287	−33	−40	−4
Per household	−1,329	−1,254	−1,249	−1,225	−1,824	−1,453	−1,101	−1,199	−1,467	−1,435	−2,844	−3,142	−2,114	−1,539
Per capita[g]	−322	−874[a]	−302	−853[a]	−450	−1,022[a]	−250	−908	−312[b]	−720	−752[b]	−1,842[c]	−574[b]	−1,176
Male-Headed Households														
State total (millions)	−1,421	−349	−1,035	−295	−386	−54	−93	−34	−93	−3	−173	−15	−27	−1
Per household	−884[d]	−937[d]	−758[d]	−911[d]	−1,591[d]	−1,113[d]	−1,022[d]	−896[d]	−1,470[b]	−1,199	−2,361[f]	−2,386[f]	−1,772[e]	−993[d]
Per capita[g]	−132[d]	−504[d]	−97[d]	−488[d]	−330[d]	−608[d]	−166[d]	−542[d]	−295[e]	−507[d]	−546[e]	−1,042[f]	−410[c]	−584[d]
Female-Headed Households														
State total (millions)	−1,522	−507	−1,348	−437	−174	−70	−32	−49	−15	−2	−113	−17	−13	−2
Per household	−2,509	−1,635	−2,486	−1,599	−2,706	−1,897	−1,421	−1,568	−1,450	−2,114	−4,132[b]	−4,393[c]	−3,412[b]	−2,246[i]
Per capita[g]	−827	−1,319	−818	−1,286	−902	−1,561	−586	−1,354	−415[b]	−1,333	−1,303[c]	−3,166[c]	−1,199[b]	−1,942[i]

a. Per-capita mean deficit differs significantly (at 5 percent level) by age of household head.

b. Foreign-born household heads under age 65 from Europe and Canada have significantly different mean deficits from their counterparts in other regions.

c. Foreign-born household heads age 65 and older from Europe and Canada have significantly different mean deficits from their counterparts in other regions.

d. Male-headed household mean deficit is significantly smaller than corresponding female-headed household mean deficit.

e. Both notes b and d, above.

f. Both notes c and d, above.

g. Found by first calculating net fiscal impact per capita for each household and then averaging over all households in the category.

Table 6.5 AVERAGE LOCAL EXPENDITURES, REVENUES, AND NET FISCAL IMPACT PER HOUSEHOLD, BY AGE AND NATIVITY STATUS OF HEAD: FY 1989–90 (IN DOLLARS)

	Total ($)		Native Born ($)		Foreign Born ($)		Foreign-Born Households by Region of Origin ($)							
							Europe/Canada		Asia		Latin America		Other	
	<65	65+	<65	65+	<65	65+	<65	65+	<65	65+	<65	65+	<65	65+
Local Expenditures[a]														
General county	716	731	708	728	768	755	752	744	741	778	803	813	785	767
General municipal	1,427	1,458	1,382	1,441	1,707	1,576	1,582	1,506	1,559	1,681	1,926	1,979	1,868	1,736
Elementary and secondary education	2,134	154	2,034	154	2,754	156	2,526	89	3,672	368	2,370	546	2,581	116
County college	49	9	48	9	56	13	55	11	52	15	61	23	56	14
AFDC	17	4	17	4	16	4	7	1	16	13	26	19	20	0
Total	4,344	2,356	4,190	2,335	5,302	2,503	4,922	2,351	6,039	2,855	5,187	3,380	5,311	2,633
Local Revenues														
Property tax	2,472	2,162	2,448	2,150	2,619	2,247	2,949	2,276	2,831	2,706	2,126	1,867	2,447	2,432
Utility tax	160	142	161	142	157	139	164	139	156	159	152	135	150	145
Total	2,632	2,304	2,609	2,292	2,776	2,386	3,113	2,415	2,987	2,865	2,278	2,002	2,597	2,577
Net Fiscal Impact[h]	−1,712	−52[b]	−1,581	−43[b]	−2,526[c]	−117[b,d]	−1,809	63	−3,053[e]	10	−2,909[e]	−1,378[f]	−2,714[e]	−56

a. See text for explanation of expenditure and revenue categories.
b. Under age 65 and age 65 + mean deficits are significantly different at 5 percent level.
c. Native- and foreign-born mean deficits differ significantly for household heads under 65.
d. Native- and foreign-born mean deficits differ significantly for household heads 65 +.
e. Foreign-born household heads under 65 from Europe and Canada have significantly lower mean deficits than their counterparts from other regions.
f. Foreign-born household heads 65 + from Europe and Canada have significantly lower mean deficits than those from Latin America.
g. Calculated as revenues minus expenditures.

ployee benefits and pension contributions, and debt service. These costs are evenly apportioned to all households in a given political jurisdiction. We assumed that, if immigrant and native households are located in the same neighborhood, they receive the same level of government benefits from general county and municipal expenditures. Therefore, differences in these costs by household type in the first two rows of table 6.5 reflect variations in the spatial distribution throughout New Jersey of the respective populations.

Households' estimated net fiscal impacts at the local level are shown in the last row of table 6.5. The net fiscal cost is either negligible or very small for senior citizen households. Elderly immigrants from Europe and Canada even appear to generate a slight surplus for other taxpayers, although the amount ($63) is not statistically different from zero. The one exception is Latin American households. Elderly Latino immigrant households incurred a local deficit of almost $1,400 per household in FY 1989–90, principally because they paid below-average amounts in property taxes and lived in urban areas in northeastern New Jersey that spent relatively large sums on general municipal functions.

The typical nonelderly household received benefits from local government that exceeded taxes paid by more than $1,700 (see table 6.5). This amount is larger than the fiscal burden these same households placed on state government in 1989–90.[16] There is a substantial nativity differential at the local level. The deficit imposed by immigrant households exceeds the one for natives by nearly $1,000 per household, or by 60 percent. This comparison hides even larger variations when migrants are disaggregated by region of origin. European migrants have fiscal costs that are relatively close to those of natives. But the fiscal impacts associated with younger immigrants from outside Europe and Canada are between 72 percent and 93 percent greater than those for their native counterparts. Given our findings at the state level, budget gaps this large might be expected for Latin American and other immigrants. But the fiscal deficit for Asian households (nearly $3,100) requires comment. Asian families have the highest average number of school-age children, and they live in school districts that spend relatively large amounts per student. The disproportionately large public school expenditure on Asian children is only partially offset by the higher-than-average property taxes paid by younger Asian families. Parallel to findings at the state level, a regression analysis using a household's net fiscal impact as the dependent variable shows that nativity status is not a statistically significant predictor when household socioeconomic and demographic factors are controlled. Latin American immigrants again are the single exception.[17]

Table 6.6 shows that the combined household sector deficit at the local level was $3.83 billion in 1989–90, approximately the same size as the aggregate deficit households imposed on state government. In contrast to the state picture, however, virtually all of the local fiscal deficit is attributable to younger households. Immigrant families are again responsible for a disproportionate share. Their fraction of the local deficit (20.5 percent) is half again as large as their portion of total households (13.5 percent). Among the immigrant population, European households' net use of local services is relatively small. Europeans and Canadians account for one-quarter of the aggregate local immigrant deficit but comprise nearly half of all foreign households. Male–female differences are generally consistent with those at the state level in the sense that net fiscal deficits attributable to female-headed households are typically significantly greater than those for male-headed households. On the other hand, with the exception of Latinos, male-headed senior citizen households are net fiscal assets at the local level and might be expected to provide a small subsidy to other taxpayers.

CONCLUSIONS

This chapter has used data from 1990 Census 5 percent PUMS files, supplemented extensively with information from state and municipal budgets, to estimate the state and local fiscal impacts of immigrant and native-born households in New Jersey. We took the household as the unit of analysis and passed each of the approximately 145,000 New Jersey households on the PUMS files under a microscope to estimate taxes paid to state and local governments and benefits received from the same jurisdictions. We do not claim that our methodology represents "best" practice, but it is better practice than many approaches taken in the past.

There are several new features of these estimates. First, they are based on a micro-level analysis instead of a top-down macro procedure that prorates government revenues and expenditures evenly across households on the basis of average cost assumptions. We attributed roughly two-thirds of FY 1989–90 current state expenditures on the noninstitutionalized population to targeted households that actually benefit from the expenditure. Just one-third of state expen-

Table 6.6 NET FISCAL IMPACT OF HOUSEHOLDS ON LOCAL GOVERNMENTS, BY AGE, SEX, AND NATIVITY STATUS OF HOUSEHOLD HEAD: FY 1989–90 (IN DOLLARS)

Net Fiscal Impact	Total N.J. Households ($)		Native Born ($)		Foreign Born ($)		Foreign-Born Households by Region of Origin ($)							
							Europe/Canada		Asia		Latin America		Other	
	<65	65+	<65	65+	<65	65+	<65	65+	<65	65+	<65	65+	<65	65+
All Households														
State total (millions)	−3,790	−36	−3,016	−26	−774	−10	−204	4	−225	<0.1	−293	−14	−51	−0.1
Per household	−1,712	−52	−1,581	−43	−2,526	−117	−1,809	63	−3,053	10	−2,909	−1,378	−2,714	−56
Per capita[e]	−415	−79[a]	−383	−72[a]	−613	−133[a]	−386	−48	−693[b]	61	−781[b]	−751[c]	−763[b]	−159
Male-Headed Households														
State total (millions)	−2,585	87	−1,970	80	−614	7	−176	13	−202	0.5	−198	−7	−38	0.9
Per household	−1,607[d]	234[d]	−1,443[d]	247[d]	−2,535[d]	146[d]	−1,940[d]	340[d]	−3,186[d]	211	−2,699[d]	−1,129[d]	−2,568[d]	656[d]
Per capita[e]	−336[d]	108[d]	−293[d]	115[d]	−574[d]	62[d]	−396	134[d]	−702	155	−661[d]	−468[d]	−681[d]	372[d]
Female-Headed Households														
State total (millions)	−1,206	−123	−1,045	−106	−160	−17	−29	−9	−23	−0.5	−95	−7	−13	−1
Per household	−1,987	−396	−1,927	−387	−2,493	−459	−1,281	−273	−2,242	−567	−3,469	−1,790	−3,270	−980
Per capita[e]	−625	−305	−608	−294	−761	−386	−347	−271	−637	−209	−1,101	−1,220	−1,074	−848

a. Per capita mean deficit differs significantly (at 5 percent level) by age of household head.

b. Foreign-born household heads under age 65 from Europe and Canada have significantly different mean deficits from their counterparts in other regions.

c. Foreign-born household heads age 65+ from Europe and Canada have significantly different mean deficits from their counterparts in other regions.

d. Male-headed household mean differs significantly from the corresponding female-headed household mean.

e. Found by first calculating net fiscal impact per capita for each household and then averaging over all households in the category.

ditures were allocated on a pro rata share basis, and these were typically costs for public goods. Second, we attached fiscal cost and benefit data to each household record, and these micro units were then compared in different ways. We contrasted the fiscal impacts of households headed by immigrants and natives. Differences by age and sex of household head and by region of origin for the foreign-born population were also featured in the analysis. Third, we viewed government expenditures on households and revenues provided by the household sector to the state and to municipalities in the broadest terms possible, which means that we were able to draw conclusions about the net fiscal impacts of different kinds of households.

We found that both immigrant and native households are net fiscal burdens on state and local government in New Jersey, receiving more in services than they pay in taxes. Part of the shortfall is made up from a variety of taxes paid by corporations and part by monies passed back from the federal government. There is typically greater variation in fiscal impacts within the foreign-born population than between immigrants and natives. Immigrant households on average have significantly larger fiscal deficits associated with them than native households at both the state and local levels. Moreover, the relative burden imposed by immigrants is greater for county and municipal governments than for the state. This conclusion is consistent with research from other states showing that local governments usually shoulder the most substantial burden in providing services to immigrant families (Rothman and Espenshade 1992). It would be useful for comparative purposes to move beyond New Jersey and to apply these micro-analytic methodologies to data from other states with large immigrant populations. Because no state is necessarily representative of the entire United States, developing additional case studies would provide a richer and more comprehensive national picture of the state and local fiscal impacts of U.S. immigration.

Our study challenges future research in four ways. First, the non-household sector needs to be brought into the analysis on both the revenue and expenditure side. We have ignored taxes paid by corporations and have interpreted most government expenditures as benefits to households, which helps to produce the conclusion that households on average receive more services than they pay for. Second, the methodology of fiscal accounting needs to move beyond single-period static analysis toward examining individuals' and households' use of public benefits and payment of taxes in a dynamic life-cycle context. Separating out age and cohort effects is impossible when the analysis is restricted to a single cross section. As a first step, the methods developed here could be applied to successive cross sections. Age and cohort effects could then be deduced from the set of cross-sectional results. Third, second-round spillover and multiplier effects need to be accounted for in more complex general equilibrium models. Immigrants' entrepreneurial activities may generate employment for other native and foreign workers. If immigrants have adverse labor market outcomes for native workers, these effects also need to be taken into account in computing fiscal impacts. Finally, estimating the fiscal impacts of immigrants is frequently a task assigned to in-house researchers working for state and local governments. These analysts are often laboring under tight budgetary and time constraints, and may face incentives to reach a predetermined conclusion. An important challenge for future research is to engage the attention of academic economists, especially public finance specialists, in examining the fiscal implications of U.S. immigration.

Notes

Financial support for this research was provided by a grant from the Andrew W. Mellon Foundation. We are grateful to the following individuals for supplying information, data, and guidance about the operations of state and local government programs: Patricia Austin, Maryann Belanger, Gerald Dowgin, Pamela Espenshade, Mary Forsberg, David Grimm, Evelyn Klingler, Robert Lupp, Linda O'Connor, Marc Pfeiffer, Deena Schorr, and Melvin Wyns. Andrei Shidlowski, from the New Jersey School Boards Association, prepared the data on per pupil expenditure. Valuable comments were received from members of the National Research Council's Panel on the Demographic and Economic Impacts of Immigration at a workshop in Irvine, California, January 25–26, 1996. Melanie Adams and Maya Smith provided skillful technical and research assistance.

1. During 1994, Arizona, California, Florida, New Jersey, New York, and Texas filed suits in federal district courts to recover costs they claim they incurred because of the federal government's failure to enforce U.S. immigration policy, protect the nation's borders, and provide adequate resources for immigration emergencies (Dunlap and Morse 1995). All six lawsuits sought compensation for the costs of imprisoning undocumented criminal aliens in state or local correctional facilities, and many included claims for public education, emergency health care, and other social services. The amounts involved ranged from $50 million in New Jersey for the 1993 costs of jailing 500 undocumented criminal felons and for future costs of new prison construction to more than $33 billion in the New York case, which sought reimbursement of all state and county costs associated with illegal immigration between 1988 and 1993 (State and Local Coalition on Immigration 1994). All six suits have been dismissed, but some states are appealing the decisions (Espenshade 1996).

2. For comprehensive reviews, see Rothman and Espenshade (1992) and Vernez and McCarthy (1995, 1996).

3. See, for example, Borjas and Trejo (1991) and Clark et al. (1994).

4. See Huddle (1993) and Clark et al. (1994) as examples.

5. There are obvious situations where discrepancies would occur, however. Not all of the state sales tax collections come from New Jersey residents. Pennsylvania and New York residents who work or shop in New Jersey contribute to the state's total sales tax revenues through their purchases. Moreover, out-of-state tourists visiting New Jersey contribute to sales tax receipts. A similar situation exists on the expenditure side. Public monies spent to build state roads provide benefits to out-of-state motorists as well as to New Jersey's residents.

6. See Borjas (1985) for an example applied to immigrants' wage mobility between 1970 and 1980, as well as Garvey (chapter 11, this volume).

7. Taxes paid by households constituted approximately 75 percent of total state tax revenue in FY 1990. The principal taxes included the gross income tax, sales and use tax, motor vehicle fees and the motor fuels tax, cigarette tax, the inheritance/estate transfer tax, business personal property tax, and the realty transfer tax.

8. Especially populous central cities are identified by the city alone. On the other hand, such sparsely settled New Jersey counties as Salem, Cape May, Warren, and Sussex are not identified separately. With the exception of these four counties, PUMAs do not cross county boundaries, so it is a fairly straightforward task to assign the residents of each PUMA to a particular county.

9. There are three types of local government expenditure on elementary and secondary education: general elementary and secondary school education, the local share of per pupil expenditure on public elementary and secondary schooling, and county vocational schools. We discuss only the second of these in the text. General elementary and secondary education expenditures constitute county-level expenses on the county superintendent of schools. All New Jersey counties, with the exception of Hunterdon, support county vocational schools that provide intensive preparation for students interested in technical occupations. Because these schools are highly specialized, they invest in costly equipment and enroll relatively few pupils.

10. Additional educational costs are incurred by limited-English-proficient (LEP) students who are eligible for additional education services through remedial skills and bilingual education programs. Unfortunately, a direct estimate of these costs was not possible with the available data. The most detailed per pupil expenditure data available for the school year 1989–90 do not separate bilingual education expenses but, rather, bundle them with expenditures on other state-sponsored education programs (New Jersey School Boards Association 1990). There was no satisfactory way to break out bilingual education costs without making gross assumptions about relative school district participation in these state programs. Consequently, our methodology assigns the same per pupil expenditure to immigrant and native school children within a given PUMA, which is not entirely appropriate because immigrants are more likely to require bilingual education programs. The problem is somewhat attenuated by the geographic concentration of immigrants in New Jersey in the larger urban cores (see Garvey, chapter 11, this volume). Per pupil expenditures are higher in the school districts serving these urban centers than in the surrounding districts, partly reflecting the higher costs of educating LEP students.

11. Equalized property tax rates correct for the fact that assessed value in New Jersey municipalities rarely equals true market value of a residence. These rates are defined such that the product of the equalized rate and the estimated market value of a residence equals the amount of property tax derived by multiplying the statutory property tax rate by assessed value.

12. We thank Robert Inman for suggesting the capitalized value approach to us.

13. In earlier work, Espenshade and King (1994) used a different approach for estimating renters' property tax contributions. They based their calculations on New Jersey guidelines (State of New Jersey 1990a; New Jersey Public Law 1990) and multiplied annual contract rent by 18 percent to approximate the fraction of rent payments that compensates owners for property taxes. This method and the capitalized value approach give identical results if the equalized tax rate is 1.76 percent and if the assumed discount rate equals 8 percent.

14. Using household-level information on the nativity status of children enrolled in public school, we can disaggregate state expenditures on public elementary and secondary school for immigrant-headed households into those for native- and foreign-born children (see the second row in the top panel of table 6.3). The average household state expenditure on native-born children in households headed by migrants from Europe and Canada is $1,142 and $44 in younger versus older households, respectively. The corresponding figures are $1,043 and $182 in Asian households, $1,161 and $269 in Latino households, and $1,089 and $44 in other immigrant households. Recalculating net fiscal impacts of immigrant households by counting only educational expenditures on foreign-born children has a dramatic effect on the results in younger households. The deficit is reduced by 71 percent for Asian households, by 40 percent for Latin American households, and by slightly more than 50 percent for other immigrant households. For younger European and Canadian families, disregarding native-born children converts a per-household fiscal deficit of $1,101 into a small surplus. However, focusing exclusively on foreign-born children in immigrant households encounters several problems. The native-born children are still someone's responsibility, and it can be argued that they are the responsibility of their immigrant parents. Moreover, disaggregating fiscal impacts at the level of individual children runs counter to our overall analysis, which takes the household—not the individual—as the appropriate unit of analysis.

15. However, when the immigrant-native differential is captured by modeling each region of origin separately, the coefficient on Latin America is still significant.

16. A deficit of this magnitude arises because we have attributed general county and municipal expenditures entirely to the household sector and because we have neglected nonhousehold sources of revenue to local governments. The latter include real estate taxes paid on commercial and industrial property, public utility taxes paid by businesses, and federal revenue sharing.

17. Once again, netting out public elementary and secondary school expenditures on native children in foreign-born households drastically reduces the implied fiscal deficit. The absolute amounts in question, on a per household basis, are $1,968 and $85 for younger and older, respectively, European and Canadian households, $2,119 and $227 for Asian households, $1,396 and $353 for Latin American households, and $1,591 and $65 in other immigrant families. In general, ignoring local educational expenditures on native children in foreign households has a stronger fiscal impact than a similar calculation at the state level.

References

Abowd, John M., and Richard B. Freeman, eds. 1991. *Immigration, Trade, and the Labor Market.* Chicago: University of Chicago Press.

Borjas, George J. 1994. "The Economics of Immigration." *Journal of Economic Literature* 32(4, December): 1667–1717.

_____. 1985. "Assimilation, Changes in Cohort Quality, and the Earnings of Immigrants." *Journal of Labor Economics* 3(4): 463–89.

Borjas, George J., and Richard B. Freeman, eds. 1992. *Immigration and the Work Force: Economic Consequences for the United States and Source Areas.* Chicago: University of Chicago Press.

Borjas, George J., and Lynette Hilton. 1996. "Immigration and the Welfare State: Immigrant Participation in Means-Tested Entitlement Programs." *Quarterly Journal of Economics*, forthcoming.

Borjas, George J., and Stephen J. Trejo. 1991. "Immigrant Participation in the Welfare System." *Industrial and Labor Relations Review* 44(2, January): 195–211.

Clark, Rebecca L., Jeffrey Passel, Wendy Zimmerman, and Michael Fix. 1994. *Fiscal Impacts of Undocumented Aliens: Selected Estimates for Seven States.* Report to the Office of Management and Budget and the Department of Justice. Washington, D.C.: Urban Institute, September.

Dunlap, Jonathan C., and Ann Morse. 1995. "States Sue Feds to Recover Immigration Costs." *NCSL Legisbrief* 3(1, January). Washington, D.C.: National Conference of State Legislatures.

Espenshade, Thomas J. 1996. "Fiscal Impacts of Immigrants and the Shrinking Welfare State." Working Paper 96-1. Princeton, N.J.: Princeton University, Office of Population Research.

Espenshade, Thomas J., and Vanessa E. King. 1994. "State and Local Fiscal Impacts of U.S. Immigrants: Evidence from New Jersey." *Population Research and Policy Review* 13: 225–56.

Fix, Michael, and Jeffrey S. Passel. 1994. *Immigration and Immigrants: Setting the Record Straight.* Washington, D.C.: Urban Institute Press.

Forsberg, Mary E. 1995. *State Aid Programs for Municipalities, 1989 and 1990.* Trenton, N.J.: Office of Legislative Services, Revenue, Finance, and Appropriations Section. Data file.

Friedberg, Rachel, and Jennifer Hunt. 1995. "The Impact of Immigrants on Host Country Wages, Employment, and Growth." *Journal of Economic Perspectives* 9(2, Spring): 23–44.

_____. 1996. "Immigration and the Receiving Economy." Paper presented at the Social Science Research Council Conference on "America Becoming/Becoming American," Sanibel Island, Fla., January 18–21.

Fullerton, Donald, and Diane Lim Rodgers. 1993. *Who Bears the Lifetime Tax Burden?* Washington, D.C.: Brookings Institution.

Garvey, Deborah L., and Thomas J. Espenshade. 1996. "Fiscal Impacts of New Jersey's Immigrant and Native Households on State and Local Governments: A New Approach and New Estimates." Working Paper 96-5. Princeton, N.J.: Princeton University, Office of Population Research.

Huddle, Donald. 1993. *The Costs of Immigration.* Washington, D.C.: Carrying Capacity Network.

Isbister, John. 1996. *The Immigration Debate: Remaking America.* West Hartford, Conn.: Kumarian Press.

Metcalf, Gilbert E. 1993. "The Lifetime Incidence of State and Local Taxes: Measuring Changes during the 1980s." NBER Working Paper 4252. Cambridge, Mass.: National Bureau of Economic Research.

New Jersey Public Law. 1990. c.61, s.2 (New Jersey Statutes Annotated c.54:4–8.58).

New Jersey School Boards Association. 1990. *1989–90 Cost of Education Index and Users' Guide.* Trenton, N.J.: NJSBA Information Systems. Computer file.

Pechman, Joseph A. 1985. *Who Paid the Taxes, 1966–85?* Washington, D.C.: Brookings Institution.

Rothman, Eric S., and Thomas J. Espenshade. 1992. "Fiscal Impacts of Immigration to the United States." *Population Index* 58(3, Fall): 381–415.

Rutgers, The State University of New Jersey. 1990. *1990 New Jersey Legislative District Data Book.* New Brunswick, N.J.: Bureau of Government Research and Department of Government Services.

State and Local Coalition on Immigration. 1994. "Three More States Sue Feds for Costs of Immigration." *Immigrant Policy News . . . The State-Local Report* (Washington, D.C.) 1(2, November 9).

————. 1996. "Legislative Outlook." *Immigrant Policy News . . . Inside the Beltway* (Washington, D.C.) 3(5, August 2).

State of New Jersey. 1990a. *Fifty-Second Annual Report of the Division of Local Government Services, 1989.* Trenton, N.J.: Department of Community Affairs, Division of Local Government Services.

————. 1990b. *Instructions for Preparing NJ Form 1040.* Trenton, N.J.: Department of the Treasury, Division of Taxation.

————. 1991. *State of New Jersey Budget: Fiscal Year 1991–1992,* by Governor Jim Florio. Trenton, N.J.: Author.

U.S. General Accounting Office. 1994. *Illegal Aliens: Assessing Estimates of Financial Burden on California.* GAO/HEHS-95-22. Washington, D.C.: U.S. Government Printing Office, November.

————. 1995. *Illegal Aliens: National Net Cost Estimates Vary Widely.* GAO/HEHS-95-133. Washington, D.C.: U.S. Government Printing Office, July.

Vernez, Georges, and Kevin McCarthy. 1995. *The Fiscal Costs of Immigration: Analytical and Policy Issues.* Center for Research on Immigration Policy. DRU-958-1-IF. Santa Monica, Calif.: RAND Corp., February.

————. 1996. *The Costs of Immigration to Taxpayers: Analytical and Policy Issues.* Santa Monica, Calif.: RAND Corp.

Yinger, John. 1982. "Capitalization and the Theory of Local Public Finance." *Journal of Political Economy* 90(5): 917–43.

Chapter Seven

IMMIGRANT EDUCATION IN NEW JERSEY: POLICIES AND PRACTICES

Ana María Villegas and John W. Young

Since the mid-1970s, the United States has experienced the largest and most diverse inflow of immigrants since the beginning of the century (Portes and Rumbaut 1990). The precise level of immigration is difficult to calculate because large numbers of both documented and undocumented immigrants entered the country during this time. Nevertheless, the 1990 Census showed nearly 20 million foreign-born individuals residing in this country. During the 1980s alone, approximately 9 million people from more than 100 different nations adopted the United States as their new home (Chavez 1995).

This sharp rise in the number of immigrants is also evident in the school population. About 2.2 million foreign-born children were enrolled in the nation's elementary and secondary schools in 1990, accounting for 5 percent of the kindergarten through 12th grade (K–12) student population that year. Ninety-two percent of these children attended public schools (American Council on Education 1994). Although the concentration of immigrant students is largest in urban centers, which are frequently the first home for newcomers (McDonnell and Hill 1993), suburban districts are enrolling more and more immigrant children, who bring with them a kaleidoscope of languages (Villegas et al. 1992). If immigrant students are to succeed in school and ultimately in the social and economic mainstream of the United States, schools must respond creatively to their unique needs. Failure to do so may result in a major loss of human potential, a price our society cannot afford in times of growing economic competition worldwide.

The recent wave of immigrant students is highly diverse, including a wide range of languages, cultures, and experiences. Unlike their predecessors who immigrated largely from Europe, immigrant students today are mostly from Asia (Vietnam, the Philippines, Korea, China, India, Laos, Cambodia, Japan), Latin America (Mexico, El Salvador, Guatemala, Nicaragua, Honduras), and the Caribbean (Haiti, the Dominican Republic, Jamaica, Cuba) (National Coalition of Advocates for Students [NCAS] 1991). Although many of these students have attended schools in their native lands, a relatively large number—especially those coming from war-ridden countries or rural areas—have had little or no schooling prior to arriving in the United States (Boothy 1986; Bui 1983; Chang 1990; Gibson 1987; Rorro 1990). Some of the children are literate in their native language, but many are not. A small fraction of the youngsters have attained some level of English language fluency before entering U.S. schools, but the overwhelming majority speak little or no English (Chang 1990). A sizable number of these students were victims of extreme poverty in their native countries, and many continue to live below the poverty level in the United States. Some of the new immigrants have suffered the traumas of war, including loss of or separation from their immediate families (Chang 1990; NCAS 1991). This wide range of experiences poses a major challenge to U.S. school systems, many of which are unprepared to respond effectively to such diverse backgrounds and needs.

Unfortunately, relatively little empirical attention has been paid to immigrant education in the United States. The full configuration of instructional programs and support services available to immigrant students has not been documented to date. Nor is there a clear understanding of the policy context for immigrant education. This lack of knowledge is regrettable because it deprives those responsible for planning and implementing programs for immigrant students of valuable information that could help improve interventions for these pupils.

To address this knowledge gap, this chapter reports the results of a study of policies and practices affecting immigrant children in one state, New Jersey. New Jersey is particularly well suited to this purpose owing to its large concentration of immigrants. As pointed out in previous chapters, whereas only 3.3 percent of the nation's population resides in New Jersey, the state contains 5.4 percent of the country's immigrant population (Espenshade 1991). Moreover, Fix and Passel (1991) have predicted that the proportion of the immigrant population will increase in New Jersey in the years to come.

The study reported here involved two major research activities. First, we surveyed school districts to obtain information both about the immigrant student population served through the New Jersey public schools during the 1991–92 school year, and about the programs and services offered to these students. In addition, we wanted to identify the districts' needs for serving this student population. Second, during the 1992–93 school year we conducted in-depth case studies of districts considered to have effective or promising programs for immigrant children. To determine the policy context for immigrant education in the state, we interviewed selected officials from the New Jersey State Department of Education.

The balance of this chapter is organized into four sections. The first of these describes the policy context for immigrant education. The second section provides an overview of the study methods. The third section summarizes the findings. Attention is given to describing the immigrant student population of the state, where immigrant students attend schools, and what type of instructional services are available to them. The chapter concludes with highlights of the major themes and issues that surfaced in the study.

POLICY CONTEXT

Despite the large numbers of immigrant students in the United States, there is no clear immigrant education policy at the federal level (McDonnell and Hill 1993). Nor does New Jersey have an immigrant education policy (Villegas 1992). What exists, instead, is a set of judicial and legislative mandates that, to a large extent, dictate the type of instructional programs and services immigrant children are entitled to, mostly by virtue of their limited proficiency with the English language.

Federal-Level Mandates

JUDICIAL ACTION

The U.S. Constitution does not expressly provide students with a right to a public education. Nevertheless, the Supreme Court has ruled in key cases that to the extent to which states offer education, *all* students are entitled to equal opportunities. Of these decisions, two are most relevant to immigrant students—*Lau v. Nichols* (414 US 563 [1974]) and *Plyler v. Doe* (457 US 202 [1982]).

In the *Lau v. Nichols* decision of 1974, the U.S. Supreme Court ruled that, under Title VI of the Civil Rights Act, schools must take affirmative steps to provide a comprehensible education to limited-English-proficient (LEP) students. According to the Court, "there is no equality of treatment merely by providing students with the same facilities, textbooks, teachers, and curriculum; for students who do not understand English are effectively foreclosed from any meaningful education."

This Supreme Court decision entitles LEP students to special instructional services until they are deemed able to benefit from a curriculum taught entirely in English. Among the special services in place in the schools to address the instructional and language needs of LEP students are programs of bilingual education (BE) and English-as-a-second-language (ESL). So long as an immigrant student has limited English proficiency, he or she qualifies for special instructional services under the *Lau v. Nichols* Supreme Court decision.

The second Supreme Court decision is more directly focused on the immigrant student population. In the *Plyler v. Doe* case of 1982, the Supreme Court ruled that, under the Equal Protection Clause of the Fourteenth Amendment, undocumented immigrant children are entitled to a public education. As a result of this decision, school districts are responsible for serving all immigrant children, regardless of their immigration status. But the question of who pays for the education of undocumented immigrant students has continued to be a point of contention, especially in states with large numbers of immigrants. In New Jersey, for example, about 16,000 undocumented immigrant students were enrolled in the public schools during the 1993–94 school year, at an approximate cost of $152 million to the state, according to a study conducted by the Urban Institute (Clark et al. 1994). In a separate report, however, the Institute has argued that, overall, immigrants pay more in taxes than they receive in public services, including education (Fix and Passel 1994). Nevertheless, as discussed later in this chapter, many New Jersey school officials who responded to our survey complained that the state and federal governments do not bear sufficient financial responsibility for educating the growing numbers of immigrant students enrolled in the public schools.

Recently, the question of who pays for the education of undocumented immigrant children was debated vigorously in the U.S. Congress as part of a broader effort to revise immigration laws. While the U.S. House of Representatives approved a provision that would allow states to deny public education to undocumented children, the U.S. Senate did not. The reconciled bill, which was signed into law by President Clinton in September 1996, does not include the schooling provision. Thus, the *Plyler v. Doe* ruling is still in effect, and the public schools continue to be responsible for educating undocumented immigrant students.

LEGISLATIVE ACTION

Immigrant students are entitled to a variety of federally funded programs, so long as they meet the qualifying criteria established for these programs. Of all federally funded programs, the most applicable to immigrant students are the Emergency Immigrant Education Act of 1984 (EIEA), Title VII of the Improving America's School Act of 1994 (previously known as Title VII of the Elementary and Secondary Education Act of 1968), and Chapter 1 of the Education Consolidation and Improvement Act of 1981 (Fix and Zimmermann 1993).

Through the EIEA, the federal government provides school districts with a small amount of money to address the needs of immigrant students. As defined by the federal government, *immigrant students* are those who were born outside the United States and have spent less than three full academic years in U.S. schools. This definition includes both documented and undocumented immigrants, as well as students of refugee status. Puerto Ricans and other students from U.S. territories or possessions are excluded (U.S. General Accounting Office 1991).

To be eligible for EIEA funding, school districts must enroll 500 or more immigrant students, or a minimum of 3 percent of their K–12 enrollment must be composed of immigrants. These federal funds, which are channeled through state Departments of Education, were approved by Congress in response to the financial crisis facing school districts with large numbers of immigrant students. The money is intended to supplement already-existing services for immigrants in eligible districts.

The federal government appropriates approximately $30 million per year for programs funded under the EIEA. In 1986, school districts received $86 per qualifying student. By 1990, the funds available per pupil had dropped to $42. Currently, districts receive less than $30 per student. The decrease in per pupil allocation is the result of increasing numbers of immigrant students entering the school system, although the yearly appropriation of funding has remained virtually unchanged over time. During the 1991–92 school year, 53 school districts in New Jersey reported receiving EIEA funds. Collectively, these districts enrolled a total of 18,425 immigrant students.

Through Title VII (the Federal Bilingual Education Act), the federal government provides funding for bilingual education programs. Grants are awarded to school districts on a competitive basis, and most of the funding is used to support transitional bilingual education programs. The intent of the grants is to build district capacity to serve language-minority students. Immigrant LEP children qualify for participation in Title VII programs. Only 8 of the 158 districts that responded to our 1991–92 school-year survey reported serving newcomers through Title VII funds.

Immigrant children who are performing substantially below grade level in reading and mathematics, along with their native-born peers also in need of academic support, are eligible to receive instructional assistance through Chapter 1, under which the federal government funds services for "educationally disadvantaged" children. The General Accounting Office estimated that during the 1989–90 school year, from one-half to two-thirds of the recent immigrants receiving EIEA support also participated in Chapter 1 programs (U.S. General Accounting Office 1991). Of the 158 districts responding to our survey, conducted in spring 1992, 126 reported using Chapter 1 funds to serve immigrant students.

State-Level Mandates

As mentioned, New Jersey, like other states, lacks an immigrant education policy. The education of immigrant children in this state is prescribed mostly by the New Jersey Bilingual Education Act of 1975 and Administrative Code (N.J.A.C. 6:31-1.4[b]/16:31-1.5[a]), which provide a legal mandate for ESL and bilingual education.

According to the regulations, New Jersey school districts are responsible for designing special programs that allow LEP students to develop academic skills while acquiring English-language proficiency. Students' English-language proficiency is determined through state-approved standardized tests, including the Language Assessment Battery (LAB) and the Maculitis Test. Districts can satisfy the state mandate in three basic ways, depending on the total number of LEP students enrolled. First, districts with 20 or more LEP students from the same language background must implement programs of bilingual education. Second, State Board of Education policy further requires that districts with 10 or more LEP students, regardless of language background (but no more than 20 from any single language group), implement ESL programs. Third, the Board recently adopted a policy requiring districts with at least 1 LEP student, but fewer than 10, to offer some type of English language service to the identified pupils.

The state gives each district a specified amount of money per year for each LEP student enrolled, so long as the student is served through an approved program of bilingual education or ESL. During the 1991–92 school year, the per pupil amount was approximately $1,000. Of the 158 districts responding to our spring 1992 survey, 134 reported using these funds to serve recent immigrant students during that school year.

In summary, this study found that the major sources of financial support for immigrant education are Chapter 1, Title VII, and EIEA funds from the federal government, and ESL/BE funds from the state. In addition, all but seven districts responding to the spring 1992 survey reported spending substantial local funds for programs and services for newcomers. Because New Jersey does not collect information about students' national origin, there is no reliable way to determine the level of funding each source provides for immigrant education.

The study also revealed that there are no education policies designed especially for immigrant students, either at the federal or state levels. The education of immigrant students in New Jersey is affected mostly by a set of federal and state mandates that prescribe the type of instructional services LEP students are entitled to by law. Taken together, this set of mandates does not address the needs of immigrant children holistically, however. For instance, it is clear that many immigrant children must be taught English, but their needs extend beyond that of learning a new language. As the findings presented in a subsequent section of this chapter show, immigrant children in New Jersey must often contend with cultural incompatibilities between home and school, which often present learning barriers. Moreover, since many newcomers to this state have had little or no schooling in their native countries, they need special attention to make up for lost time. Most lack familiarity with the U.S. school system, which is as alien to some of them as the English language itself. Others need support in dealing with the psychological stress associated with immigration. This is especially true for those youngsters immigrating from countries that have undergone social upheaval. Unfortunately, the lack of an immigrant education policy has resulted in fragmented services for immigrant students.

STUDY METHODS

This study adopted the definition of *immigrant student* used by the federal government in awarding districts funds under the EIEA. As mentioned earlier, this category includes immigrant students who have spent less than three full academic years in U.S. schools. The decision to use this definition was debated vigorously by the project's advisory committee and staff. For one thing, Puerto Ricans constitute a sizable proportion of the student enrollment in New Jersey, and their exclusion from the study was questioned by several committee members. Although technically not qualifying as immigrants, as defined by the federal government, the schooling needs of Puerto Rican children are similar to those of immigrants, including the need to learn a new language and adapt to a new culture. Also debated by the advisory committee was the EIEA definition's narrow focus on recent immigrants. After all, the immigrant experience does not end automatically after the initial three years in this country.

Despite the obvious limitations, the committee agreed to use the EIEA definition of an immigrant student on both substantive and pragmatic grounds. Substantively, the initial years in U.S. schools present a unique set of challenges to immigrant students who must learn a new language and adapt to a new sociocultural environment. Although this learning and adaptation process is never fully accomplished during the initial three years in the United States, the cultural shock associated with it is felt most acutely during this time. Thus, the initial period in the host country merits special research attention. From a practical viewpoint, school districts are familiar with the EIEA definition of immigrant students. Because these federal funds are awarded based on a per pupil formula, school districts seeking assistance must keep an accurate count of the number of students who qualify as immigrants according to the EIEA definition. By using the EIEA definition, narrow as it is, both the accuracy and reliability of the data were increased.

To qualify for participation in the survey, a school district had to enroll at least 10 students of limited English proficiency. Because the New Jersey State Department of Education does not collect information on the total number of immigrants enrolled in each school district, the number of LEP pupils was used as a proximal indicator for the target population. According to New Jersey State Department of Education personnel, a large proportion of LEP students in the state are immigrants. As indicated earlier, any district with 10 or more LEP students is required to provide ESL instruction to the identified pupils. These districts, therefore, seemed most suited to our purposes. Of the 591 districts in the state, 253 met the criterion for participation in this facet of the study. All 53 school districts that had received EIEA funds during the 1991–92 school year were included in the sample.

Of the 253 districts selected to participate in our spring 1992 survey, 161 returned completed questionnaires, producing a respectable 64 percent response rate. Among the 53 EIEA-funded districts, 38 surveys were received, for an even higher response rate of 70 percent. Responding districts were geographically representative of the state and of the population of all districts surveyed. It should be noted that about one-half of the surveyed districts were in the northern part of the state, reflecting the distribution of the general population as well as of the immigrant population.

Twelve school districts with promising programs and services for immigrant students were selected as case study sites out of 33 districts originally nominated. The sites selected from this pool included a mix of geographic regions, urban and suburban locations, district size, district wealth, ethnic composition of the immigrant student population, and type of intervention programs. Two strategies were used to collect data: interviews and review of relevant documents. The case-study portion of the study was conducted during the 1992–93 school year.

RESULTS

The results of the study are organized into three broad areas—immigrant students and where they attend schools, difficulties experienced by the school districts serving this student population, and instructional programs provided to immigrant students in the state.

Immigrant Students in New Jersey: Who Are They and Where Do They Attend School?

Because the New Jersey Department of Education does not collect data on the national origin of its student population, there is no precise count of immigrant students in the state. Table 7.1 summarizes information about immigrant enrollments in New Jersey's public schools based on the results of the survey. Specifically, the table shows a total of 17,129 immigrant students. This number, although seemingly low, is consistent with the narrow definition of immigrant student adopted by the study. It approximates the number of immigrant students served in New Jersey through EIEA during the 1991–92 school year, which totalled 18,425 according to the state Department of Education. It should be mentioned that 16 districts did not report their immigrant enrollments because they found it either too difficult to calculate

Table 7.1 IMMIGRANT ENROLLMENT IN DISTRICTS RESPONDING TO SURVEY,
BY GEOGRAPHIC AREA OF ORIGIN
($N = 145$)

Area of Origin	Frequency	Percentage
Central or South America	5,422	32
Asia	3,901	23
Europe (including Russia)	3,290	19
Caribbean (including Cuba)	2,597	15
Middle East	576	3
Pacific Islands	547	3
Africa	251	2
Other	545	3
Total	17,129	100

reliable numbers or they feared that providing this information might be interpreted as noncompliance with the intent of *Plyler v. Doe* (1982).

An independent estimate of the number of immigrant students in the state was constructed by Espenshade (personal communication to authors, June 1992). Using data collected by the U.S. Bureau of the Census in the late 1980s, Espenshade calculated that New Jersey had approximately 19,965 recent immigrants (residing fewer than four years in the United States) of school age (5–21 years old). When using a more inclusive definition of *immigrant student*, one that includes all foreign-born school-age students regardless of length of residence in the United States, the estimate rose to over 58,000. Puerto Ricans were excluded from the count. Examined collectively, the data suggest that the immigrant school-age population in New Jersey is somewhere in the range of 19,000 (when a restrictive definition of *immigrant student* is used) to approximately 60,000 (when using the broader definition of *foreign born*).

Table 7.1 also shows the diversity among the immigrant population in New Jersey public schools. The schools enrolled recently arrived immigrant students from Central and South America, Asia, Europe, the Caribbean, the Middle East, the Pacific Islands, and Africa. Central and South America were the geographic regions most numerously represented; nearly one-third (32 percent) of the identified immigrant students were from these areas. Following this group in number were Asian students, who accounted for nearly one-fourth (23 percent) of the total. Europeans were the next largest group, comprising 19 percent of the identified immigrants. Students from the Caribbean followed in number, encompassing another 15 percent of enrolled immigrants. Children from the Middle East, the Pacific Islands, and

Africa were represented in the schools as well, but in much smaller proportions.

According to the New Jersey Department of Education, students of limited English proficiency in the state (many of whom are recent immigrants) represented over 100 different language groups during the school year. Spanish, however, was the language most frequently spoken by these students. This claim was corroborated by our finding that the largest numbers of recent immigrants in the schools were from Central and South America, geographic areas in which Spanish prevails. In addition to Spanish, the other major languages spoken by New Jersey immigrants include Portuguese, Korean, French Creole, Gujarati, Japanese, Arabic, Polish, Vietnamese, Cantonese, Mandarin, and Italian. This linguistic diversity presented challenges to school systems, particularly for those that enrolled immigrants from numerous language groups.

Immigrant enrollment trends provide additional insight into the impact of recent immigration in New Jersey schools. Trend data are summarized in table 7.2. The table shows that during the five years preceding the survey, two-thirds (66 percent) of the districts had experienced an increase of 5 percent or more in their immigrant enrollments. Only 5 percent of the respondents reported a decrease in the total number of immigrants enrolled during this time. This finding suggests that the steady rise in the numbers of immigrants in the public school sector, which began nearly two decades ago, had not yet leveled off. It also supports Fix and Passel's (1991) earlier-cited prediction that this trend toward increased immigration will continue for some time to come.

Information about the type of school districts (i.e., district wealth) attended by immigrants from different geographic areas is summarized in table 7.3. For purposes of this analysis, respondents were categorized according to the district factor group (DFG) designation assigned by the New Jersey Department of Education. The DFG is an

Table 7.2 DISTRICT ENROLLMENT TREND IN IMMIGRANT STUDENT
POPULATION, 1987–92

(N = 154)

Enrollment Trend	Frequency	Percentage
Significant increase (increase of > 25%)	41	27
Slight increase (increase of 5–25%)	60	39
Little change (no more than 5%)	44	29
Slight decrease (decrease of 5–25%)	5	3
Significant decrease (decrease of > 25%)	4	2

Table 7.3 AVERAGE PERCENTAGE OF IMMIGRANT STUDENTS FROM DIFFERENT
AREAS OF ORIGIN, BY DISTRICT WEALTH: 1991–92 SCHOOL YEAR

| | District Factor Group | | |
Area of Origin	A–C (n = 43) (%)	D–G (n = 51) (%)	H–J (n = 61) (%)
Central/South America	37	28	17
Asia	15	30	49
Europe	22	20	18
Caribbean	14	6	3
Other	12	16	13
Total	100	100	100

indicator of the socioeconomic status of citizens in each district, and it ranges from letter A (for the lowest socioeconomic districts) to J (for the highest socioeconomic districts).

As shown in table 7.3, students from Central and South America as well as the Caribbean, many of whom are Spanish speakers, were found in larger proportions in the less-affluent districts (those in the A–C category). By contrast, the wealthiest districts (H–J) enrolled proportionately more Asian immigrants. European students were fairly evenly distributed across districts of varying wealth.

Difficulties Experienced by New Jersey School Districts in Serving Immigrant Students

The immigrant student population has enriched the linguistic and cultural fabric of the public schools in New Jersey. Many districts, however, have found themselves not fully prepared to serve this diverse population, and some continue to struggle to address the needs of immigrant children. Table 7.4 gives insight into the difficulties experienced by the districts in serving the new wave of immigrant students. As the table shows, the reported difficulties are related to district wealth.

The overriding concern reported by districts (80 percent of the respondents) was that of teaching the growing numbers of LEP students effectively (table 7.4). Poor and affluent districts alike expressed difficulties initiating new programs of bilingual and ESL instruction or expanding existing services to accommodate their rapidly changing student body. Because poor (mostly urban) districts enrolled many

Table 7.4 DIFFICULTIES REPORTED BY DISTRICTS IN SERVING IMMIGRANT
STUDENTS BY FACTOR GROUPS: 1991–92 SCHOOL YEAR

	District Factor Group			
	A–C	D–G	H–J	Total
	(n = 43)	(n = 51)	(n = 61)	(n = 155)
Reported Difficulty	%	%	%	%
Teaching large numbers of LEP students effectively	88	76	77	80
Handling the frequent mobility of immigrant students	63	57	41	52
Lack of preparation of school professionals in dealing with immigrant students	33	47	42	41
Teaching immigrant students who lack prior school experiences	58	41	31	41
Finding bilingual teachers	37	20	20	25
Lack of state and/or federal funding	30	22	16	22

more immigrant students, the problem was especially intense in these
settings.

The frequent mobility of immigrant students was identified by over
half the districts (52 percent) as an obstacle to success in teaching
these pupils (table 7.4). For example, one particular school with a large
immigrant population started the 1991–92 academic year with a total
enrollment of 500 students. A gradual increase in the number of students was observed each month until May 1992, when the enrollment
peaked at 554 students. One month later, the enrollment dropped to
450, a decrease of more than 100 students during the last month of
school. In September 1992, the same school enrolled 524 students, a
sizable increase over the June figure. According to the school principal, enrollment decreases at the end of one school year and increases
at the beginning of the next school year are typical. Unfortunately, the
number of full-time teaching equivalent (FTE) positions that schools
receive for any single academic year is based on enrollment figures
for the previous June. This practice sets schools with a large immigrant population and a severe immigrant mobility problem at a major
disadvantage. As the table shows, student mobility problems were
experienced least intensely by the wealthiest districts.

According to school personnel who were interviewed during the
second phase of the study, the search for better and more permanent
employment leads immigrant families to move frequently. Furthermore, inadequate and undependable housing, a byproduct of poverty,
contributes to the pattern of high mobility. These residential changes

force immigrant children to transfer from school to school, sometimes within the same school district, but often across district lines. The result is interrupted schooling and disrupted learning.

Lack of preparation on the part of school professionals in serving immigrant students was reported as a major concern by 41 percent of responding districts (table 7.4). Children who do not understand English do not have access to a comprehensible education when English is the language of instruction. To be effective with this student population, teachers need specialized skills. Cultural clashes between home and school also create learning barriers for immigrant students. For example, class discussions requiring students to express personal opinions on a given topic clash with the previous schooling experience of many immigrant students who were taught to memorize opinions of authorities. Teachers who lack sensitivity to cultural differences can misinterpret the behavior of immigrant students and develop negative impressions of their academic and social skills. Unfortunately, the New Jersey teaching force is not adequately prepared to deal with these linguistic and cultural issues in the classroom. Nor are many educators in the state adept at helping newcomers deal with the psychological stress associated with their transition into the United States. Not surprisingly, concern over the lack of preparation among educators was voiced most vigorously by more affluent suburban schools, which until the late 1980s had not enrolled significant numbers of immigrant students.

Another major obstacle reported by 41 percent of the districts was that of teaching older immigrant students who come to the United States without prior schooling in their native country (table 7.4). This phenomenon, although evident in both poor and wealthy districts, was most marked in the less-affluent urban settings. According to personnel from these districts, "academically delayed" students tend to come from war-torn countries or rural areas in Central America or from rural parts of the Caribbean. Because these students often lack literacy skills in their native language, teachers find it difficult to instruct them in bilingual classes with other LEP students who are close to age-appropriate levels of literacy skills in their first language. Although recognizing that special services are required for these students, districts seem at a loss for strategies to effectively address this need.

One-quarter of the responding districts reported difficulties hiring and retaining teachers who have bilingual certification (table 7.4). This problem was especially evident in the less-affluent urban districts, where bilingual education was most widely used. Recruiting staff seems to be especially problematic for districts seeking teachers who are bilingual in English and a language other than Spanish. Urban districts often complained that suburban districts lured away their trained Spanish-speaking bilingual teachers by offering them better salaries. This practice attests to an ongoing competition between and among districts in the state for scarce bilingual resources. A related problem was finding bilingual counselors.

Lack of federal and state funding to support programs for immigrant students was also identified by 22 percent of the districts as a barrier (table 7.4). Again, this problem was reported with greater frequency by urban districts, which generally have a weaker local tax base for education. A few school administrators, mostly from suburban districts, complained vehemently that local communities were unfairly expected to assume the major share of the cost of educating increasing numbers of immigrant students. They felt that the federal government should either provide considerably more money for immigrant education or reduce the number of immigrants entering the United States legally and illegally. This position, however, was voiced only by a few survey respondents.

To summarize, the difficulties associated with serving immigrant students are numerous and vary by district. As might be expected, problems were more pronounced in the less-affluent districts. Proportionately, a greater number of the poorer districts reported challenges in teaching large numbers of LEP students effectively, in handling the frequent mobility of immigrant students, in teaching immigrant students who lack prior school experiences, in finding bilingual teachers, and in obtaining state and/or federal funding. In contrast, the lack of preparation of school professionals was more problematic for the wealthier districts. These findings were not surprising, given that, on average, poorer districts enrolled many more immigrant students.

Major Instructional Programs for Immigrant Students

The study survey revealed that school districts in New Jersey serve recent immigrant students primarily through two types of instructional programs—English-as-a-Second-Language and Bilingual Education.[1] Both ESL and BE programs enrolled LEP students in general, whether native born or foreign born. As evident from table 7.5, ESL was more widely used to serve immigrant students than BE. Two-thirds of the districts implemented ESL programs solely, but just slightly more than one-fifth of the sites used BE programs (which include an ESL component) alone. About one-tenth of the districts

Table 7.5 SPECIAL INSTRUCTIONAL PROGRAMS SERVING NATIVE- AND
FOREIGN-BORN LEP STUDENTS: 1991–92 SCHOOL YEAR
(N = 158)

Program	Frequency	Percentage
ESL only	105	66
Bilingual education only (with ESL component)	35	22
Both ESL and BE programs	18	11

had both ESL and BE programs. In brief, ESL programs existed in 77 percent of the districts, whereas BE was used in only 33 percent of the sites. This finding contradicts the perception held by many New Jersey residents that bilingual education is the primary mode of instruction for immigrant students.

ESL Programs

Table 7.6 summarizes relevant information about the ESL programs in the surveyed districts. As is evident from the table, many of the ESL students were new immigrants. Specifically, newcomers comprised 80 percent or more of the ESL students in 51 districts. Another 38 districts estimated that 50–79.9 percent of their ESL students were new immigrants. Thus, newcomers accounted for at least 50 percent of the ESL enrollments in three-fourths of the responding districts. The other students enrolled in ESL programs include Puerto Ricans, immigrants who have been in the United States longer than three years, and youngsters who were born in this country to immigrant parents and had not developed English language fluency prior to entering school. Table 7.6 also shows the distribution of ESL programs across grade levels. From the table it is clear that ESL programs were concentrated in elementary schools. Overall, 91 percent of the districts reported having ESL in the elementary grades, compared to only 29 percent at the middle school level and 30 percent in the high school grades.

Five types of ESL programs were reported in place by the responding districts—pullout, class period, high-intensity, in-class, and resource center (see appendix 7.A for a description of each type of program). It should be noted that regardless of program type, all ESL instruction in New Jersey is provided to students on a part-time basis, usually for one to three class periods per day. Typically, the students spend the remainder of the school day in mainstreamed classes in which English is the sole medium of instruction. Table 7.6 shows that pullout and class period ESL prevail in the state. Pullout instruction

Table 7.6 PROFILE OF ESL PROGRAMS IN NEW JERSEY: 1991–92 SCHOOL YEAR

	Frequency	Percentage
Percentage Immigrant Students (n = 120):		
80.0 or more	51	43
50.0–79.9	38	32
25.0–49.9	17	14
10.0–24.9	7	6
Less than 10	7	6
Grade Level (n = 121):		
Elementary school	110	91
Middle school	35	29
High school	36	30
Type of Program (n = 123):		
Pullout	108	88
Class period	86	70
High-intensity	53	43
In-class	16	13
Resource center	9	7
Other	9	7
Program Changes for Immigrant Students (n = 123):		
Materials	75	62
Curriculum	64	52
Staff development	55	45
Staffing	47	38
No changes needed	23	19
Changes needed: none made	4	3
Other	12	10

was reported by 88 percent of the districts, and the class period approach by 70 percent. Also used with frequency, but to a lesser extent than the pullout and class period designs, was the high-intensity approach (reported by 43 percent of the districts). These data demonstrate that school districts often combined two or more types of ESL instruction in serving immigrant students.

The districts were asked if they had made any changes recently in their ESL programs to render them more effective for immigrant students. This information is summarized in table 7.6 as well. The changes most frequently reported were in materials and curriculum. Seventy-five districts (62 percent) adapted existing materials or created new ones, and 64 districts (52 percent) modified the established curriculum. These changes were intended to make the materials and curriculum more culturally inclusive of the new immigrant population, to address the students' specific language needs, and to build on their strengths. In addition, 55 districts reported concentrating more of their staff development efforts on issues related to immigrants. In another 47 districts, ESL positions were added to meet the needs of the growing number of newcomers. Twenty-three districts reported no need for program changes because their ESL curricula had been designed originally for the specific immigrant groups served. Another 4 districts, however, reported that their ESL programs needed changes, but admitted none had been made due to budgetary constraints. Among the respondents, 12 districts reported changes other than those mentioned here; these included creating summer programs and using peer tutors in middle and secondary schools.

BILINGUAL EDUCATION PROGRAMS

A total of 53 districts, accounting for about one-third of the sites, reported implementing some form of bilingual education. These included 35 districts that used BE programs only and another 18 districts that implemented both BE and ESL programs (see table 7.5). In BE programs, students are taught academic concepts through their native language. In addition, the pupils receive intensive ESL instruction during portions of the day. Frequently, academic content is reinforced in English. It should be emphasized that every program of bilingual education, as defined by the New Jersey Administrative Code, must have an ESL instructional component. According to New Jersey law, bilingual education programs must be offered daily and should include all required courses and activities available to all students in the district. Bilingual education programs in New Jersey are furthermore transitional. That is, students judged to have acquired sufficient English language skills to derive benefit from content area instruction taught solely in English are "exited" from the program and "mainstreamed" into "regular" classes. Typically, this transition is completed within three to five school years.

Table 7.7 outlines the extent to which bilingual education programs serve immigrant students in New Jersey. As shown, new immigrants accounted for at least 50 percent of enrollments in 33 of the districts reported to offer BE programs. This represented 62 percent of the responding districts. Whereas bilingual education existed at all grade levels (elementary, middle, high school), it prevailed in elementary schools. All 53 districts that reported serving immigrants through bilingual education provided this service at the elementary level. Bilingual instruction, however, was also reported with frequency at the middle level (by 37 districts, or 70 percent of the sites) and in high school grades (by 38 districts, or 72 percent of the sites).

Table 7.7 PROFILE OF BILINGUAL EDUCATION PROGRAMS IN NEW JERSEY: 1991–92 SCHOOL YEAR

	Frequency	Percentage
Percentage of Immigrant Students (n = 53):		
80.0 or more	20	37
50.0–79.9	13	25
25.0–49.9	11	20
10.0–24.9	4	8
Less than 10	5	10
Grade Level (n = 53):		
Elementary school	53	100
Middle school	37	70
High school	38	72
Type of Program (n = 53):		
Full bilingual program		
Self-contained	24	45
Departmentalized	13	25
Proficiency-level	10	19
Partial bilingual		
Part-time bilingual	35	66
Bilingual resource	8	15
Bilingual tutorial	7	13
Alternative to bilingual education		
High-intensity ESL	38	72
Program Changes for		
Immigrant Students (n = 53):		
Materials	35	66
Staff development	28	53
Staffing	28	53
Curriculum	26	49
No changes needed	12	23
Changes needed: none made	3	6
Other	5	9

Descriptions of the types of bilingual programs approved by the State Board of Education are found in appendix 7.B. There are three primary types of bilingual programs—self-contained classrooms, proficiency-level instruction, and departmentalized programs. School districts with relatively small numbers of LEP students are permitted by the State Board of Education to implement alternative instructional options that are less comprehensive in scope than a full bilingual program. These alternatives are part-time bilingual instruction, bilingual resource services, bilingual tutorials, and high-intensity ESL.

Alternatives may be used only as a phase-in step to a full bilingual program.

Information about the types of bilingual education programs implemented in New Jersey is shown in table 7.7. Interestingly, the two most commonly used program types in the state—high-intensity ESL and part-time bilingual instruction—are alternatives to full bilingual programs. In high-intensity ESL programs (implemented in 38 districts, or 72 percent of the respondents), ESL instructional methods are used without the aid of the students' native language. Part-time bilingual programs (implemented in 35 districts, or 66 percent of the sites) have a certified bilingual teacher who instructs the students for only a portion of the school day. The three full bilingual program types were used far less frequently than the high-intensity ESL and bilingual part-time alternatives. This was due largely to the scarcity of bilingual teachers in the state. Of the full-time options, the self-contained design was most often used, reported by 24 districts, or 45 percent of the sites. Nearly all of these programs were in elementary schools.

Many districts reported making changes in their bilingual education programs to accommodate the needs of the immigrant students. The changes most frequently cited were in instructional materials (by 35 districts), staff development and staffing (by 28 districts each), and curriculum (by 26 districts) (table 7.7). Although 12 districts reported not needing program changes, 3 others admitted to having to modify their programs but lacking the resources to do so. Five districts reported other changes, including initiating summer programs and promoting staff awareness of cultural differences.

COMPARISON OF DISTRICTS OFFERING BILINGUAL EDUCATION AND ESL PROGRAMS

Table 7.8 provides information about the district context in which bilingual and ESL programs were implemented in New Jersey during the 1991–92 school year. It should be noted that this analysis is limited to districts with either ESL or BE programs; the 18 districts that implemented both types of instructional programs are not included. Table 7.8 makes evident that, when compared to districts with ESL programs, bilingual districts enrolled more than twice as many students, two-and-a-half times the proportion of minorities, more than three times the proportion of LEP pupils, and over three times the proportion of immigrants. Districts with bilingual programs also served over twice the proportion of immigrants from Central/South America and the Caribbean. In contrast, ESL districts enrolled proportionately more than twice as many Asian immigrants. Moreover,

Table 7.8 SELECTED CHARACTERISTICS OF DISTRICTS BY PROGRAM TYPE: 1991–92 SCHOOL YEAR

	Bilingual Education (n = 35)	ESL Only (n = 105)
Average student enrollment	5,102	2,375
Average percentage minority	52	21
Average percentage LEP	10	3
Average percentage immigrant	7	2
Average total immigrants	357	48
Average percentage immigrants by area of origin		
Central/South America	40	22
Caribbean	14	4
Asia	19	42
Europe	16	17
Other	11	15
Percentage of programs by district factor group		
A–C (less affluent)	61	17
D–G	29	35
H–J (most affluent)	10	48

BE programs were most frequently found in poor districts, whereas ESL programs were most often implemented in wealthier districts.

In brief, the findings reported in this chapter show that immigrant students in New Jersey do not share a single educational experience. The kinds of students with whom they attend school and the schooling they receive vary. The relative wealth of the school district is the major variable in determining the characteristics of the immigrant students' educational experience. The wealthier districts enrolled a larger portion of newcomers from Asian backgrounds and served them mostly through ESL programs. The lower-wealth districts, by contrast, enrolled proportionately more immigrant students, especially those from Spanish-speaking countries, and served them largely through some form of bilingual education.

CONCLUSIONS

The rise of immigration to the United States has had a profound impact on the public schools. Schooling has traditionally functioned as a major means of successfully integrating newcomers into the economic, social, and political fabric of this country. However, many school districts are finding it difficult to carry out this critical responsibility. This New Jersey study offers several insights that might inform discussion about immigrant education elsewhere.

A salient finding from this investigation is the notable absence of an immigrant education policy. As a result, the education of immigrant students is shaped largely by a number of legislative and judicial federal and state mandates that primarily address the rights of LEP students to a comprehensible education. This study revealed that many districts, despite their good intentions, deal with the needs of immigrant students in an ad hoc manner, an approach that often proves ineffectual. While focusing on the students' English language needs, the related cultural, psychological, and social barriers are left largely unattended. We learned that cultural incompatibilities between home and school, the stress of the immigrant experience, and the precarious economic conditions of many immigrant families—the latter of which often lead to frequent mobility—influence the learning process in profound ways. Unless schools adopt a comprehensive approach to addressing the multiple barriers immigrant students must overcome, the schools' ability to integrate newcomers to the United States is reduced. Because no state in this country currently has an immigrant education policy, we suspect this problem also afflicts schools elsewhere.

Immigrant students are not alone in their need for assistance. Like native-born students with limited proficiency in English, most immigrant students need to develop their English-language skills. Not unlike many African American students, immigrant pupils often experience a cultural dissonance between home and school. And, like too many at-risk students, many newcomers suffer from the disadvantages of poverty. Immigrant students, however, constitute a special group with unique characteristics and needs that stem from their newcomer status. To meet the special needs of newcomers, school districts need a system for identifying immigrant students upon enrollment. Although *Plyler v. Doe* prohibits school districts from asking parents for documentation of their children's legal status in this country, it does not bar them from inquiring at initial registration about the youngsters' place of birth and date of entry into the United States. Districts need this information to serve the students appropriately.

This study also revealed that the makeup of the immigrant student population has changed dramatically over time. Whereas white Europeans accounted for the majority of newcomers in the past, now Hispanics and Asians constitute the overwhelming majority. New immigrant students, as a group, also speak many more languages than immigrant students of the past. This change in the flow and makeup of the immigrant student population has challenged New Jersey school systems to launch massive professional development programs to prepare their staffs to both understand and address the needs of the growing number of newcomers. Unfortunately, many districts in the state have been caught less than adequately prepared for this task. We suspect that this is the case in other states as well. This study suggests that the preparation of administrators, teachers, and other school personnel is one of the most important factors in serving immigrant students well. In setting spending priorities, professional development for inservice teachers and other educators merits special consideration. In addition, teacher education programs should be encouraged to produce more bilingual and ESL teachers to meet the growing demand for personnel with this type of preparation.

Two other major challenges New Jersey districts have had to contend with are developing instructional programs for students who have little or no literacy in their native language or have received less than age-appropriate education in their own countries, as well as handling the frequent mobility of immigrant students. Again, we believe that school districts in other states are dealing with similar difficulties. Research is needed to devise creative and effective solutions to these problems.

Lastly, this study showed that New Jersey districts have had to address the multiple needs of increasing numbers of immigrant children with relatively little financial support from the federal government. While increasing appropriations for the Emergency Immigrant Education Act is not likely within the current political climate, the federal government could allocate a portion of the money it currently invests in professional development for school personnel and in teacher education to prepare educators specifically to work effectively with immigrant students.

Immigrant education in the 1990s presents new challenges: today's society is dramatically different from the society that greeted the large numbers of immigrants at the beginning of the century. The demand for physical labor to build industries of the past has yielded to the need for sophisticated technological expertise. This puts more pressure on schools to educate youth to high levels of excellence. Failure to do so has more serious repercussions today than ever before.

Note

1. The districts reported using a variety of sources to pay for these programs, including state funds earmarked for bilingual education, Chapter 1, Title VII, and local taxes. The study did not examine how the different funding sources were combined, however. Information collected through visits to the case-study sites suggests that Chapter 1 funds were used mostly to help students improve their reading and writing skills in English, sometimes (but not always) using ESL methods.

References

American Council on Education. 1994. "The Foreign-Born Population of the 1990s: A Summary Profile." *Research Briefs* 5(6): 1–12.

Boothy, N. 1986. "Children and War." *Cultural Survival Quarterly* 10(4): 28–30.

Bui, T. H. 1983. "Meeting the Needs of Indochinese Students." *Momentum* 14(1): 20–22.

Chang, H. N. 1990. *Newcomer Programs: Innovative Efforts to Meet the Educational Challenges of Immigrant Students.* San Francisco: California Tomorrow Immigrant Students Project.

Chavez, L. 1995. "What to Do about Immigration." *Commentary* 99(3): 29–35.

Clark, R. L., J. S. Passel, W. N. Zimmermann, and M. E. Fix. 1994. *Fiscal Impacts of Undocumented Aliens: Selected Estimates for Seven States.* Washington, D.C.: Urban Institute.

Espenshade, T. J. 1991. *Demographic and Socioeconomic Characteristics of New Jersey's Language-Minority School-Age Population.* Unpublished report submitted to the Andrew W. Mellon Foundation. Photocopy.

Fix, Michael, and J. S. Passel. 1991. *The Door Remains Open: Recent Immigration to the United States and a Preliminary Analysis of the Immigration Act of 1990.* Program for Research on Immigration Policy Paper PRIP-UI-14. Washington, D.C.: Urban Institute.

————. 1994. *Immigration and Immigrants: Setting the Record Straight.* Washington, D.C.: Urban Institute.

Fix, M., and W. Zimmermann. 1993. *Educating Immigrant Children: Chapter 1 in the Changing City.* Washington, D.C.: Urban Institute Press.

Gibson, M. A. 1987. "The School Performance of Immigrant Minorities: A Comparative View." *Anthropology and Education Quarterly* 18(4): 262–75.

McDonnell, L. M., and P. T. Hill. 1993. *Newcomers in American Schools: Meeting the Educational Needs of Immigrant Youth.* Santa Monica, Calif.: RAND Corp.

National Coalition of Advocates for Students. 1991. *New Voices: Immigrant Students in U.S. Public Schools.* NCAS Research and Policy Report. Boston: Author.

NCAS. *See* National Coalition of Advocates for Students.

Portes, A., and R. G. Rumbaut. 1990. *Immigrant America: A Portrait.* Berkeley: University of California Press.

Rorro, G. L. 1990. *Haitian Voices: Considerations for the Classroom Teacher.* Trenton, N.J.: New Jersey Department of Education.

U.S. General Accounting Office. 1991. *Immigrant Education: Information on the Emergency Immigrant Education Act Program.* GAO Pub. No. HRD-91-50. Washington, D.C.: Author.

Villegas, A. M. 1992. *Working Effectively with Immigrant Students.* Princeton, N.J.: Educational Testing Service.

Villegas, A. M., B. Bruschi, B. C. Clewell, J. Gant, P. Goertz, M. Joy, and T. Wlodkowski. 1992. *Immigrant Education in New Jersey: Programs, Services, and Policies: Case Studies of Districts with Effective Programs.* Princeton, N.J.: Educational Testing Service.

APPENDIX 7.A
ENGLISH-AS-A-SECOND-LANGUAGE PROGRAM TYPES

Districts that have 10 or more LEP students, but fewer than 20 of any single language group, must provide at least one of the following types of ESL instruction.

Pullout ESL: Small groups of students at the elementary level are drawn from regular classrooms by grade and/or language proficiency and are provided ESL instruction in other areas of the building that are approved for instructional activities.

Class period ESL: Students receive ESL for high school credit at the secondary level as a scheduled class period. Students are grouped according to grade and/or language proficiency.

In-class ESL: Small groups of students at the elementary level receive ESL instruction by the ESL teacher in the regular classroom.

High-intensity ESL: Students are grouped for an intensive ESL program of two or more periods that include standard ESL instruction as well as instruction in reading and other content areas using an ESL approach.

Resource center ESL: Students are drawn from various schools in the district and are placed in a magnet center for both ESL and regular program instruction. This allows for better grouping when instruction is provided in the ESL program.

In New Jersey, school districts with 20 or more LEP students of the same language group must provide at least one of the seven types of bilingual education programs listed below. Those designated by an asterisk (*) are *alternatives* that districts with small numbers of limited-English-proficient students may implement.

a. *Self-contained bilingual program:* Students remain in the same classroom for their academic day, receiving all formal instruction from the same bilingual teacher via the language in which they are most proficient, as well as developing second-language concepts, fluency, and literacy skills.

b. *Proficiency-level bilingual program:* Students are placed in self-contained bilingual classrooms according to their level of language proficiency. Based upon the proficiency level of the class, students are instructed in (1) primarily their native language, (2) both their native language and English, or (3) primarily English.

c. *Departmentalized bilingual program for secondary grades:* Students receive instruction in the content areas from bilingual teachers who are also certified in the content areas.

*d. *Alternative bilingual part-time program:* This alternative program model may provide instruction in reading and mathematics by a bilingual teacher for at least 90 minutes plus an additional 30 minutes for ESL instruction.

*e. *Alternative bilingual resource program at the elementary level:* This program option is for LEP students who have very strong academic skills in their native language, combined with proficiency in reading and writing in English, but lack strong aural/oral proficiency. Bilingual resource room services are provided daily by a certified bilingual teacher in identified subjects and with specific assignments on an individual basis.

*f. *Alternative bilingual tutorial:* Students are provided a standard ESL class, a second period of bilingual instruction in a required content area, and a third period as a tutorial activity to cover subject areas based upon student need.

*g. *Alternative high-intensity ESL:* Students receive two or more class periods a day of ESL instruction, with one period as the standard ESL class. The second period is either a tutorial where needed content is studied through ESL methods and techniques or a reading period taught by ESL methods and techniques.

Chapter Eight

EFFECTS OF PARENTS' PLACE OF BIRTH AND ETHNICITY ON BIRTH OUTCOMES IN NEW JERSEY

Nancy E. Reichman and Genevieve M. Kenney

Immigration into the United States from Latin America has increased dramatically in recent decades. The Immigration and Nationality Act Amendments of 1965, by revoking the system of national origin quotas and making visas easier to obtain in general, contributed significantly to this trend. Whereas Latin Americans comprised only 26 percent of legal immigrants entering the United States from 1941 to 1950, 40 percent of legal immigrants from 1951 to 1960 were from Latin America (Passel and Edmonston 1994). Although Latinos continued to represent roughly 40 percent of legal immigrants through the 1980s (Passel and Edmonston 1994), the size of the legal immigrant flow from all countries increased from roughly 2.5 million people between 1951 and 1960 to over 7.3 million people from 1981 to 1990 (Borjas 1994). Thus, legal Latin American immigrants to the United States during the 1980s numbered almost 3 million. Legal immigration from Mexico, the largest single source of immigrants to the United States, increased from about 0.3 million people in the 1950s to almost 1.7 million during the 1980s (Borjas 1994). The flow of illegal immigrants has also consisted of an increasing share of Latinos. By 1980, Mexicans alone represented approximately half of the nation's estimated 2–4 million undocumented immigrants (Warren and Passel 1987).

As a result of this surge of Latin American immigration and the relatively high fertility rates of Latinos (Mendoza 1994), an increasing and significant proportion of the United States population is of Hispanic ethnicity.[1] Persons of Latin American descent comprised approximately 6.8 percent of the U.S. population in 1980. That figure increased to 9.3 percent in 1991, representing more than 22 million people (Mendoza 1994). Hispanics are expected to number 31 million by the year 2000 (Delgado 1993). According to the U.S. Bureau of the Census (1995), births to Hispanic mothers represented 14.3 pecent of all births in 1990 (based on data from 48 states and the District of

Columbia), up from 9.9 percent of 1985 births (based on data from only 23 states and the District of Columbia).

Concurrent with the Latin American influx into the United States has been an increasing national concern over the problem of low birthweight, which has been associated with a variety of long-term health problems and conditions such as neurodevelopmental handicaps, cerebral palsy, and respiratory tract conditions (Hack, Klein, and Taylor 1995), as well as with learning disorders (Chaikind and Corman 1991). Although the rate of low birthweight[2] in the United States declined steadily between 1970 and 1985, this trend reversed itself slightly from 1985 to 1991. Throughout, the rate of low birthweight among blacks remained approximately twice that for whites. Overall, low birthweight stood at 6.94 percent of all live births in the United States in 1990 ("Increasing Incidence of Low Birthweight" 1994). In 1990, past and present low birthweight allegedly added an extra $2 billion to the nation's health care bill (Cooper 1992).

Past research has generally shown that the rate of low birthweight among Hispanics is similar to that of non-Hispanic whites. However, since the Hispanic community consists of individuals from a number of different countries, economic situations, political circumstances, and length of time in the United States, aggregation could mask important differences in the rates of low birthweight among the different Hispanic subgroups. In light of the increasing proportion of U.S. births to Hispanics, the pressing concern of low birthweight in the United States, and the heterogeneity of the Hispanic community, there is a need to investigate the prevalence of low birthweight for different Hispanic subgroups. Identification of those groups most at risk for adverse birth outcomes, if any, could be used to facilitate the targeting of social programs designed to improve birth outcomes among high-risk women living in poverty.

The effects of parents' birthplace and ethnicity on prenatal care usage and birth outcomes have been studied little, owing in large part to the dearth of data sufficiently rich to facilitate investigation of these variations. This study uses data on single live in-state births to New Jersey residents in 1989 and 1990 to estimate the effects of both of these attributes on prenatal care usage and birthweight. Major emphasis is placed on Latin American birthplaces and ethnicities. This is one of the few studies on the subject to employ a multivariate framework. The investigation of this issue is important in New Jersey, where immigrants now comprise over 12 percent of the population, and "persons of Spanish origin" also represent roughly the same proportion of New Jersey residents (New Jersey Department of Labor

1995). Furthermore, as some claim that New Jersey, more than any other state, resembles the United States as a whole in racial and ethnic composition (U.S. Congress 1994), the findings from New Jersey may be indicative of what prevails in the United States as a whole.

The section following reviews findings from past research on the effects of maternal birthplace and Hispanic ethnicity on both birthweight and the risk factors for low birthweight. The third section describes the data and presents a descriptive analysis. The fourth section examines the analytical framework used in this study. The fifth section presents multivariate analyses highlighting the effects of birthplace and ethnicity on prenatal care usage and birth outcomes. The final section contains a summary and conclusions.

BACKGROUND AND LITERATURE

This study attempts to isolate the effects of maternal birthplace and ethnicity on birthweight and on prenatal care delay, with a major focus on Hispanic women in New Jersey. A growing body of literature, mostly focusing on pieces of this puzzle, has indicated that there is considerable variation in both birthweight and the various risk factors for low birthweight among different Hispanic subgroups. Major findings from this body of research are presented after a brief overview of the data sources most widely used in these studies. For clarity of presentation, the summary of findings is organized into the following broad categories: ethnicity and birthweight, birthplace and birthweight, and differences in risk factors for low birthweight. Owing to the small number of studies investigating the relationship between birthplace and risk factors, the last category presents findings for different ethnic groups as well as for different birthplaces. The section ends with a short summary of major points from past studies.

Data on Birthplace, Ethnicity, Risk Factors, and Birth Outcomes

Few data sets are available containing information on the health and behaviors of various Latino subpopulations. It was not until 1989 that identifiers for Hispanic subgroups were included on the standard birth and death forms used by most states. In 1993, the Surgeon General's National Hispanic/Latino Health Initiative recognized that *Healthy People 2000* (U.S. Department of Health and Human Services 1990), a set of 300 national health promotion goals, contained a paucity of objectives for the Hispanic population (Delgado 1993; Delgado and Estrada 1993). Since state and local funding decisions are regularly tied to *Healthy People 2000* objectives, it was felt that the health needs of Hispanics were likely overlooked and underserviced (Delgado 1993; Delgado and Estrada 1993). A result has been a concerted effort to mandate placement of Hispanic subgroup identifiers on all Department of Health and Human Services surveys and forms.

Most studies on birth outcomes and prenatal care usage of Latinos have used either the National Vital Statistics system or the Hispanic Health and Nutrition Examination Survey (HHANES), a one-time survey conducted by the National Center for Health Statistics from 1982 to 1984. As of 1983, the former included identifiers for Hispanic subgroups on birth certificates in 23 states plus the District of Columbia, accounting for over 90 percent of the Hispanic population in the United States based on estimates from the 1980 Census (Mendoza et al. 1991). The HHANES sampled Mexican Americans from five southwestern states, Cuban Americans from Dade County, Florida, and Puerto Ricans from the metropolitan New York City area (containing parts of Connecticut, New Jersey, and New York). This data set contains detailed demographic and medical information obtained through interviews and physical examinations. A patchwork picture can be compiled based on the results of studies that have used these data sources to investigate the effects of birthplace and ethnicity on low birthweight and its risk factors.

Ethnicity and Birthweight

Mendoza et al. (1991), using both of the data sources just described, compared the rates of low birthweight of mainland Puerto Ricans, Mexican Americans, and Cuban Americans. They found that Puerto Ricans had the highest rates of low birthweight, whereas the other groups fared much better. Reflecting a generally acknowledged paradox, Mexican American women had outcomes very similar to those of Cuban Americans, despite the social and economic disadvantages of the former as compared to the latter. Consistent with Mendoza et al., Becerra et al. (1991), using 1983 and 1984 Vital Statistics data, found that infants born to Puerto Rican mothers were at the highest risk of low birthweight, and that those born to Cuban women were at the lowest risk among these three Hispanic groups.

Birthplace and Birthweight

Mendoza et al. (1991) found some indication that foreign-born mothers, particularly Mexicans, had lower rates of low birthweight than did U.S.-born women belonging to the same ethnic group. The results from Becerra et al. (1991) and a HHANES study by Guendleman et al. (1990) also suggest that first-generation immigrants, particularly those from Mexico, may be at an advantage. According to Guendleman et al., Mexican-Americans themselves represent a heterogeneous group, characterized by wide variations in health and behaviors. They estimated that U.S.-born Mexicans are at a 60 percent higher risk for delivering a low birthweight baby than are Mexican-born U.S. residents. They also reported that the rate of low birthweight for Mexican women born in the United States was almost on par with that of the overall United States black population.

Differences in Risk Factors for Low Birthweight

Puerto Rican women appear to have risk factors that make them more likely than other Hispanics to have a low birthweight birth. Cubans exhibit many fewer of these risk factors. As discussed earlier, however, Mexicans present a mixed picture. For ease of discussion both in this section and later in the chapter, risk factors are categorized as (1) demographic and economic and (2) medical and behavioral. The former group includes the age of the mother (teenage mothers and mothers over 35 years of age are more likely to have adverse outcomes), as well as marital status, education, poverty, and health insurance: Unwed motherhood, lack of education, poverty, and lack of health insurance are all risk factors for low birthweight. The medical and behavioral set of risk factors includes the quantity and quality of prenatal care, as well as the following, all of which are associated with low birthweight births: alcohol consumption, cigarette smoking, drug usage, prior infant mortality, previous terminations, short birth intervals, low weight gain in pregnancy, preterm births, high parity, and hypertension. Medical and behavioral risk factors also include diabetes, which is associated with increased birthweight. Except where explicitly stated otherwise, the following discussion focuses on ethnicity, rather than birthplace, and its association with the various risk factors for low birthweight.

Demographic and Economic Risk Factors

According to Stroup-Benham and Trevino (1991), who used a subsample of women ages 15–45 years from the HHANES data, Puerto Ricans appear to be the most economically disadvantaged. Cubans, on the other end of the spectrum, had the highest levels of education and were the most likely to be employed. Although Puerto Ricans were the least likely to be employed, they were the most likely to have health insurance, partly since Puerto Rico's status as a U.S. territory qualifies those born in Puerto Rico, subject to eligibility requirements, for Medicaid (Mendoza et al. 1992). According to Solis et al. (1990) and Trevino et al. (1991), Mexicans were the least likely among Hispanics to have health insurance.[3] Stroup-Benham and Trevino (1991) also found that Mexican and Cuban women of reproductive age were more likely to be married than were Puerto Ricans.

Medical and Behavioral Risk Factors

In general, it appears that Mexicans are the least likely to obtain medical services (Solis et al. 1990; Trevino et al. 1991), including prenatal care (Moore and Hepworth 1994). Furthermore, according to Guendleman (1994), Mexican immigrants receive less prenatal care than do U.S.-born Mexicans. Stroup-Benham and Trevino (1991) found Mexicans to have the highest rates of both fertility and miscarriages. Few findings have been reported on weight gain during pregnancy by Hispanic subgroups. A study by Felice et al. (1986) did find that Mexican American teenagers had higher weight gain than did both their white and black counterparts. Mendoza et al. (1991) found that preterm deliveries, which are more prevalent for Hispanics in general than for non-Hispanic whites, were least common for Cubans and were most prevalent for Puerto Ricans.

According to the Council on Scientific Affairs (1991), Hispanics, particularly Puerto Ricans and Mexicans, are much more likely than non-Hispanic whites to suffer from both diabetes and hypertension. Marks, Garcia, and Solis (1990) found that Puerto Ricans tend to have the least-balanced diet of the three Hispanic groups. According to Haynes et al. (1990), Cubans and Puerto Ricans are heavier users of tobacco than are Mexicans. Amaro et al. (1990) found Puerto Ricans to have the highest reported use of marijuana and cocaine. In addition, they found that U.S.-born Hispanics in all three groups, both men and women, reported use of these substances more often than did their non–U.S.-born counterparts.

Summary of Findings from Past Research

Data sets containing information on birth outcomes and prenatal care usage among Latinos by birthplace, ethnicity, or both are few and far between. The limited number of existing studies shows evidence of considerable variation in both birth outcomes and risk factors for low birthweight by Hispanic subgroup. Past research suggests that Puerto Rican women, both island-born and mainland-born, appear to be most at risk for poor birth outcomes, whereas Cuban women, regardless of birthplace, are the least at risk. Regardless of birthplace, Mexicans appear to be at high risk based on socioeconomic measures. However, they tend to refrain from potentially harmful behaviors such as smoking and alcohol consumption. Nevertheless, the favorable birth outcomes of Mexicans, despite the socioeconomic disadvantages of this group and its tendency to underutilize health care services, have baffled many researchers. Finally, isolated studies have indicated that, within certain ethnic groups, those born in the United States are more at risk for adverse birth outcomes than are the foreign born.

DATA AND DESCRIPTIVE ANALYSIS

The primary data set used in this analysis contains 1989 and 1990 files, collected by the New Jersey Department of Health, that link Vital Statistics birth records with uniform billing hospital discharge data for single live in-state births to New Jersey residents. Insurance information was obtained from the uniform bill, while most of the other measures used in this analysis were from the birth records. Blacks and whites were analyzed separately, since past research has indicated racial differences in the effects of prenatal risk factors on birth outcomes (Corman, Joyce, and Grossman 1987).[4] The analysis focuses on infant birthweights and usage of prenatal care of women born in the United States, Cuba, Mexico, and Puerto Rico. Table 8.1 indicates the percentage of linked births associated with each of these maternal birthplaces, the percentage of births for each birthplace for which the father was U.S.-born, and the percentage white by maternal birthplace. Although women born in many other countries live in New Jersey, the data were not disaggregated for other foreign-born groups.

   Tables 8.2 and 8.3 present the prenatal care usage and birth outcome measures by race and maternal birthplace, respectively. The two pre-

Table 8.1 CHARACTERISTICS OF LINKED DATA SET BY MATERNAL BIRTHPLACE

	Birthplace of Mother			
	United States	Cuba	Mexico	Puerto Rico[a]
Percentage of all linked births, 1989–90[b]	78.08	0.60	0.53	3.10
For Each Birthplace:				
Percentage of fathers born in United States	97.23	35.98	7.80	34.92
Percentage white	78.88	94.55	90.55	95.39
Number of observations	168,504	1,288	1,132	6,693

a. Although Puerto Rico is technically part of the United States, it was shown earlier in the text that the health and behaviors of this group differ substantially from those of individuals born in the rest of the United States. As such, Puerto Rican–born U.S. residents are treated as a separate group.

b. Percentages of linked births do not sum to 100 percent because maternal birthplace was listed as *not classifiable* for 37,745 births. In addition, extremely small numbers of women were born in the Virgin Islands, Guam, and Canada; women born in these locations were excluded from the analysis. A study performed by the Center for Health Statistics in New Jersey found a high degree of accuracy in the maternal birthplace coding for 1992. The numbers of women born in the United States, Cuba, Mexico, and Puerto Rico in 1989 and 1990 are consistent in magnitude with the counts found to be accurate for 1992. In addition, the numbers of those listed as *nonclassifiable* in 1989 and 1990 are similar in magnitude to the sum of those listed as being born in the *rest of the world* plus those listed as *nonclassifiable* in 1991 and 1992. Therefore, it appears likely that most of the nonclassifiables in 1989 and 1990 were from the *rest of the world* (i.e., not born in the United States, Cuba, Mexico, Puerto Rico, Virgin Islands, Guam, or Canada).

natal care measures are the probability of initiating prenatal care in the first trimester of pregnancy and the probability of receiving no prenatal care at all.[5] The birth outcome measures are the birthweight of the newborn in grams and the probability of delivering a low birthweight baby. When the sample sizes were sufficient, the data were disaggregated by ethnicity into non-Hispanic, Mexican, Puerto Rican, Cuban, Central and South American, and other Hispanic. The notes to table 8.2 indicate which groups had insufficient cell sizes, as well as how these groups were treated for the purposes of this analysis. For clarity of presentation, the foreign-born were not as disaggregated by ethnicity as were the U.S.-born.

The rate of low birthweight in New Jersey for all races combined in 1990, at 5.8 percent, compared favorably with the corresponding figure cited earlier for the United States as a whole. However, tables 8.2 and 8.3 indicate that there were considerable variations in both pre-

Table 8.2 OUTCOME MEASURES (MEANS) FOR BLACK MOTHERS BY BIRTHPLACE AND ETHNICITY

| | | Mother's Birthplace[a] | | | | | | |
| | | United States | | Other Hispanic[b] | Mexico | Puerto Rico | "Not Classifiable" or "Rest of the World" | |
	All Blacks	Non-Hispanic	Puerto Rican				Hispanic	Non-Hispanic
No prenatal care	0.043	0.052	0.023	0.014	0.012	0.022	0.003	0.002
Care initiated in first trimester	0.627	0.603	0.632	0.648	0.214	0.652	0.707	0.739
Birth Outcomes:								
Low birthweight (<2500 grams)	0.117	0.126	0.068	0.102	0.036	0.060	0.050	0.089
Birthweight (grams)	3,142.43	3,120.82	3,205.00	3,179.56	3,259.95	3,281.16	3,345.61	3,241.96
Number of observations[c]	42,319	31,559	261	577	84	184	1,021	6,040

a. Since there were only 38 black women born in Cuba, these observations were excluded from the analysis.

b. Excludes Mexicans, Cubans, and Central/South Americans, who comprised very few of the native black births. The cell sizes were as follows: U.S.-born Mexican blacks (n = 31), U.S.-born Cuban blacks (n = 9), U.S.-born Central/South American blacks (n = 23).

c. For a given birthplace, the sum of the number of observations in table 8.2 plus the number of observations in table 8.3 is less than the total number of observations for that birthplace in table 8.1. Whereas tables 8.2 and 8.3 include only black and white women, respectively, table 8.1 includes women of all races. In addition, within each birthplace group, the number of observations varies for the different outcome measures owing to missing values. The number of observations, as denoted in tables 8.2 and 8.3, indicates the minimum number of observations in a given column. For the latter reason, the total number of blacks indicated above is greater than the sum of the numbers of observations in a given column. In addition, the total number of blacks includes black women born in the Virgin Islands. Guam, and Canada.

Table 8.3 OUTCOME MEASURES (MEANS) FOR WHITE MOTHERS BY BIRTHPLACE AND ETHNICITY

| | | | Mother's Birthplace | | | | | | | | "Not Classifiable" or "Rest of the World" | |
| | | | United States | | | | | | | | | |
	All Whites	Non-Hispanic	Mexican	Puerto Rican	Cuban	Central/South America	Other Hispanic	Cuba	Mexico	Puerto Rico	Hispanic	Non-Hispanic
No prenatal care	0.005	0.003	0.020	0.021	0.003	0.009	0.013	0.003	0.020	0.018	0.008	0.007
Care initiated in first trimester	0.862	0.902	0.737	0.670	0.878	0.736	0.740	0.912	0.467	0.651	0.718	0.835
Birth Outcomes:												
Low birthweight (<2500 grams)	0.044	0.039	0.053	0.079	0.045	0.059	0.056	0.047	0.054	0.075	0.048	0.042
Birthweight (grams)	3,432.53	3,461.56	3,396.56	3,242.23	3,401.86	3,340.06	3,334.09	3,381.36	3,299.16	3,263.72	3,380.98	3,414.65
Number of observations[a]	163,572	120,300	205	6,121	327	424	1,606	1,191	961	5,980	10,683	10,859

a. For a given birthplace, the sum of the number of observations in table 8.2 plus the total number of observations in table 8.3 is less than the total number of observations for that birthplace in table 8.1. Whereas tables 8.2 and 8.3 include only black and white women, respectively, table 8.1 includes women of all races. In addition, within each birthplace group, the number of observations varies for the different outcome measures owing to missing values. The number of observations, as denoted in tables 8.2 and 8.3, indicates the minimum number of observations in a given column. For the latter reason, the total number of whites indicated above is greater than the sum of the numbers of whites in the disaggregated groups presented. In addition, the total number of whites includes white women born in the Virgin Islands, Guam, and Canada.

natal care usage and birth outcomes among different racial, ethnic, and immigrant groups. Overall, both prenatal care usage and outcomes were markedly worse for blacks than for whites.

Table 8.2 indicates that non-Hispanic U.S.-born black mothers were more likely to receive no prenatal care and less likely to receive first-trimester care than most other black mothers. The relative birthweight outcomes for this group were also poor. In terms of risk factors, U.S.-born black mothers in New Jersey in 1989 and 1990 were less likely to be married, more likely to be teenagers, and more likely to consume cigarettes and alcohol than were their foreign-born black counterparts (not shown in table 8.2).[6] The Puerto Rican women, both mainland-born and island-born, were the most likely black women to be on Medicaid. Those born in Mexico and Puerto Rico had the lowest levels of education of all of the black groups. Cigarette and alcohol consumption were lower for black women born in Mexico than for any of the other black groups.

Non-Hispanic U.S.-born whites were much more likely to use prenatal care, and to do so within the first trimester, than all other whites except the island-born Cubans. In general, the mainland-born and island-born Puerto Ricans were the least likely among whites to be married and the most likely to be on Medicaid (not shown in table 8.3). Mainland-born Puerto Ricans and U.S.-born Central/South American mothers were much more likely than other whites to be teenagers. Among all of the white groups, the women born in Mexico were the least likely to consume both alcohol and tobacco. Regardless of birthplace, the Mexicans and Puerto Ricans were the least educated of the white groups. Finally, white Cubans (born anywhere) had the highest mean weight gain in pregnancy, whereas white Mexicans (born anywhere) had the lowest weight gain.

Table 8.3 reveals evidence of the "Mexican paradox" described earlier. White Mexican women, both U.S.-born and Mexican-born, were roughly six times more likely than U.S.-born non-Hispanic whites to receive no prenatal care. Furthermore, white women born in Mexico were only half as likely as U.S.-born non-Hispanic whites to receive first trimester care, and U.S.-born whites of Mexican descent were also at increased risk of initiating care beyond the first trimester. However, the Mexican birth outcomes for whites did not reflect this lack of care. Hence, the Mexican paradox seemingly holds for whites in New Jersey.

Consistent with much of the past research, which studied women from geographical areas other than New Jersey and time periods earlier than 1989 and 1990, table 8.3 indicates that Puerto Rican whites had poorer prenatal care usage and birth outcomes than Mexicans and Cubans. Whether born in Puerto Rico or not, they initiated care later than did all other whites except those born in Mexico. They had rates of "no care" high enough to put them on par with the Mexican-born and Mexican U.S.-born whites. They also had the lowest mean birthweights and highest rates of low birthweight among all whites. In contrast, table 8.2 indicates that the prenatal care usage and birth outcomes of Puerto Rican blacks compared favorably to those of other blacks.

In contrast to the findings of other studies (i.e., Becerra et al. 1991; Guendleman et al. 1990; Mendoza et al. 1991), there is no evidence in these data that Mexican U.S.-born women are at higher low birth-weight risk than women born in Mexico, or that the Mexican U.S.-born rate of low birthweight is comparable to that for blacks. In fact, few differences were detected between the outcomes of U.S.-born and foreign-born women belonging to the same ancestral group. However, in keeping with past research, the U.S.-born women had consistently higher rates of reported smoking and alcohol usage than their foreign-born counterparts in the same ethnic group.

ANALYTICAL FRAMEWORK AND EMPIRICAL IMPLEMENTATION

This analysis is based upon the economic theory of family behavior developed by Becker and Lewis (1973) and by Willis (1973) and frequently applied in the analysis of infant health and birth outcomes (Corman and Grossman 1985; Corman, Joyce, and Grossman 1987; Frank et al. 1992; Grossman and Joyce 1990; Joyce 1987a, b; Joyce and Grossman 1990a, b; Rosenzweig and Schultz 1982, 1983, 1988). For the purposes of this study, the behavioral model can be written as follows:

$$birthweight = f_1(prenatal\ care,\ sex\ of\ the\ infant,\ health$$
$$insurance\ coverage,\ medical\ risk\ factors,$$
$$alcohol\ usage,\ cigarette\ smoking,\ number\ of$$
$$other\ children,\ previous\ loss\ of\ child,\ prior$$
$$terminations,\ recent\ live\ birth,\ age\ of\ the$$
$$mother,\ parents'\ birthplaces\ and\ ethnicities,\ z)\quad(8.1)$$

$$prenatal\ care,\ alcohol\ usage,\ smoking = f_j(p,\ y,\ k)\quad j = 2\ to\ 4$$
$$(8.2)–(8.4)$$

Equation (8.1) represents an infant health production function, whereby an infant's birthweight is expressed as a function of a set of basic health inputs and risk factors. Most of the risk factors for low birthweight were described earlier in the subsection on "Differences in Risk Factors for Low Birthweight." In addition, the sex of the infant is also expected to affect birthweight. On average, females are born 3 to 4 ounces lighter than male infants (Guttmacher 1986). The birthweight equation also contains a set of unobserved factors (z), which includes drug usage, diet, and the infant's biological endowment (e). Equations (8.2) to (8.4) represent demand functions for prenatal care, alcohol consumption, and cigarette smoking, as a function of price (p) and income (y) measures, and a set of other factors (k), some of which may be unobserved (for example, e). The input demand functions are theoretically derived from a demand function for infant health, which is obtained by the maximization of the parents' utility function subject to production and resource constraints. One of these constraints is the birthweight production function represented by equation (8.1).

A major objective of this study is to identify the roles of birthplace and ethnicity on birthweight. Rosenzweig and Schultz (1982, 1983, 1988) argued that z, the unobserved factors in equation (8.1), are likely to be correlated with input usage. Thus, ordinary least squares estimation would yield biased estimates of the effects of inputs on birth outcomes. To address this issue, this study places emphasis on reduced-form estimation, wherein the prenatal inputs modeled in equations (8.2)–(8.4) are excluded from the estimation of equation (8.1).[7]

This study also examines the roles of birthplace and ethnicity on the acquisition of prenatal care. Since p and y are not directly ascertainable in this case, several individual characteristics were used as proxy variables. The personal characteristics typically employed in this type of analysis include marital status, education, health insurance status, and age of the mother. In addition, smoking and alcohol, previous terminations, number of other children, and previous loss of a child are hypothesized to reflect the general degree of wantedness of the current pregnancy, and would therefore be expected to influence the level of care as well (Grossman and Joyce 1990). The father's birthplace may also serve as a proxy variable for p or y, or it may reflect the degree of assimilation in the United States.

The primary question that this study seeks to answer is whether maternal birthplace and ethnicity have distinct effects on prenatal care usage and birthweight, all else equal. The analysis controls for a variety of known risk factors and estimates the effects of birthplace and ethnicity beyond their effects on the observed explanatory variables. Table 8.4 describes the variables that are used in the analysis and indicates the expected sign for each variable, where applicable. Sets of dichotomous variables were used for both ethnicity and birthplace. The black regressions contain birthplace indicators for Mexico, Puerto Rico, and "other non-U.S.," and dummy variables for both Puerto Rican and "other Hispanic" ethnicities. The white regressions contain dichotomous birthplace variables for Cuba, Mexico, Puerto Rico, and "other non-U.S.," as well as indicators for Central/South American, Cuban, Mexican, Puerto Rican, and "other Hispanic" ethnicities. For all of the regressions, the excluded birthplace category is the United States and the reference ethnic category is "non-Hispanic."

The descriptive analysis, presented in the previous section, indicates that there were systematic differences by birthplace and ethnicity in prenatal care usage and birth outcomes. However, the multivariate analysis controls for many of the risk factors that also vary by ethnicity and birthplace. Therefore, it is not clear a priori whether the birthplace and ethnicity effects revealed by the descriptive analysis will be significant in a multivariate context. It is also possible that birthplace and ethnicity are correlated with unobserved factors in the birthweight and prenatal care models (z and k, respectively), leading to significant birthplace and ethnicity effects in the multivariate models. Different rates of drug usage, dietary habits, cultural norms and values, fluency in the English language, and kinship network patterns are all thought to have an impact on reproductive behavior and birth outcomes. None of these variables, however, could be included in the analysis due to the limitations in the data. Thus, findings of any significant effects of birthplace and/or ethnicity beyond their effects on the control variables can most likely be at least partially explained by some or all of these attributes and behaviors.

MULTIVARIATE ANALYSIS

The multivariate results are presented in tables 8.5, 8.6, and 8.7. The following discussion focuses initially on the birthplace and ethnicity results, and then on findings pertaining to the other risk factors. Table 8.5 presents race-specific logistic regression results for two different prenatal care outcomes—first-trimester care and no prenatal care. Based on these results, birthplace and ethnicity appear to be strong determinants of prenatal care usage for both blacks and whites. Being born in Mexico significantly decreases the probability that both blacks and whites will obtain first-trimester care, all else equal. Mexican ethnicity is associated with decreased rates of first-trimester care for whites. In contrast, Mexican birthplace significantly decreases the probability of receiving no prenatal care for both blacks and whites, controlling for insurance status and the other covariates. Being born in Puerto Rico does not appear to be important in explaining prenatal care usage of either blacks or whites. For whites, Puerto Rican ethnicity significantly decreases the probability of first-trimester care and increases the likelihood of no prenatal care, all else equal. In contrast, Puerto Rican ethnicity appears to decrease the probability of a black woman receiving no prenatal care.

Tables 8.6 and 8.7 present race-specific regression results for two outcome measures—birthweight and low birthweight. The former are estimated by ordinary least squares (OLS) and the latter are estimated by logistic regression (logit). Two different models for each outcome are presented. In each case, the first column presents the reduced-form model in which the birth outcome is expressed as a function of its exogenous determinants only. The second model adds controls for smoking, alcohol, the month of prenatal care initiation,[8] and maternal weight gain. It is notable that the coefficients are similar in magnitude across specifications, even when controlling for prenatal care delay. Due to their clearer relevance in terms of policy implications, more attention is paid here to the results for low birthweight than to those for birthweight itself.

In general, the birthplace effects on low birthweight are much stronger for blacks than for whites. For blacks, both birthplace (except for Puerto Rico) and ethnicity are significant even after controlling for numerous risk factors. Both foreign birthplace and Hispanic ethnicity appear to significantly reduce the risk of low birthweight of blacks relative to those who are either U.S.-born and/or non-Hispanic, other things equal. In contrast, birthplace is uniformly insignificant in explaining low birthweight for whites. Ethnicity also appears to matter little for whites. A major exception, however, is Puerto Rican ethnicity, which appears to significantly increase the probability of low birthweight for whites, even after controlling for a host of risk factors. Another exception is that Central/South American and "other Hispanic" ethnicities appear to reduce birthweight when controlling for prenatal care delay, maternal weight gain, smoking, and alcohol in addition to the reduced-form determinants.

Based on the low birthweight model that controls for smoking, alcohol, maternal weight gain, and prenatal care delay, Puerto Rican

Table 8.4 DESCRIPTION OF VARIABLES

Variable Name	Description	Expected Sign (+/−)			
		Birthweight	Low Birthweight	First Trimester	No Care
Outcome Measures:					
Birthweight	Weight of infant at birth (grams)				
Low birthweight	Dichotomous variable that equals 1 if infant weighed less than 2,500 grams at birth				
First-trimester care	Dichotomous variable that equals 1 if woman received care in first trimester of pregnancy				
No care	Dichotomous variable that equals 1 if woman was reported as receiving no prenatal care				
Demographic and Economic Risk Factors:					
Married	Dichotomous variable that equals 1 if woman was married	+	−	+	−
Education	Years of education attained by mother	+	−	+	−
Mother over 35	Dichotomous variable that equals 1 if woman was over 35 years of age at time of delivery	−	+	+	
Teenage mother	Dichotomous variable that equals 1 if woman was less than 20 years of age at time of delivery		+	−	+
Medicaid	Dichotomous variable that equals 1 if woman received Medicaid	−	+	−	+
Self-pay	Dichotomous variable that equals 1 if woman paid for delivery out of pocket	−	+	−	+
Other insurance	Dichotomous variable that equals 1 if woman received government health insurance other than Medicaid		+	−	+
Uninsured	Dichotomous variable that equals 1 if woman was uninsured	−	+	−	+

Medical and Behavioral Risk Factors:

Variable	Definition				
Female	Dichotomous variable that equals 1 if baby was female	−	+		
Smoking	Dichotomous variable that equals 1 if woman reported smoking cigarettes at any time during pregnancy	−	+	−	+
Alcohol	Dichotomous variable that equals 1 if woman reported alcohol consumption at any time during pregnancy	−	+	−	+
Recent live birth	Dichotomous variable that equals 1 if woman had another live birth within previous 20 months	−	+	−	+
Number of other children	Number of previous live births still living				
Prior loss of child	Dichotomous variable that equals 1 if woman had at least one prior live birth that later died				
Previous termination(s)	Dichotomous variable that equals 1 if woman had at least one prior induced or spontaneous termination				
Hypertension	Dichotomous variable that equals 1 if woman was diagnosed as having pregnancy-related hypertension	−	+		
Diabetes	Dichotomous variable that equals 1 if woman was diagnosed as having diabetes	+	−		

Other Factors:

Variable	Definition
Born in Cuba	Dichotomous variable that equals 1 if mother was born in Cuba
Born in Mexico	Dichotomous variable that equals 1 if mother was born in Mexico
Born in Puerto Rico	Dichotomous variable that equals 1 if mother was born in Puerto Rico
Born in other non-U.S.	Dichotomous variable that equals 1 if mother's birthplace was "Not Classifiable" or "Rest of the World"
Central/South American ethnicity	Dichotomous variable that equals 1 if woman was of Central/South American ethnicity
Cuban ethnicity	Dichotomous variable that equals 1 if woman was of Cuban ethnicity
Mexican ethnicity	Dichotomous variable that equals 1 if woman was of Mexican ethnicity

Table 8.4 DESCRIPTION OF VARIABLES (continued)

Variable Name	Description	Expected Sign (+/−)			
		Low Birthweight	Birthweight	First Trimester	No Care
Puerto Rican ethnicity	Dichotomous variable that equals 1 if woman was of Puerto Rican ethnicity				
Other Hispanic ethnicity	Dichotomous variable that equals 1 if woman was of "other Hispanic" ethnicity				
Father born in United States	Dichotomous variable that equals 1 if father of baby was born in United States				
Low weight gain in pregnancy	Weight gain less than 25 pounds during pregnancy	+	−		
Month of prenatal care initiation	Month during pregnancy in which prenatal care was initiated (from 1 to 9)	+	−		

Table 8.5 LOGIT RESULTS—PRENATAL CARE EQUATIONS

	Blacks		Whites	
	First Trimester	No Care	First Trimester	No Care
Constant	−0.161	−2.298**	0.733**	−4.340**
Demographic and Economic Risk Factors:				
Married	0.529**	−0.881**	0.709**	−1.302**
Education	0.101**	−0.125**	0.089**	−0.063
Mother over 35	0.317**	−0.494**	0.302**	−0.088
Teenage mother	−0.584**	0.076	−0.729**	0.314**
Medicaid	−0.614**	0.542**	−1.088**	0.504**
Self-pay	−0.919**	1.420**	−1.234**	1.932**
Other insurance	−0.661**	0.162	−1.222**	0.101
Uninsured	−0.482*	0.112	−1.484**	1.226**
Medical and Behavioral Risk Factors:				
Smoking	−0.186**	0.468**	−0.444**	0.576**
Alcohol	−0.484**	0.604**	−0.013	0.491**
Recent live birth	−0.639**	0.671**	−0.520**	0.687**
Number of other children	−0.202**	0.268**	−0.207**	0.300**
Prior loss of child	0.066	−0.349*	0.076	0.035
Previous termination(s)	−0.049	−0.011	−0.002*	−0.366**
Mother's Birthplace:				
Cuba			0.166	−0.127
Mexico	−1.400**	−2.020*	−0.682**	−0.858*
Puerto Rico	0.088	−0.393	−0.066	−0.167
Other non-U.S.	0.303**	−0.830**	−0.231**	−0.198
Mother's Ethnicity:				
Central/South American			−0.167**	−0.502**
Cuban			0.439**	−0.225
Mexican			−0.459**	0.716
Puerto Rican	0.162	−0.929*	−0.190**	0.293*
Other Hispanic	0.129	−1.256**	−0.200**	0.009
Father born in United States	0.317**	−0.616**	0.407**	−0.732**
Chi-squared	5897.021** (20 degrees of freedom)	1978.576 (20 degrees of freedom)	22,656.012** (24 degrees of freedom)	1683.168** (24 degrees of freedom)
Number of observations	34,304	34,304	138,382	138,382

*Significant at .05 level.
**Significant at .01 level.

Table 8.6 REGRESSION RESULTS—BIRTHWEIGHT EQUATIONS (Blacks)

	Blacks			
	Birthweight (grams)		Low Birthweight (<2500 grams)	
	OLS	OLS	logit	logit
Constant	2,974.4**	3,290.0**	−1.428**	−2.763**
Demographic and Economic Risk Factors:				
Married	93.6**	58.4**	−0.289**	−0.177**
Education	15.0**	7.3**	−0.052**	−0.023*
Mother over 35	−23.4	−25.9	0.170*	0.209**
Teenage mother	36.1**	16.2	−0.280**	−0.217**
Medicaid	−47.0**	−13.8	0.152**	0.038
Self-pay	−113.5**	−63.6**	0.408**	0.216**
Other insurance	−43.9	−44.5	−0.066	−0.156
Uninsured	12.9	−8.3	−0.182	−0.072
Medical and Behavioral Risk Factors:				
Female	−114.5**	−118.0**	0.181**	0.209**
Smoking		−176.2**		0.508**
Alcohol		−115.2**		0.385**
Recent live birth	−68.6**	−33.3**	0.224**	0.114*
Number of other children	8.4**	28.3**	0.008	−0.066**
Prior loss of child	−122.5**	−108.7**	0.449**	0.403**
Previous termination(s)	−16.9*	−10.6	0.145**	0.121**
Hypertension	−178.6**	−184.1**	0.884**	0.997**
Diabetes	183.3**	179.4**	−0.230	−0.201
				(continued)

ethnicity increased the probability of low birthweight for whites by 1.8 percentage points, which is almost half the rate of low birthweight for non-Hispanic whites. This large effect cannot be explained by differences in any of the observed risk factors. It is reasonable to conjecture that some of this effect operates through prenatal care: table 8.5 shows that whites of Puerto Rican ethnicity are both less likely to get first-trimester care and more likely to obtain no prenatal care than whites who are non-Hispanic. However, when controlling for prenatal care in the low birthweight equation, the coefficient on Puerto Rican ethnicity remained comparable to that in the reduced form model. Thus, Puerto Rican ethnicity appears to have significant

Table 8.6 REGRESSION RESULTS—BIRTHWEIGHT EQUATIONS (Blacks)
        (*continued*)

	Blacks			
	Birthweight (grams)		Low Birthweight (<2500 grams)	
	OLS	OLS	logit	logit
Mother's Birthplace:				
Mexico	185.4**	126.4*	−1.630**	−1.377*
Puerto Rico	93.6	61.9	−0.296	−0.178
Other non-U.S.	120.3**	61.3**	−0.481**	−0.250**
Mother's Ethnicity:				
Puerto Rican	97.5**	41.8**	−0.822**	−0.529*
Other Hispanic	68.5**	35.9*	−0.330**	−0.222
Father born in United States	58.4**	26.0**	−0.222**	−0.112**
Other Controls:				
Low weight gain in pregnancy		−233.2**		0.989**
Month of prenatal care initiation		−17.2**		0.060**
R^2	0.043**	0.098**		
Chi-squared			742.392** (21 degrees of freedom)	1655.987** (25 degrees of freedom)
Number of observations	38,260	34,268	38,260	34,268

*Significant at .05 level.
**Significant at .01 level.

adverse low birthweight effects beyond its indirect effects through prenatal care.

To a certain extent, the multivariate analysis supports the so-called Mexican paradox. Women born in Mexico and those of Mexican ethnicity are less likely to receive prenatal care in the first trimester than their U.S.-born and non-Hispanic counterparts, yet they appear not to be at increased risk for adverse birth outcomes when controlling for numerous risk factors.[9] Mexican women born in Mexico are even less likely than other ethnic Mexicans to receive first-trimester care, other things equal. Again, the birth outcomes do not reflect this propensity. Thus, since Mexicans are relatively unlikely to get first-trimester care but are also relatively unlikely to experience a poor

Table 8.7 REGRESSION RESULTS—BIRTHWEIGHT EQUATIONS (Whites)

| | Whites | | | |
| | Birthweight (grams) | | Low Birthweight (<2500 grams) | |
	OLS	OLS	logit	logit
Constant	3,269.5**	3,488.6**	−2.351**	−3.499**
Demographic and Economic Risk Factors:				
Married	71.7**	38.7**	−0.352**	−0.216**
Education	11.3**	4.2**	−0.051**	−0.021**
Mother over 35	−30.3**	−31.8**	0.309**	0.330**
Teenage mother	−27.1**	−29.5**	0.056	0.038
Medicaid	−63.8**	−37.6**	0.231**	0.155**
Self-pay	−65.0**	−38.0**	0.372**	0.224**
Other insurance	−1.0	7.8	−0.134	−0.243
Uninsured	−59.5**	−25.7	−0.041	−0.148
Medical and Behavioral Risk Factors:				
Female	−135.8**	−134.3**	0.202**	0.197*
Smoking		−206.2**		0.720**
Alcohol		−2.8		0.090
Recent live birth	−35.6**	−22.9**	0.137**	0.044
Number of other children	46.3**	52.9**	−0.155*	−0.202*
Prior loss of child	−46.4**	−37.2**	0.437**	0.392**
Previous termination(s)	−6.2	−0.6	0.147**	0.123**
Hypertension	−158.9**	−157.7**	1.240**	1.302**
Diabetes	65.7**	79.2**	0.057	−0.009

(continued)

birth outcome, the Mexican paradox is in this sense reflected in these data.

In contrast to the findings from past studies and from this study's descriptive analysis, however, the multivariate analysis indicates that Mexicans are not at increased risk of getting no prenatal care. In fact, when controlling simultaneously for the multiple causal factors, it appears that women born in Mexico actually are at reduced risk of obtaining no prenatal care. Thus, when reconciling the risks of obtaining no care and experiencing poor birth outcomes, there is no apparent Mexican paradox.

The results on the demographic and behavioral risk factors accord well with those from past research (Corman and Grossman 1985; Corman, Joyce, and Grossman 1987; Frank et al. 1992; Grossman and

Table 8.7 REGRESSION RESULTS—BIRTHWEIGHT EQUATIONS (Whites)
          (continued)

	Whites			
	Birthweight (grams)		Low Birthweight (<2500 grams)	
	OLS	OLS	logit	logit
Mother's Birthplace:				
Cuba	−41.4	−52.9*	0.047	0.109
Mexico	−19.7	−25.1	−0.322	−0.460
Puerto Rico	−2.4	−9.0	−0.001	0.021
Other non-U.S.	−7.5	−25.8**	−0.082	−0.002
Mother's Ethnicity:				
Central/South				
American	−3.2	−23.8**	−0.032	0.092
Cuban	−15.0	−27.6	−0.021	0.063
Mexican	−28.2	−44.1	0.168	0.290
Puerto Rican	−109.3**	−131.0**	0.319**	0.422**
Other Hispanic	−4.9	−27.6**	−0.004	0.122
Father born in United				
States	25.6**	21.5**	−0.092**	−0.051
Other Controls:				
Low weight gain in				
pregnancy		−157.9**		0.915**
Month of prenatal				
care initiation		−6.6**		0.033**
R^2	0.047**	0.079**		
Chi-squared			1504.084**	2736.181**
			(25 degrees	(29 degrees
			of freedom)	of freedom)
Number of observations	149,234	138,231	149,234	138,231

*Significant at .05 level.
**Significant at .01 level.

Joyce 1990; Joyce 1987a, b; Joyce and Grossman 1990a, b); Rosenzweig and Schultz 1982, 1983, 1988). The demographic and economic risk factors for prenatal care delay, birthweight, and low birthweight, which are generally significant, are consistent in direction with the behavioral models outlined in the section titled "Analytical Framework and Empirical Implementation." These strong and significant results underscore the importance of socioeconomic status on reproductive behavior and birth outcomes. As expected, those enrolled in Medicaid, both blacks and whites, are more likely to delay care, to obtain no care, and to have a low birthweight baby than are women with private health insurance. Teenage pregnancy significantly reduces the likelihood of both blacks and whites obtaining first-trimester care and significantly increases the likelihood for whites of going without care, all else equal. Marital status and education also significantly affect prenatal care usage and birth outcomes in the hypothesized directions. Most of the medical and behavioral risk factors are also significant and of the expected signs. Smoking is highly and uniformly significant in explaining both prenatal care delay and poor birth outcomes for blacks and whites. Pregnancy-related hypertension also consistently affects both birthweight and low birthweight in the expected directions.

CONCLUSION

The descriptive analysis of birth outcomes and prenatal care usage in New Jersey reveals birthplace and ethnicity differences that are consistent with past research. For whites in particular, island-born and mainland-born Puerto Ricans had both the worst prenatal care usage and the poorest birth outcomes among Hispanics. The poor birth outcomes of this group, however, cannot be explained by inadequate prenatal care usage alone. U.S.-born Mexicans and women born in Mexico, who face similar socioeconomic circumstances as Puerto Ricans and are also relatively unlikely to obtain first-trimester care, did not have birth outcomes that reflected these conditions. At the other end of the spectrum, Cubans had prenatal care usage and outcomes on par with U.S.-born non-Hispanic whites. Some of the ethnic and birthplace differences became insignificant in a multivariate context. For example, U.S.-born Mexicans and women born in Mexico had high rates of no prenatal care. Yet, when controlling for the determinants of prenatal care usage such as insurance status, these groups no longer appeared to be at increased risk for obtaining no care. However, some of the birthplace and ethnicity effects persisted even after controlling for the observed risk factors, suggesting that there may be important unobserved factors associated with birthplace and ethnicity.

Puerto Ricans in New Jersey, born in Puerto Rico or not, are a group identified by this study to be at high risk for poor birth outcomes. Overall, mainland and island-born Puerto Rican whites are twice as likely to have a low birthweight baby as their U.S.-born non-Hispanic white counterparts. These Puerto Rican groups are characterized by relatively low rates of marriage, high rates of teenage motherhood, low levels of education, high rates of Medicaid, high rates of smoking, and high rates of both late and no prenatal care. Yet, the multivariate analysis indicates that even after controlling for these factors, there are still significant and sizable negative effects from belonging to these groups. One of the unobserved factors that might contribute to these effects is income.[10] According to Lemann (1991), "what leaps out at anyone who takes even a casual look at the census data is that Puerto Ricans are the worst-off ethnic group in the United States. For a period in the mid-1980's nearly half of all Puerto Rican families were living in poverty (p. 96)." Other factors may be related to diet (Marks, Garcia, and Solis 1990), drug usage (Amaro et al. 1990), or life-style factors such as stress, as well as emotional, financial, and practical support from one's extended family and community (Guendleman 1994). In addition, poor birth outcomes have been linked to the sporadic use of prenatal care once such care has been initiated, possibly due to lack of transportation, language barriers, or distrust of the medical estab-lishment (Alexander and Korenbrot 1995). It is possible that these barriers to quality care may vary by birthplace or ethnicity.

Although the purpose of this study was to investigate the roles of birthplace and ethnicity on prenatal care usage and birthweight, the results illustrate the already well-documented differences in these outcomes by race.[11] Specifically, non-Hispanic U.S.-born blacks in New Jersey are consistently and dramatically at risk, compared to all other groups, of receiving no prenatal care and of having low birth-weight babies. The rate of low birthweight for this group was 20 percent higher than that of the second most at-risk group. U.S.-born non-Hispanic blacks also had the highest rate of obtaining no prenatal care, making them at least twice as likely to go without care as any other group. In addition, the rate of late care among U.S.-born non-Hispanic blacks was second only to that of foreign-born Mexicans. In contrast, non-Hispanic U.S.-born whites in New Jersey were at the lowest risk of receiving no care, of obtaining late care, and of deliv-ering a low birthweight baby. Thus, the foremost demographic risk factor for both inadequate prenatal care and low birthweight appears to be race.

From a public policy standpoint, the results from this study indicate that programs attempting to improve birth outcomes should target two identifiable groups: non-Hispanic blacks and Puerto Ricans.[12] It is possible that there are additional foreign-born groups particularly at risk, but they could not be identified from these data owing to the large number of births falling under the "not classifiable" or "rest of the world" category for maternal birthplace. Because aggregation might hide important birthplace differences within that category, it is important that more detailed birthplace information be made available. Indeed, there appear to be significant variations in both prenatal behaviors and birth outcomes within the fast-growing Asian community (Rumbaut and Weeks 1989). Unfortunately, disaggregated effects for Asian subgroups could not be identified with these data.

This analysis underscores the importance of risk factors such as smoking and hypertension, indicating that successful smoking cessation programs and better treatment for hypertension during pregnancy would result in improved birth outcomes. It is also possible that the Medicaid program could improve birth outcomes by further increasing the use of prenatal care through greater outreach efforts or additional changes in the enrollment system.[13] Both non-Hispanic blacks and Puerto Ricans are heavily enrolled in Medicaid, yet both groups are at high risk of obtaining late or no prenatal care. However, as both of these groups are also disproportionately poor, it is unlikely that Medicaid changes alone will reduce the effects of the risk factors associated with poverty.

Resolution of the "Mexican paradox" might shed some light on how to improve poor birth outcomes. Poor prenatal care usage translates into unfavorable birth outcomes for non-Hispanic blacks and Puerto Ricans, yet Mexicans have far superior birth outcomes despite similarly high rates of late care. Several hypotheses explaining this paradox have been proposed. According to Mason (1991: 482), "the caring, supporting role of the extended family, which is a tradition in the Mexican American culture, and the more frequent presence of the baby's father, must . . . make a difference." In addition, Mexicans have lower rates of drug use and relatively balanced diets (Guendleman 1994). Perhaps the favorable outcomes of Mexicans reflect their propensity to obtain at least some care during pregnancy despite numerous risk factors for not doing so. The multivariate results indicate that whites born in Mexico are actually at *reduced* risk of obtaining no prenatal care, implying that receiving some minimum amount of prenatal care may be even more important in some cases than obtaining early care.

This study has identified many factors that explain the poor prenatal care usage and birth outcomes of Puerto Ricans and non-Hispanic blacks in New Jersey. Reducing these risk factors and also the rates of no care and late care for these groups would improve birth outcomes. Other factors, such as diet, stress, and drug usage, also appear to be important but are unobserved. Resolution of the Mexican paradox and a better understanding of the role of culture on prenatal behavior might identify factors that significantly affect birth outcomes independently of prenatal care delay and poverty, as would the identification of factors underlying the association of Hispanic ethnicity and foreign birthplace with improved birth outcomes among blacks.

Whereas this study focused almost exclusively on New Jersey, there are lessons to be learned that have national implications. As indicated earlier, births to Hispanics have been increasing dramatically nationwide. This trend is expected to continue; thus, it is becoming increasingly important to understand patterns in birth outcomes within this heterogeneous community. This study revealed considerable variation in both prenatal care usage and low birthweight among different Hispanic subgroups. Some of the patterns revealed by this study, which unlike past research analyzed Cubans outside of South Florida and Mexicans outside of the Southwest, are consistent with findings by others. For example, Cuban whites were found to have favorable prenatal care usage relative to non-Hispanic whites, and Puerto Rican whites were found to be at high risk for delivering low birthweight babies relative to their non-Hispanic white counterparts. In contrast to past studies, however, Mexican-born women in New Jersey appear to have no birthweight advantage relative to other Mexicans of the same race, indicating that it is important to study groups in different locations. In general, the results underscore the importance of race, ethnicity, and maternal birthplace in targeting programs aimed at improving prenatal care usage and birth outcomes among the poor. The results also reinforce the strong association between many known risk factors and low birthweight. In particular, the results for smoking and hypertension have clear implications for the design of comprehensive prenatal care programs.

Notes

1. The term *Hispanic* generally refers to people from Spain, as well as those from other Spanish-speaking countries; however, for the purposes of this discussion, the terms *Hispanic* and *Latino* are used interchangeably to refer strictly to persons of Latin American descent.

2. The rate of low birthweight is generally defined as the percentage of all live births in which the infant weighed less than 2,500 grams (about 5½ pounds) at birth.

3. Since the time period covered by these studies, the Omnibus Budget Reconciliation Act (OBRA) of 1986 has mandated Medicaid coverage of labor and deliveries, but not

prenatal care, for financially eligible undocumented women. The finding of lower usage of prenatal care in the current study by some of the foreign-born women on Medicaid may reflect this OBRA 1986 provision.

4. There are additional racial classifications in the data: Asians, American Indians, and "Other." However, the number of American Indians is very small, and the lack of detailed birthplace information precludes a meaningful analysis for the other two groups.

5. The prenatal care measures in tables 8.2 and 8.3 were based on the month that care was initiated (ranging from one to nine plus a category for no prenatal care). Thus, the women in the first-trimester care group initiated care in months one, two, or three of their pregnancies. The *no care* women includes those who were reported as receiving no care.

6. Means for all of the risk factors discussed in this section are available upon request.

7. There has been some discussion in the literature about whether education and marital status belong in the birthweight equation in their own right, reflecting reproductive efficiency, or whether these measures work primarily through prenatal care (Corman and Grossman 1985; Joyce et al. 1992; Rosenzweig and Schultz 1982). In the reduced-form estimation, this issue does not come into play, since the determinants of the prenatal inputs, rather than the inputs themselves, are used. Therefore, both education and marital status are included in the birthweight equation.

8. The month of prenatal care initiation measure contained in the data ranges from one to nine, with a separate category indicating that the woman received no prenatal care. The prenatal care timing measure constructed for the present analysis grouped those reported as receiving no care with those initiating care in the ninth month.

9. These results apply to both black and white Mexicans. However, in the case of blacks, only foreign-born Mexicans were included in the analysis. Moreover, the sample size for this group, at 84 women, is relatively small. However, as there is no indication in these data that the paradox does not apply to blacks as well as whites, this discussion focuses on Mexicans of both races.

10. Unfortunately, this data set contains no direct measure of income. Instead, Medicaid and education were used as proxies for income in this analysis.

11. It is important to note that the risk factors are not held constant when making comparisons by race. Therefore, these risk factors should be examined carefully when making racial inferences from the present analysis. However, the full birthweight model (which contains smoking, alcohol, prenatal care delay, and weight gain) was run on the pooled black and white data, with a dichotomous variable for race. The results from this auxiliary regression indicate that the observed characteristics, such as marital status, teenage pregnancy, and insurance status, account for only 26 percent of the difference between the black and white mean birthweights.

12. The results clearly indicate that Puerto Rican whites are at high risk for poor prenatal care usage and adverse birth outcomes. Although the results also indicate that Puerto Rican blacks have favorable prenatal care usage and birth outcomes compared to U.S.-born non-Hispanic blacks, the descriptive statistics in tables 8.2 and 8.3 show that Puerto Rican blacks and Puerto Rican whites have similar prenatal care usage and birth outcomes. Thus, the policy implications in this section focus on all Puerto Ricans, and not just on Puerto Rican whites.

13. On February 1, 1988, the state of New Jersey inaugurated HealthStart, a special prenatal care program for pregnant women on Medicaid. This program includes outreach, outstationing, and other features intended to improve the use of prenatal care among Medicaid women in the state. A recent evaluation of the HealthStart program (Reichman and Florio forthcoming) has suggested that the program has been effective in reducing prenatal care delay and is associated with reduced rates of low birthweight among blacks.

References

Alexander, G., and C. Korenbrot. 1995. "The Role of Prenatal Care in Preventing Low Birth Weight." *The Future of Children* 5: 103–20.

Amaro, H., R. Whitaker, G. Coffman, and T. Heeren. 1990. "Acculturation and Marijuana and Cocaine Use: Findings from HHANES 1982–1984." *American Journal of Public Health 80* (suppl): 54–60.

Becerra, J., C. Hogue, H. Atrash, and N. Perez. 1991. "Infant Mortality among Hispanics: A Portrait of Heterogeneity." *Journal of the American Medical Association* 265: 217–21.

Becker, G., and H. Lewis. 1973. "On the Interaction between the Quantity and Quality of Children. *Journal of Political Economy* 81: S279–88.

Borjas, G. 1994. "The Economics of Immigration." *Journal of Economic Literature* 32: 1667–1717.

Chaikind, S., and H. Corman. 1991. "The Impact of Low Birthweight on Special Education Costs." *Journal of Health Economics* 10: 291–311.

Cooper, M. 1992. "Infant Mortality: Why Is the U.S. Death Rate High Compared with Other Nations?" *CQ Researcher* 2: 641–64.

Corman, H., and M. Grossman. 1985. "Determinants of Neonatal Mortality Rates in the U.S." *Journal of Health Economics* 4: 213–36.

Corman, H., Joyce, T., and M. Grossman. 1987. "Birth Outcome Production Functions in the United States." *Journal of Human Resources* 22: 339–60.

Council on Scientific Affairs. 1991. "Hispanic Health in the United States." *Journal of the American Medical Association* 265: 248–52.

Delgado, J. 1993. "Improving Data Collection Strategies." In *One Voice, One Vision—Recommendations to the Surgeon General to Improve Hispanic/Latino Health.* Washington, D.C.: U.S. Department of Health and Human Services, Public Health Service, June.

Delgado, J., and L. Estrada. 1993. "Improving Data Collection Strategies." *Public Health Reports* 108: 540–45.

Felice, M., M. Shragg, M. James, and D. Hollingworth. 1986. "Clinical Observations of Mexican American, Caucasian, and Black Pregnant Teenagers." *Journal of Adolescent Health Care* 7: 305–10.

Frank, R., D. Strobino, D. Salkever, and C. Jackson. 1992. "Updated Estimates of the Impact of Prenatal Care on Birthweight Outcomes by Race." Journal of Human Resources 27: 629–42.

Grossman, M., and T. Joyce. 1990. "Unobservables, Pregnancy Resolutions, and Birthweight Production Functions in New York City." *Journal of Political Economy* 98: 983–1007.

Guendleman, S. 1994. "Mexican Women in the United States." *Lancet* 344: 352.

Guendleman S., J. Gould, M. Hudes, and B. Eskenazi. 1990. "Generational Differences in Perinatal Health among the Mexican American Population: Findings from HHANES, 1982–84." *American Journal of Public Health* 80 (suppl.): 61–65.

Guttmacher, A. 1986. *Pregnancy, Birth, and Family Planning: The Definitive Work.* New York: E. P. Dutton.

Hack, M., N. Klein, and H. Taylor. 1995. "Long Term Developmental Outcomes of Low Birthweight Infants." *The Future of Children* 5(1): 176–96.

Haynes S., C. Harvey, H. Montes, H. Nickens, and B. Cohen. 1990. "Patterns of Cigarette Smoking among Hispanics in the United States: Results from HHANES, 1982–84. *American Journal of Public Health* 80 (suppl.): 47–53.

"Increasing Incidence of Low Birthweight—United States, 1981–91." 1994. *Morbidity and Mortality Weekly Report* 43(18): 335–39.

Joyce, T. 1987a. "The Demand for Health Inputs and Their Impact on the Black Neonatal Mortality Rate in the U.S." *Social Science and Medicine* 24: 911–18.

————. 1987b. "The Impact of Induced Abortion on Black and White Birth Outcomes in the U.S." *Demography* 24: 229–44.

Joyce, T., and M. Grossman. 1990a. "The Dynamic Relationship between Low Birthweight and Induced Abortion in New York City: An Aggregate Time-Series Analysis." *Journal of Health Economics* 9: 273–88.

————. 1990b. "Pregnancy Wantedness and the Early Initiation of Prenatal Care." *Demography* 27: 1–17.

Joyce, T., A. Racine, and N. Mocan. 1992. "The Consequences and Costs of Maternal Substance Abuse in New York City: A Pooled Time-Series, Cross-Section Analysis. *Journal of Health Economics* 11: 297-314.

Lemann, N. 1991. "The Other Underclass." *Atlantic Monthly* 268: 96–110.

Marks, G., M. Garcia, and J. Solis. 1990. "Health Risk Behaviors of Hispanics in the United States: Findings from HHANES, 1982–84." *American Journal of Public Health* 80 (suppl.): 20–26.

Mason, J. 1991. "Reducing Infant Mortality in the United States through 'Healthy Start.' " *Public Health Reports* 106: 479–83.

Mendoza, F. 1994. "The Health of Latino Children in the United States." *The Future of Children* 4: 43–72.

Mendoza, F., S. Ventura, L. Saldivar, K. Baisden, and R. Martorell. 1992. "The Health Status of U.S. Hispanic Children." In *Health Policy and the Hispanic,* edited by A. Furino. Boulder, Colo.: Westview Press.

Mendoza, F., S. Ventura, R. Valdez, R. Castillo, L. Saldivar, K. Baisden, and R. Martorell. 1991. "Selected Measures of Health Status for Mexican-American, Mainland Puerto Rican, and Cuban-American Children." *Journal of the American Medical Association* 265: 227–32.

Moore P., and J. Hepworth. 1994. "Use of Perinatal and Infant Health Services by Mexican-American Medicaid Enrollees." *Journal of the American Medical Association* 272: 297–304.

New Jersey Department of Labor. 1995. *Characteristics of Persons in New Jersey.* New Jersey State Data Center.

Passel, B., and J. Edmonston. 1994. "Ethnic Demography: U.S. Immigration and Ethnic Variations." In *Immigration and Ethnicity: The Integration of America's Newest Arrivals,* edited by B. Edmonston and J. Passel. Washington D.C.: Urban Institute Press.

Reichman, N., and M. Florio. Forthcoming. "The Effects of Enriched Prenatal Care Services on Medicaid Birth Outcomes in New Jersey." *Journal of Health Economics* (forthcoming).

Rosenzweig, M., and T. Schultz. 1982. "The Behavior of Mothers as Inputs to Child Health: The Determinants of Birth Weight." In *Economic Aspects of Health,* edited by Victor R. Fuchs (53–93). Chicago: University of Chicago Press, for the National Bureau of Economic Research.

————. 1983. "Estimating a Household Production Function: Heterogeneity, the Demand for Health Inputs, and Their Effects on Birth Weight." *Journal of Political Economy* 91: 723–46.

————. 1988. "The Stability of Household Production Technology: A Replication." *Journal of Human Resources* 23: 535–49.

Rumbaut, R., and J. Weeks. 1989. "Infant Health among Indochinese Refugees: Patterns of Infant Mortality, Birthweight, and Prenatal Care in Comparative Perspective." *Research in the Sociology of Health Care* 8: 137–96.

Solis, J., G. Marks, M. Garcia, and D. Shelton. 1990. "Acculturation, Access to Care, and Use of Preventive Services by Hispanics: Findings from HHANES, 1982–84." *American Journal of Public Health* 80 (suppl.): 11–19.

Stroup-Benham, C., and F. Trevino. 1991. "Reproductive Characteristics of Mexican-American, Mainland Puerto Rican, and Cuban-American Women: Data from the Hispanic Health and Nutrition Examination Survey." *Journal of the American Medical Association* 265: 222–26.

Trevino, F., M. Moyer, R. Valdez, and C. Stroup-Benham. 1991. "Health Insurance Coverage and Utilization of Health Services by Mexican Americans, Mainland Puerto Ricans, and Cuban-Americans." *Journal of the American Medical Association* 265: 233–37.

U.S. Bureau of the Census. 1995. *Statistical Abstract of the United States.* Washington, D.C.: Author.

U.S. Congress, House. 1994. Subcommittee on Census and Population of the Committee on Post Office and Civil Service. *America's Changing Profile: Hearing before the Subcommittee on Census and Population of the Committee on Post Office and Civil Service.* 102d Cong. 2d sess. (May–September 1992), Serial No. 102-64. Washington D.C.: U.S. Government Printing Office.

U.S. Department of Health and Human Services. 1990. *Healthy People 2000: National Health Promotion and Disease Prevention Objectives.* Pub.

No. (PHS) 91-50212. U.S. Public Health Service. Office of the Assistant Secretary for Health, Office of Disease Prevention and Health Promotion. Washington D.C.: U.S. Government Printing Office.

Warren, R., and J. Passel. 1987. "A Count of the Uncountable: Estimates of Undocumented Aliens Counted in the 1980 United States Census." *Demography* 24: 375–93.

Willis, R. 1973. "A New Approach to the Economic Theory of Fertility Behavior." *Journal of Political Economy* 81: S14–S64.

Chapter Nine

MIGRANTS AND SETTLERS: POLITICAL OPPORTUNITIES AND POLITICAL BEHAVIORS AMONG NEW JERSEY IMMIGRANTS

Louis DeSipio

The rapid increase in immigration to the United States over the past 30 years has caused some scholars and elected leaders to question both the political loyalty and political adaptability of these new immigrants. Concerns about immigrant loyalty are not new in American political history. Each large wave of immigration has engendered similar concerns and has challenged the political order to ensure the incorporation of new Americans (Fuchs 1990). Unlike previous periods of high immigration, however, the incorporation of today's immigrants can be studied while the process is occurring.

The locus of much of this political adaptation is communities where immigrants reside. Many of the opportunities for community activity and political involvement are shaped locally. Thus, scholars can not only investigate contemporary political adaptation as it occurs, but they can also identify variations that speed or slow the process. To the extent that local- or state-level scholarship on immigrant political adaptation exists, it has focused on the Southwest, Miami, and New York City (de la Garza, Menchaca, and DeSipio 1994; Lamphere 1992; Moore and Pinderhughes 1994). This scholarly neglect of other immigrant-receiving areas is unfortunate because these less-studied areas offer lessons not available in the regions that have received the overwhelming majority of recent immigrants. New Jersey, for example, offers a unique laboratory to examine immigrant political adaptation. Its immigrant population includes both recent- and long-term immigrants. Their origins are diverse, with no one nation or region dominating the pool. Finally, their numbers are sufficiently large that New Jersey immigrants, including those who comprise the newer immigrant populations, have been able to influence the outcomes of electoral politics.

The need to examine the state impact of immigration results from the vast expansion and diversification of the immigrant flow that began in 1965, with changes to the 1952 Immigration and Nationality Act. Most immigrants prior to 1965 came from Europe; after 1965, with the abolishment of the national origins quota system, Latin America and Asia dominated the flow. The 1965 act also established family unification as the guiding principle of U.S. immigration law. This principle has allowed a steady increase in the number of immigrants arriving in the United States each year. In the 1990s, between 700,000 and 900,000 immigrants arrive annually to establish permanent residence in the United States (U.S. Immigration and Naturalization Service 1996). Although this annual level of immigration dipped slightly in 1994 and 1995, it will not decline dramatically without statutory change.[1] After five years (three years if married to a U.S. citizen), these immigrants become eligible for naturalization.

This change in the source and numbers of immigrants has spurred extensive academic and public policy debate, particularly regarding the economic contributions of immigrants, the skills and knowledge they bring to the United States, and the consequences of this immigration for the United States (Borjas 1990; Bouvier and Grant 1994; Brimelow 1995; Fuchs 1990; Jasso and Rosenzweig 1990; Simon 1989). Scholarship on other forms of immigrant political, linguistic, and social adaptation has been less voluminous (Edmonston and Passel 1994; Gutiérrez 1995; Pachon and DeSipio 1994).

This chapter examines the political adaptation of contemporary immigrants in New Jersey. To investigate this process, I focus on three categories of political attitudes and behaviors among newer immigrants—political attachment and naturalization, community-level nonelectoral politics, and electoral politics. I find that immigrants to New Jersey are demonstrating attitudinal and behavioral attachments to U.S. politics, including some forms of local, mostly nonelectoral, political activity. Low levels of U.S. citizenship acquisition, however, preclude electoral activity.

THE FOREIGN BORN IN NEW JERSEY

New Jersey has long been a part of U.S. immigration history. In fact, Ellis Island sits, in part, on land to which New Jersey lays claim. The island's ambiguous relationship to the states of New York and New Jersey will likely be resolved soon by the U.S. Supreme Court. In 1990

New Jersey had the fifth highest number of foreign-born residents of any state in the nation (see table 9.1). Aside from their sheer numbers, the foreign born in New Jersey are interesting for several other reasons. New Jersey's immigrants are heterogeneous in origin, they consist of both recent immigrants and longer-term residents, and they are dispersed throughout the state. Thus, unlike the more frequently studied immigrants of California and Texas, New Jersey's immigrants are much more a cross section of 20th-century immigration to the United States. This section of the chapter describes the state's foreign-born residents as a background to a discussion of their political attitudes and political behaviors.

As Western and Kelly note in chapter 2 of this volume, New Jersey's foreign-born population is unique in that it traces its origins to all parts of the world. These diverse origins create a heterogeneous racial and ethnic mix among the foreign born in New Jersey. According to the U.S. Bureau of the Census (1993b), nearly 60 percent of New Jersey's foreign born are white, 21 percent are Asian, and 10 percent are black. Approximately 30 percent report that they are of Hispanic origin. If national trends hold, between 80 percent and 90 percent of Hispanics report themselves to be racially white, approximately 10 percent to be black, and the remainder as racially mixed. Thus, New Jersey's immigrants are roughly equally divided between whites of primarily European origin, Hispanics, and Asians. This contrasts sharply with most other large immigrant-receiving states where one racial or ethnic population dominates.

The racial and ethnic diversity of New Jersey's immigrants is reflected also in their national origins. Fully 28 countries composed 1 percent or more of New Jersey's 1990 foreign-born population (see table 9.2). Ten of these countries are in Europe and 6 are in Asia. Of the 12 in the Americas, 7 are in Spanish-speaking Latin America, and 5 are non–Latin American. The 3 countries of origin with the most

Table 9.1 STATES WITH FIVE LARGEST FOREIGN-BORN POPULATIONS: 1990

State	Foreign-Born Population	Percentage of State Foreign Born	Number Naturalized	Percentage of Immigrants Naturalized
California	6,458,825	21.7	2,017,610	31.2
New York	2,851,861	15.9	1,297,020	45.5
Florida	1,662,601	12.9	713,505	42.9
Texas	1,524,436	7.6	515,190	33.8
New Jersey	966,610	12.5	470,936	48.7

Source: U.S. Bureau of the Census (1993b).

Table 9.2 COUNTRIES OF ORIGIN COMPOSING 1 PERCENT OR MORE OF NEW
JERSEY'S FOREIGN-BORN POPULATION: 1990

Place of Birth	Number	Percentage	Rank Order, Top Ten
Europe			
Germany	51,234	5.3	4
Greece	14,056	1.5	
Hungary	10,219	1.1	
Ireland	14,716	1.5	
Italy	74,820	7.7	1
Poland	40,280	4.2	7
Portugal	35,703	3.7	10
Spain	10,196	1.1	
United Kingdom	37,718	3.9	8
Soviet Union	19,680	2.0	
Asia			
China	17,729	1.8	
India	52,918	5.5	3
Japan	15,232	1.6	
Korea	31,086	3.2	
Philippines	40,488	4.2	6
Taiwan	13,842	1.4	
North America			
Canada	17,759	1.8	
Cuba	63,415	6.6	2
Dominican Republic	36,582	3.8	9
El Salvador	13,673	1.4	
Haiti	15,961	1.7	
Jamaica	21,351	2.2	
Mexico	13,422	1.4	
South America			
Brazil	10,133	1.0	
Colombia	42,339	4.4	5
Ecuador	21,839	2.3	
Guyana	10,028	1.0	
Peru	21,239	2.2	
Africa (none)			
Oceania (none)			

Source: U.S. Bureau of the Census (1992).
Notes: Table excludes individuals born abroad of American parents. Although such
individuals were born abroad, they were U.S. citizens at birth and did not have the
traditional experiences of immigrants. The (former) Soviet Union includes the following
geopolitical entities: Armenia, Azerbaijan, Byelarus, Georgia, Kazakhstan, Kyrgyzstan,
Moldavia, Russia, Tajikistan, Turkmenistan, Ukraine, and Uzbekistan.

New Jersey residents—Italy, Cuba, and India—are also geographically dispersed.

This diversity of origins also appears in a quick examination of countries of origin of U.S. immigrants who upon arrival in 1993 reported to the U.S. Immigration and Naturalization Service (INS) that they would be residing in New Jersey.[2] In 1993, the country sending the largest numbers of immigrants to New Jersey was the Dominican Republic (see table 9.3). This country's 5,176 emigrants accounted for just 10 percent of the 50,285 who reported that they would reside in New Jersey. Four other countries provided 5 percent or more of New Jersey's 1993 immigrants. Three were Asian—China, India, and the Philippines—and one European—Poland. With the exception of Africa and Oceania, whose countries sent only small numbers of emigrants to New Jersey, all continents are represented in the contemporary flow of immigrants to the state.

Western and Kelly (chapter 2, table 2.3) highlight a second characteristic of New Jersey's foreign-born population—namely, that it includes both recent and long-term immigrants. Many of New Jersey's foreign born of European origin arrived before 1965. Asians and Latin Americans, on the other hand, tend to be more recent immigrants, with the majority arriving after 1975. There are exceptions to these broad generalizations. Whereas Cubans are a continuing part of the immigrant flow to New Jersey, they do not follow the patterns of other Latin American immigrants; large numbers of Cubans arrived in the 1960s and early 1970s (Rogg 1974). Nor are all European immigrants long-term residents of the United States. The states of the former Soviet Union, Poland, and Ireland have sent increasing numbers of migrants in recent years to the United States. As table 9.3 indicates, these countries provide an important share of today's immigrants to New Jersey as well.

This mixture of old and new immigrants gives New Jersey the highest naturalization rate of the five states with large foreign-born populations (table 9.1). Almost half of New Jersey's immigrants are naturalized citizens. New York, which also has a mixture of old and new immigrants, has a similarly high naturalization rate.

This heterogeneity also appears in the wide disparity in naturalization rates by race and ethnicity. Slightly more than 57 percent of the white foreign-born New Jerseyites had become naturalized (see table 9.4). Blacks, Asians, and Latinos, all of whom have high percentages among the recent immigrants, have naturalization rates in the 30 to 40 percent range. Factors that influence these different rates are discussed later in the chapter. For now, however, it is important

Table 9.3 COUNTRY OF ORIGIN OF NEW IMMIGRANTS TO NEW JERSEY AND SELECTED METROPOLITAN STATISTICAL AREAS: FISCAL YEAR 1993

	New Jersey		Newark MSA		Bergen-Passaic MSA		Jersey City MSA		Middlesex-Somerset-Hunterdon MSA	
	Number	%	Number	%	Number	%	Number	%	Number	%
Total Intended Immigration	50,285		13,551		12,931		8,754		7,371	
Canada	437	0.9	145	1.1	58	0.4	12	0.1	79	1.1
China	2,548	5.1	511	3.8	381	2.9	336	3.8	818	11.1
Colombia	2,170	4.3	715	5.3	736	5.7	441	5.0	126	1.7
Cuba	783	1.6	158	1.2	43	0.3	535	6.1	23	0.3
Dominican Republic	5,176	10.3	675	5.0	1,970	15.2	1,456	16.6	762	10.3
Ecuador	1,265	2.5	416	3.1	227	1.8	511	5.8	56	0.8
El Salvador	923	1.8	330	2.4	135	1.0	362	4.1	41	0.6
Germany	225	0.4	67	0.5	42	0.3	9	0.1	36	0.5
Guatemala	485	1.0	148	1.1	73	0.6	96	1.1	50	0.7
Guyana	710	1.4	375	2.8	65	0.5	179	2.0	60	0.8
Haiti	970	1.9	768	5.7	31	0.2	56	0.6	13	0.2
Honduras	480	1.0	126	0.9	60	0.5	192	2.2	53	0.7

Hong Kong	355	0.7	83	0.6	49	0.4	34	0.4	120	1.6
India	4,725	9.4	818	6.0	892	6.9	829	9.5	1,450	19.7
Iran	221	0.4	49	0.4	88	0.7	12	0.1	31	0.4
Ireland	1,012	2.0	218	1.6	304	2.4	125	1.4	86	1.2
Jamaica	1,138	2.3	470	3.5	351	2.7	26	0.3	92	1.2
Korea	1,069	2.1	148	1.1	573	4.4	50	0.6	113	1.5
Mexico	462	0.9	69	0.5	158	1.2	72	0.8	51	0.7
Pakistan	619	1.2	105	0.8	110	0.9	98	1.1	149	2.0
Peru	2,073	4.1	534	3.9	893	6.9	362	4.1	166	2.3
Philippines	4,637	9.2	1,216	9.0	911	7.0	1,090	12.5	640	8.7
Poland	3,887	7.7	1,078	8.0	1,586	12.3	318	3.6	406	5.5
Soviet Union	1,875	3.7	693	5.1	439	3.4	93	1.1	276	3.7
Taiwan	927	1.8	263	1.9	149	1.2	61	0.7	265	3.6
United Kingdom	950	1.9	244	1.8	166	1.3	61	0.7	167	2.3
Vietnam	937	1.9	233	1.7	25	0.2	129	1.5	88	1.2
Other	9,226	18.3	2,896	21.4	2,416	18.7	1,209	13.8	1,154	15.7

Source: U.S. Immigration and Naturalization Service (1994: tables 17 and 19).

Notes: Data are based on the intended state and city of residence as reported by immigrants to the United States. The U.S. Immigration and Naturalization Service does not require that immigrants report any subsequent changes in residence. Columns may not add up to 100 due to rounding.

Table 9.4 NATURALIZATION RATES FOR RACIAL AND ETHNIC GROUPS AMONG
NEW JERSEY'S FOREIGN BORN: 1990

Racial/ Ethnic Group	Total Foreign Born	Percentage of New Jersey Foreign-Born Population	Number Naturalized	Percentage Naturalized
White	579,022	59.9	334,083	57.7
Black	92,856	9.6	31,709	34.1
Asian	198,923	20.6	78,088	39.3
American Indian	1,667	0.2	458	27.5
Other	94,142	9.7	26,598	28.3
Hispanic[a]	290,627	30.1	101,146	34.8
New Jersey	966,610		470,936	48.7

Source: U.S. Bureau of the Census (1993b).
a. Hispanics can be of any race. Traditionally, between 80 and 90 percent of Hispanics nationally are classified in racial terms as white and the remainder are black. In 1990, an increasing number of Hispanic respondents indicated that they were of mixed race.

to note that the political opportunities available to the foreign born in New Jersey vary considerably for different nationality groups depending on their citizenship status. Analytically, the political behaviors of the long-term residents also present a problem. Over time, their political behaviors have become largely indistinguishable from those of second- and third-generation immigrants whose political behaviors do not regularly have a clear ethnic dimension (Alba 1990; Fuchs 1990). As a result, I examine the political attitudes and behaviors of immigrant populations who arrived in the 1960s and thereafter.

The final background characteristic of New Jersey's foreign-born population relates to its dispersion throughout the state (see figure 2.1 in Western and Kelly, chapter 2). Four of the state's 21 counties have 20 percent or more foreign-born residents. One—Hudson County—is more than one-third foreign born. Just 12 counties have less than 10 percent foreign born. Of the counties with the greatest concentrations of foreign-born residents, 5 are in the northeastern corner of the state—Hudson, Passaic, Union, Bergen, and Essex counties. Just one—Middlesex county—is in the center of the state. These high-concentration counties are analytically important not just for the density of the foreign-born population but also because they are the destination of the majority of contemporary immigrants to the state. As table 9.3 indicates, these areas received approximately two-thirds of New Jersey's immigrants in 1993. This high-concentration, immigrant-receiving region of the state is the area most likely to see political activity among the new immigrant groups. As I will suggest, this area, and particularly Hudson County, has seen the highest levels of immigrant politics.

In sum, New Jersey has a higher number of foreign-born residents than all but four other states. New Jersey is unique among the top five, however, in that its foreign-born population is diverse along several dimensions. No one nation or region dominates the flow of immigrants to the state. Their numbers include both immigrants from earlier eras of immigration as well as contemporary immigrants, and immigration to the state is not concentrated in a major city, but, instead, in a region of the state. These factors make study of immigrant political behavior difficult, but at the same time create opportunities for immigrants to express themselves in the political arena. The following discussion highlights these opportunities and explores how immigrants are responding.

NATURALIZATION AND POLITICAL ATTACHMENT AMONG NEW JERSEY IMMIGRANTS

One primary measure of political attachment among immigrants is their formal attachment to the United States by becoming U.S. citizens (DeSipio and de la Garza 1992). Naturalization offers a status virtually indistinguishable from that of the native born. With the two exceptions of not being able to serve as president and the rare possibility of denaturalization if a court finds that the applicant lied in his or her naturalization application, naturalized U.S. citizens are entitled to all the rights and privileges of the native born. Despite this opportunity, many New Jersey immigrants have not become naturalized. This raises the question of whether immigrants desire attachment to the United States. Although there is no single answer to this question, the results of two surveys to be discussed here indicated a high level of political loyalty to the United States among immigrants and, equally important, revealed that many more immigrants desire citizenship than are able to achieve this goal (de la Garza et al. 1992; Pachon and DeSipio 1994). The remainder of this section discusses possible reasons for the gap between immigrant attachment to the United States and successful completion of naturalization.

Several examples I offer come from the Latino community. This reflects my own research interests, as well as the fact that Latinos have been by far the most studied (DeSipio 1987, 1996b; Pachon 1987).

Immigrant Attachment to the United States

Although there is no comprehensive survey of immigrant political attitudes, two recent surveys of Latino political attitudes and behaviors offer insights into immigrant attachment to the United States. These surveys[3]—the 1988 National Latino Immigrant Survey (NLIS) (Pachon and DeSipio 1994)[4] and the 1989–90 Latino National Political Survey (LNPS) (de la Garza et al. 1992)[5]—have indicated that Latino immigrants develop an attachment to the United States and to U.S. political values relatively quickly after their arrival. These national patterns of attachment to the United States appeared to be even stronger among New Jersey Latino[6] immigrants than among Latino immigrants nationally.

The great majority of Latino immigrants surveyed nationally and all of the survey respondents in New Jersey reported that they intended to make the United States their permanent home. More than 97 percent of NLIS respondents reported that they "presently plan to make the United States their permanent home." In New Jersey, all 129 answered in the affirmative. Residential intentions alone, of course, do not reflect political attachment. Latino immigrants also indicated that they have very positive attitudes toward life in the United States. Both in New Jersey and nationally, 79 percent reported that life is better here than in their countries of origin. Moreover, they expected their children's lives to be better than their own; approximately 90 percent of parents, both nationally and in New Jersey, expressed this view.

Nonnaturalized immigrants also expressed strong attachment to the United States. On one indicator—the answer to the question of whether life is better in the United States or in the country of origin—nonnaturalized New Jersey Latino immigrants proved to be more strongly attached. Fully 87 percent reported that life was better in the United States. This rate was somewhat higher than the 80 percent of Latino denizens nationally who gave that response.

A final indication of this emerging attachment to the United States is found in the LNPS. Nearly 60 percent of New Jersey foreign-born Latinos (almost all Cubans) reported an "extremely strong" love for the United States. Just 4 percent reported that this feeling of attachment was not very strong. These New Jersey rates represented stronger feelings for the United States than among Latino immigrants nationally, where 25 percent reported extremely strong feelings for the United States and 8 percent reported "not very strong" love. Among the nonnaturalized New Jersey respondents, reported levels of love for the United States were not quite as high, with 50 percent reporting extremely strong feelings and 6 percent reporting not very strong feelings. In sum, New Jersey's Latino immigrants—whether naturalized or not—reported that they were attached to the United States and see their lives as evolving in this country.

A final measure is perhaps the most compelling indicator of attachment to the United States. Both surveys asked respondents whether their primary political attachments lie with their country of origin or the United States. As might be predicted, the NLIS found that nationally the noncitizens were more likely to report allegiance to their countries of origin than to the United States. The ratio was about 2:1 (61 percent to 33 percent). Interestingly, a majority of noncitizen Latinos in New Jersey reported a stronger attachment to the United States than to their home countries (58 percent to 33 percent). Thus, not only do New Jersey Latino noncitizens express a generalized attachment to life in the United States, but the majority also reported a political attachment.

Although there are no data on which to base similar claims for non-Latino immigrants in New Jersey, these findings indicate a strong attachment, affection, and even budding loyalty to the United States among Latino immigrants. Clearly, the interests and incentives for naturalization vary from immigrant to immigrant and, by extension, from immigrant community to immigrant community. Latino naturalization rates in New Jersey, however, are comparable to those of immigrants from other regions of the world (although they are lower than those of Europeans, who have been resident in the United States for much longer than other immigrant groups). Consequently, it is not unreasonable to assume that these levels of affinity to the United States are matched in other immigrant populations.

Naturalization in New Jersey Immigrant Communities

Despite this apparent attachment, several measures indicate that many eligible immigrants in New Jersey have not naturalized. Table 9.4 shows that approximately half of New Jersey's foreign-born population had naturalized. This figure is misleading, however. It shows the percentage naturalized of *all* immigrants. Some of these immigrants are ineligible, such as those with fewer than five years of legal residence, undocumented immigrants, and children (unless the parent seeks naturalization). The INS does not keep records that enable one to determine how many naturalization-eligible immigrants are present in the United States at any time because it does not maintain records of permanent-resident immigrants who emigrate or die; thus, it is not possible to construct a percentage naturalized of eligible immigrants. (Liang [1994] has developed an estimate for emigration and mortality among 1973 emigrants). With these limitations in mind, table 9.5 reports naturalization rates among New Jersey's foreign born, by county. These data demonstrate that the counties with the highest share of foreign born have the lowest levels of naturalized citizens. This finding is not surprising; however, the counties with the largest share of foreign-born residents are those receiving the largest numbers of new immigrants, who are the least likely to naturalize. This phenomenon influences political behaviors. In these counties where immigrants' numbers offer the greatest likelihood of political influence, high rates of noncitizenship limit the practical political influence they can have.

The survey data on Latino immigrants offer a more precise indication of true naturalization rates. The NLIS found that approximately 52 percent of New Jersey's eligible Latino immigrants have natural-

Table 9.5 NEW JERSEY ADULT NATURALIZATION RATE, BY COUNTY: 1990

County	Total Adult Foreign Born	Total Naturalized	Percentage Naturalized
Atlantic	12,235	7,394	60.4
Bergen	135,028	74,240	55.0
Burlington	17,852	11,148	62.4
Camden	20,818	12,407	59.6
Cape May	2,305	1,638	71.1
Cumberland	5,818	3,976	68.3
Essex	108,702	47,583	43.8
Gloucester	6,403	4,348	67.9
Hudson	153,929	66,066	42.9
Hunterdon	5,090	3,323	65.3
Mercer	25,809	13,563	52.6
Middlesex	86,553	44,591	51.5
Monmouth	39,126	24,926	63.7
Morris	40,940	22,650	55.3
Ocean	25,419	19,771	77.8
Passaic	78,599	35,968	45.8
Salem	1,265	896	70.8
Somerset	24,829	14,066	56.7
Sussex	5,904	4,037	68.4
Union	82,994	40,657	49.0
Warren	3,556	2,308	64.9
Statewide	883,174	455,556	51.6

Source: U.S. Bureau of the Census (1993a).

ized. Nationally, just 34 percent of eligible Latino immigrants have naturalized. It is not possible to say if these higher-than-average naturalization rates among eligible New Jersey Latino immigrants can be applied to the unadjusted rates for other immigrant populations.

PREDICTORS OF NATURALIZATION

There are several possible reasons for these levels of citizenship attainment. The first is perhaps the most obvious, but is also the most often overlooked in the scholarship on naturalization: the longer an immigrant has resided in the United States, the higher the likelihood of naturalization. The second explanation pertains to the individual characteristics of immigrants. Certain sociodemographic traits, immigration characteristics, and associational patterns have been found to increase the likelihood of naturalization. Finally, a third explanation relates to the administration of naturalization. Many immigrants who are interested in seeking U.S. citizenship and who have taken steps toward that are deterred by the INS's administration of naturalization. Although no single factor explains the gap between attachment to the United States and low levels of citizenship, taken as a whole, these factors present a picture of immigrant populations with higher levels of interest in joining the polity than raw naturalization rates suggest.

The initial scholarship on naturalization posited that cultural differences among various nationalities influenced the potential for Americanization. Early scholars of U.S. naturalization assumed that Southern and Eastern Europeans were less able to become Americans than were Northern and Western Europeans. These assumptions were not rigorously tested, and for approximately 20 years they dominated the popular understanding of who naturalized and who did not (U.S. Immigration Commission 1911). Beginning in the 1920s, however, scholars more carefully began to examine the propensity to naturalize and found that length of residence explained most differences in nationality—and regional—naturalization rates (Gavit 1971 [1922]). On average, nationalities that had been in the United States for the longest average periods had the highest naturalization rates. Thus, nationality differences explained little, at least for turn-of-the-century immigrants. This finding appears to hold for New Jersey immigrants. As I have indicated, the group with the highest naturalization rates— Europeans—has lived in New Jersey the longest. Among Latinos, Cubans were the most likely to have naturalized; they have lived in New Jersey the longest.

Bernard (1936) initiated a second wave of scholarship by assessing individual socioeconomic differences as predictors of naturalization. What factors distinguish immigrants who naturalize from those who do not? Although there is no comprehensive national study of immigrants, several recent studies (each relying on different pools of immigrants) have identified clusters of factors—sociodemographic characteristics, attitudinal and associational traits, and immigration characteristics—that supplement length of residence as a predictor of naturalization. All naturalization scholars to some degree look at the sociodemographic characteristics of immigrants (Barkan and Khokolov 1980; DeSipio 1996b; Jasso and Rosenzweig 1990; Portes and Mozo 1985; Yang 1994). These include such factors as higher incomes, white-collar employment, professional status, homeownership, years of education, and English-language abilities. The married are more likely to naturalize than the unmarried, and women more likely than men.

Certain immigration experiences appear to influence naturalization as well (DeSipio 1996b). Immigrants who arrived as young children were more likely to naturalize than are those who arrived in the United States as teenagers or adults. Also, immigrants who migrated to the United States for political reasons were more likely to naturalize than those who migrated for economic reasons.

Other scholars find attitudinal and associational variables, such as roots in the United States, attitude toward life in the United States, and social identification as an American, to be positive predictors of naturalization (García 1981; Portes and Curtis 1987). Immigrants who associated mostly with noncitizens were less likely to naturalize (DeSipio 1996b). Immigrant community attitudes also influenced naturalization. Jones-Correa (1994) found that an "ideology of return [to the home country]" among organizational members discouraged naturalization among Latinos in Queens, New York.

The final category of variables relates to characteristics at the time of immigration that shape the settlement experience. Positive factors include visa categories, with immigrants who entered as refugees and skilled workers more likely to naturalize than other immigrants (Jasso and Rosenzweig 1985, 1990). Emigration for political reasons has also been found to increase the likelihood of naturalization (Jasso and Rosenzweig 1990; Portes and Mozo 1985). In light of these other factors that have a positive influence on naturalization, a rather counterintuitive finding by one scholar is that the higher the home country's per capita gross national product (GNP), the lower the likelihood of naturalization (Yang 1994). Although per capita GNP raises the opportunity costs of migrating to the United States, once that decision is made, these immigrants bring with them many of the sociodemographic traits (education, professional status, income, and, perhaps, English-language skills) that predict naturalization.

The study of characteristics at immigration has also reviewed national and regional origin differences. Jasso and Rosenzweig (1985) found that immigrants from Africa and Asia were more likely than average to naturalize, whereas immigrants from Mexico were less likely than average to naturalize. Portes and Mozo (1985) found that immigrants from Canada and Mexico were less likely to naturalize than nationals of other countries, controlling for sociodemographic factors. Finally, controlling for sociodemographic, associational, and immigration-related factors, DeSipio (1996b) has found that among Latinos, Cubans and Dominicans were more likely than Mexicans to begin the naturalization process and to become U.S. citizens.

These sociodemographic characteristics, immigration experiences, and associational characteristics that indicate a propensity to naturalize suggest that New Jersey immigrants will be somewhat more likely to naturalize than immigrants in other states. Although there is wide variation among New Jersey immigrants, the state attracts many immigrants with characteristics that predict naturalization. As Western and Kelly find in chapter 2, New Jersey receives many immigrants with high levels of formal education and professional occupations. The geographic dispersion of the immigrants increases the likelihood that immigrants will associate with U.S. citizens as well as non-U.S. citizens. Finally, Mexicans and Canadians comprise a small share of the state's immigrants. Thus, these findings predict that New Jersey will see higher rates of naturalization than are found in other states.

Each factor discussed so far varies from individual to individual. The final deterrent to naturalization—the administration process—influences some nationalities more than others and some geographic areas more than others. The administration of naturalization is highly decentralized, resulting in differing treatment of applicants from one INS district office to another. The impact of this administrative inconsistency is difficult to measure, but two recent studies of the INS's administration of the naturalization program demonstrate possible impacts (U.S. Immigration and Naturalization Service 1990; U.S. Congress 1988). First, immigrants from different countries and regions have different administrative denial rates (DeSipio and Pachon 1992). Overall, applicants from Latin America, the Spanish- and English-speaking Caribbean, and Africa have higher-than-average denial rates. Each of these regions sends large numbers of immigrants to New Jersey. This, in part, may reflect different immigrant skill and education levels, but also may reflect the INS's organizational culture in areas with high numbers of applications. Second, the variety of experiences of individual naturalization applicants who go before the INS may, in turn, lead to confusion in immigrant populations that could discourage some interested immigrants from seeking naturalization. Finally, some INS offices have higher-than-average rates of unsuccessful applicants. In both the 1988 and 1990 studies on the INS's administration of the naturalization program, the Newark INS district office was among the *most likely* to formally deny an application or to encourage the applicant to withdraw his or her application under threat of being denied. Almost one in three applicants who applied for naturalization in Newark did not succeed in their first effort. No studies of this question have been performed since 1990. The Newark district office plays a key role in the state's naturalization profile. If these patterns from the late 1980s continue, they suggest that New Jersey immigrants seeking naturalization would face greater administrative discouragement than immigrants in other states.

In sum, naturalization is far from automatic among immigrants interested in becoming U.S. citizens. The statutory requirements and bureaucratic administration make naturalization seem a difficult goal for many immigrants. One optimistic note for advocates of immigrant naturalization is that the incentive structure for naturalization may soon change. Provisions in the recently enacted Welfare Reform and Immigration legislation to deny social welfare benefits to noncitizens have combined with the anti-immigrant message of California's Proposition 187, as well as an administrative requirement to replace aging green cards, to bring about a national surge of naturalization applications (DeSipio 1996a). This surge has also been felt in New Jersey, where the INS has had to shift personnel from airport duties and extend hours to evenings and Saturdays to meet a record demand for naturalization (Peet 1995). Although future data will better reveal the long-term impact on naturalization among New Jersey residents, recently released INS data show the beginning of what could be a steady increase; naturalization increased from 16,598 in fiscal year (FY) 1992 to 18,495 in FY 1993 and to a record high of 24,618 in FY 1994 (U.S. Immigration and Naturalization Service 1996: table 50). Despite this unprecedented interest, however, naturalization's statutory requirements and INS's administration ensure that interest alone will not guarantee a successful outcome.

NEW JERSEY IMMIGRANT POLITICAL BEHAVIOR

The high level of non-U.S. citizenship among New Jersey's immigrant community complicates discussion about politics in traditional terms. Most discussions of politics in the United States focus on participation in U.S. elections, an activity prohibited to most non-U.S. citizens.[7] There are, nevertheless, other measures of interest in politics. Again, these examples are drawn almost exclusively from New Jersey's Latino community. Specifically, I examine two types of political activity among Latino immigrants based on the survey data— community organizational activity and forms of electoral politics for which immigrants are eligible. In the final subsection, I move away from the survey data to look at a specific example of community-level electoral politics, both as a way of suggesting the opportunities for immigrant political influence and of pointing out limitations on this political potential.

Community Organizational Activity

Throughout the history of U.S. immigration, one of the first manifestations of immigrant political activity has been local organizing to meet specific needs. These organizations often begin with a focus on the sending community or sending country and take the form of fraternal organizations designed to provide assistance to new immigrants or to those left in the home country. As the immigrants' awareness of the receiving community increases and their sense of political efficacy grows, they create or join organizations designed to meet local needs. These needs can be political—over the allocation of government resources—or fraternal. In either case, organizational membership shows a degree of engagement with U.S. political society.

Among the New Jersey Latino immigrants eligible for citizenship surveyed in the National Latino Immigrant Survey (Pachon and De-Sipio 1994), more than 80 percent were active in some form of community organizational activity, a rate slightly higher than that of Latino immigrants nationally (74 percent). The most common of these community activities was membership in a church. Admittedly, church membership is more a matter of faith than one of desire for collective activity. Excluding those New Jersey immigrants whose only community organizational membership is churches, the share who are active in their community drops to just over one-third (34 percent). The next most frequently mentioned community organiza-

tion among New Jersey immigrants was a parent-teacher organization.[8]
Others mentioned included social clubs, national origin clubs, and
unions. These community organizations can offer more than just solidarity; they offer the opportunity for inter-ethnic contact. Both nationally and in New Jersey, however, this did not occur. Most non-
church organizations to which Latino immigrants belonged have
memberships that are majority Latino.

Approximately one-third of New Jersey Latino immigrants, then,
were active in nonelectoral organizations in their communities. Although these rates may indicate a distance from politics, they could
also indicate a core of immigrants who are developing an awareness
of needs beyond their own. In terms of potential mobilization, these
community group members offer an easy target for communitywide
naturalization efforts.

Individual Political Activity

In terms of the broad range of electoral political activities, not being
a U.S. citizen precludes few activities—noncitizens cannot vote and
cannot stand for office. As voting and holding office are the ends of
much work in electoral politics, many immigrants may well choose
not to participate in other forms of electoral political activity. Interestingly, despite these limitations, immigrants are involved in a variety of individual political activities. I examine two categories of activity here: first, political activities in the countries of origin; and,
second, electoral activities other than voting in U.S. elections.

Activity in elections abroad offers one possible insight into the
potential for activity in the United States. Previous activity could
serve as a learning experience for types of political activism or as a
lesson for the efficacy of political involvement. These data, from the
National Latino Immigrant Survey (Pachon and DeSipio 1994), should
be viewed with some caution because the opportunities for political
involvement varied considerably in the Latin American countries of
origin. Overall, more than two-thirds of foreign-born residents of New
Jersey who immigrated to the United States as adults participated in
the politics of their home countries. These activities ranged from the
relatively passive—following politics in the news (51 percent)—to the
more complex—participating in a march (49 percent). Few (4 percent)
reported that they had voted in their home countries. The nonnaturalized were slightly less likely to report that they had followed
politics in the news and marched than were the naturalized. The
home-country participation rates for New Jersey immigrants—citizen

and noncitizen alike—were significantly higher than was the national average for Latinos in the NLIS (Pachon and DeSipio 1994: table 5.9).

Among New Jersey's noncitizens, nearly 73 percent engaged in U.S. electoral politics in some manner. Again, New Jersey immigrants proved to be more active than Latino immigrants from other states; just 64 percent of Latino immigrants in other states took part in some form of political behavior other than voting. Of these, the most common activity for New Jersey Latino immigrants was following politics in the news, but the awareness of U.S. politics that this indicates should not be discounted. Approximately one-half had participated more actively, including activities such as writing letters about a political issue or marching in political rallies. Again, this rate exceeded the rate for Latinos nationally (33 percent).

Although these home country and nonelectoral forms of participation are indirect indicators of the potential for good citizenship if these immigrants subsequently naturalize, they do indicate a population with political skills developed in their home countries and some preliminary engagement in U.S. politics. These findings, particularly those concerning engagement in U.S. politics, should offer a counterweight to the low naturalization rates discussed in the previous section. Latino immigrants in New Jersey, then, are not disengaged from U.S. politics. Instead, they are developing an awareness that has not yet resulted in naturalization. Based on these data, the statutory and bureaucratic impediments loom larger as factors keeping them from full U.S. political access.

Electoral Politics

Because the majority of New Jersey's immigrants are not U.S. citizens, they do not have a direct ability to influence electoral outcomes with their votes. One indirect ability is, nevertheless, very important. The census counts them, and their numbers contribute to the construction of electoral districts. Thus, in areas with large numbers of immigrants, noncitizens fill out the population of districts that come to be perceived as Latino or Asian districts. This phenomenon of creating, for example, a Latino district with a relatively small Latino U.S. citizen population and a somewhat larger Latino non-U.S. citizen population, is particularly evident in states with large and geographically dispersed immigrant populations, such as California, Texas, and Florida (de la Garza and DeSipio 1996). It is partially responsible for the vast expansion since 1980 in the numbers of municipal, school board, judicial, and county districts electing Latinos to office. The pattern is also evident at higher levels of office, including state legislative and congressional districts. Clearly, the combined noncitizen and co-ethnic U.S. citizen population must be quite large to encourage the formation of districts at these levels. New Jersey gained such a congressional district in 1991. This district offers a tool for viewing the indirect involvement of immigrants in electoral politics.

In the redistricting that followed the 1990 Census, the New Jersey Legislature created a congressional district—the 13th, comprising most of Hudson County—with a strong likelihood of electing a Latino (Nieves 1992a, b). State Senator and Union City Mayor Robert Menendez seized the opportunity created by the legislature and ran for this seat. His victory, both in the primary (68 percent to 32 percent) and in the general election (64 percent to 31 percent) clearly demonstrated that his appeal extended beyond the district's Latino population, which numbers approximately 41 percent. He had ties to the Democratic Party machine and had served in local and state electoral offices for almost 20 years (sometimes holding municipal and state office simultaneously) (*New York Times* 1992).

Menendez's victory is interesting for reasons beyond his status as New Jersey's first Latino elected to Congress. Menendez was born in the United States in 1954 of Cuban-born parents, distinguishing him both from foreign-born Latinos who comprise a majority of the Latinos in his district and from the Cubans who began arriving in northern New Jersey in large numbers in 1959. Clearly, elected leaders develop ties to various constituencies and these constituencies do not have to be made up of co-ethnics or people who share a particular trait or characteristic. Menendez's priorities as mayor—drug education, bringing police into schools for education and enforcement, child care programs, and recycling—as well as his agenda in Congress—targeted tax incentives and promotion of enterprise zones—are representative of community needs in Hudson County (Barone and Ujifusa 1993: 835–37).

A second interesting element in the 13th district is that its creation was spurred in large part by the nonparticipants. Although exact figures are not available, it is safe to estimate that at least half of voting-age Latinos in Menendez's district are noncitizens. Had the decision to form a Latino district been driven by the Latino citizen population of no more than 20 percent, it is less likely that such a district would have been created. This may or may not pose a dilemma for Menendez and other similarly situated Latino or Asian elected officials; they must symbolically represent the noncitizen and their co-ethnics while depending on a racial and ethnic coalition for reelection. The phenomenon is only beginning to appear and merits further study. This ability to constitute the foundation for a district, however, must be recognized as one implicit power of noncitizen communities. Further, the ability to vote for co-ethnics and to see them elected may offer an incentive for naturalization and, later, for participation. Latino immigrants in Menendez's district or in other Latino districts shape the structure of the local political debates by their numbers before their citizenship status or electoral influence would ensure that opportunity.

These opportunities for non-U.S. citizens to influence electoral politics indirectly may change before the next round of redistricting. The Supreme Court has debated the constitutionality of the provisions of the Voting Rights Act that mandate the creation of minority districts. Although the role of noncitizens in promulgating these districts has not been a focus of the Court's attention, this may change when the courts examine a districting case involving two Latino districts in Texas (Bush v. Vera).

CONCLUSIONS

New Jersey's immigrants are at an interesting stage in their political development. Although the majority are excluded from formal participation due to noncitizenship, their numbers are sufficiently large to ensure that the electoral system will take them into account in decisions of consequence. This attention would seem to be merited. Attitudinally, many have made the attachment to the United States that the nation expects of its immigrants prior to formal acceptance through naturalization. The gap between this attachment to the United States and citizenship is not unique to New Jersey. Were these immigrants to begin to formalize that attachment in greater numbers, they would have the skills and interests to apply their citizenship. Several indicators suggest that these immigrants bring a sense of political efficacy and have begun to engage in their communities, particularly in the schools, through nonelectoral political activity.

What New Jersey's immigrants (and immigrants nationally) offer, then, is a challenge to the political system. This is not a challenge to American values or to the American system of government, as some would assert, but instead a challenge to facilitate their political incorporation. The recent surge in demand for naturalization may well bring the political needs of immigrants to the attention of the polity.

Were the nation to study what it asks of immigrants seeking citizenship and what prevents them from reaching their goals, the experiences of New Jersey immigrants would offer a rich case study.

New Jersey immigrants merit study for a second reason. Much of the contemporary scholarship on immigrants and immigrant acculturation has been driven by the experiences of immigrants in the new immigrant-receiving states, particularly in the Southwest and Florida. New Jersey, on the other hand, represents a potentially different model, joined by New York, Massachusetts, and, perhaps, Illinois. These states have large numbers of both recent and long-term immigrants from all parts of the world. No single nationality or region dominates their immigrant populations. Further, these states' immigrants have a wider range of economic, educational, and age characteristics. Perhaps most important for the question of political adaptation, they have a range of experiences with naturalization. Thus, the study of immigrants in New Jersey promises a more nuanced portrait of the question of how U.S. society incorporates its new members.

Notes

1. During the most recent session of Congress, members introduced several proposals to reduce the annual level of legal immigration. These proposals ranged from a three-year suspension of all immigration to the establishment of a firm ceiling of 550,000 annual immigrants. In the interest of passing legislation to reduce the number of undocumented immigrants, Congress did not bring these proposals to a vote. Analysts expect that Congress will revisit legal immigration levels in the next Congress.

2. The INS does not verify these intended residences, and there is no requirement that immigrants report their moves to the INS. The next point at which the government becomes aware of the location of specific immigrants is when they apply for naturalization.

3. Both surveys were designed to be nationally representative; thus, they are not necessarily representative of all Latino immigrants in New Jersey.

4. The primary focus of the NLIS was Latino immigrant attitudes toward and experiences with naturalization. As a result, the sample includes permanent resident Latino immigrants with the five years of residence necessary for naturalization. Nationally, the NLIS included 1,636 respondents, of whom 129 resided in New Jersey. Survey methodology and descriptive findings are contained in Pachon and DeSipio (1994).

5. The LNPS sample included the three largest Latino national-origin groups—Mexican Americans, Puerto Ricans, and Cuban Americans—as well as a control group of non-Hispanic whites in 38 cities and 2 rural counties nationwide (García et al. 1989). The sample included both U.S.- and foreign-born Latinos. Survey methodology and descriptive findings are contained in de la Garza et al. (1992).

Of the 3,415 respondents nationwide, 84 were foreign-born residents of New Jersey, all but 1 of whom was of Cuban birth. Because of the relatively low number of New Jersey foreign-born respondents and the overwhelmingly Cuban origins of these respondents, I used LNPS data selectively in this analysis. Unless otherwise noted, my source is the NLIS.

6. Because of the small sample sizes, I am hesitant to perform subgroup analysis on Latino respondents to the NLIS. These respondents included immigrants from 14 nations. No one country comprises a majority, though Cuba is the largest single country of origin, with 42 percent of the New Jersey respondents. The other large countries of origin in the NLIS are El Salvador, the Dominican Republic, Panama, and Colombia.

7. Some jurisdictions permit non-U.S. citizens to vote in certain types of elections. New York City, for example, grants them school council election votes. I have found no evidence that New Jersey jurisdictions permit noncitizen voting.

8. The LNPS (de la Garza et al. 1992) found that 61 percent of New Jersey immigrant parents had met with their children's teachers and attended Parent-Teacher Association meetings, slightly more than half (53 percent) had met with the principal of their children's schools, and 33 percent had attended a school board meeting. Clearly the focus of school-related activity is children. Nevertheless, these activities indicate immigrants' engagement in their communities.

References

Alba, Richard D. 1990. *Ethnic Identity: The Transformation of White America.* New Haven, Conn.: Yale University Press.

Alvarez, Robert. 1987. "A Profile of the Citizenship Process among Hispanics in the United States." *International Migration Review* 21 (Summer): 327–51.

Barkan, E. R., and N. Khokolov. 1980. "Socioeconomic Data as Indices of Naturalization Patterns in the United States: A Theory Revisited." *Ethnicity* 7: 159–90.

Barone, Michael, and Grant Ujifusa. 1993. *The Almanac of American Politics, 1994.* Washington, D.C.: National Journal, Inc.

Bernard, William. 1936. "Cultural Determinants of Naturalization." *American Sociological Review* 1(6, December): 943–53.

Borjas, George J. 1990. *Friends or Strangers: The Impact of Immigrants on the U.S. Economy.* New York: Basic Books.

Bouvier, Leon F., and Lindsey Grant. 1994. *How Many Americans? Population, Immigration, and the Environment.* San Francisco: Sierra Club Books.

Brimelow, Peter. 1995. *Alien Nation: Common Sense about America's Immigration Disaster.* New York: Random House.

de la Garza, Rodolfo O., and Louis DeSipio. 1996. "Latinos and the 1992 Elections: A National Perspective." In *Ethnic Ironies: Latino Politics in the 1992 Elections,* edited by Rodolfo O. de la Garza and Louis DeSipio (3–50). Boulder, Colo.: Westview Press.

de la Garza, Rodolfo O., Martha Menchaca, and Louis DeSipio. 1994. *Barrio Ballots: Latino Politics in the 1990 Elections.* Boulder, Colo.: Westview Press.

de la Garza, Rodolfo O., Louis DeSipio, F. Chris García, John A. García, and Angelo Falcón. 1992. *Latino Voices: Mexican, Puerto Rican, and Cuban Perspectives on American Politics.* Boulder, Colo.: Westview Press.

DeSipio, Louis. 1987. "Social Science Literature and the Naturalization Process." *International Migration Review* 21(2, Summer): 390–405.

———. 1996a. "Are We Incorporating the Next Generation? Citizenship and Naturalization among U.S. Immigrants." *Harvard Journal of Hispanic Policy* 9 (May): 7–24.

———. 1996b. *Counting on the Latino Vote: Latinos as a New Electorate.* Charlottesville: University Press of Virginia.

DeSipio, Louis, and Rodolfo O. de la Garza. 1992. "Making Them Us: The Political Incorporation of Immigrant and Non-immigrant Minorities." In *Nations of Immigrants: Australia, the United States, and International Migration*, edited by Gary Freeman and James Jupp (202–215). Melbourne: Oxford University Press.

DeSipio, Louis, and Harry P. Pachon. 1992. "Making Americans: Administrative Discretion and Naturalization." *UCLA Chicano/Latino Law Review* 12 (Spring): 52–66.

Edmonston, Barry, and Jeffrey S. Passel, eds. 1994. *Immigration and Ethnicity: The Integration of America's Newest Arrivals.* Washington, D.C.: Urban Institute Press.

Espenshade, Thomas J. 1994. *A Stone's Throw from Ellis Island: Economic Implications of Immigration to New Jersey.* Lanham, Md.: University Press of America.

Fuchs, Lawrence H. 1990. *The American Kaleidoscope: Race, Ethnicity, and the Civic Culture.* Hanover, N.H.: University Press of New England.

García, F. Chris, John A. García; Angelo Falcón, and Rodolfo O. de la Garza. 1989. "Studying Latino Politics: The Development of the Latino National Political Survey." *PS: Political Science and Politics* 22: 848–52.

García, John A. 1981. "Political Integration of Mexican Immigrants: Explorations into the Naturalization Process." *International Migration Review* 15(4): 608–25.

———. 1987. "The Political Integration of Mexican Immigrants: Examining Some Political Orientations." *International Migration Review* 21(2, Summer): 372–89.

Gavit, John. 1971 (1922). *Americans by Choice.* Montclair, N.J.: Patterson Smith.

Grenier, Guillermo, and Alex Stepik, eds. 1992. *Miami Now! Immigration, Ethnicity, and Social Change.* Gainesville: University Press of Florida.

Guest, A. M. 1980. "The Old–New Distinction and Naturalization: 1900." *International Migration Review* 14(4): 492–510.

Gutiérrez, David G. 1995. *Walls and Mirrors: Mexican Americans, Mexican Immigrants, and the Politics of Ethnicity.* Berkeley: University of California Press.

Jasso, Guillermina, and Mark R. Rosenzweig. 1985. "What's in a Name? Country of Origin Influences on the Earnings of Immigrants in the United States." *Bulletin* #85-4. Minneapolis: University of Minnesota, Economic Development Center, June.

————. 1990. *The New Chosen People: Immigrants in the United States.* New York: Russell Sage Foundation.

Jones-Correa, Michael. 1994. "Between Two Nations: The Political Life of Latin American Immigrants in New York City." Ph.D. Dissertation, Princeton University, Princeton, N.J.

Lamphere, Louise, ed. 1992. *Structuring Diversity: Ethnographic Perspectives on the New Immigration.* Chicago: University of Chicago Press.

Liang, Zai. 1994. "On the Measurement of Naturalization." *Demography* 31 (3, August): 525–48.

Moore, Joan, and Rachel Pinderhughes. 1994. *In the Barrios: Latinos and the Underclass Debate.* New York: Russell Sage Foundation.

New York Times, The. 1992. "Menendez to Seek Congressional Seat," April 8: B4 (v. 141).

Nieves, Evelyn. 1992a. "A Campaign Reflects Hispanic Growth." *New York Times,* October 30: B4 (v. 142).

————. 1992b. "A New House District Could Make History: A Democrat Wants to Be New Jersey's First Hispanic Congressman." *New York Times,* October 29: B7 (v. 142).

Pachon, Harry. 1987. "An Overview of Citizenship in the Hispanic Community." *International Migration Review* 21(2, Summer): 299–310.

Pachon, Harry, and Louis DeSipio. 1994. *New Americans by Choice: Political Perspectives of Latino Immigrants.* Boulder, Colo.: Westview Press.

Peet, Judy. 1995. "Citizenship Requests Soar on Policy Shifts, Fears." *Newark Star-Ledger,* January 15: Section One, Page One.

Portes, Alejandro, and Robert L. Bach. 1985. *Latin Journey: Cuban and Mexican Immigrants in the United States.* Berkeley and Los Angeles: University of California Press.

Portes, Alejandro, and John Curtis. 1987. "Changing Flags: Naturalization and Its Determinants among Mexican Immigrants." *International Migration Review* 21(2, Summer): 352–72.

Portes, Alejandro, and Rafael Mozo. 1985. "The Political Adaptation Process of Cubans and Other Ethnic Minorities in the United States: A Preliminary Analysis." *International Migration Review* 16(1): 35–63.

Portes, Alejandro, and Alex Stepik. 1994. *City on the Edge: The Transformation of Miami.* Berkeley: University of California Press.

Rogg, Eleanor M. 1974. *The Assimilation of Cuban Exiles: The Role of Community and Class.* New York: Aberdeen Press.

Simon, Julian L. 1989. *The Economic Consequences of Immigration.* Cambridge, Mass.: Basil Blackwell.

U.S. Bureau of the Census. 1992. "The Foreign-Born Population by Place of Birth for New Jersey: 1990." 1990 Census, Special Tabulations. Washington, D.C.: U.S. Bureau of the Census, Ethnic and Hispanic Branch, Population Division.

————. 1993a. "1990 Age, Nativity, and Citizenship for the United States, and Counties." CPH-L-114. Washington, D.C.: U.S. Bureau of the Census, Ethnic and Hispanic Branch, Population Division.

————. 1993b. "1990: The Foreign-Born Population by Race, Hispanic Origin, and Citizenship for the United States." CPH-L-134. Washington, D.C.: U.S. Bureau of the Census, Ethnic and Hispanic Branch, Population Division.

U.S. Congress. Senate. Committee on the Judiciary. 1988. *Report on Returns, Nonfiles, and Other Unadjudicated Naturalization Applications.* 100th Cong., 2d sess. Washington, D.C.: Government Printing Office.

U.S. Immigration and Naturalization Service. 1990. "Report on Citizenship Applications Returned/Nonfiled." Washington, D.C.: Author. Photocopy.

————. 1994. *1993 Statistical Yearbook of the Immigration and Naturalization Service.* Springfield, Va.: National Technical Information Service.

————. 1996. *1994 Statistical Yearbook of the Immigration and Naturalization Service.* Springfield, Va.: National Technical Information Service.

U.S. Immigration Commission. 1911. *Reports of the Immigration Commission.* Washington, D.C.: U.S. Government Printing Office.

Yang, Philip Q. 1994. "Explaining Immigrant Naturalization." *International Migration Review* 28(3): 449–77.

Part Three

PROCESSES OF
IMMIGRANT ADAPTATION

IMMIGRATION AND FERTILITY IN NEW JERSEY: A COMPARISON OF NATIVE AND FOREIGN-BORN WOMEN

Deanna Pagnini

The childbearing behavior of native and foreign-born women has been a subject of interest for many years. At the turn of the century, fears about race suicide due to the low fertility of native-born white women and the high fertility of immigrants from Southern and Eastern Europe fueled considerable concern in both the popular and academic presses (Pagnini and Morgan 1990). Today we see some of the same concerns about immigration and fertility, although they are usually less about race suicide than about the perceived costs to the public of immigrants having more children than native-born Americans. For example, one woman who was discussing the children of Mexican immigrants said that "I didn't breed them. I don't want to feed them" (Kozol 1995).

The fertility of immigrant and native-born women is an especially pertinent issue in New Jersey, which ranks fourth highest in the percentage of state residents who were born outside the United States. From a planning perspective, the distribution of the immigrant population and their fertility patterns will determine the amount of resources and services that will need to be directed to them. For example, whether bilingual educational programs are needed in a community obviously depends on the number of children in that area who do not speak English. Those children may have been born in the United States to immigrant parents, or they may have been born outside of the United States and migrated with their parents.

For scholars, one of the most interesting questions surrounding immigration is the extent to which immigrants retain the customs and values of their countries of birth or adopt the practices of the country to which they move. The childbearing behavior of immigrant women is often used as an indicator of their assimilation into American society: Do their fertility patterns mirror those of the women in the countries they left, or does their fertility behavior become similar to that of American women?

According to proponents of the assimilation, or adaptation, hypothesis, the longer immigrant women have resided in the United States, the more likely it is that they will resemble native-born women in their childbearing behavior. Residence in the United States leads immigrant women to adopt the norms and values of the dominant society, and these values are expressed in childbearing behavior. More important than just the number of years women live in the United States, however, is the timing of their initial move to this country. If women moved here as children, they will have had more time to be influenced by American society before beginning to have children. Their country of birth should then have little effect on their fertility.

This assimilation hypothesis makes an often untested assumption: that there is *one* fertility regime in the United States that influences immigrant women. This assumption is critical when discussing comparisons between native and foreign-born women. Although we no longer aggregate all foreign-born women into one category, most research lumps all native-born women into one category. However, we know that there are racial, ethnic, and class differences in the timing of fertility and completed family size within the American population (Cherlin 1992; Rindfuss, Morgan, and Swicegood 1988), and so aggregating all native-born women may mask important differences.

This chapter uses individual-level fertility data from the 1990 Census to describe and analyze the fertility behavior of women in New Jersey. The research addresses several questions. Do foreign-born women in New Jersey have higher fertility than native-born women? The data show that as a group immigrant women do bear more children than do native-born women. I then move beyond this simple native–foreign contrast to examine which groups have higher or lower fertility than the native born (who have also been disaggregated into detailed racial and ethnic groups).

Previous research has shown that place of birth does affect fertility. The question is whether these differences are due to underlying nativity differences in the preference for large or small families or whether they are the result of differences in the sociodemographic composition of the groups. I use individual-level data to address this issue by examining whether place of birth has an effect once individual sociodemographic characteristics are controlled for. I use two measures of fertility: children ever born (a cumulative measure) and whether a woman has an own-child under age three in the household (a current measure).

In contrast to work by other researchers in the field, I disaggregate the native-born population into detailed racial and ethnic categories.

I also disaggregate the foreign-born population by place of birth and by whether the women moved to the United States as children or as adults. The results demonstrate that asking whether foreign-born women have higher fertility than native-born women is too simplistic a question—the answer depends upon the fertility measure, the comparison group used, and whether fertility is adjusted for differences in background characteristics.

PREVIOUS RESEARCH ON IMMIGRATION AND FERTILITY

A number of studies have examined the relationship between immigration and fertility for both historical (i.e., Morgan, Watkins, and Ewbank 1994) and contemporary populations (i.e., Ford 1985, 1990; Kahn 1988, 1994). Several studies simply document the differences between native and foreign-born women, whereas others analyze the determinants of fertility behavior. Some studies focus specifically on the behavior of a single ethnic group (Bean and Swicegood 1985), whereas others compare the fertility of different immigrant groups. Although they use different groups and methodologies, these studies demonstrate the importance of controlling for the individual characteristics of the women as well as for their place of birth.

Ford (1985) used census data from 1970 and 1980 to compare the standardized means of children ever born for native and foreign-born women. She found that when the foreign-born women were aggregated as a group, the fertility of native-born and foreign-born women was virtually indistinguishable.[1] This aggregation masked substantial variation, however, as revealed when individual countries/regions were examined. For example, women from Mexico had considerably higher fertility than the native born, and women from Central America, Russia, the Middle East, Israel, and the Caribbean had slightly higher fertility than the native born, findings that were attributed to the higher fertility in the women's countries of origin. In an examination of recent fertility, Ford (1985) found that immigrant women—with the exception of Cuban, British, and Canadian women—were more likely than native-born women to have a child under the age of three. Women who migrated recently may have had their fertility patterns disrupted, and thus they may have been "making up" some of their fertility at older ages.

According to Kahn (1994), data from the 1980 Census show that the higher fertility of immigrant women can be explained by differences in age, education, income, and ethnic compositions between native and foreign-born women. Once these factors were controlled for, immigrant and native-born women had similar childbearing patterns. When future childbearing expectation data from the Current Population Survey were examined, however, immigrant women expressed the desire for more children than did native-born women, even after controlling for these other variables. Thus, although behaviorally the two groups of women were similar, they professed different total childbearing intentions. Kahn (1988) has also used the 1980 Public Use Microdata Sample (PUMS) data to examine the effects of the sending country on fertility assimilation in the United States by including data on the net reproduction rate (NRR) of the country of origin. She found that the NRR had less of an effect for those who were more assimilated, as measured by the ability to speak English and duration of residence in the United States.

Ford's (1990) study of the effects of duration of residence in the United States for immigrant women tested two complementary hypotheses: assimilation (long-term) and disruption (short-term). The disruption hypothesis states that fertility is interrupted for a time immediately after migration. Ford found that fertility for the most recent immigrants was lower than for immigrants who migrated earlier. After a period of time, however, these fertility differentials disappeared. She found more evidence for the short-term disruption model than for the assimilation model, partly because no one has defined how long it should take for immigrants to become "assimilated."

Instead of using census data to compare the fertility of a number of immigrant groups with native-born women, Rumbaut and Weeks (1986) studied the fertility of one specific group, the Indochinese, who moved from a society characterized by high fertility to the United States. They used data from the Indochinese Health and Adaptation Research Project (IHARP), based in San Diego County, to calculate a total fertility rate of 5.75 for Indochinese women; the U.S. equivalent was 1.8. When disaggregated by ethnicity, all five Indochinese ethnic groups had much higher fertility than the native-born population. They found that first-wave immigrants had lower fertility than those who came later, which may be due to the fact that first-wave immigrants tended to have higher levels of education. Within each group, they discovered that those "respondents who have made the greatest progress in terms of economic and cultural adjustment to their new environment have the lowest levels of fertility" (p. 453).

In the same vein, Jaffe and Cullen (1975) examined the fertility of Puerto Rican women born on the island as well as on the mainland

United States, and found that island-born women had higher fertility. They attributed this higher fertility to differences in education, marital status, and employment between the two groups. They asserted that "completion of high school is tantamount to taking on the demographic characteristics of the non-Spanish U.S. White population" (p. 197).

These studies have shown that there has been wide variation in the fertility of immigrant women, which is dependent both upon place of birth and individual characteristics such as education and age. As discussed by Western and Kelly in chapter 2 of this volume, the state of New Jersey differs from the rest of the country in its distribution of immigrants' countries of origin. New Jersey has a higher percentage of immigrants from Europe than the country as a whole, and European women tend to have low fertility rates. New Jersey also has a lower concentration of Latin American immigrants, especially from Mexico, who tend to have higher fertility. Given these differences in the composition of immigrant women, one might expect that the difference between the fertility of native and foreign-born women would be smaller in this state than in the country as a whole. I now turn to an examination of the fertility of New Jersey residents.

DATA

Because this chapter focuses on the fertility of women in New Jersey, only a limited number of possible data sources are available. The objective is to compare the fertility of foreign-born and native-born women by detailed place of birth/ethnicity categories. Ideally there would be a data set including detailed fertility information as well as a large number of foreign-born women. Unfortunately, these data do not exist at the state level. National-level fertility surveys (such as the National Survey of Family Growth) include extremely detailed fertility data, but they do not have detailed place-of-birth categories of women, nor do they include enough respondents from New Jersey to analyze the state separately. Aside from surveys, the other possible data source is the U.S. Census. Given the need for detailed data on women in New Jersey, I traded the quality and detail of information available in fertility surveys for the large quantity of respondents in the 1990 Census. The 1990 5 percent PUMS data file for New Jersey thus provides the data for these analyses. The sample chosen includes all women ages 15–64 who appeared in the 1990 PUMS data. Since both completed and current fertility were being analyzed, I needed women who are currently in their childbearing years, along with those who have completed their fertility. The sample includes 137,746 women. Of those, 115,054 were born in the United States and 22,692 were born in other countries.

The only direct fertility variable in the census is the question on the number of children ever born. Although this information is usually reliable, the measure does have several problems, owing to the fact that only the total number of children ever born is reported; thus, there is no fertility schedule of when each child was born, and age-specific or total fertility rates cannot be calculated. For the women who moved to the United States when they were children, one can safely assume that their children were born here. For immigrant women who migrated as adults, however, where their children were born is unknown. For native-born women, even if they are New Jersey residents now, their children may not have been born in the state. Children ever born is still a useful measure, however. The fertility behavior of all New Jersey women, no matter where or when it took place, still has an effect on the state. For example, if the children are young, they are likely to be living with their parents and going to school in the state. Among younger women who have not yet finished their fertility careers, differences in children ever born by age can indicate differences in the timing of fertility. Even if two groups end up with an equal number of children ever born at the end of their childbearing years, the timing patterns may have been different.

The second fertility variable is a measure of recent fertility—whether a woman has an own child under three years of age in the household. Unlike earlier public use census files, there is no "mom-link" variable identifying the mother of each child. Following previous work (i.e., Rutherford and Cho 1978), I used questions on children ever born, relationship to household head, marital status, and age to identify the mothers of children under age three. Rutherford and Cho (1978), in a comparison of this method with National Vital Statistics data, found that own-child "estimates of contemporary age-parity-specific fertility in the United States are reasonably accurate at the ages and parities at which most births occur" (p. 576). In the United States, most young children reside with their mothers, so fostering out of children is not a large problem. Two other groups of people are missed in this sample, however. If the mother has died, the child will not be counted in the sample. If the child died, there would also be no record. Given the relatively low rates of infant mortality and female mortality at the childbearing ages, however, this measure should be fairly accurate.

SAMPLE DESCRIPTION

Figures 10.1 and 10.2 present the number of women ages 15–44 and 45–64, respectively, in the 1990 New Jersey PUMS data by nativity. The native-born population is disaggregated by race and ethnicity, and the foreign-born population by place of birth and whether the women moved to the United States as children or adults.[2]

Figure 10.1 shows that the majority of women of childbearing age in New Jersey are native-born non-Hispanic whites, followed by native-born non-Hispanic blacks. The next most prevalent groups are women born in Europe, Central America, East Asia, Puerto Rico,[3] and South America. No other group included more than 2,000 women. The recent increases in immigration from Latin America and Asia are apparent in these distributions. The foreign-born women appear to be fairly evenly split from sending regions with high fertility (i.e., South America, Central America) and those with low fertility (i.e., Europe, Canada).

Canadians, island-born Puerto Ricans, and Europeans were the most likely to move to the United States as children. South Asians, East Asians, and Africans were more likely to move as adults (see figure 10.1). Those who moved to the United States as children have had more time to be exposed to American childbearing norms and values and are not subject to possible short-term disruption effects on their fertility from the migration experience. As stated, it seems reasonable to assume that women who came to the United States as children had their own children in this country. Those who came to the United States as adults may have had their children in their sending country, in the United States, in a third country, or in some combination thereof.

Figure 10.2 includes only women who have completed their childbearing (ages 45–64). In contrast to their younger counterparts, significantly more older women were born in Europe, reflecting earlier waves of immigration to New Jersey. Except for Europeans and Central Americans, there are fewer than 1,000 women in all other nativity categories. Most of these older women appear to have moved to the United States as adults, so some or all of their childbearing may have taken place in

Figure 10.1 NUMBER OF WOMEN AGES 15–44 IN NEW JERSEY 1990 PUMS, BY PLACE OF BIRTH

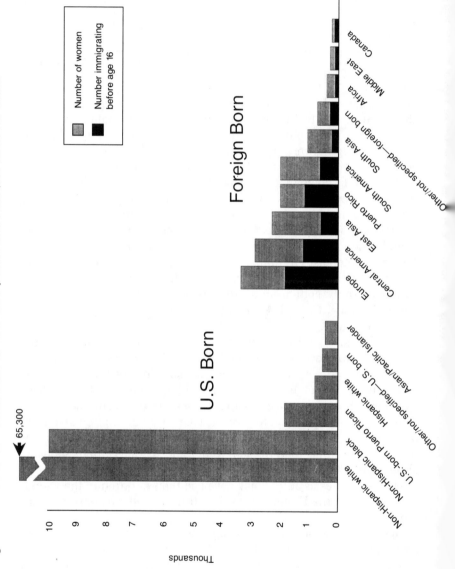

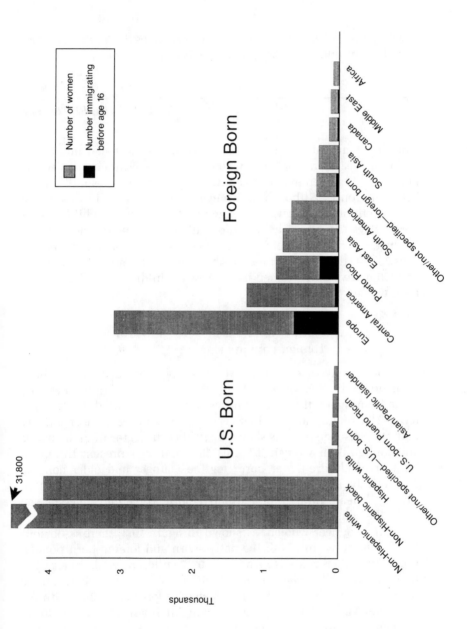

their countries of origin. The next section examines the fertility behavior of both the younger and older cohorts of New Jersey women.

CUMULATIVE FERTILITY

One direct measure of cumulative fertility is the mean number of children ever born. For those who have completed their fertility, the number of children ever born allows one to compare overall fertility between groups. Although the younger women are still in the midst of their childbearing careers, comparing the number of children ever born by age category provides information about the timing of childbearing, as well as simply the quantity. As shown below, for women ages 15–44, the mean number of children ever born indicates that as of 1990, native-born women had 0.3 fewer children than did foreign-born women.[4]

Mean Number of Children Ever Born
Native-born women: 1.51
Foreign-born women: 1.80

As previously discussed, however, simply comparing native-born with foreign-born women can be misleading. The foreign-born women come from many different countries, which have varied fertility patterns. The assumption that there is one native-born American fertility pattern is also suspect, as shown by further disaggregating the native and foreign-born women. Figures 10.3 and 10.4 present the mean number of children ever born[5] for the younger and older cohorts, respectively, and show that there is not a strict native/foreign-born divide. Instead, immigrant and native-born women are interspersed along the continuums.

For the younger women, as shown in figure 10.3, there is obvious heterogeneity within both the native-born and foreign-born populations. The values range from a low of 0.37 children ever born for U.S.-born Asian/Pacific Islanders to a high of 1.97 for island-born Puerto Rican women. There are several clusters of fertility values, with African and Middle Eastern women having high fertility, then a cluster of women whose values range between 1.2 and 1.4 (including native-born blacks), followed by a cluster of women with lower fertility levels. The ordering of foreign-born women along the children ever-born continuum closely corresponds to the ordering of their birth regions in terms of total fertility rates (Population Reference Bureau 1990).

Figure 10.3 MEAN NUMBER OF CHILDREN EVER BORN TO NEW JERSEY WOMEN AGES 15–44, BY PLACE OF BIRTH

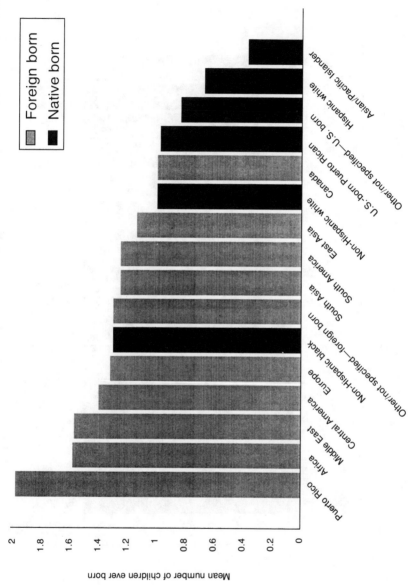

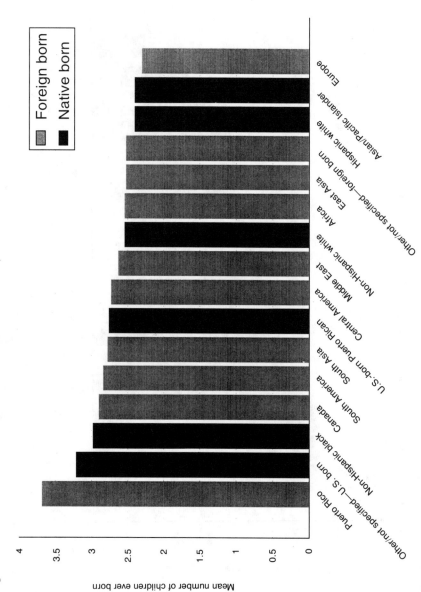

Figure 10.4 MEAN NUMBER OF CHILDREN EVER BORN TO NEW JERSEY WOMEN AGES 45–64, BY PLACE OF BIRTH

Except for Puerto Rican and European women (who are higher in the order than expected), the order is exactly the same.[6] Because the mean number of children ever born for younger women is influenced by the age distribution of the population, completed fertility must be examined as well.

Figure 10.4 depicts completed fertility for older women. In terms of total number of children ever born, island-born Puerto Ricans had more children than other women, followed by U.S.-born women whose race/ethnicity was not specified, followed by U.S.-born blacks. All of the other women have relatively similar completed fertility levels, with European women and native-born women who are Hispanic whites or Asian/Pacific Islanders having the lowest levels. Thus, when examining children ever born by nativity, we find that for completed fertility, there is some variation between groups, but it is not a simple native-born/foreign-born dichotomy. Of course, these women were bearing their children at a different historical point than today, but it does help to dispel the notion that immigrant women bear children at a much higher rate than native-born women.

Because fertility behavior is influenced by more than country of origin, however, this study also examined the effect of place of birth once other factors that affect fertility are controlled for. In other words, is it simply compositional differences between the populations that explain the variation in fertility (Kahn 1994)? Are some immigrant groups characterized by higher levels of education, which lead to lower fertility? To answer these questions, this study employed a multivariate analysis.

Based on previous research on fertility and the availability of data in the census, three other sets of independent variables besides place of birth were included in the models. Although nonmarital fertility rates have been increasing in the United States over the past 30 years, those who are/were married should have higher fertility. The relationship of marital status to fertility should be especially strong for the older cohorts of women, in which nonmarital fertility was highly stigmatized (Pagnini and Rindfuss 1993). Marital status was coded as never married, formerly married (divorced, widowed, separated), and currently married.

The relationship of educational attainment to fertility has been well documented (Cherlin 1994; Rindfuss et al. 1988). School roles and motherhood roles are usually incompatible. Women with higher educational attainments tend to have fewer children and to have them at older ages. Educational differences between immigrant and native-born women are thought to account for part of the difference in fertility behavior (i.e., Kahn 1994). For these analyses, educational attainment was coded as less than high school, high school graduate, any college, and any graduate education. The final set of independent variables measures the woman's age at the time of the census in categories; the expectation is that older women will have more children. Among the women who have completed their fertility, however, there may be some variation based on historical patterns.

The dependent variable is the number of children ever born, and the estimator used is ordinary least squares (OLS) regression.[7] The results are represented graphically in figure 10.5. A bar on the right-hand side of the zero line signifies a positive coefficient, and a bar on the left-hand side signifies a negative coefficient. If there is no bar, then that coefficient was either zero or extremely close to it. Those coefficients that are statistically significant have asterisks next to them. The reference categories are in parentheses.

Figure 10.5 presents the results for all New Jersey residents ages 15–64. In terms of the control variables, this study found that those who never married or were previously married have significantly lower numbers of children ever born than do those who were married at the time of the census. As predicted by previous research, educational attainment has a negative relationship with fertility—the higher the level of educational attainment, the lower the number of children ever born. Age should have a positive relationship to total fertility, which this study demonstrates. Within the older cohorts (those older than 50), there is little differentiation by age. These results all support previous fertility research, but this study was more interested in determining whether controlling for these variables eliminates differences between native and foreign-born women.

Examining the results for place of birth, two groups of women were identified: those whose fertility does not differ from or is lower than the reference group (native-born non-Hispanic whites) and those who have significantly higher fertility. Native and foreign-born women appear in each of these groups. Some native-born women have higher fertility than some of the foreign-born women, which suggests that aggregating all native-born women together and assuming they have the same fertility pattern will yield misleading conclusions. The foreign-born women whose fertility did not differ from or was lower than the reference category are all women who migrated from low-fertility regions (Europe, East Asia, and Canada). Within the native-born population, Hispanic whites and Asian/Pacific Islanders were all similar to non-Hispanic whites.

The women with the highest numbers of children ever born either came from high-fertility regions (Puerto Rico, Middle East, South Asia, Central America, South America, and Africa) or were born in the United States of African American or Puerto Rican heritage. This study found that controlling for sociodemographic characteristics does not completely eliminate fertility differentials between groups, which implies that compositional differences are an incomplete explanation for fertility differentials. Race, ethnicity, and region of birth have an independent, additive effect on the fertility of certain groups of women. For the foreign-born women with low fertility, however, it was not possible to determine whether they were adopting the fertility patterns of native-born white women in the United States or were reflecting the fertility regimes of their regions of origin.

Whereas these results demonstrate the overall differences between various immigrant and native-born groups, this study also wanted to determine how much variation there is between immigrant women. Because many explanations for fertility differentials have focused on the role of assimilation, it is possible to test whether fertility varies by language attainment or citizenship, or whether the woman migrated as an adult or child. Those who speak English would be more likely to be influenced by American norms and values, whereas those who became citizens have made a commitment to reside in the United States. As previously stated, women who migrated as adults not only have had less exposure to the prevailing fertility views but also may be more affected by the disruption process of migration itself (Ford 1990). Is there less variation between regions of birth for those who came as children than for those who came as adults? Figure 10.6 presents the regression results for both of these groups.

Examining the results for those who came to the United States as children, one finds that marital status, education, and age again have the expected results (see figure 10.6). Two variables were added to the models that measure assimilation: citizenship and the ability to speak English.[8] Not surprisingly, since those who moved as children have been in the United States for a number of years, these two variables did not have significant effects. In terms of place of birth, only island-born Puerto Ricans, Central Americans, and other/nonspecified foreign-born women have significantly different fertility than European immigrants. Place of birth has no significant effect for any of the other women. If the assimilation hypothesis were correct, this is the result one would expect to find. Perhaps because of the proximity of New Jersey to Puerto Rico and the ease of travel between the two

Figure 10.5 OLS REGRESSION RESULTS ON CHILDREN EVER BORN, TO NEW JERSEY WOMEN AGES 15–64

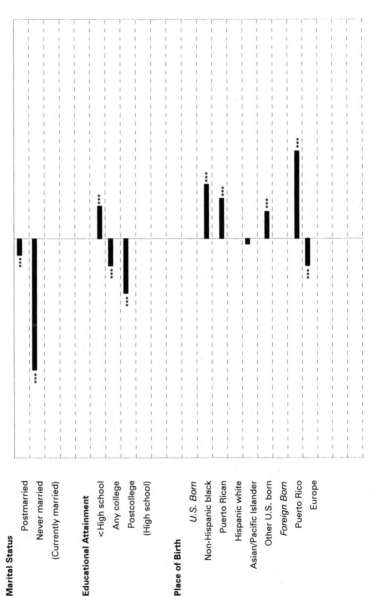

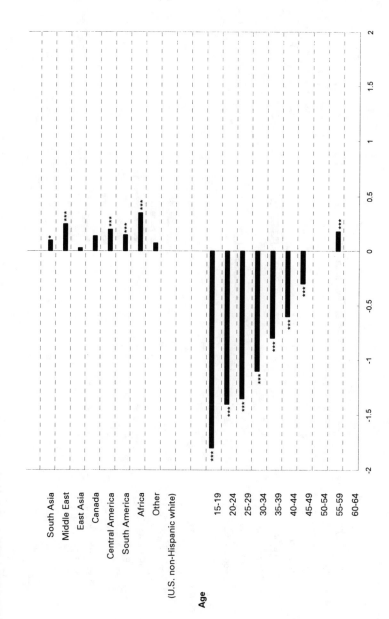

Intercept 2.71***, R^2 .40, N 137,746, *p<.05, **p<.01, ***p<.001

Figure 10.6 OLS REGRESSION RESULTS ON CHILDREN EVER BORN TO NEW JERSEY IMMIGRANT WOMEN, 1990

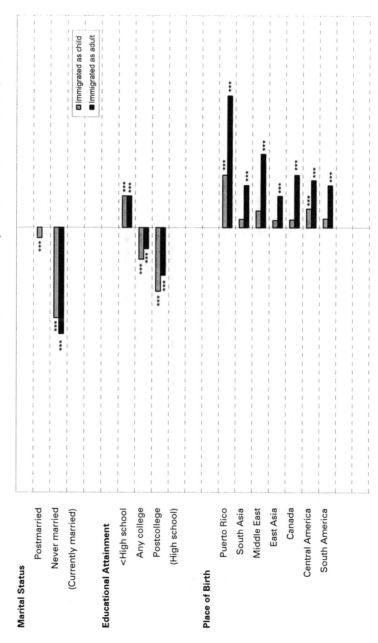

Marital Status

Postmarried

Never married

(Currently married)

Educational Attainment

<High school

Any college

Postcollege

(High school))

Place of Birth

Puerto Rico

South Asia

Middle East

East Asia

Canada

Central America

South America

☐ Immigrated as child
■ Immigrated as adult

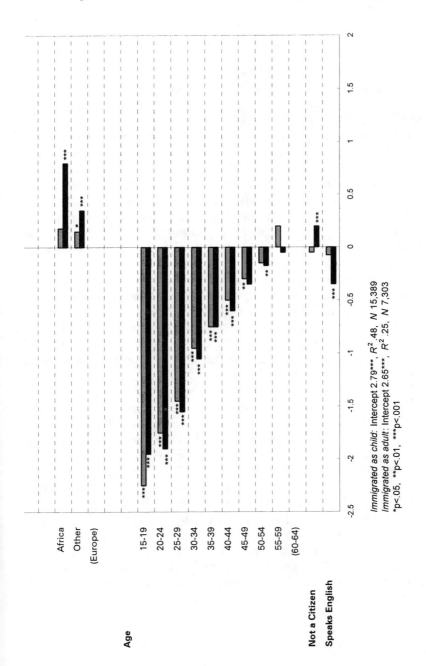

places, island-born women are still influenced by the fertility norms of their place of birth.

Among women who migrated as adults, however, different results were found, with region of birth and the assimilation variables having more significance. Those who have not become citizens have higher fertility, as do those who cannot speak English, both of which are consistent with an assimilation hypothesis. Even after controlling for the compositional differences between groups, women from every place of birth category had significantly higher fertility than European-born women. Thus, nativity matters more for women who came to the United States as adults rather than children. These results suggest that foreign-born women who migrated as adults were significantly influenced by the fertility norms of their regions of birth. These models, however, did not allow detection of any disruption effect of the migration process itself.

To summarize the cumulative fertility analyses, this study found that the mean number of children ever born was fairly similar among women who completed their fertility. Fertility was much more diverse for the women in the midst of their fertility careers, but the levels do mirror recent fertility levels in the regions of origin for the foreign born (Population Reference Bureau 1990). When the native-born women were disaggregated by race and ethnicity, no one pattern of native-born fertility was found.

Once the study controlled for other variables, place of birth was still found to be a significant predictor of the number of children ever born for certain groups. Place of birth had the most effect for women who migrated to the United States as adults, whereas it mattered little for women who migrated as children. These models all included women up to age 64, many of whom completed their childbearing well before the census data were collected. Although this behavior took place in the past, however, the fertility patterns of older women continue to have an effect on the educational, demographic, and labor force composition of the state. Unfortunately, no information was available on the timing of childbearing for older women, although this information was available for younger women. I turn now to an analysis of recent fertility.

RECENT FERTILITY

To examine recent fertility, I used a measure constructed from the household information—whether a woman has a child under age three in the household. Although, as stated, this measure is not perfect—some infants may have died, some mothers may have died, or some children may not be living with their mothers—the impact of these missing groups is likely to be small.[9]

For women ages 15–44, foreign-born women are slightly more likely to have an own child under three years of age in their household than are native-born women:

Percentage Having an Own Child under Age Three
Native-born women: 10.1
Foreign-born women: 10.7

As previously shown, however, simply comparing native and foreign-born women can be misleading. Figure 10.7 presents the percentage of New Jersey women with a child under age three by the nativity and race categories. The percentages range from a high of 18.7 for African women and 16.7 for Middle Eastern women to a low of 4.7 for native-born Asian/Pacific Islanders. Except for these three extremes, the other women are closely clustered.

What happens to these patterns when compositional differences are controlled for? Because the dependent variable is categorical (either a woman had a birth or did not), a logit regression was used.[10] I used the same set of control variables as in the analyses of cumulative fertility. I expected marital status to have the same effect on recent fertility as it had on cumulative fertility: women currently or formerly married should be more likely to have a child under age three. The relationship between education and recent fertility is not as clear-cut as when discussing cumulative fertility. Fertility rates among older, more educated, women have increased in recent years, which may be reflected in current fertility (Morgan 1994). Age should have a curvilinear relationship to recent fertility—that is, one would expect the youngest and oldest women to have the lowest likelihoods of having a child under age three.

Figure 10.8 presents the regression results for all New Jersey women ages 15–44. As expected, marital status has a significant effect and age has a significant, curvilinear effect. The effect of education is not linear. Women with less than a high school education were less likely to have had a birth than women with either a high school or college education, whereas graduate education had no effect.

Are the effects of place of birth different for current fertility than for cumulative fertility? Only three groups of women were more likely than the reference group (native-born non-Hispanic whites) to have had a child under age three, and two of those groups are native-born

Figure 10.7 PERCENTAGE OF NEW JERSEY WOMEN AGES 15–44 WITH CHILD UNDER AGE THREE, BY PLACE OF BIRTH

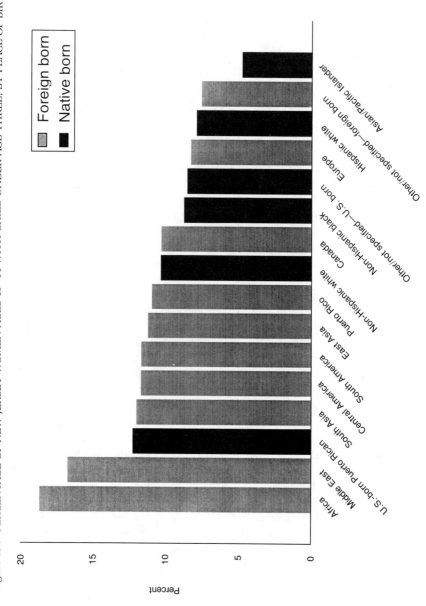

(Puerto Ricans and non-Hispanic blacks). One immigrant group had a higher probability of having had a birth—African-born women. Six groups of women had a significantly lower likelihood of having had a birth—two native-born and four foreign-born. Three of those immigrant groups came from regions with low recent fertility rates themselves (Europe, South Asia, and East Asia). From figure 10.8, one can conclude that only African immigrants were likely to have had higher recent fertility than native-born whites, but that American-born Puerto Ricans and blacks had higher fertility. Surprisingly, given this study's findings in the cumulative fertility analysis, island-born Puerto Rican women were essentially identical to the native-born non-Hispanic whites. This finding may reflect the short-term disruption effects of migration, which I test in the next analyses.

Are there similar patterns between immigrants once the study's measures of assimilation are controlled for? Figure 10.9 presents the logit results for foreign-born women only, comparing women who moved to the United States as children with those who moved as adults. For the foreign-born women who came as children, marital status and age have the expected effects, whereas educational attainment, citizenship, and ability to speak English have no significant impact. After controlling for these factors, only women born in Puerto Rico appear to have different fertility than European-born women.

When the findings for women who came to the United States as adults are examined, somewhat different results are found. Women who had some postcollege education were more likely to have a child under age three than any other group. Perhaps this is the result of a "catch-up" effect for these women—either they may have postponed childbearing while seeking a degree or while migrating (Ford 1990). One would expect there to be more variation in place-of-birth effects between women who came to the United States as adults, since they would have had more time to be exposed to the fertility regimes of their birthplace. This idea is supported by the results. Citizenship and the ability to speak English, which had a significant effect on cumulative fertility for adult immigrants, do not affect the likelihood of having a child under age three. In the short term, these variables may not have a large effect, but they may have a long-term effect on cumulative fertility.

Foreign-born women from Puerto Rico, the Middle East, Canada, Central America, South America, and Africa all had higher probabilities of having at least one child under age three. Except for Canadian women, all these women came from regions with high fertility rates. If there were a disruption effect on fertility, one would expect to see

Figure 10.8 LOGIT REGRESSION RESULTS ON WHETHER WOMAN HAS CHILD UNDER AGE THREE: ALL NEW JERSEY WOMEN AGES 15–44

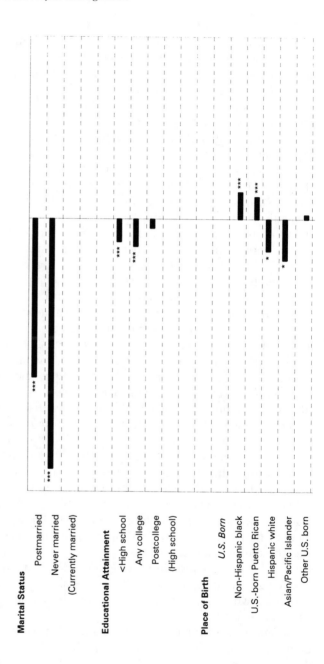

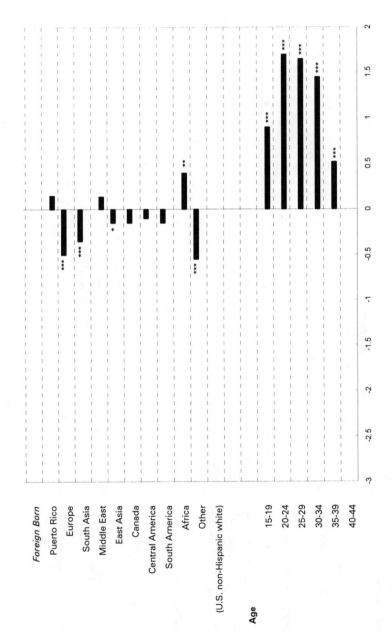

Intercept -2.31, Chi-square 11067.211, df 25, N 94,023, *p<.05, **p<.01, ***p<.001

Figure 10.9 LOGIT REGRESSION RESULTS ON WHETHER AN IMMIGRANT WOMAN HAS A CHILD UNDER AGE THREE

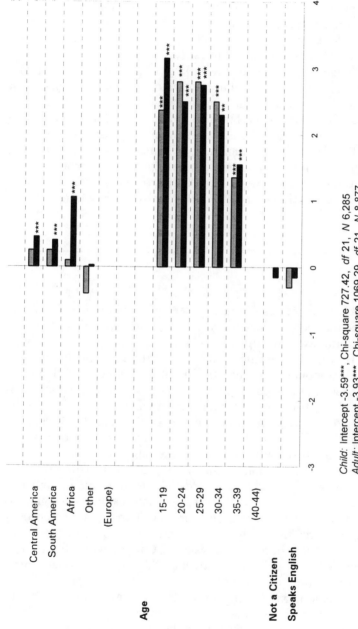

Child: Intercept -3.59***, Chi-square 727.42, *df* 21, *N* 6,285
Adult: Intercept -3.93***, Chi-square 1069.29, *df* 21, *N* 8,877
*p<.05, **p<.01, ***p<.001

it in recent fertility, but the findings show that women who migrated as adults from high fertility regions had higher recent fertility, even controlling for compositional differences between groups.

This study's measure of recent fertility (whether a woman has a child under age three) may be the variable of most interest to policymakers, since these are the children who are likely to be using health care resources now, and educational resources in the near future. The unadjusted distribution did show that foreign-born women were more likely to have a child under age three than were native-born white women. However, once compositional differences were adjusted for, the only immigrant group found to have significantly higher fertility than native-born whites was African-born women. Several groups, in fact, had significantly lower fertility than native-born whites.

CONCLUSION

Although New Jersey has a higher percentage of immigrants from low-fertility countries than does the rest of the United States, the fertility of immigrant women appears to be higher than for native-born women. However, these simple comparisons between the native- and foreign-born populations mask important within-group differences. When the mean number of children ever born was examined, individual subgroups of native- and foreign-born women were found to be interspersed along a continuum. That is, there is substantial heterogeneity within the populations of native- and foreign-born women, and the fertility distributions typically overlap.

One possible explanation for this heterogeneity of fertility patterns concerns the extent to which the populations differ on a number of characteristics that influence fertility decision making. Do compositional differences in age, marriage, or educational patterns account for the differences in fertility between groups, or does the region of birth have an effect beyond these factors? Comparing all the women in the New Jersey sample, this study found that including the control variables did eliminate some of the variation between groups of native- and foreign-born women, but region of birth was still significant for a number of women. Women who migrated from regions of high fertility tended to have more children than women who were born in lower fertility regions. If the foreign-born women came from low-fertility regions and have low fertility within the United States, it was not possible to distinguish between adaptation to American fertility norms or adherence to fertility norms from their countries.

The assimilation hypothesis has guided much of the research on immigrant fertility, and asserts that those who have been in the United States the longest, those who become citizens, and those who speak English should have fertility patterns that are more like those of women born in the United States than in their countries of origin. Support for the assimilation hypothesis was found when the fertility of immigrant women was analyzed. Between-group differences disappeared for the most part for those women who had come to the United States as children, whereas they remained for the women who came to the United States as adults. These results held both for cumulative and recent fertility. These findings parallel those of Kahn (1988), who also found that the age at which women immigrated to the United States affected the total number of children ever born, as did the ability to speak English and educational attainment.

An especially interesting group is Puerto Rican women, because it is possible to identify both those who were born on the island, as well as those born in the United States. Island-born Puerto Rican women generally have the highest fertility levels. Because of the amount of travel between the United States and Puerto Rico, one would expect U.S.-born Puerto Rican women to be affected by the fertility regimes of both countries (Jaffe and Cullen 1975). Whereas island-born women can also travel between the countries, the culture may be more pertinent for women born in Puerto Rico. U.S.-born Puerto Rican women did display fertility behavior that was between the extremes of native-born whites and island-born Puerto Rican women, a finding that confirms Jaffe and Cullen's (1975) work of 20 years earlier and lends support to the assimilation hypothesis.

Would these findings hold up if national-level data were examined instead of data specific to New Jersey? The distributions show that if only immigrants are compared with the native born without adjusting for compositional factors, some groups of immigrant women are indeed found to be having more children. Some of these high-fertility groups are underrepresented in New Jersey, and thus other states may have higher numbers of foreign-born children or native-born children whose parents are immigrants or may have a more stark native/foreign-born contrast in fertility. Would the compositional variables have different effects on national data? This study's results are consistent with Kahn's (1994) national-level analyses, in that the compositional differences did have similar effects for women in New Jersey. As opposed to this study, Kahn found that including these variables eliminated the differences between native- and foreign-born women, but this study had data from a different year and included a different sample.

This research has also shown, however, that it is misleading to assume that there is one fertility regime for the native-born population. Non-Hispanic blacks had fertility rates that equaled some of the high rates of certain ethnic groups, and native-born Asian/Pacific Islanders had fertility that was much lower. Further work on comparative fertility at the national level should disaggregate native-born women by race and ethnicity, rather than treat them as one standard-bearing group.

Notes

The helpful comments of participants at the "Conference on Impacts of Immigration to New Jersey" (at Princeton University, May 18–19, 1995), especially those of Thomas J. Espenshade, are gratefully acknowledged, as is the preparation of the figures by Amy Worlton.

1. Since the children ever born measure is related to the age composition of a population, the measure was standardized to the native-born population's age distribution.

2. Those who came to America at age 16 or younger were categorized as child immigrants. Data on time of immigration are not available by single year, but were condensed into categories. I took the midpoint of each category as the year of immigration. Those who came before 1950 were assigned an immigration year of 1945, so there is likely to be more miscoding of child/adult immigrants for the oldest women.

3. Although women born in Puerto Rico are not technically "immigrants," I am including them with the foreign born. This strategy allows us to examine whether there are differences in fertility between Puerto Ricans born on the island and those born in the United States.

4. For the United States as a whole, there was an approximate .25 difference between the mean numbers of children ever born to foreign-born and native-born women, which is close to the difference I calculated in New Jersey (U.S. Bureau of the Census 1989).

5. Since the mean number of children ever born is likely to be affected by the age composition of the population, I standardized them using the non-Hispanic white population. The results were similar, so I am presenting the unstandardized results; the standardized values are available upon request.

6. The ordering (from highest to lowest) is Africa, the Middle East, Central America, South Asia, South America, Puerto Rico, East Asia, the United States, Canada, and Europe.

7. There is some debate about whether OLS is the proper estimator for a dependent variable such as children ever born, which is a count variable. When the dependent variable has a large range of values, however, OLS provides reasonable estimates and the results are easily interpretable. This set of data fits that criterion.

8. Women were coded as being able to speak English so long as they could speak the language at all, even if they were unable to speak it well.

9. Given the racial differences in infant mortality in the United States, one would expect that African American children would be undercounted the most. When the regression results are examined, however, blacks still are found to have a higher likelihood of having a child under age three.

10. The numbers in figure 10.8 are the logit coefficients from the regressions. They represent the change in log odds of having a child under age three versus not having a child under age three. The coefficients can be exponentiated to give the percentage increase/decrease in the odds of having a child under age three.

References

Bean, Frank D., and C. Gray Swicegood. 1985. *Mexican American Fertility Patterns.* Austin: University of Texas Press.

Cherlin, Andrew J. 1992. *Marriage, Divorce, Remarriage,* 2d ed. Cambridge, Mass.: Harvard University Press.

Ford, Kathleen. 1985. "Declining Fertility Rates of Immigrants to the United States (with Some Exceptions)." *Sociology and Social Research* 70(1): 68–70.

———. 1990. "Duration of Residence in the United States and the Fertility of U.S. Immigrants." *International Migration Review* 24(1): 34–68.

Jaffe, A. J., and Ruth M. Cullen. 1975. "Fertility of the Puerto Rican Origin Population—Mainland United States and Puerto Rico: 1970." *International Migration Review* 9(2): 193–209.

Kahn, Joan R. 1988. "Immigrant Selectivity and Fertility Adaptation in the United States." *Social Forces* 67(1): 108–28.

———. 1994. "Immigrant and Native Fertility during the 1980s: Adaptation and Expectations for the Future." *International Migration Review* 28(3): 501–19.

Kozol, Jonathan. 1995. "Spare Us the Cheap Grace." *Time Magazine,* December 11: 96.

Morgan, S. Philip, Susan Cotts Watkins, and Douglas Ewbank. 1994. "Generating Americans: Ethnic Differences in Fertility." In *After Ellis Island: Newcomers and Natives in the 1910 Census,* edited by Susan Cotts Watkins. (83–124). New York: Russell Sage Foundation.

Pagnini, Deanna L., and S. Philip Morgan. 1990. "Intermarriage and Social Distance among U.S. Immigrants at the Turn of the Century." *American Journal of Sociology* 96(2): 405–32.

Pagnini, Deanna L., and Ronald R. Rindfuss. 1993. "The Divorce of Marriage and Childbearing: Changing Attitudes and Behavior in the United States." *Population and Development Review* 19(2): 331–47.

Population Reference Bureau. 1990. "World Population Data Sheet." Washington, D.C.: Author.

Rindfuss, Ronald R., S. Philip Morgan, and C. Gray Swicegood. 1988. *First Births in America*. Berkeley: University of California Press.

Rumbaut, Ruben G., and John R. Weeks. 1986. "Fertility and Adaptation: Indochinese Refugees in the United States." *International Migration Review* 20(2): 428–66.

Rutherford, Robert D., and Lee-Jay Cho. 1978. "Age-Parity-Specific Birth Rates and Birth Probabilities from Census or Survey Data on Own Children." *Population Studies* 32(2): 567–81.

U.S. Bureau of the Census. 1989. *Fertility of American Women: June 1988*. Current Population Reports. Ser. P-20, no. 436. Washington, D.C.: Author.

Chapter Eleven

IMMIGRANTS' EARNINGS AND LABOR-MARKET ASSIMILATION: A CASE STUDY OF NEW JERSEY

Deborah L. Garvey

The question of how well immigrants perform in the United States labor market has become a contentious policy issue, largely as a result of increased immigration rates in the postwar period. Per capita immigrant inflow to the United States has exhibited a secular upward trend since the end of World War II (U.S. Immigration and Naturalization Service 1996), and during the 1980s the country received the largest influx of immigrants in any decade since the 1920s (Butcher and Card 1991). These trends are expected to continue well beyond the turn of the century. Concerns about the ability of recent immigrants to apply their skills successfully in the U.S. labor market have intensified as a result of the shift in immigrants' origins away from more developed European countries and toward Latin America and Asia (Borjas 1994; Jasso and Rosenzweig 1990).

These policy issues first prompted researchers in the late 1970s to examine the ability of recent immigrants to assimilate into the U.S. labor market. Early cross-sectional studies of the U.S. labor-market performance of immigrant men (Borjas 1982; Carliner 1980; Chiswick 1978, 1980b) yielded two striking conclusions: first, although immigrants' earnings at arrival are lower than those of the native born, their experience-earnings profiles are steeper than those of similarly skilled native workers; and, second, there exists an "overtaking age" at about 10 to 15 years after arrival where the earnings-experience profiles of native-born and foreign-born workers with the same observed socioeconomic characteristics cross. These findings had the remarkable implication that not only do the earnings of the foreign born "catch up" to natives' earnings with experience in the U.S. labor market, but they actually surpass native earnings after a relatively brief period in the United States.

A human capital framework (Greenwood and McDowell 1986) is often called upon to explain the first result. Immigrants' earnings in the initial postarrival period are observed to be quite low relative to immigrants with longer stays in the United States and the native born, as a result of the imperfect international transferability of human capital. New immigrants have low productivity and consequently low earnings in the U.S. labor market because of the specificity of their formal educations, skill sets, and labor-market experience to the labor market of their countries of origin. However, those who migrate for reasons of economic improvement have strong incentives to engage in more intensive investment in U.S.-specific human capital relative to the native born, because they must recoup the costs of immigration.[1] With duration in the United States, then, immigrants accumulate U.S.-specific human capital by acquiring additional schooling, on-the-job training or skill certification, by improving their English language ability,[2] and by developing effective job-search techniques, knowledge, and experience relevant to the U.S. labor market. Thus, immigrants' productivity and earnings rise with length of stay in the United States, asymptotically approaching the productivity and earnings of the native born.

This explanation is not sufficient, however, to account for the existence of an overtaking age. Chiswick (1978) appealed to unobserved heterogeneity in the characteristics of immigrants relative to the native born to explain his second and more startling result. He posited that immigrants are favorably self-selected, relative to the overall population of their countries of origin, for characteristics favorable to labor market success. As a consequence, they are likely to "have more innate ability or motivation relevant to the labor market" (p. 901) than the native born. Thus, upon accumulation of the skills necessary to transfer fully their acquired human capital to the U.S. labor market, foreign-born workers can be expected to earn more than native-born workers who are otherwise similar in all observed characteristics.

The immigration assimilation literature subsequent to Chiswick leaned heavily on the assumptions of self-selection and "stationarity"[3] of immigrant characteristics across cohorts that were implicit in his theoretical framework. Researchers relied exclusively on cross-sectional data to estimate human capital earnings functions. Not surprisingly, Chiswick's results were confirmed and extended to female immigrants (Chiswick 1980b; Long 1980), and to certain subgroups of the immigrant population (e.g., Hispanics [Borjas 1982]). The empirical result that immigrants fully assimilate into the U.S. labor market within 10 to 15 years after arrival became accepted as fact.

It was not until 1985 that Borjas pointed out that cross-sectional analyses of immigrant earnings using a single data set suffer from a

critical identification problem.[4] A researcher cannot separately identify aging and cohort effects using a single cross section of data.
Hence, the positive correlation observed in the literature between
duration in the United States and increased earnings of immigrants
may arise as a result of either an aging effect (immigrant cohorts do
indeed assimilate into the U.S. labor market over time and experience
significant earnings growth) and/or a cohort effect (the observed
growth results from a secular decline in the skill mix of recently
admitted immigrants relative to older immigrant cohorts). Borjas proposed disentangling the aging and cohort effects by constructing a
synthetic cohort data set consisting of the 1970 and 1980 Censuses.
He found that the decomposition of immigrants' earnings into within-
cohort earnings growth and across-cohort earnings growth over the
decade yields very different results from simple cross-sectional estimates. He discovered that within-cohort earnings growth is much
slower than the relatively rapid growth implied by cross-sectional
analyses. His results indicate that immigrants' earnings will seldom,
if ever, surpass those of the native born over the life cycle. By contrast,
a significant fraction of the relative earnings growth observed in cross-
sectional regression estimates is accounted for by differentials in earnings across cohorts at the same point in their U.S. life cycles. Hence,
Borjas concluded that the observed improvement over time in immigrants' earnings relative to those of the native born is due not to labor-
market assimilation but reflects a secular decline in the skill mix that
enables immigrants to perform well in the U.S. labor market relative
to the native born. Borjas (1987) ascribed the strong across-cohort
effect to a decline in immigrant "quality," brought about by the shift
in the national origin mix away from relatively well-educated European immigrants and toward less-educated immigrants from Asia and
Latin America that resulted from the Immigration and Nationality Act
Amendments of 1965. Borjas (1995) subsequently confirmed these
results for the decade of the 1980s by extending his analysis to 1990
Census data.

   This chapter critically reexamines Borjas' findings using the Public
Use Microdata Samples (PUMS) from the 1980 and 1990 Censuses for
the state of New Jersey. My purpose is to investigate whether increases
in immigrant earnings observed in the cross section are as strongly
biased by quality differentials across cohorts for the decade of the
1980s as Borjas found to be the case in a national sample. The empirical analysis presented here assesses whether previous findings at the
national level are readily applicable to a high-immigrant concentration state with a relatively well-educated population and a

technology-oriented industrial structure. The analysis demonstrates that the growth in immigrants' real earnings observed in cross section is robust to a decomposition into its within-cohort and across-cohort components. Most immigrant groups experienced steady growth in their real earnings within cohorts, both absolutely and relative to the native born, over the decade. By contrast, there is little evidence to support the notion of a precipitous secular decline in the quality of immigrant cohorts. In some instances there even appears to be a slight increase in the skill mix of recent immigrant cohorts relative to earlier cohorts, although this effect is essentially zero when immigrants are compared to the native born. Overall, the coefficient on years since migration is biased little in the cross section by the confusion of aging and cohort effects. Indeed, the cross-sectional analysis appears to capture fairly well immigrants' acquisition of U.S.-specific human capital.

My findings suggest that immigrant assimilation is a complex phenomenon not adequately captured in national-level data sets. State-level case studies provide richer detail on the demographic characteristics of immigrants and natives and the regional labor markets in which they work than do national studies. The latter necessarily abstract from the diversity of the immigrant and native labor-market experience at the local level by emphasizing a global perspective. Additional case studies conducted on data from other high-immigrant concentration states are clearly required to provide a more comprehensive picture of the diversity of immigrants' labor-market assimilation experiences.

The remainder of the chapter is divided into four sections. The second section presents a theoretical framework for the decomposition of immigrants' earnings into within-cohort and across-cohort components. This framework is then applied to the analysis of immigrants' earnings in the third section and to the relative earnings of immigrants in the fourth section. The fifth section concludes the discussion.

THEORETICAL FRAMEWORK AND METHODOLOGY

The following review of the nonidentification of aging and cohort effects in cross-sectional regression analyses of immigrants' earnings, and the construction of synthetic cohorts from multiple cross-sectional data sets to solve this identification problem, closely follows Borjas (1985, 1994).

In cross-sectional analyses of the earnings of immigrants, a human capital earnings function of the following form is commonly estimated:

$$\ln(y_i) = X_i\beta + \gamma_1 YSM_i + \gamma_2(YSM_i)^2 + \epsilon_i, \qquad (11.1)$$

where y_i is the ith immigrant's annual wage and salary income, X_i is a vector of i's socioeconomic characteristics (e.g, potential labor-market experience,[5] marital status, and educational attainment), years since migration (YSM_i) measures the duration of stay in the United States, $(YSM_i)^2$ allows for nonlinearities in the economic returns to time in the United States, and ϵ_i is a normally distributed error term.

When total potential labor-market experience is included as an element of X, γ_1 and γ_2 then measure the differential return to labor-market experience acquired in the United States rather than in the country of origin. Hence, when γ_1 is estimated to be significantly positive and γ_2 slightly negative, as is the case in the cross-section literature on immigrant assimilation, these results are interpreted as supporting the predictions of the human capital model. Investment in U.S.-specific human capital enables immigrants to rapidly increase their productivity relative to the native born, at a decreasing rate over time, thereby generating future earnings growth. A steeper experience-earnings profile that gradually flattens over time is thus observed for immigrants relative to the native born.

There are two potential factors that bias estimates of γ_1 in cross-sectional analyses. First, if immigrants who eventually return to their countries of origin are a nonrandom sample of their immigrant cohorts or if the incentives to emigrate differ systematically by immigrant cohort, then γ_1 will be biased (Jasso and Rosenzweig 1988). For example, if relatively successful immigrants are more likely to emigrate, γ_1 will be biased down, because earlier cohorts will be selected to include relatively less-successful immigrants, whereas more recent cohorts will contain a more representative sample of the immigrant ability distribution. It is difficult, if not impossible, to estimate these "vintage" effects because of the paucity of data on emigration. Although this chapter makes no attempt to disentangle the effects of return migration on the earnings growth of immigrants, it is important to note that cross-sectional analyses are plagued by the same selectivity problem.

A second potential factor that biases estimates of γ_1 in the cross section is the assumption of stationarity in the characteristics of immigrant cohorts (net of selective emigration and pure aging effects) that is required to give a time-series interpretation to the coefficient. It is valid to say that a recently arrived immigrant will earn, on average, p percent more 10 years from now than today, because he was observed to earn p percent less than the cohort that arrived 10 years earlier, only if there is no secular change in the characteristics of immigrant cohorts (i.e., no cohort effect).[6]

The bias due to the violation of the stationarity assumption depends on the direction of the cohort effect. If recently admitted immigrant cohorts have fewer skills that are transferable to the U.S. labor market than earlier immigrant cohorts, due perhaps to changes in immigration policy that favor family reunification over occupational preferences, then γ_1 will be biased upward (see figure 11.1).[7] The degree of immigrant assimilation into the U.S. labor market will consequently be overstated in the cross section. On the other hand, if recent immigrant cohorts are more highly skilled relative to earlier cohorts, owing, say, to political changes in sending countries that result in emigration of those at the upper end of the skill and income distributions, then γ_1 will be biased downward.

Figure 11.1 COHORT EFFECTS AND CROSS-SECTION EXPERIENCE-EARNINGS PROFILES OF IMMIGRANTS

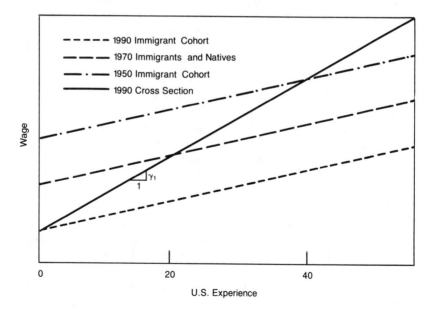

Source: Adapted from Borjas (1994).

It is likely that the assumption of no cohort effect is violated in the postwar period for several reasons. Political upheavals and institutional changes in Southeast Asia, the former Communist bloc, and Latin and South America have likely changed the migration calculus in favor of selectively skilled workers. Implementation of the Immigration and Nationality Act Amendments of 1965 altered the national origin mix toward less-developed source countries, whose immigrants do not perform as well in the U.S. labor market (Borjas 1987). Hence, it is misleading to draw inferences on the degree of immigrant assimilation in the labor market from estimates of γ_1 and γ_2 derived from equation (11.1).

To correct for the likely bias introduced in cross-sectional estimates of γ_1, it is convenient to partition the observed cross-sectional change in an immigrant cohort's earnings into its two components: a within-cohort component and an across-cohort component. Consider foreign-born men ages 18 to 54 with nonzero earnings in the 1980 Census and a "matched" sample of men aged 28 to 64 with nonzero earnings in the 1990 Census.[8] A typical cross-sectional analysis of immigrants' earnings in each census would take the form:

$$\ln(y_{80}) = X\delta_{80} + \alpha_{75}D_{75} + \alpha_{70}D_{70} + \alpha_{65}D_{65}$$
$$+ \alpha_{60}D_{60} + \alpha_{50}D_{50} + \alpha_{LT50}D_{LT50} + \epsilon_{80} \tag{11.2}$$

$$\ln(y_{90}) = X\delta_{90} + \beta_{85}D_{85} + \beta_{80}D_{80} + \beta_{75}D_{75} + \beta_{70}D_{70}$$
$$+ \beta_{65}D_{65} + \beta_{60}D_{60} + \beta_{50}D_{50} + \beta_{LT50}D_{LT50} + \epsilon_{90}, \tag{11.3}$$

where X[9] is defined as in equation (11.1), the D_k are immigrant cohort dummies for the five-year cohorts back to 1950 and the open-ended cohort prior to 1950, and the α_k and β_k are regression coefficients on the cohort dummies in the 1980 and 1990 earnings equations, respectively. Define k for the postwar cohorts for whom earnings data are present in both the 1980 and 1990 Censuses: (1) 1975–79, (2) 1970–74, (3) 1965–69, (4) 1960–64, and (5) 1950–59.[10] Then the preceding earnings regressions yield two predicted earnings equations:

$$\hat{y}_{80.k} = \overline{X}_k\hat{\delta}_{80} + \hat{\alpha}_k \tag{11.4}$$

$$\hat{y}_{90.k} = \overline{X}_k\hat{\delta}_{90} + \hat{\beta}_k, \tag{11.5}$$

where $\overline{X}_k$ represents the mean socioeconomic characteristics of immigrant cohort k in 1990. Hence, $\hat{y}_{80.k}$ is the average (natural logarithm of) earnings of a member of cohort k in 1980, and $\hat{y}_{90.k}$ is the average log earnings of a member of cohort k in 1990. Borjas (1985) noted these predicted earnings are net of "pure aging" effects. However, these aging effects may introduce bias in predicted earnings as defined here because one controls for 1990 socioeconomic characteristics in the prediction of 1980 earnings. If immigrants acquire additional education, improve their English-language proficiency, or otherwise alter their socioeconomic characteristics along any dimension other than time during the decade, the mean socioeconomic characteristics of the cohort are changed. Hence, within-cohort earnings growth is biased downward to the extent that immigrants improve their mean characteristics.[11]

Despite this potential source of bias, the critical assumption in cross-sectional analyses is indeed that *all* cohorts have the same average socioeconomic characteristics. Hence, the stationarity assumption permits one to define:

$$\hat{y}_{90,k+10} = \overline{X}_k \hat{\delta}_{90} + \hat{\beta}_{k+10}, \tag{11.6}$$

where $\hat{y}_{90,k+10}$ is the average (natural logarithm of) earnings of a member of the cohort that arrived 10 years after cohort k.

Using definitions (11.5) and (11.6), a cross-sectional regression then predicts that the growth in earnings for cohort k over the decade is given by:

$$\hat{y}_{90,k} - \hat{y}_{90,k+10} = \hat{\beta}_k - \hat{\beta}_{k+10}, \tag{11.7}$$

which measures the degree of labor-market assimilation of the cohort.[12]

Note that cross-sectional equation (11.7) can be decomposed into its two components:

$$\hat{y}_{90,k} - \hat{y}_{90,k+10} = (\hat{y}_{90,k} - \hat{y}_{80,k}) + (\hat{y}_{80,k} - \hat{y}_{90,k+10}), \tag{11.8}$$

where the first component gives the within-cohort growth in immigrants' earnings, and the second component gives the across-cohort growth. The within-cohort growth term measures the increase in real earnings experienced by a cohort over the decade. Note that the across-cohort term captures earnings growth of two immigrant cohorts, k and $(k + 10)$, who are at exactly the same point in their U.S. life cycles. That is to say, if cohort k has been in the United States n years in 1980, then cohort $(k + 10)$ has also been in the United States n years in 1990. To the extent that immigrants' skills have deteriorated (improved) across cohorts, the across-cohort term will be positive (negative), thus biasing upward (downward) the estimate of immigrants' earnings growth yielded by equation (11.7) in the cross section.

The difficulty with the preceding measure of growth in immigrants' earnings is that it does not take into account aggregate labor-market conditions that may selectively affect immigrants' earnings independently of their socioeconomic characteristics. For example, as New Jersey's economy strengthened during the mid-1980s, economic returns to characteristics exogenously increased. The within-cohort term is biased upward whereas the across-cohort term is biased downward to the extent that favorable labor market conditions exogenously influenced earnings. It is preferable to estimate the growth in immigrants' earnings *relative* to those of the native born to correct for any bias introduced by omitting aggregate labor-market controls from the regression.[13] This chapter's discussion of the measurement of growth in immigrants' earnings relative to the native born parallels the previous discussion of absolute immigrant earnings growth, and is detailed in appendix 11.A.

ANALYSIS OF IMMIGRANTS' EARNINGS

The data used for this study were obtained from the 5 percent PUMS of the 1980 and 1990 Censuses for New Jersey. The analysis was restricted to men ages 18 to 54 in the 1980 Census and to men ages 28 to 64 in the 1990 Census who had positive earnings and nonzero weeks worked in the reference year.[14] Immigrants accounted for 10.9 percent of the 1980 sample of male wage and salary earners and 16 percent of the 1990 sample.[15] The 5-percentage-point increase in the immigrant share of wage earners likely reflects a confluence of two factors: net migration to New Jersey of immigrant workers relative to the native born over the decade and differential patterns of labor supply behavior between immigrant and native-born workers.

The distribution of foreign-born male wage earners by region and country of origin in 1990 is given in table 11.1. The shift in immigration away from European countries toward Asia and Latin America observed in the national data also holds true for immigration to New Jersey. Note the decline in the proportion of immigrants from Europe, Canada, and Australia. Among immigrants who arrived prior to 1960, these groups accounted for almost 80 percent of all immigrants, whereas their proportion declined to just slightly over 20 percent of recent arrivals. The concomitant increase in immigration from the Western Hemisphere and Asia is also evident. These groups comprised approximately 17 percent of immigrants who arrived prior to

Table 11.1 PERCENTAGE DISTRIBUTION OF FOREIGN-BORN ADULT MEN BY
COUNTRY OF ORIGIN AND IMMIGRANT COHORT, NEW JERSEY: 1990

| | Period of Immigration (%) | | | | | | |
Country of Origin	1985–90	1980–84	1975–79	1970–74	1960–69	Before 1960	Overall
Europe/Canada[a]	**20.3**	**16.7**	**24.8**	**27.8**	**40.2**	**78.9**	**33.0**
Canada	1.2	0.6	1.0	0.6	1.4	2.7	1.2
Italy	0.8	1.0	2.6	6.1	11.6	19.4	6.5
Germany	1.1	0.7	0.7	1.2	3.1	15.2	3.2
Poland	3.8	3.0	2.4	2.3	4.0	4.6	3.4
Portugal	3.4	3.4	7.0	6.3	4.0	1.2	4.2
United Kingdom	2.7	2.6	2.6	0.9	3.0	6.1	2.9
Southeast and East Asia	**21.3**	**16.3**	**18.4**	**13.5**	**8.9**	**2.3**	**13.7**
China/Taiwan	4.0	4.7	5.2	3.0	3.7	1.1	3.7
Korea	4.7	3.4	3.8	2.5	1.0	0.5	2.7
Philippines	5.0	5.1	4.9	5.5	2.7	0.1	4.0
Middle East and South Asia	**14.5**	**16.2**	**15.3**	**14.1**	**7.6**	**3.8**	**12.1**
India	9.6	10.8	8.1	8.6	4.0	0.7	7.2
Central America/Caribbean	**18.2**	**21.8**	**18.4**	**22.6**	**25.6**	**8.1**	**19.8**
Cuba	1.6	5.6	1.1	9.3	15.4	4.8	6.7
Dominican Republic	4.2	4.2	4.7	2.9	3.3	0.3	3.4
Jamaica	2.0	2.4	4.0	2.3	1.6	0.4	2.1
Other America[b]	**17.9**	**17.8**	**12.9**	**15.1**	**12.8**	**3.4**	**13.9**
Colombia	5.3	6.8	3.7	4.9	4.3	0.4	4.5
Peru	3.6	4.4	2.6	3.2	1.2	0.2	2.6
Africa	**3.6**	**6.8**	**6.3**	**3.7**	**1.6**	**1.1**	**3.9**
Not reported	**4.1**	**4.5**	**3.9**	**3.3**	**3.4**	**2.4**	**3.7**
Total	100.0	100.0	100.0	100.0	100.0	100.0	100.0

Note: Sample includes men ages 28–64 who had nonzero wage or salary income in the
reference year, 1989. Proportions are calculated on the weighted sample.
a. Includes English-speaking developed countries (Ireland, Australia, New Zealand,
and Oceania).
b. Excludes Canada.

1960, whereas their proportion of recent arrivals was well over 70
percent.

It would be incorrect to conclude from this secular shift in region
of origin that the relative skill mix of immigrants has declined. Immigrants from India, for example, comprised nearly 30 percent of
Asian immigrants in recent cohorts, and Chinese and Korean immigrants accounted for another 25 percent (see table 11.1). These immigrant groups are highly educated relative both to other immigrant
groups and to the native born (see table 11.2). Among immigrants
from Latin America, arrivals from Cuba, the Dominican Republic,
Colombia, and Peru predominate. These groups appear to be less well-

Table 11.2 EDUCATIONAL ATTAINMENT AND EARNINGS OF NATIVE-BORN AND FOREIGN-BORN MEN: 1990

Panel A. Weighted Mean Educational Attainment and Earnings of Native-Born Men, by Ethnic Group, 1990

	Non-Hispanic Whites	Non-Hispanic Blacks	Non-Cuban Hispanics	Cubans	Asians	Other Ethnic Groups
Educational attainment[a]	11.75	10.25*	8.95*	11.17	13.07*	10.60*
Annual earnings	$44,692	$26,670*	$25,719*	$38,504	$42,050	$28,954*
N	1,103,028	140,368	55,521	2,018	3,234	2,381

Panel B. Weighted Mean Educational Attainment and Earnings of Foreign-Born Men, by Ethnic Group, 1990

	Non-Hispanic Whites	Non-Hispanic Blacks	Non-Cuban Hispanics	Cubans	Asians	Other Ethnic Groups
Educational attainment	10.64**	10.86**	9.06	9.56**	13.40	10.95
Annual earnings	$41,981**	$26,820	$23,110**	$32,835	$41,440	$25,693
N	96,877	19,233	59,340	17,367	56,955	1,379

Note: Sample includes men ages 28–64 who had nonzero wage or salary income in the reference year.
a. See note 16 in text for interpretation of educational attainment.
*Indicates mean is significantly different from that of non-Hispanic native-born whites at 5 percent level.
**Indicates foreign-born mean is significantly different from that of native-born counterparts at 5 percent level.

equipped for success in the U.S. labor market. They generally possess weaker skill sets (as proxied by educational attainment)[16] and have lower earnings compared to their native-born counterparts and non-Hispanic whites.

Tables 11.3 and 11.4 provide a snapshot of the industrial and occupational classification of immigrants relative to the native born. Not surprisingly, the foreign born are underrepresented relative to the native born in sectors that are traditionally reserved for the native born, such as public administration and the military. Unlike other research (Altonji and Card 1991), however, in which the immigrant distribution in agriculture is relatively greater than that of the native born, in New Jersey the immigrant share in agriculture is smaller than that of the native born, albeit insignificantly. This likely results from sampling variability introduced by the small role agriculture plays in New Jersey's service-oriented economy. On the other hand, both durable and nondurable manufacturing are high-immigrant share industries, and immigrants are also significantly overrepresented in the occupations that predominate in this sector, especially machine operators, fabricators, and laborers. Not surprisingly, the relative immigrant share in service occupations is significantly higher, particularly in private household and food service occupations, and lower in professional and technical occupations that require higher skills.

This descriptive analysis appears to support other findings in the literature suggesting that, in general, immigrants possess fewer of the skills required for success in the U.S. labor market than do their native-born counterparts, and as a consequence, immigrants have lower earnings. In the empirical analysis following, these stylized facts are subjected to more rigorous scrutiny.

As a starting point and basis for comparison with the cross-sectional literature on immigrant assimilation, a simple human capital earnings function was estimated for male wage and salary earners in the 1990 Census. Key parameter estimates are given in table 11.5 and the full set of parameter estimates is given in appendix table 11.A-1. After controlling for educational attainment,[17] differential returns to education for the foreign born, potential labor-market experience,[18] marital status, duration in the United States, whether a disability is present that limits work, standard metropolitan statistical area (SMSA) of residence, industry, occupation, and English-ability controls, these results generally replicate conventional findings based on a single cross-section of data. The coefficient on foreign born is slightly negative, but insignificant, for all ethnic groups except non-Hispanic whites. It indicates that newly arrived immigrants earn

Table 11.3 INDUSTRY CLASSIFICATION OF FOREIGN-BORN WAGE EARNERS, BY IMMIGRANT COHORT, AND NATIVE-BORN WAGE EARNERS: 1990

Industry	Immigrant Cohort (%)					Immigrant Overall (%)	Native Born (%)	Relative Immigrant Share (%)[a]
	1980–90	1970–79	1960–69	1950–59	Before 1950			
Agriculture, forestry, and fishing	1.39	0.47	0.49	0.47	0.26	0.82	0.95	0.86
Mining	0.33	0.21	0.16	0.13	0.42	0.24	0.20	1.20
Construction	10.44	9.87	9.98	9.90	10.58	10.13	9.60	1.06
Nondurable manufacturing	12.17	14.13	14.77	14.11	14.80	13.53	10.41	1.30*
Durable manufacturing	13.31	14.31	13.44	15.44	16.24	13.93	10.70	1.30*
Transport, public utilities, and communications	7.45	10.19	10.67	10.25	9.02	9.22	12.84	0.72*
Wholesale and retail trade	23.55	19.79	19.22	19.05	15.84	20.91	17.11	1.22*
Finance, insurance, and real estate	6.61	6.06	6.90	5.66	4.24	6.35	7.83	0.81*
Services	23.11	22.56	21.67	20.25	26.31	22.46	23.25	0.97
Public administration	1.47	2.13	2.35	4.44	2.29	2.17	6.46	0.34*
Armed forces	0.16	0.29	0.36	0.30	0	0.25	0.66	0.37*
Total	100	100	100	100	100	100	100	
N	94,895	72,842	50,712	25,727	6,975	251,151	1,306,550	

Note: Sample includes men ages 28–64 who had nonzero wage or salary income in the reference year. Proportions are calculated on the weighted sample.

a. Relative immigrant share is calculated by dividing the percentage of foreign-born workers employed in an industry by the percentage of native-born workers in that industry. If foreign-born and native-born workers are equally represented in an industry, the ratio is one. The concentration ratio is greater (less) than one as foreign-born workers are overrepresented (underrepresented) in an industry relative to the native born.

*Indicates relative immigrant share is significantly different from one at 5 percent level.

Table 11.4 OCCUPATION CLASSIFICATION OF FOREIGN-BORN WAGE EARNERS, BY IMMIGRANT COHORT, AND NATIVE-BORN WAGE EARNERS: 1990

Occupation	Immigrant Cohort (%)					Immigrant Overall (%)	Native Born (%)	Relative Immigrant Share (%)[a]
	1980–90	1970–79	1960–69	1950–59	Before 1950			
Manager and professional	26.15	29.42	32.58	32.18	42.01	29.46	33.77	0.87*
Technical, sales, and administrative support	20.05	19.87	18.52	19.77	19.64	19.65	23.48	0.84*
Service occupations	12.31	8.83	8.22	9.18	6.72	10.00	8.49	1.18*
Farming, forestry, and fishing	1.25	0.57	0.52	0.56	0.19	0.81	0.97	0.83
Precision production, craft, and repair	15.39	17.29	20.51	23.09	18.81	17.86	16.86	1.06
Operators, fabricators, and laborers	24.79	23.98	19.50	15.22	12.63	22.17	16.25	1.36*
Military occupations	0.06	0.04	0.15	0	0	0.06	0.18	0.35*
Total	100	100	100	100	100	100	100	
N	94,895	72,842	50,712	25,727	6,975	251,151	1,306,550	

Note: Sample includes men ages 28–64 who had nonzero wage or salary income in the reference year. Proportions are calculated on the weighted sample.

a. Relative immigrant share in an occupation is analogous to the relative immigrant share in an industry given in table 11.3.

*Indicates relative immigrant share is significantly different from one at 5 percent level.

between 2 percent and 22 percent less than their native-born counterparts, all else equal. The foreign-born coefficient is slightly positive, but insignificant, for non-Hispanic whites. The estimate implies that all else equal, white non-Hispanic immigrants earn approximately 5 percent more upon arrival than native-born non-Hispanic whites.[19]

These results confirm Chiswick's (1978) finding that immigrants have steeper experience-earnings profiles than similarly skilled native-born workers.[20] The coefficient estimates on the variables measuring differential returns to U.S. labor-market experience (YSM and YSM^2) imply that immigrants' earnings "catch up" with and then overtake those of the native born within 1 year (among whites and non-Cuban Hispanics) to 15 years (among Asians).

These results are robust to Chiswick's (1978) parsimonious specification of the human capital earnings regression. When controls for English-language ability, occupation, and industry are removed (see appendix table 11.A-2), the coefficient on foreign born becomes more negative, but generally remains insignificant, except for Asian and Cuban immigrants.[21] The existence of an overtaking age within 10–20 years of residence in the United States, though, is still preserved for all immigrant groups.

The decomposition of cross-sectional growth in immigrants' earnings into its within-cohort and across-cohort components was accomplished by estimating equations (11.2) and (11.3) on the pooled 1980 and 1990 immigrant sample. The results are presented in table 11.6. The Consumer Price Index for the Northeast region was used to express 1989 earnings in 1979 constant dollars. The covariates included only those variables in Chiswick's (1978) parsimonious specification of appendix table 11.A-2 (potential labor-market experience and its square, marital status, whether a work-limiting disability was present, the six educational categories, whether one resided in an SMSA, and duration in the United States), so that the indicator variables for foreign birth absorbed any of the differential returns to skills associated with immigrant status. Two changes were made to Chiswick's specification. The linear duration variable (years since migration) was replaced with immigrant cohort indicators to allow for a more flexible functional form for the returns to duration and to permit identification of each cohort. Also, indicator variables for each SMSA were replaced with an indicator "resides in an SMSA" for simplicity of presentation.[22] The δ vector of economic returns to immigrant characteristics was constrained to be the same for all cohorts within a census, but was allowed to vary across censuses.[23]

Table 11.5 REGRESSION ANALYSIS OF EARNINGS OF FOREIGN-BORN AND NATIVE-BORN MEN, BY ETHNIC GROUP: 1990
(STANDARD ERRORS IN PARENTHESES)

Regression Coefficients Dependent Variable: log (salary)	Non-Hispanic Whites	Non-Hispanic Blacks	Non-Cuban Hispanics	Cubans[a]	Asians[a]
Educational Attainment					
Not more than elementary	0.066	-0.105	0.177	0.063	0.067
	(0.060)	(0.133)	(0.098)	(0.059)	(0.059)
High school dropout	0.082	-0.157	0.229*	0.074	0.076
	(0.057)	(0.131)	(0.099)	(0.057)	(0.057)
Completed high school	0.159*	-0.044	0.412*	0.150*	0.149*
	(0.057)	(0.131)	(0.099)	(0.057)	(0.057)
Postsecondary/associate's degree	0.267*	0.092	0.509*	0.259*	0.255*
	(0.057)	(0.132)	(0.099)	(0.056)	(0.056)
Bachelor's degree	0.441*	0.321*	0.682*	0.435*	0.428*
	(0.057)	(0.134)	(0.101)	(0.057)	(0.057)
Professional/graduate degree	0.596*	0.417*	0.874*	0.591*	0.580*
	(0.057)	(0.137)	(0.108)	(0.057)	(0.057)
Foreign * Educational Attainment				(0.117)	(0.057)
Not more than elementary	-0.143	-0.292	-0.199	-0.562*	-0.285
	(0.091)	(0.288)	(0.121)	(0.158)	(0.160)
High school dropout	-0.167	-0.069	-0.280*	-0.456*	-0.319*
	(0.090)	(0.280)	(0.120)	(0.160)	(0.146)
Completed high school	-0.234*	-0.107	-0.399*	-0.559*	-0.283*
	(0.089)	(0.276)	(0.119)	(0.159)	(0.140)
Postsecondary/associate's degree	-0.229*	-0.076	-0.403*	-0.556*	-0.170
	(0.089)	(0.276)	(0.121)	(0.159)	(0.138)
Bachelor's degree	-0.234*	-0.147	-0.509*	-0.565*	-0.219
	(0.090)	(0.279)	(0.130)	(0.169)	(0.136)
Professional/graduate degree	-0.226*	-0.135	-0.410*	-0.475*	-0.142
	(0.090)	(0.283)	(0.140)	(0.168)	(0.136)

Experience	0.038*	0.036*	0.020*	0.039*	0.039*
	(0.001)	(0.004)	(0.004)	(0.001)	(0.001)
(Experience²)ᵃ	−0.001*	−0.001*	<−0.001*	−0.001*	−0.001*
	(<0.001)	(<0.001)	(<0.001)	(<0.001)	(<0.001)
Log weeks worked	0.956*	1.001*	0.882*	0.952*	0.948*
	(0.008)	(0.017)	(0.019)	(0.008)	(0.008)
Married	0.254*	0.177*	0.202*	0.264*	0.261*
	(0.006)	(0.017)	(0.019)	(0.006)	(0.006)
Foreign born	0.051	−0.224	−0.019	−0.187	−0.228
	(0.093)	(0.278)	(0.118)	(0.178)	(0.137)
Years since migration	0.007*	0.039*	0.033*	0.042*	0.021*
	(0.003)	(0.010)	(0.005)	(0.010)	(0.005)
(Years since migration²)ᵃ	<−0.001	−0.001*	−0.001*	−0.001*	<−0.001*
	(<0.001)	(<0.001)	(<0.001)	(<0.001)	(<0.001)
Has disability that limits work	−0.239*	−0.244*	−0.135*	−0.245*	−0.240*
	(0.012)	(0.035)	(0.043)	(0.012)	(0.012)
Constant	4.942*	5.100*	5.317*	5.069*	4.958*
	(0.098)	(0.388)	(0.148)	(0.107)	(0.132)
Adjusted R²	0.384	0.471	0.448	0.388	0.389
N	65,024	6,845	5,361	60,889	62,841

Note: The sample includes men ages 28–64 who worked in the reference year and had nonzero wage or salary income. Controls are included for SMSA of residence, industry, occupation, and English-language ability. See appendix table 11.A-1 for the complete ordinary least squares regression specification.

a. Foreign-born Cubans and Asians were compared to native-born non-Hispanic whites rather than to their native-born counterparts because of insufficient sample sizes.

*Indicates coefficient is significantly different from zero at 5 percent level.

Table 11.6 DECOMPOSITION OF CROSS-SECTIONAL GROWTH IN IMMIGRANT
EARNINGS, BY ETHNIC GROUP: 1980–90 (F-TESTS IN PARENTHESES)

Group and Year of Immigration	Cross-Sectional Growth	Within-Cohort Growth	Across-Cohort Growth
Non-Hispanic Whites			
1975–79	0.1351	0.1896	−0.0545
	(10.76*)	(20.83*)	(1.67)
1970–74	0.0142	0.0634	−0.0492
	(0.13)	(2.53)	(1.41)
1965–69	0.0527	0.1258	−0.0731
	(1.74)	(10.23*)	(3.22)
1960–64	0.1085	0.1305	−0.0219
	(7.22*)	(9.83*)	(0.29)
1950–59	0.0524	0.1146	−0.0622
	(3.28)	(13.36*)	(3.81)
Non-Hispanic Blacks			
1975–79	0.2462	0.2459	0.0004
	(8.04*)	(6.90*)	(0.00)
1970–74	0.2031	0.2286	−0.0255
	(6.64*)	(6.65*)	(0.08)
1965–69	0.2459	0.3478	−0.1019
	(6.46*)	(9.47*)	(1.03)
1960–64	−0.0911	0.1931	−0.2842
	(0.49)	(1.09)	(3.37)
1950–59	−0.0991	0.0761	−0.1752
	(0.26)	(0.10)	(0.88)
Non-Cuban Hispanics			
1975–79	0.3612	0.3309	0.0304
	(74.93*)	(44.22*)	(0.47)
1970–74	0.2907	0.1632	0.1275
	(55.28*)	(14.10*)	(9.71*)
1965–69	0.0906	0.2041	−0.1134
	(3.36)	(15.26*)	(4.63*)
1960–64	0.0972	0.0733	0.0239
	(2.46)	(0.94)	(0.15)
1950–59	0.066	0.0252	0.0404
	(0.62)	(0.06)	(0.28)

(continued)

The estimates given in table 11.6 indicate that most immigrant cohorts experienced real wage growth in the cross section and that
nearly all the growth during the 1980s resulted from real earnings
growth within the cohort.[24] For example, the cross-sectional regression predicts that non-Hispanic black immigrants who arrived between 1975 and 1979 experienced 24.6 percent real wage growth on
average over the decade. The within-cohort growth term indicates that

Table 11.6 (continued)

Group and Year of Immigration	Cross-Sectional Growth	Within-Cohort Growth	Across-Cohort Growth
Cubans			
1975–79	0.3729	0.4420	−0.0691
	(3.71)	(4.54*)	(0.13)
1970–74	0.2859	0.3423	−0.0565
	(11.44*)	(17.02*)	(0.38)
1965–69	−0.0183	0.3014	−0.3197
	(0.01)	(17.17*)	(4.06*)
1960–64	0.2448	0.2703	−0.0255
	(9.90*)	(12.87*)	(0.10)
1950–59	0.0483	0.3141	−0.2658
	(0.26)	(6.75*)	(7.83*)
Asians			
1975–79	0.2728	0.2414	0.0314
	(50.00*)	(27.71*)	(0.51)
1970–74	0.2313	0.2555	−0.0242
	(33.04*)	(26.73*)	(0.25)
1965–69	0.2110	0.2103	0.0007
	(17.27*)	(11.10*)	(0.00)
1960–64	0.2059	0.1352	0.0706
	(8.57*)	(1.78)	(0.69)
1950–59	0.1043	0.1847	−0.0804
	(1.06)	(1.86)	(0.59)

Source: Appendix tables 11.A-3 and 11.A-4.
*Indicates F-test is significant at 5 percent level.

all of this growth resulted from real wage growth within the cohort, and was not an artifact of earnings differences over cohorts at the same point in their U.S. life cycles.

One of the most striking features of the decomposition is that, for many immigrant cohorts, the within-cohort growth in real earnings actually exceeds that predicted in the cross section over the decade. This implies that the earnings of more recent immigrants were greater than those of earlier cohorts at the same duration in the United States. Consider, for example, Cuban immigrants who arrived in the second half of the 1960s. Cross-sectional earnings growth for the cohort was an insignificant − 2 percent. However, the cohort actually experienced significant wage growth of 30 percent over the decade. This growth in real earnings was obscured by cohort differentials in earnings: the cohort of the late 1970s was relatively more successful in the labor market in 1990 than the cohort of the late 1960s had been in 1980.

Caution should be used when interpreting these negative across-cohort effects as indicative of an improvement in the labor-market capabilities (or "quality") of more recent immigrants. Note that the only cohorts for which such effects are significant are the Cuban cohorts of the 1950s and late 1960s and the 1965–69 cohort of non-Cuban Hispanics. The Cuban estimates may well be driven by the "brain drain" that resulted in the years immediately following the 1959 Cuban revolution. These highly skilled immigrants would likely be more successful upon arrival in the United States than the cohort who arrived 10 years prior had been, as a result of high selectivity in favor of immigrants with skills most valued by the U.S. labor market and with a network of contacts that enabled them to emigrate.[25]

Two important conclusions may be drawn from table 11.6. First, the within-cohort growth in earnings experienced by immigrants varied both across cohorts of the same ethnic group and across ethnic groups. Within-cohort growth was generally stronger for more recent cohorts than for earlier cohorts. This reflects the fact that most immigrants migrate in early adulthood, when returns to experience are likely to be greatest. Second, the within-cohort growth in real earnings was especially strong for Cubans, other Hispanics, and blacks, and less so for white immigrants. These results are consistent with the hypothesis that there was little, if any, change across immigrant cohorts in their ability to adapt to the U.S. labor market. Hence, one would reject the hypothesis that there has been a secular decline in the "quality" of immigrants to New Jersey.

GROWTH IN RELATIVE EARNINGS OF IMMIGRANTS

The measure of growth in immigrants' real earnings in the last decade presented in table 11.6 does not control for changes in aggregate market conditions that affected New Jersey during the period. If aggregate labor-market or demand conditions were such that immigrants' earnings were positively affected independently of their socioeconomic characteristics, then the within-cohort growth term is biased upward. It is thus preferable to estimate the growth in immigrants' earnings relative to a base of the native born.

Pooled immigrant and native samples were used to estimate the human capital earnings functions of equations (11.2) and (11.3) in the text and equations (A.1) and (A.2) in appendix 11A. Dummy variables indicating the census from which a worker was drawn and whether the worker was an immigrant or a native were interacted with the covariates to produce a superset of explanatory variables. The δ vector of returns to immigrant characteristics was constrained to be the same for all immigrant cohorts within a census, but was allowed to vary across censuses, while the λ vector of returns to native characteristics was permitted to vary across censuses for the native born. The cross-sectional growth in the relative earnings of immigrants was then decomposed into its within-cohort and across-cohort components as given by equation (A.4) in appendix 11A. Within-cohort growth in relative earnings indicates the degree to which immigrants' and natives' earnings-experience profiles converge over time. The across-cohort term measures the change in relative earnings of adjacent immigrant cohorts at the same point in their U.S. life cycles. A positive value for the latter term indicates that the relative earnings capacity of immigrant cohorts with the same duration in the United States declined over time, thus biasing upward the rate of earnings convergence observed in the cross section.

The decomposition of relative growth in immigrants' earnings is given in table 11.7. The results indicate that the real earnings growth observed within immigrant cohorts is robust to controls for aggregate labor-market conditions. For example, the cross-sectional regression predicts that non-Hispanic black immigrants who arrived between 1975 and 1979 experienced 24.6 percent average real wage growth over the decade. The within-cohort relative growth term indicates that almost all of this growth (0.1951/0.2462 ≃ 80%) resulted from real wage growth of immigrants relative to the native born. The growth in real earnings was slightly (although insignificantly) overstated by cohort differences in relative earnings: the 1975–79 immigrant cohort had slightly higher earnings in 1980 relative to the native born than the 1985–89 cohort did in 1990.

Although within-cohort relative earnings growth is of a lower magnitude than that observed in the immigrant sample, the basic finding that most immigrant cohorts experienced at least some real growth in their relative earnings remains unaltered. As in the immigrant sample, within-cohort relative earnings growth is observed to be strongest for blacks, Asians, and non-Cuban Hispanics, which indicates these groups made the greatest gains relative to their native-born counterparts. It is interesting to note, however, that the earnings growth of Cuban immigrants relative to the non-Hispanic native white population were not as great as those observed in the immigrant sample.

Table 11.7 DECOMPOSITION OF CROSS-SECTIONAL GROWTH IN RELATIVE
IMMIGRANT EARNINGS, BY ETHNIC GROUP: 1980–90
(F-TESTS IN PARENTEHSES)

Group and Year of Immigration	Cross-Sectional Growth	Within-Cohort Growth	Across-Cohort Growth
Non-Hispanic Whites			
1975–79	0.1351	0.0844	0.0507
	(12.83*)	(4.80*)	(1.69)
1970–74	0.0142	−0.0396	0.0538
	(0.15)	(1.13)	(1.94)
1965–69	0.0527	0.0179	0.0348
	(2.07)	(0.24)	(0.84)
1960–64	0.1085	0.0276	0.0810
	(8.61*)	(0.51)	(4.65*)
1950–59	0.0524	0.0129	0.0395
	(3.91*)	(0.19)	(1.74)
Non-Hispanic Blacks			
1975–79	0.2462	0.1951	0.0511
	(7.81*)	(4.10*)	(0.24)
1970–74	0.2031	0.1752	0.0279
	(6.44*)	(3.65)	(0.09)
1965–69	0.2459	0.2813	−0.0354
	(6.27*)	(5.86*)	(0.12)
1960–64	−0.0911	0.1328	−0.2239
	(0.47)	(0.49)	(2.00)
1950–59	−0.0991	−0.0526	−0.0465
	(0.25)	(0.04)	(0.06)
Non-Cuban Hispanics			
1975–79	0.3612	0.2675	0.0937
	(73.14*)	(24.10*)	(3.57)
1970–74	0.2907	0.1248	0.1659
	(53.95*)	(6.34*)	(12.30*)
1965–69	0.0906	0.1778	−0.0872
	(3.28)	(8.84*)	(2.10)
1960–64	0.0972	0.0493	0.0479
	(2.40)	(0.36)	(0.48)
1950–59	0.0656	0.0135	0.0521
	(0.60)	(0.01)	(0.37)

(continued)

Despite this somewhat arbitrary choice of reference group, though, Cuban immigrant cohorts still enjoyed positive real wage growth over the decade.

Across-cohort growth in relative immigrant earnings, although somewhat more positive than in the immigrant sample, was rarely significant. Two important cohorts for which the term was signifi-

Table 11.7 (continued)

Group and Year of Immigration	Cross-Sectional Growth	Within-Cohort Growth	Across-Cohort Growth
Cubans[a]			
1975–79	0.3729	0.2822	0.0907
	(4.92*)	(2.44)	(0.30)
1970–74	0.2859	0.1416	0.1442
	(15.15*)	(3.77)	(3.23)
1965–69	−0.0183	0.1323	−0.1507
	(0.02)	(4.32*)	(1.19)
1960–64	0.2448	0.1655	0.0792
	(13.11*)	(6.35*)	(1.31)
1950–59	0.0483	0.1296	−0.0813
	(0.34)	(1.51)	(0.95)
Asians[a]			
1975–79	0.2728	0.1458	0.1270
	(52.70*)	(10.50*)	(8.73*)
1970–74	0.2313	0.1919	0.0394
	(34.82*)	(15.64*)	(0.67)
1965–69	0.2110	0.1474	0.0636
	(18.20*)	(5.66*)	(1.21)
1960–64	0.2059	0.0762	0.1297
	(9.03*)	(0.59)	(2.44)
1950–59	0.1043	0.1158	−0.0116
	(1.12)	(0.77)	(0.01)

Note: F-test for cross-sectional growth differs slightly from that in table 11.6 because the regression was estimated on the pooled immigrant and native sample.
a. Foreign-born Cubans and Asians were compared to native-born non-Hispanic whites due to insufficient sample sizes.
*Indicates F-test is significant at 5 percent level.

cantly positive were the 1970–74 cohort of non-Cuban Hispanics and the 1975–79 Asian cohort.[26] The effect observed for the Hispanic cohort may reflect a shift in the relative composition of immigrants from economic migrants to refugees between the early 1970s and the early 1980s. Immigrants from El Salvador, Honduras, and Peru, countries torn by civil strife in the period, composed a larger fraction of the Hispanic immigrant flow in the early 1980s than during any other period in the postwar era. Since refugees migrate primarily for political, not economic, reasons and are less likely to have engaged in intensive preparation for their migration, they might be expected to do less well in the labor market upon arrival than economic migrants. The decline in growth of relative earnings of the most recent Asian cohort as compared to the 1975–79 cohort appears to reflect a marked decline in educational attainment among Indians and, to a lesser extent, lower educational achievement among Chinese, Korean, and Taiwanese immigrants. It must be noted, however, that even these cohorts' experience-earnings profiles exhibited convergence with those of the native born, albeit at a lesser rate than that implied in the cross section.

The key conclusion to draw from table 11.7 is that, although the rate of growth in the relative earnings of immigrants is overstated in the cross-sectional regression, most immigrant cohorts did indeed experience positive wage growth relative to their native counterparts during the 1980s. Hence, one cannot reject the hypothesis that immigrants' earnings-experience profiles are converging to those of the native born.

CONCLUSION

This chapter scrutinizes Borjas' findings (1985, 1995) of declining immigrant "quality" in the postwar period and investigates whether this conclusion is applicable to a high-immigrant concentration state with a well-educated work force and a technology-oriented industrial structure. The empirical analysis demonstrates that the growth in real earnings of immigrant cohorts observed in cross-sectional data, although somewhat overstated, is insensitive to a decomposition into its within-cohort and across-cohort components. Most immigrant cohorts experienced steady growth in real earnings over the decade, both absolutely and relative to their native-born counterparts. On the other hand, there is little evidence to support the hypothesis of a precipitous secular decline in the "quality" of immigrant cohorts. Indeed, there appears to be little significant change in the skill mix of recent immigrant cohorts relative to earlier cohorts. Overall, the results provide strong evidence that New Jersey's immigrants have successfully assimilated into the local labor market.

These conclusions require further examination, however. My results are not immediately generalizable to the immigrant population of the United States as a whole. The technology- and service-oriented nature of the New Jersey economy attracts immigrants who are better educated and more highly skilled relative to the overall immigrant population.[27] The potential bias of selective migration of immigrants is further exacerbated by the relative ease with which immigrants can cross state boundaries. If immigrants who find it difficult to succeed in the New Jersey labor market simply migrate to a bordering state, then within-cohort growth in immigrants' earnings will be biased upward. If such outmigration as a result of labor-market failure is undertaken differentially among immigrants and the native born, bias will be imparted to estimates of within-cohort growth in the relative earnings of immigrants. Borjas' (1995) findings, using national data, that immigrants did not successfully assimilate into the U.S. labor market over the decade of the 1980s, might be taken as prima facie evidence that selectivity bias drives my findings of immigrant assimilation. If selectivity bias is found to be a problem, it calls into question the reliability of assimilation results obtained from state-level analyses.

As a test of the selectivity hypothesis, I decomposed earnings growth in the cross section into its within-cohort and across-cohort components using 1970 and 1980 Census data for New Jersey.[28] If the real wage growth enjoyed by New Jersey's foreign-born population during the 1980s were purely an artifact of selectivity effects, one would expect New Jersey's immigrants to have experienced similar absolute and relative earnings growth during the 1970s. Such a finding would be expected, given that immigrants in New Jersey at the time of the 1980 Census also possessed skill sets differentially favorable to labor market success.[29] The state's immigrants were more highly skilled on average than the immigrant population of the United States, and their educational attainment compared favorably with that of natives. The results of the 1970/1980 earnings growth decomposition, although frequently insignificant, mimic Borjas' (1995) findings: immigrants enjoyed little real wage growth, either absolutely or relative to the native born, over the decade of the 1970s. There is also evidence of a slight decline in immigrant "quality," as measured by positive across-cohort (relative) earnings growth estimates.

These results refute a simple immigrant selectivity story as the only explanation for the disparity between my evidence of assimilation for New Jersey's immigrant population and Borjas' (1995) findings of declining immigrant quality over the decade of the 1980s. Educational attainment of New Jersey's immigrants in the 1980 Census, both in absolute terms and relative to the native born, resembled the 1990 distribution shown in table 11.2 (Garvey 1994). It appears, therefore, that selective outmigration of immigrants or natives who fared poorly in New Jersey's labor market in the 1970s does not account for the observed within-cohort earnings growth of immigrants over the decade of the 1980s.

My findings for the 1970s confirm that the successful assimilation of immigrants into New Jersey's labor market observed during the

1980s cannot be wholly explained by the relative high skills and educational attainment of New Jersey's immigrant population. If this were the entire story, immigrants should also have experienced real earnings growth over the decade of the 1970s. Changes in the wage structure over the 1980s resulted in a rapid rise in returns to skills over the period and may partially account for the observed immigrant labor market assimilation (Juhn, Murphy, and Pierce 1993). New Jersey's industrial structure is characterized by high-technology and skilled service sectors that require highly educated workers. As returns to skills increased, these regional labor market effects exerted a stronger independent influence on the relative growth of immigrants' earnings.

Variations in structural effects across local labor markets may not be adequately captured in aggregate national-level data sets, such as those used by Borjas (1985, 1995). As a result, national-level studies of immigrant performance in the U.S. labor market may not fully describe the complex assimilation experience of immigrants into regional labor markets that are characterized by vastly different occupational and industrial structures. Further case studies using data from other high-immigrant concentration states are necessary to develop a comprehensive picture of immigrants' labor-market assimilation experience.

Notes

I am indebted to David Card, Dexter Chu, Thomas Espenshade, Henry Farber, Cynthia Harper, Karen Needels, Jim Heum Park, Cecilia Rouse, and to participants at the "Conference on Impacts of Immigration to New Jersey" (at Princeton University, May 18–19, 1995), as well as at the Department of Economics' Labor Lunch, for their helpful advice and comments.

1. The same argument can be extended to refugees, who migrate primarily for ideological or political reasons to avoid persecution. Such migrants may possess skills that are less readily transferable to the U.S. labor market, and as a result, they may perform worse initially relative to economic immigrants. However, the prohibitive cost of return migration provides greater incentive for such migrants to invest more heavily in U.S.-specific human capital than economic migrants and thus, they may have steeper earnings-experience profiles (Chiswick 1980a). Borjas (1982) found, for example, that Cubans have greater postimmigration investments in schooling than other Hispanic immigrants.

2. Reviews of the literature and analyses of the interplay of English-language proficiency and earnings are found in Bloom and Grenier (1993) and Chiswick and Miller (1992,

1995). Espenshade and Fu (1996) analyzed the acquisition of English language skills by immigrants within a life-course framework.

3. Under stationarity, one assumes that average socioeconomic and demographic characteristics related to labor market success are constant across immigrant cohorts.

4. See Heckman and Robb (1985) for a discussion of the identifiability of aging and cohort effects in earnings regressions.

5. Potential labor-market experience measures the number of years a worker could be in the labor force, under the assumptions that workers complete their schooling without interruption and do not work while attending school. The definition of potential labor-market experience used in this chapter—age minus years of schooling minus 5—is adopted from the literature.

6. Note that p equals $(10\hat{\gamma}_1 - 100\gamma_2) \cdot 100$ in this example, when YSM equals 10.

7. For a discussion of the theoretical and empirical implications for immigrant performance in the U.S. labor market of the shift in the immigration policy from occupational to family reunification preferences, see Borjas (1994) and Borjas and Bronars (1991).

8. The adjacent census samples do not actually represent the same men; hence, they are called "synthetic" cohorts. Differences arise for several reasons. First, the census sample is a 5-percent sample of enumerated persons; thus, by design, it does not cover the population universe. To the extent that there are differences in enumeration procedures across censuses that differentially affect the ability to count subgroups of the immigrant population or immigrants relative to natives, the two samples will not match. Second, as noted earlier, there is also likely to be selective return migration across immigrant cohorts and countries of origin. Differential interstate migration of immigrants and natives may also alter immigrant cohort size and composition over the decade. Third, if there are differential patterns over time of mortality, of disability that prevents work, or of labor supply behavior across immigrant cohorts or among immigrants and native-born workers, then the two census samples will not be perfectly matched. Note that these weaknesses are also inherent in cross-sectional analyses of census data.

9. Note that the X vector does not include a constant. This permits inclusion of the full set of immigrant cohort dummies without introducing perfect collinearity in the regressors.

10. Coefficient estimates for the immigrant cohort that arrived prior to 1950 are not reported because the cohort is an amalgamation of several cohorts that cannot be separately identified. This cohort comprised approximately 6 percent of the 1980 sample of immigrant males and 3 percent of the 1990 sample.

11. Chiswick (1986) noted that this bias is likely to be more severe for Cuban immigrants and other refugee groups that invest in more postimmigration schooling relative to other immigrant groups. However, within-cohort earnings growth is likely biased downward even *within* a national origin group. Newly arrived immigrants invest in more U.S.-specific human capital, as they acquire skill in navigating the U.S. labor market and fluency in English, than older immigrant cohorts (Espenshade and Fu 1996). Differences in legal status may also have a differential impact on earnings (Jasso and Rosenzweig 1988). Illegal immigrants and nonresident legal immigrants may experience lower returns to work than permanent residents, because their labor-market activities are constrained by legal requirements or a desire to remain undetected by immigration authorities. Within-cohort earnings growth is then understated to the extent that immigrants naturalize or become legal permanent residents. Hence, one would expect within-cohort earnings growth to be most biased for recent immigrant cohorts.

12. Note that cross-sectional earnings growth given in equation (11.7) is exactly defined for all cohorts with the exception of the 1950 cohort. Under the assumption that im-

migrant arrivals in the 1950s are similarly distributed over time to those of the 1960s, this term is defined as a simple weighted average of the two five-year cohorts of the 1960s:

$$\hat{y}_{90.50} - \hat{y}_{90.60} = \hat{\beta}_{50} - \frac{1}{2}[\hat{\beta}_{60} + \hat{\beta}_{65}].$$

13. Bias still remains in longitudinal analyses of immigrants' earnings, even after controlling for labor-market conditions, if the degree of complementarity of immigrants and native-born workers in production changes over time (Grossman 1982). Note that such biases plague cross-sectional analyses as well.

14. The criterion of nonzero weeks worked for wage and salary earners resulted in a negligible loss of 0.15 percent of the 1980 sample and less than 0.01 percent of the 1990 sample.

15. The 1990 Census provides weights that permit the sample to be weighted to the population level. Descriptive statistics are presented for the weighted sample. The regression analysis of growth in immigrants' earnings is performed on the unweighted 1990 and 1980 samples. See DuMouchel and Duncan (1983) for an analysis of circumstances when weighted regression of stratified samples is preferable to unweighted regression. In this study's model, where β is assumed to vary by population stratum, there is no rationale for preferring weighted to unweighted regression in estimating the population β.

16. Educational attainment is reported in the 1990 Census as the highest level of schooling completed or the highest degree received by the respondent. This classification does not always correspond to single years of completed schooling, as is the case in the 1980 Census. The increment to completed schooling represented by a response category varies from approximately one year to an unspecified number of years (e.g., completed a professional, master's, or doctoral degree). Mean educational attainment in table 11.2 therefore does *not* give the mean years of completed schooling. A value of 9 corresponds to completion of the 12th grade, but no diploma; 10 to a high school graduate; 11 to some college education; 12 and 13 to an associate's degree; 14 to a bachelor's degree; and 15 through 17 to a master's through doctoral degree.

17. For compatibility, educational attainment is defined as a categorical variable in both censuses, with groupings delineated according to hypothesized threshold values. Hence, whether elementary school was completed, whether one completed high school or dropped out, whether postsecondary education was pursued, whether one possessed a bachelor's degree, and whether one held a postgraduate degree form the six educational attainment categories. The baseline category is no formal schooling completed.

18. Calculation of potential labor market experience (age − schooling − 5) is not straightforward in the 1990 Census because of the way educational attainment is reported (see note 16). To obtain the number of years spent in school, each grade was assumed to take one year to complete. The average number of years was assigned for response categories that encompassed more than one grade. A bachelor's degree was assumed to take four years beyond high school, a master's degree an additional two years beyond college, and the average professional/doctoral degree was assumed to be completed four years after the bachelor's degree. These definitions did not appear to impart a systematic bias to the coefficients on experience, which tended to be of the same magnitude as those found in the literature.

19. These results, which imply less of a disadvantage to being foreign born than is commonly found in the cross-section literature, are influenced by the inclusion of controls for English-language ability in the regressions. Difficulty with English is highly correlated with being foreign born, and is strongly negatively related to earnings (Chiswick and Miller 1992). The negative association of foreign-born status and earnings is thus attenuated when one controls for foreign birth and English-language ability simultaneously. Indeed, the coefficient on foreign born in the non-Hispanic white regres-

sion becomes (insignificantly) negative upon omission of the English-ability variables. Regression estimates of table 11.5 without controls for English-language fluency are available from the author upon request.

20. Potential labor-market experience and its square measure the return to an additional year spent in labor-market activities for both the native born and the foreign born. The variable "years since migration" (YSM) and its square (YSM^2) are calculated as the number of years a foreign-born worker has spent in the United States. Both variables equal zero for the native born. Hence, YSM and YSM^2 give the differential return to U.S. labor market experience for the foreign born. It is equivalent to interacting the potential labor market experience variables with nativity status.

21. These findings imply that the nativity status indicator serves as a proxy for English-language ability and its effects on occupational attainment.

22. Specification tests indicated that there was essentially no difference in the explanatory power of the two sets of SMSA variables.

23. This was accomplished by defining an indicator for the census from which the observation was drawn and interacting it with the covariates to produce a superset of explanatory variables.

24. Recall that if immigrants' skills deteriorated (improved) across cohorts, the across-cohort term would be positive (negative), thus biasing upward (downward) the cross-sectional estimates of immigrants' earnings growth reported in the first column of table 11.6.

25. It seems unlikely that favorable aggregate labor market conditions in 1990 relative to 1980 explain this result, since one would need to posit that such conditions selectively affected Hispanic immigrants.

26. Recall that a significantly positive estimate of across-cohort relative earnings growth indicates that the skill mix of recent immigrant cohorts relative to the native born has declined over time, thus biasing upward the estimate of immigrants' relative earnings growth in the cross section.

27. Evidence of such differences is documented by Western and Kelly in chapter 2 of this volume.

28. The results are available from the author upon request.

29. See Garvey (1994) for a socioeconomic and demographic profile of New Jersey's immigrant population from 1950 to 1980.

References

Altonji, Joseph G., and David Card. 1991. "Immigration, Trade, and the Labor Market." In *Immigration, Trade, and the Labor Market*, edited by John M. Abowd and Richard B. Freeman. Chicago and London: University of Chicago Press.

Bloom, David E., and Gilles Grenier. 1993. "Language, Employment and Earnings in the United States: Spanish-English Differentials from 1970 to 1990." NBER Working Paper 4584. Cambridge, Mass.: National Bureau of Economic Research.

Borjas, George J. 1982. "The Earnings of Male Hispanic Immigrants in the United States." *Industrial and Labor Relations Review* 35(3): 343–53.

_____. 1985. "Assimilation, Changes in Cohort Quality, and the Earnings of Immigrants." *Journal of Labor Economics* 3(4): 463–89.

_____. 1987. "Self-Selection and the Earnings of Immigrants." *American Economic Review* 77(4): 531–53.

_____. 1994. "The Economics of Immigration." *Journal of Economic Literature* 32(4): 1667–1717.

_____. 1995. "Assimilation and Changes in Cohort Quality Revisited: What Happened to Immigrant Earnings in the 1980's?" *Journal of Labor Economics* 13(2): 201–45.

Borjas, George J., and Stephen G. Bronars. 1991. "Immigration and the Family." *Journal of Labor Economics* 9(2): 123–48.

Butcher, Kristin F., and David Card. 1991. "Immigration and Wages: Evidence from the 1980's." *American Economic Review* 81(2): 292–96.

Carliner, Geoffrey. 1980. "Wages, Earnings and Hours of First, Second, and Third Generation American Males." *Economic Inquiry* 18(1): 87–102.

Chiswick, Barry R. 1978. "The Effect of Americanization on the Earnings of Foreign-Born Men." *Journal of Political Economy* 86(5): 897–921.

_____. 1980a. *An Analysis of the Economic Progress and Impact of Immigrants.* Report prepared for the Employment and Training Administration, U.S. Department of Labor. Washington, D.C.: National Technical Information Service.

_____. 1980b. "Immigrant Earnings Patterns by Sex, Race, and Ethnic Groupings." *Monthly Labor Review* 103(10): 22–25.

_____. 1986. "Is the New Immigration Less Skilled than the Old?" *Journal of Labor Economics* 4(2): 168–92.

Chiswick, Barry R., and Paul W. Miller. 1992. "Language in the Immigrant Labor Market." In *Immigration, Language and Ethnicity: Canada and the United States,* edited by Barry R. Chiswick. Washington, D.C.: American Enterprise Institute Press.

_____. 1995. "The Endogeneity between Language and Earnings: International Analyses." *Journal of Labor Economics* 13(2): 246–88.

DuMouchel, William H., and Greg J. Duncan. 1983. "Using Sample Survey Weights in Multiple Regression Analyses of Stratified Samples." *Journal of the American Statistical Association* 78(383): 535–43.

Espenshade, Thomas J., and Haishan Fu. 1996. "An Analysis of English-Language Proficiency among U.S. Immigrants." *American Sociological Review.* Forthcoming.

Garvey, Deborah L. 1994. "The Role of Immigrants in New Jersey's Economy." In *A Stone's Throw from Ellis Island: Economic Implications of Immigration to New Jersey,* edited by Thomas J. Espenshade. Lanham, Md.: University Press of America.

Greenwood, Michael J., and John M. McDowell. 1986. "The Factor Market Consequences of U.S. Immigration." *Journal of Economic Literature* 24(4): 1738–72.

Grossman, Jean Baldwin. 1982. "The Substitutability of Natives and Immigrants in Production." *Review of Economics and Statistics* 54(4): 596–603.

Heckman, James J., and Richard Robb. 1985. "Using Longitudinal Data to Estimate Age, Period, and Cohort Effects in Earnings Equations." In *Cohort Analysis in Social Research: Beyond the Identification Problem*, edited by William M. Mason and Stephen E. Feinberg. New York: Springer Verlag.

Jasso, Guillermina, and Mark R. Rosenzweig. 1986. "Family Reunification and the Immigration Multiplier: U.S. Immigration Law, Origin-Country Conditions, and the Reproduction of Immigrants." *Demography* 23(3): 291–311.

———. 1988. "How Well Do U.S. Immigrants Do? Vintage Effects, Emigration Selectivity, and Occupational Mobility." *Research in Population Economics* 6: 229–53.

———. 1990. *The New Chosen People: Immigrants in the United States.* New York: Russell Sage Foundation.

Juhn, Chunhui, Kevin Murphy, and Brooks Pierce. 1993. "Wage Inequality and the Rise in the Returns to Skill." *Journal of Political Economy* 101(3): 410–42.

Long, James E. 1980. "The Effect of Americanization on Earnings: Some Evidence for Women." *Journal of Political Economy* 88(3): 620–29.

U.S. Immigration and Naturalization Service. 1996. *Statistical Yearbook of the Immigration and Naturalization Service, 1994.* Washington, D.C.: U.S. Government Printing Office.

APPENDIX 11.A   DECOMPOSITION OF RELATIVE GROWTH IN IMMIGRANTS' EARNINGS

This study defines a human capital earnings equation for the native born in each census as follows:

$$\ln(y_{80,n}) = X\lambda_{80} + \alpha_n + \epsilon_{80} \qquad (A.1)$$

$$\ln(y_{90,n}) = X\lambda_{90} + \beta_n + \epsilon_{90}, \qquad (A.2)$$

where X is defined as in the immigrant equations, and α_n and β_n are constant terms. Thus, the predicted earnings for a native-born worker who is similar in all observed characteristics to the average immigrant in cohort k are given in each year as:

$$\hat{y}_{80,n} = \overline{X}_k \hat{\lambda}_{80} + \hat{\alpha}_n \qquad (A.3)$$

$$\hat{y}_{90,n} = \overline{X}_k \hat{\lambda}_{90} + \hat{\beta}_n, \qquad (A.4)$$

where $\overline{X}_k$ is again the mean socioeconomic characteristics of immigrant cohort k in 1990, and $\hat{y}_{80,n}$ and $\hat{y}_{90,n}$ are the average (log) earnings of a native-born worker who is statistically similar to the average member of immigrant cohort k.

Using equations (11.5) and (11.6) in the text and (A.4), above, the cross-sectional growth in the *relative* earnings of immigrants is then given by:

$$(\hat{y}_{90,k} - \hat{y}_{90,n}) - (\hat{y}_{90,k+10} - \hat{y}_{90,n}) = \hat{y}_{90,k} - \hat{y}_{90,k+10} \qquad (A.5)$$

$$= \hat{\beta}_k - \hat{\beta}_{k+10},$$

which is exactly equivalent to the cross-sectional growth in immigrant earnings given in equation (11.7) in the text. Hence, the comparison of immigrants relative to a native-born base does not affect cross-sectional estimates of immigrant earnings growth.

Decomposing equation (11.A.5) yields:

$$\hat{\beta}_k - \hat{\beta}_{k+10} = [(\hat{y}_{90,k} - \hat{y}_{80,k}) - (\hat{y}_{90,n} - \hat{y}_{80,n})] \qquad (A.6)$$

$$+ [(\hat{y}_{80,k} - \hat{y}_{90,k+10}) - (\hat{y}_{80,n} - \hat{y}_{90,n})],$$

where the first term in brackets gives within-cohort relative earnings growth and the second term in brackets gives across-cohort relative earnings growth. The within-cohort term gives the rate at which immigrants' earnings profiles approach those of the native born. The across-cohort term measures the growth in relative earnings of immigrant cohorts at the same point in their U.S. life cycles. A positive value of this second term indicates that the skill mix of recent immigrant cohorts relative to the native born has declined over time, thus biasing upward the cross-sectional estimate of immigrants' (relative) earnings growth.

Table 11.A-1 CROSS-SECTIONAL REGRESSION OF EARNINGS OF FOREIGN-BORN AND NATIVE-BORN MEN, BY ETHNIC GROUP: 1990, FULL SPECIFICATION (STANDARD ERRORS IN PARENTHESES)

Regression Coefficients Dependent Variable: log (salary)	Non-Hispanic Whites	Non-Hispanic Blacks	Non-Cuban Hispanics	Cubans[a]	Asians[a]
Educational Attainment					
Not more than elementary	0.066	−0.105	0.177	0.063	0.067
	(0.060)	(0.133)	(0.098)	(0.059)	(0.059)
High school dropout	0.082	−0.157	0.229*	0.074	0.076
	(0.057)	(0.131)	(0.099)	(0.057)	(0.057)
Completed high school	0.159*	−0.044	0.412*	0.150*	0.149*
	(0.057)	(0.131)	(0.099)	(0.057)	(0.057)
Postsecondary/associate's degree	0.267*	0.092	0.509*	0.259*	0.255*
	(0.057)	(0.132)	(0.101)	(0.056)	(0.056)
Bachelor's degree	0.441*	0.321*	0.682*	0.435*	0.428*
	(0.057)	(0.134)	(0.108)	(0.057)	(0.057)
Professional/graduate degree	0.596*	0.417*	0.874*	0.591*	0.580*
	(0.057)	(0.137)	(0.117)	(0.057)	(0.057)
Foreign * Educational Attainment					
Not more than elementary	−0.143	−0.292	−0.199	−0.562*	−0.285
	(0.091)	(0.288)	(0.121)	(0.158)	(0.160)
High school dropout	−0.167	−0.069	−0.280*	−0.456*	−0.319*
	(0.090)	(0.280)	(0.120)	(0.160)	(0.146)
Completed high school	−0.234*	−0.107	−0.399*	−0.559*	−0.283*
	(0.090)	(0.280)	(0.120)	(0.160)	(0.146)
Postsecondary/associate's degree	−0.229*	−0.076	−0.403*	−0.556*	−0.170
	(0.089)	(0.276)	(0.121)	(0.159)	(0.138)
Bachelor's degree	−0.234*	−0.147	−0.509*	−0.565*	−0.219
	(0.090)	(0.279)	(0.130)	(0.169)	(0.136)
Professional/graduate degree	−0.226*	−0.135	−0.410*	−0.475*	−0.142
	(0.090)	(0.283)	(0.140)	(0.168)	(0.136)
Experience	0.038*	0.036*	0.020*	0.039*	0.039*
	(0.001)	(0.004)	(0.004)	(0.001)	(0.001)

(continued)

Table 11.A-1 CROSS-SECTIONAL REGRESSION OF EARNINGS OF FOREIGN-BORN AND NATIVE-BORN MEN, BY ETHNIC GROUP: 1990, FULL SPECIFICATION (STANDARD ERRORS IN PARENTHESES) (continued)

Regression Coefficients Dependent Variable: log (salary)	Non-Hispanic Whites	Non-Hispanic Blacks	Non-Cuban Hispanics	Cubans[a]	Asians[a]
$(\text{Experience})^2$	-0.001^*	-0.001^*	$<-0.001^*$	-0.001^*	-0.001^*
	(<0.001)	(<0.001)	(<0.001)	(<0.001)	(<0.001)
Log weeks worked	0.956^*	1.001^*	0.882^*	0.952^*	0.948^*
	(0.008)	(0.017)	(0.019)	(0.008)	(0.008)
Married	0.254^*	0.177^*	0.202^*	0.264^*	0.261^*
	(0.006)	(0.017)	(0.019)	(0.006)	(0.006)
Foreign born	0.051	-0.224	-0.019	-0.187	-0.228
	(0.093)	(0.278)	(0.118)	(0.178)	(0.137)
Years since migration	0.007^*	0.039^*	0.033^*	0.042^*	0.021^*
	(0.003)	(0.010)	(0.005)	(0.010)	(0.005)
$(\text{Years since migration})^2$	<-0.001	-0.001^*	-0.001^*	-0.001^*	$<-0.001^*$
	(<0.001)	(<0.001)	(<0.001)	(<0.001)	(<0.001)
SMSA					
Atlantic City	0.139^*	0.152^*	0.103	0.141^*	0.135^*
	(0.025)	(0.067)	(0.084)	(0.025)	(0.025)
New York (Bergen)	0.264^*	0.226^*	0.294^*	0.268^*	0.273^*
	(0.021)	(0.065)	(0.065)	(0.021)	(0.021)
Paterson/Clifton/Passaic	0.193^*	0.096	0.157^*	0.202^*	0.195^*
	(0.023)	(0.064)	(0.061)	(0.023)	(0.023)
Jersey City	0.119^*	0.133^*	0.186^*	0.148^*	0.122^*
	(0.024)	(0.063)	(0.059)	(0.024)	(0.024)
New Brunswick/Perth Amboy	0.216^*	0.239^*	0.243^*	0.226^*	0.209^*
	(0.021)	(0.062)	(0.062)	(0.022)	(0.021)
Newark	0.261^*	0.155^*	0.224^*	0.263^*	0.257^*
	(0.021)	(0.053)	(0.059)	(0.021)	(0.021)
Long Branch/Asbury Park	0.238^*	0.115	0.292^*	0.242^*	0.240^*
	(0.022)	(0.063)	(0.072)	(0.022)	(0.022)
Philadelphia	0.124^*	0.108^*	0.111	0.129^*	0.121^*
	(0.021)	(0.055)	(0.064)	(0.021)	(0.021)

Trenton	0.136* (0.023)	0.079 (0.063)	0.233* (0.077)	0.137* (0.024)	0.131* (0.024)
Cape May and Salem counties	0.075* (0.025)	0.194* (0.080)	0.222 (0.137)	0.083* (0.026)	0.078* (0.026)
Hunterdon County	0.217* (0.025)	0.152 (0.179)	0.101 (0.142)	0.229* (0.025)	0.221* (0.025)
Ocean County	0.122* (0.022)	0.073 (0.088)	0.149 (0.081)	0.129* (0.022)	0.121* (0.022)
Sussex and Warren counties	0.138* (0.023)	0.206 (0.129)	0.443* (0.111)	0.143* (0.023)	0.138* (0.023)
English-Speaking Ability					
Speaks English very well	0.200* (0.067)	0.062 (0.339)	0.216* (0.039)	0.074 (0.079)	0.215 (0.110)
Speaks English well	0.093 (0.067)	−0.101 (0.344)	0.157* (0.039)	−0.015 (0.080)	0.152 (0.111)
Does not speak English well	0.033 (0.069)	0.008 (0.351)	0.101* (0.038)	0.012 (0.078)	0.076 (0.113)
Industry Classification					
Mining	0.332* (0.061)	0.525* (0.262)	−0.104 (0.169)	0.316* (0.063)	0.317* (0.061)
Construction	0.300* (0.034)	0.199 (0.118)	−0.105 (0.111)	0.303* (0.035)	0.306* (0.034)
Nondurable manufacturing	0.340* (0.034)	0.236* (0.117)	−0.116 (0.110)	0.353* (0.035)	0.350* (0.034)
Durable manufacturing	0.283* (0.034)	0.207 (0.116)	−0.121 (0.109)	0.295* (0.035)	0.297* (0.034)
Transport/communications/public utilities	0.313* (0.034)	0.295* (0.116)	−0.033 (0.111)	0.324* (0.035)	0.327* (0.034)
Wholesale/retail trade	0.195* (0.034)	0.112 (0.116)	−0.208 (0.109)	0.209* (0.034)	0.211* (0.034)
Finance/insurance/real estate	0.423* (0.034)	0.174 (0.119)	0.026 (0.113)	0.438* (0.035)	0.440* (0.035)

(continued)

Table 11.A-1 CROSS-SECTIONAL REGRESSION OF EARNINGS OF FOREIGN-BORN AND NATIVE-BORN MEN, BY ETHNIC GROUP: 1990, FULL SPECIFICATION (STANDARD ERRORS IN PARENTHESES) (continued)

Regression Coefficients Dependent Variable: log (salary)	Non-Hispanic Whites	Non-Hispanic Blacks	Non-Cuban Hispanics	Cubans[a]	Asians[a]
Service	0.128*	0.080	-0.232*	0.137*	0.146*
	(0.033)	(0.115)	(0.108)	(0.034)	(0.034)
Public administration	0.260*	0.274*	-0.143	0.267*	0.274*
	(0.035)	(0.118)	(0.118)	(0.035)	(0.035)
Armed forces	-0.129*	-0.191	-0.694*	-0.121*	-0.114*
	(0.051)	(0.137)	(0.161)	(0.052)	(0.052)
Occupational Classification					
Manager/professional	0.394*	0.258*	0.528*	0.377*	0.385*
	(0.034)	(0.102)	(0.106)	(0.035)	(0.034)
Technical/sales/administrative	0.240*	0.089	0.279*	0.223*	0.225*
	(0.034)	(0.101)	(0.104)	(0.035)	(0.035)
Service occupations	0.061	-0.038	0.181	0.058	0.055
	(0.035)	(0.101)	(0.104)	(0.036)	(0.035)
Military occupations	0.354*	0.374*	0.682*	0.352*	0.365*
	(0.082)	(0.173)	(0.257)	(0.083)	(0.081)
Precision production, craft, and repair	0.213*	0.109	0.344*	0.205*	0.208*
	(0.034)	(0.102)	(0.104)	(0.035)	(0.035)
Operators/fabricators/laborers	0.062	0.004	0.191	0.053	0.053
	(0.034)	(0.100)	(0.103)	(0.035)	(0.035)
Has disability that limits work	-0.239*	-0.244*	-0.135*	-0.245*	-0.240*
	(0.012)	(0.035)	(0.043)	(0.012)	(0.012)
Constant	4.942*	5.100*	5.317*	5.069*	4.958*
	(0.098)	(0.388)	(0.148)	(0.107)	(0.132)
Adjusted R^2	0.384	0.471	0.448	0.388	0.389
N	65,024	6,845	5,361	60,889	62,841

Note: Sample includes men ages 28–64 who worked in the reference year and had nonzero wage or salary income.

a. Foreign-born Cubans and Asians were compared to native-born non-Hispanic whites rather than to their native-born counterparts because of insufficient sample sizes.

*Indicates coefficient is significantly different from zero at 5 percent level.

CROSS-SECTIONAL REGRESSION OF EARNINGS OF FOREIGN-BORN AND NATIVE-BORN MEN, BY ETHNIC GROUP: 1990, SIMPLE SPECIFICATION (STANDARD ERRORS IN PARENTHESES)

Regression Coefficients Dependent Variable: log (salary)	Non-Hispanic Whites	Non-Hispanic Blacks	Non-Cuban Hispanics	Cubans[a]	Asians[a]
Educational Attainment					
Not more than elementary	0.040	-0.154	0.151	0.038	0.041
	(0.061)	(0.135)	(0.100)	(0.061)	(0.061)
High school dropout	0.089	-0.211	0.234*	0.082	0.082
	(0.059)	(0.133)	(0.101)	(0.058)	(0.058)
Completed high school	0.198*	-0.080	0.458*	0.189*	0.188*
	(0.058)	(0.133)	(0.101)	(0.058)	(0.058)
Postsecondary/associate's degree	0.360*	0.099	0.601*	0.350*	0.348*
	(0.058)	(0.134)	(0.103)	(0.058)	(0.058)
Bachelor's degree	0.610*	0.397*	0.885*	0.601*	0.597*
	(0.058)	(0.136)	(0.109)	(0.058)	(0.058)
Professional/graduate degree	0.765*	0.503*	1.102*	0.756*	0.751*
	(0.059)	(0.138)	(0.117)	(0.058)	(0.058)
Foreign * Educational Attainment					
Not more than elementary	-0.108	-0.248	-0.166	-0.519*	-0.352*
	(0.093)	(0.289)	(0.123)	(0.161)	(0.164)
High school dropout	-0.105	-0.022	-0.257*	-0.428*	-0.326*
	(0.092)	(0.280)	(0.123)	(0.163)	(0.150)
Completed high school	-0.154	-0.061	-0.383*	-0.509*	-0.282*
	(0.090)	(0.276)	(0.122)	(0.162)	(0.143)
Postsecondary/associate's degree	-0.141	-0.005	-0.396*	-0.486*	-0.150
	(0.091)	(0.277)	(0.124)	(0.161)	(0.141)
Bachelor's degree	-0.139	-0.107	-0.516*	-0.473*	-0.186
	(0.091)	(0.280)	(0.133)	(0.171)	(0.139)
Professional/graduate degree	-0.121	-0.041	-0.419*	-0.446*	-0.088
	(0.091)	(0.284)	(0.143)	(0.170)	(0.139)
Experience	0.040*	0.042*	0.020*	0.042*	0.041*
	(0.001)	(0.004)	(0.004)	(0.001)	(0.001)
$(Experience)^2$	-0.001*	-0.001*	< -0.001*	-0.001*	-0.001*
	(<0.001)	(<0.001)	(<0.001)	(<0.001)	(<0.001)

(continued)

Table 11.A-2 CROSS-SECTIONAL REGRESSION OF EARNINGS OF FOREIGN-BORN AND NATIVE-BORN MEN, BY ETHNIC GROUP: 1990, SIMPLE SPECIFICATION (STANDARD ERRORS IN PARENTHESES) (continued)

Regression Coefficients Dependent Variable: log (salary)	Non-Hispanic Whites	Non-Hispanic Blacks	Non-Cuban Hispanics	Cubans[a]	Asians[a]
Log weeks worked	0.980*	1.015*	0.893*	0.975*	0.971*
	(0.008)	(0.017)	(0.019)	(0.008)	(0.008)
Married	0.277*	0.186*	0.226*	0.288*	0.286*
	(0.006)	(0.018)	(0.019)	(0.006)	(0.006)
Foreign born	−0.114	−0.336	−0.165	−0.330	−0.344*
	(0.093)	(0.279)	(0.120)	(0.176)	(0.139)
Years since migration	0.009*	0.040*	0.039*	0.044*	0.026*
	(0.003)	(0.010)	(0.005)	(0.010)	(0.005)
(Years since migration)[a]	<−0.001	−0.001*	−0.001*	−0.001*	<−0.001*
	(<0.001)	(<0.001)	(<0.001)	(<0.001)	(<0.001)
SMSA					
Atlantic City	0.123*	0.109	0.084	0.125*	0.117*
	(0.025)	(0.068)	(0.086)	(0.025)	(0.025)
New York (Bergen)	0.303*	0.223*	0.339*	0.307*	0.312*
	(0.022)	(0.065)	(0.066)	(0.022)	(0.022)
Paterson/Clifton/Passaic	0.227*	0.100	0.166*	0.236*	0.229*
	(0.024)	(0.065)	(0.062)	(0.024)	(0.024)
Jersey City	0.143*	0.131*	0.202*	0.174*	0.151*
	(0.024)	(0.064)	(0.061)	(0.024)	(0.024)
New Brunswick/Perth Amboy	0.254*	0.241*	0.274*	0.263*	0.247*
	(0.022)	(0.063)	(0.064)	(0.022)	(0.022)

Newark	0.302*	0.147*	0.245*	0.304*	0.298*
	(0.021)	(0.054)	(0.060)	(0.021)	(0.021)
Long Branch/Asbury Park	0.272*	0.100	0.331*	0.275*	0.273*
	(0.022)	(0.063)	(0.074)	(0.022)	(0.022)
Philadelphia	0.148*	0.090	0.114	0.152*	0.144*
	(0.021)	(0.056)	(0.066)	(0.021)	(0.021)
Trenton	0.166*	0.064	0.229*	0.167*	0.162*
	(0.024)	(0.063)	(0.079)	(0.024)	(0.024)
Cape May and Salem counties	0.077*	0.155	0.271	0.085*	0.080*
	(0.026)	(0.081)	(0.140)	(0.026)	(0.026)
Hunterdon County	0.256*	0.145	0.127	0.267*	0.260*
	(0.026)	(0.182)	(0.146)	(0.026)	(0.026)
Ocean County	0.137*	0.058	0.182	0.143*	0.134*
	(0.023)	(0.089)	(0.083)	(0.023)	(0.023)
Sussex and Warren counties	0.166*	0.217	0.496*	0.170*	0.164*
	(0.023)	(0.130)	(0.114)	(0.023)	(0.023)
Has disability that limits work	-0.257*	-0.263*	-0.134*	-0.262*	-0.257*
	(0.013)	(0.036)	(0.044)	(0.013)	(0.013)
Constant	5.368*	5.310*	5.513*	5.375*	5.409*
	(0.069)	(0.155)	(0.138)	(0.069)	(0.068)
Adjusted R^2	0.352	0.454	0.419	0.357	0.389
N	65,024	6,845	5,361	60,889	62,841

Note: Sample includes men ages 28–64 who worked in the reference year and had nonzero wage or salary income.

a. Foreign-born Cubans and Asians were compared to native-born non-Hispanic whites rather than to their native-born counterparts because of insufficient sample sizes.

*Indicates coefficient is significantly different from zero at 5 percent level.

Table 11.A-3 POOLED REGRESSION ANALYSIS OF EARNINGS OF NATIVE- AND FOREIGN-BORN MEN, BY ETHNIC GROUP
(STANDARD ERRORS IN PARENTHESES)

Regression Coefficients Dependent Variable: log (salary)	Non-Hispanic Whites	Non-Hispanic Blacks	Non-Cuban Hispanics	Cubans	Asians
Native Born, 1990					
Experience	0.042	0.045	0.0280	0.042	0.042
	(0.001)	(0.004)	(0.005)	(0.001)	(0.001)
(Experience)^2	-0.001	-0.001	<-0.001	-0.001	-0.001
	(<0.001)	(<0.001)	(<0.001)	(<0.001)	(<0.001)
Log weeks worked	0.981	1.047	0.926	0.981	0.981
	(0.008)	(0.019)	(0.028)	(0.008)	(0.008)
Married	0.286	0.172	0.261	0.286	0.286
	(0.006)	(0.020)	(0.028)	(0.006)	(0.006)
Has disability that limits work	-0.267	-0.273	-0.143	-0.267	-0.267
	(0.013)	(0.039)	(0.056)	(0.013)	(0.013)
Not more than elementary	0.037	-0.166	0.147	0.037	0.037
	(0.060)	(0.145)	(0.104)	(0.059)	(0.059)
High school dropout	0.095	-0.226	0.269	0.095	0.095
	(0.057)	(0.142)	(0.106)	(0.057)	(0.057)
Completed high school	0.212	-0.092	0.493	0.212	0.212
	(0.057)	(0.143)	(0.106)	(0.057)	(0.057)
Postsecondary/associate's degree	0.380	0.091	0.651	0.380	0.380
	(0.057)	(0.143)	(0.109)	(0.057)	(0.057)
Bachelor's degree	0.643	0.400	0.959	0.643	0.643
	(0.057)	(0.145)	(0.114)	(0.057)	(0.057)
Professional/graduate degree	0.806	0.502	1.185	0.806	0.806
	(0.057)	(0.147)	(0.123)	(0.057)	(0.057)
In an SMSA	0.074	0.001	-0.065	0.074	0.074
	(0.007)	(0.048)	(0.054)	(0.007)	(0.007)
Constant	4.911	4.720	4.926	4.911	4.911
	(0.065)	(0.165)	(0.163)	(0.065)	(0.065)

Immigrant, 1990

Experience	0.027 (0.004)	0.019 (0.011)	0.016 (0.005)	0.006 (0.008)	0.032 (0.005)
(Experience)²	<-0.001 (<0.001)	<-0.001 (<0.001)	-0.001 (<0.001)	<-0.001 (<0.001)	-0.001 (<0.001)
Log weeks worked	1.022 (0.026)	0.751 (0.057)	0.873 (0.028)	0.888 (0.056)	0.904 (0.029)
Married	0.165 (0.025)	0.238 (0.060)	0.198 (0.028)	0.448 (0.055)	0.262 (0.038)
Has disability that limits work	-0.151 (0.051)	-0.002 (0.166)	-0.088 (0.077)	-0.154 (0.118)	0.120 (0.092)
Not more than elementary	-0.005 (0.070)	-0.373 (0.277)	-0.020 (0.077)	-0.364 (0.154)	-0.377 (0.149)
High school dropout	0.060 (0.073)	-0.233 (0.277)	-0.046 (0.080)	-0.237 (0.165)	-0.454 (0.137)
Completed high school	0.128 (0.072)	-0.141 (0.275)	0.045 (0.080)	-0.216 (0.168)	-0.317 (0.131)
Postsecondary/associate's degree	0.295 (0.073)	0.061 (0.278)	0.161 (0.083)	-0.085 (0.169)	-0.085 (0.130)
Bachelor's degree	0.554 (0.074)	0.219 (0.282)	0.332 (0.091)	0.127 (0.180)	0.128 (0.128)
Professional/graduate degree	0.729 (0.074)	0.378 (0.285)	0.634 (0.097)	0.323 (0.178)	0.330 (0.129)
In an SMSA	0.106 (0.033)	-0.062 (0.185)	0.060 (0.096)	-0.308 (0.130)	0.013 (0.072)
Arrived 1985–90	4.816 (0.129)	5.985 (0.397)	5.262 (0.173)	5.874 (0.306)	5.547 (0.189)
Arrived 1980–84	4.925 (0.131)	6.162 (0.397)	5.373 (0.174)	5.907 (0.293)	5.658 (0.191)
Arrived 1975–79	4.951 (0.132)	6.231 (0.403)	5.623 (0.177)	6.247 (0.321)	5.819 (0.195)

(continued)

Table 11.A-3 POOLED REGRESSION ANALYSIS OF EARNINGS OF NATIVE- AND FOREIGN-BORN MEN, BY ETHNIC GROUP (continued)

(STANDARD ERRORS IN PARENTHESES)

Regression Coefficients Dependent Variable: log (salary)	Non-Hispanic Whites	Non-Hispanic Blacks	Non-Cuban Hispanics	Cubans	Asians
Arrived 1970–74	4.940	6.365	5.663	6.193	5.890
	(0.133)	(0.408)	(0.179)	(0.298)	(0.197)
Arrived 1965–69	5.004	6.477	5.713	6.229	6.030
	(0.133)	(0.413)	(0.182)	(0.296)	(0.201)
Arrived 1960–64	5.048	6.274	5.760	6.437	6.096
	(0.134)	(0.420)	(0.187)	(0.299)	(0.207)
Arrived 1950–59	5.079	6.276	5.802	6.381	6.167
	(0.134)	(0.438)	(0.198)	(0.304)	(0.219)
Arrived before 1950	5.131	5.908	5.932	6.345	6.163
	(0.138)	(0.526)	(0.235)	(0.360)	(0.289)
Native Born, 1980					
Experience	0.076	0.063	0.056	0.076	0.076
	(0.001)	(0.003)	(0.005)	(0.001)	(0.001)
(Experience)^2	-0.001	-0.001	-0.001	-0.001	-0.001
	(<0.001)	(<0.001)	(<0.001)	(<0.001)	(<0.001)
Log weeks worked	1.105	1.025	1.026	1.105	1.105
	(0.006)	(0.016)	(0.025)	(0.006)	(0.006)
Married	0.261	0.222	0.130	0.261	0.261
	(0.007)	(0.019)	(0.030)	(0.007)	(0.007)
Has disability that limits work	-0.217	-0.199	-0.180	-0.217	-0.217
	(0.014)	(0.041)	(0.064)	(0.014)	(0.014)
Not more than elementary	0.126	0.329	0.038	0.126	0.126
	(0.083)	(0.182)	(0.131)	(0.083)	(0.083)
High school dropout	0.215	0.364	0.171	0.215	0.215
	(0.082)	(0.181)	(0.133)	(0.082)	(0.082)
Completed high school	0.429	0.558	0.393	0.429	0.429
	(0.082)	(0.181)	(0.133)	(0.082)	(0.082)

Postsecondary/associate's degree	0.520 (0.082)	0.699 (0.182)	0.576 (0.136)	0.520 (0.082)	0.520 (0.082)
Bachelor's degree	0.813 (0.082)	1.017 (0.185)	0.919 (0.149)	0.813 (0.082)	0.813 (0.082)
Professional/graduate degree	0.929 (0.083)	1.081 (0.186)	1.038 (0.148)	0.929 (0.082)	0.929 (0.082)
In an SMSA	0.035 (0.008)	0.037 (0.052)	−0.034 (0.068)	0.035 (0.008)	0.035 (0.008)
Constant	3.883 (0.085)	3.948 (0.196)	4.271 (0.169)	3.883 (0.085)	3.883 (0.085)
Immigrant, 1980					
Experience	0.057 (0.004)	0.034 (0.013)	0.053 (0.006)	0.047 (0.008)	0.053 (0.009)
(Experience)^2	−0.001 (<0.001)	−0.001 (<0.001)	−0.001 (<0.001)	−0.001 (<0.001)	−0.001 (<0.001)
Log weeks worked	1.116 (0.028)	1.092 (0.065)	1.083 (0.036)	1.115 (0.051)	1.150 (0.041)
Married	0.242 (0.027)	0.240 (0.084)	0.140 (0.040)	0.156 (0.055)	0.216 (0.053)
Has disability that limits work	−0.255 (0.061)	−0.243 (0.207)	−0.053 (0.120)	−0.410 (0.128)	0.247 (0.141)
Not more than elementary	0.093 (0.085)	−0.258 (0.288)	−0.091 (0.112)	−0.175 (0.260)	−0.442 (0.283)
High school dropout	0.181 (0.090)	−0.631 (0.290)	−0.099 (0.117)	−0.212 (0.268)	−0.485 (0.272)
Completed high school	0.304 (0.088)	−0.108 (0.285)	0.070 (0.116)	−0.076 (0.265)	−0.366 (0.263)
Postsecondary/associate's degree	0.494 (0.090)	−0.051 (0.296)	0.124 (0.121)	0.012 (0.269)	−0.269 (0.263)
Bachelor's degree	0.664 (0.092)	−0.012 (0.315)	0.302 (0.142)	0.240 (0.275)	0.144 (0.261)

(continued)

Table 11.A-3 POOLED REGRESSION ANALYSIS OF EARNINGS OF NATIVE- AND FOREIGN-BORN MEN, BY ETHNIC GROUP
(STANDARD ERRORS IN PARENTHESES) (continued)

Regression Coefficients Dependent Variable: log (salary)	Non-Hispanic Whites	Non-Hispanic Blacks	Non-Cuban Hispanics	Cubans	Asians
Professional/graduate degree	0.859	0.128	0.573	0.291	0.221
	(0.091)	(0.309)	(0.134)	(0.275)	(0.260)
In an SMSA	0.048	0.311	0.225	−0.303	−0.030
	(0.044)	(0.284)	(0.146)	(0.176)	(0.122)
Arrived 1975–79	3.931	4.277	3.988	4.621	4.527
	(0.137)	(0.416)	(0.227)	(0.379)	(0.315)
Arrived 1970–74	4.037	4.440	4.164	4.667	4.544
	(0.138)	(0.428)	(0.228)	(0.364)	(0.317)
Arrived 1965–69	4.045	4.393	4.181	4.755	4.742
	(0.139)	(0.430)	(0.230)	(0.364)	(0.319)
Arrived 1960–64	4.072	4.419	4.358	4.932	4.867
	(0.140)	(0.424)	(0.236)	(0.366)	(0.323)
Arrived 1950–59	4.118	4.463	4.455	4.854	4.882
	(0.141)	(0.450)	(0.234)	(0.371)	(0.333)
Arrived before 1950	4.112	4.187	4.473	4.722	4.488
	(0.144)	(0.467)	(0.276)	(0.433)	(0.376)

Table 11.A-4 MEANS OF INDEPENDENT VARIABLES IN 1990 CROSS SECTION

	Immigrant Cohort							
Group	1985–90	1980–84	1975–79	1970–74	1965–69	1960–64	1950–59	Before 1950
White								
EXP	17.56	19.73	22.16	25.99	27.26	27.79	30.71	35.31
EXPSQ	387.65	480.61	598.73	792.63	873.74	900.92	1055.41	1330.73
LNWEEK	3.75	3.83	3.83	3.86	3.86	3.86	3.85	3.82
MARRY	0.78	0.80	0.83	0.87	0.84	0.86	0.85	0.86
HEALTH	0.02	0.01	0.02	0.03	0.03	0.03	0.05	0.04
ELEM	0.07	0.11	0.16	0.23	0.20	0.15	0.11	0.09
LSHS	0.10	0.10	0.09	0.15	0.14	0.12	0.13	0.10
HSDIP	0.22	0.17	0.17	0.21	0.22	0.25	0.24	0.24
COLL	0.12	0.21	0.17	0.13	0.13	0.20	0.22	0.15
BA/BS	0.20	0.16	0.20	0.12	0.14	0.12	0.16	0.20
MA/PROF	0.28	0.22	0.17	0.14	0.15	0.14	0.14	0.20
SMSA	0.97	0.94	0.94	0.95	0.92	0.90	0.89	0.89
Black								
EXP	19.18	17.91	20.61	22.33	26.05	23.64	32.53	40.60
EXPSQ	453.75	407.49	529.14	600.53	779.75	671.22	1174.98	1697.90
LNWEEK	3.70	3.75	3.80	3.88	3.86	3.80	3.78	3.85
MARRY	0.77	0.69	0.71	0.78	0.77	0.76	0.75	0.6
HEALTH	0.02	0.01	0.03	0.04	0.04	0	0.06	0
ELEM	0.09	0.07	0.08	0.04	0.06	0.05	0.19	0.2
LSHS	0.12	0.15	0.13	0.16	0.10	0.22	0.06	0.4
HSDIP	0.37	0.24	0.28	0.19	0.26	0.16	0.38	0.2
COLL	0.25	0.20	0.21	0.27	0.26	0.22	0.25	0.2
BA/BS	0.09	0.20	0.20	0.14	0.17	0.27	0.06	0
MA/PROF	0.06	0.11	0.10	0.19	0.14	0.08	0.06	0
SMSA	0.99	0.98	0.99	0.98	0.98	0.97	0.88	1.00
Non-Cuban Hispanics								
EXP	20.17	20.12	21.52	25.22	28.81	27.73	32.06	36.35
EXPSQ	511.43	498.06	567.23	735.05	954.95	910.38	1150.33	1385.26
LNWEEK	3.71	3.76	3.75	3.79	3.81	3.85	3.86	3.67
MARRY	0.67	0.66	0.72	0.80	0.80	0.78	0.80	0.76
HEALTH	0.02	0.02	0.04	0.03	0.02	0.02	0.04	0
ELEM	0.23	0.20	0.17	0.20	0.20	0.09	0.17	0.18
LSHS	0.19	0.21	0.26	0.23	0.19	0.18	0.23	0.18
HSDIP	0.23	0.27	0.25	0.28	0.26	0.21	0.16	0.12
COLL	0.16	0.19	0.18	0.19	0.21	0.28	0.16	0.24
BA/BS	0.08	0.06	0.08	0.05	0.07	0.12	0.17	0
MA/PROF	0.06	0.04	0.04	0.04	0.05	0.07	0.10	0.24
SMSA	0.98	0.99	0.98	0.98	0.99	0.99	0.97	0.88

(continued)

Table 11.A-4 MEANS OF INDEPENDENT VARIABLES IN 1990 CROSS SECTION (continued)

	Immigrant Cohort							
Group	1985–90	1980–84	1975–79	1970–74	1965–69	1960–64	1950–59	Before 1950
Cubans								
EXP	25.04	27.24	27.30	30.60	27.66	26.31	35.04	39.79
EXPSQ	769.82	863.70	954.33	1161.02	980.11	834.87	1357.36	1705.75
LNWEEK	3.67	3.72	3.90	3.85	3.84	3.88	3.75	3.50
MARRY	0.66	0.68	0.74	0.84	0.82	0.79	0.80	0.86
HEALTH	0.06	0.03	0.09	0.03	0.05	0.03	0.03	0
ELEM	0.23	0.30	0.09	0.33	0.19	0.10	0.29	0
LSHS	0.34	0.21	0.26	0.18	0.14	0.10	0.20	0.14
HSDIP	0.11	0.21	0.22	0.15	0.20	0.21	0.19	0.43
COLL	0.20	0.18	0.17	0.16	0.21	0.30	0.21	0.14
BA/BS	0	0.04	0.09	0.09	0.11	0.14	0.04	0
MA/PROF	0.09	0.01	0.09	0.07	0.13	0.16	0.07	0.14
SMSA	1.00	1.00	1.00	0.98	0.96	0.94	0.97	0.86
Asians								
EXP	16.60	16.66	18.76	22.79	23.68	26.00	27.90	35.44
EXPSQ	372.77	357.85	418.89	576.84	608.83	729.27	847.21	1316.56
LNWEEK	3.71	3.84	3.86	3.86	3.88	3.90	3.93	3.95
MARRY	0.84	0.86	0.90	0.92	0.95	0.91	0.91	0.89
HEALTH	0.02	0.01	0.01	0.02	0.03	0.02	0	0
ELEM	0.03	0.02	0.02	0.01	0.01	0	0	0
LSHS	0.05	0.06	0.04	0.02	0.01	0	0	0.11
HSDIP	0.11	0.11	0.11	0.06	0.04	0.03	0.02	0.33
COLL	0.14	0.14	0.15	0.11	0.10	0.09	0.11	0
BA/BS	0.39	0.34	0.30	0.37	0.19	0.22	0.26	0.11
MA/PROF	0.27	0.32	0.37	0.42	0.64	0.66	0.61	0.44
SMSA	0.98	0.97	0.98	0.96	0.98	0.96	0.98	1.00

Chapter Twelve

HOMEOWNERSHIP ATTAINMENT OF NEW JERSEY IMMIGRANTS

Nancy McArdle

Homeownership historically has been a powerful symbol of the American Dream and a major aspiration for immigrants to the United States. It provides a yardstick of economic success and continues to be a prime mechanism for asset accumulation and the conveyance of wealth between generations (Joint Center for Housing Studies 1993). Homeowners are able to tap into equity to help finance education and business ventures, they can profit through housing price appreciation, and arguably they have a larger stake in the well-being of their communities. Lending institutions devoted to helping immigrants of particular nationalities achieve homeownership have played an important role in the economic development of the United States. Generations of immigrants have struggled to attain a home of their own and have used it to establish an economic base in their new country. According to a recent survey of immigrant attitudes toward homeownership, immigrants are almost three times as likely as all adults to cite homebuying as their foremost priority (Fannie Mae 1995).

The 1980s saw a dramatic surge in the number of immigrants entering the United States; over 40 percent of all the foreign born in the United States in 1990 entered during that decade. Due to the changes brought about by the 1965 amendments to the Immigration and Nationality Act, recent immigrants are primarily Asians and Latin Americans, as opposed to Europeans who made up the majority of previous immigrant waves. This study explores the success of these new immigrants in achieving homeownership in New Jersey and compares their progress to that of previous immigrants and of native-born households.

Using microdata from the 1980 and 1990 Censuses of Population and Housing (5 percent Public Use Microdata Sample files for New Jersey), I compare homeownership rates for the 10 largest immigrant groups in New Jersey (plus Puerto Ricans)[1] by period of entry into the

United States with rates achieved by native-born whites[2] and minorities. Second, I use logistic regression to analyze those factors that influence variation in homeownership between immigrants and the native born, and decompose these differences into those attributable to endowment and behavioral effects. The study further examines immigrant progress in achieving homeownership over the 1980s by tracing the experiences of synthetic age cohorts over time. In addition, I recognize that, in some ways, not all "homeownership" is the same, and I describe the different unit types and home values of houses owned by distinct immigrant groups.

Whereas this study focuses on immigrants residing in the state of New Jersey, many of my conclusions hold true for immigrants in a national context as well. I include a summary of findings at the national level, indicating that the New Jersey experience, although taking place among immigrants from somewhat different nationality groups than those most widely represented in the United States as a whole, is representative of overall patterns of immigrant homeownership progress.

OVERALL HOMEOWNERSHIP RATES

In 1990, immigrants headed 460,000 New Jersey households,[3] 16.6 percent of all households in the study and 13.1 percent of homeowner households.[4] This represents increases over 1980 of 18.7 percent in the number of all households headed by immigrants and of 17.9 percent in the number of owner households. Homes owned and occupied by immigrants comprised 15.9 percent of all owner-occupied homes valued over $200,000 in 1990. Overall, immigrants had a homeownership rate of 51.2 percent, compared to a rate of 72.7 percent for native-born whites and 38.5 percent for native-born minorities. Nationally, immigrants had a homeownership rate of 47.9 percent, compared to 69.3 percent for native-born whites. Thus, immigrants in New Jersey fare about the same in achieving homeownership as they do in the nation as a whole. Immigrant homeownership rates, however, vary dramatically by period of entry into the United States (entry cohort) as well as by place of birth (see figure 12.1).

Homeownership rates clearly rise with length of residency in the United States, from 24.1 percent for immigrants who entered during the 1980s to 52.6 percent for 1970s immigrants. Immigrants who entered before 1965 achieved a homeownership rate of 69.4 percent by

Figure 12.1 NEW JERSEY HOMEOWNERSHIP RATES: 1990

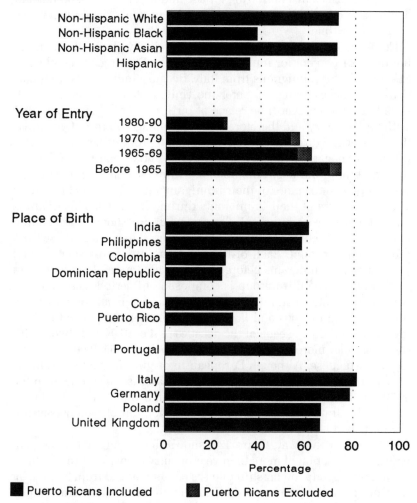

Source: 1990 Census, New Jersey PUMS 5 percent file.

1990. However, because the year of entry is closely correlated with age, a prime predictor of homeownership, this result is unsurprising. Furthermore, whereas the higher ownership rates of long-term immigrants compared to recent entrants suggest that immigrants "catch up" with the native born the longer they reside in the United States, this interpretation is suspect if significant differences exist in immigrant "quality" across cohorts. Later sections of this chapter address both these issues by controlling for age and other socioeconomic and demographic variables and by tracing the progress of particular age cohorts over time.

Homeownership rates also vary dramatically by place of birth, ranging from 24 percent for immigrants from the Dominican Republic to 81.4 percent for immigrants from Italy. Because immigrants from particular countries tended to enter the United States in waves, which ebbed and flowed over time, place of birth may be closely correlated with year of entry and therefore with current age. To initially address this concern, figure 12.1 groups immigrants from different countries into four categories, roughly according to entry cohort. Members of the first group, Indians, Colombians, Filipinos, and Dominicans, all sent 40 percent or more of their immigrants during the 1980s and 30 percent or more of their immigrants during the 1970s. This group is termed the "new immigrants." The second group, shown at the bottom of figure 12.1, is composed of Germans, Poles, Italians, and those from the United Kingdom. Each of these nationality groups sent over 60 percent of its immigrants before 1965, and are termed the "long-term immigrants." The third group is composed of Puerto Ricans and Cubans, whose pattern and timing of entry has been much smoother and not as marked by ebbs and flows. Approximately 20 percent of each group entered during each of the decades of the 1970s and 1980s, with the remainder more heavily concentrated before 1965. The last group is the Portuguese. Although European in origin, their entry profile is very unlike that of other European groups and is concentrated in the 1970s, with significant entry continuing into the 1980s.[5] Appendix 12.A-1 illustrates in more detail the distribution of New Jersey immigrants by place of birth and year of entry.

Grouped in this way, figure 12.1 shows that immigrant homeownership is a function of more than year of entry alone. Within the "new immigrant" group, ownership rates as of 1990 ranged from 24 percent for Dominicans to 61 percent for Indians. Interestingly, there is much more variation within the new immigrant group than within the more long-term groups. It would be enlightening to investigate whether this similarity in homeownership rates among European immigrant groups existed shortly after they entered the United States or whether they became more equal over time. The 1930 Census of Housing for New Jersey reveals that the major immigrant groups at that time had the following homeownership rates: Italy, 48.2 percent; Germany, 55.5 percent; Poland, 47.4 percent; and the United Kingdom, 48.2 percent

(U.S. Bureau of the Census [henceforth, Census Bureau] 1933). These data suggest that the dramatic differences between the ownership rates of some of the major new immigrant groups in New Jersey are unusual when viewed in a historic context.

DETERMINANTS OF HOMEOWNERSHIP VARIATION

Whereas figure 12.1 presents a snapshot of immigrant homeownership rates in 1990, it does little to explain *why* homeownership rates differ among these groups. Logistic regression allows for the analysis of the factors influencing the variation in homeownership between the native born and the foreign born and between immigrants from different countries of origin. Table 12.1 provides a description of the regression variables, whereas appendixes 12.B-1 and 12.D-1 present sample means and correlations of the independent variables with TENURE.

The first model, run on the entire New Jersey household sample, includes a set of socioeconomic and demographic independent variables as well as a set of dummy variables indicating race, ethnicity, foreign-born status, and year of entry (for immigrants). The second model is restricted to the top 10 immigrant groups in New Jersey (plus those born in Puerto Rico) and assesses the importance of country of birth in predicting homeownership. Logistic regression, using maximum likelihood estimation, is preferred over ordinary least squares (OLS) regression in assessing dichotomous dependent variables such as homeownership because the standard errors of the coefficients in OLS may be biased due to heteroscedasticity, and the probability estimates will systematically lie outside the 0 to 1 range (Pindyck and Rubenfeld 1981). Briefly, the expected effects of the economic and demographic control variables are as follows:

Age Individuals typically pass through a housing "life cycle"— forming households in their early 20s, moving to homeownership in their mid-20s to 30s, trading up to homes with more amenities in their late 30s to 40s, and then, at times, trading down to smaller homes or moving into assisted-living situations in old age. Homeownership is expected to be positively associated with age, although the relationship is nonlinear (Moore 1991). Age squared is included to account for this nonlinearity.

Income In most cases, a home is the most costly good a household will ever purchase. Most households do not buy a home outright,

Table 12.1 DESCRIPTION OF VARIABLES

Dependent Variable	
TENURE	Probability that household head is a homeowner.
Independent Variables	
Income	Total household income, in thousands of dollars.
Age	Age of respondent in years.
Agesq	Age squared. Used to account for nonlinear relationship between age and TENURE. Generally, the probability of homeownership increases with age at a decreasing rate.
Noncitizen	Dummy variable indicating whether respondent is a U.S. citizen. Noncitizen is coded as "1," citizen as "0."
Household type	A three-category variable, coded as two dummy variables. Single-person household is the omitted category. "Married-couple household" and "other household" are the remaining categories.
Occupation	A four-category variable, coded as three dummy variables. "Employed in a nonprofessional/managerial occupation" is the omitted category. The remaining categories are "employed in a professional/managerial position," "not in the labor force and under age 62," and "not in the labor force and over age 61."
House value	Median house value (self-reported) of owner-occupied housing in the respondent's PUMA (Public Use Microdata Area). Value is in thousands of dollars and is reported on the PUMS as a categorical value. For this analysis, the midpoint of each range was used.
Race/Ethnicity/ Immigrant Status	A nine-category variable distinguishing race/ethnicity/ immigrant year of entry status. Coded as eight dummy variables: native-born non-Hispanic blacks, non-Hispanic Asians, non-Hispanic others, Hispanics, immigrants entered before 1965, immigrants entered 1965–69, immigrants entered 1970–79, immigrants entered 1980–89. Native-born non-Hispanic whites are the omitted category.
Year of entry	A four-category variable distinguishing year of entry into the United States (for immigrants only). Coded as three dummy variables: entered 1965–69, 1970–79, and 1980–90. "Entered before 1965" is the omitted category. This variable is used as an alternative to the Race/Ethnicity/Immigrant Status variable when the analysis is limited to immigrants only.
Place of birth	An 11-category variable distinguishing country of birth for 10 largest immigrant groups in New Jersey and those born in Puerto Rico. Asian Indians are the omitted category.

but finance it through a mortgage. Income is important both in accumulating a down payment and in allowing the household to pass the income requirement hurdle of lending institutions. This study uses current income, but permanent income has also been shown to be an important determinant of homeownership (Struyk 1976). The probability of owning is expected to rise with income.

Area Median Home Value   Housing affordability is a function of both income and housing cost. Hypothetically, after controlling for income, the lower the median home value (a proxy for purchase price and carrying costs) in a household's residential area, the higher the probability of owning. Thus, median area home value should be negatively related to homeownership.

Household Type   Married-couple households are by far the most likely household type to own (Moore 1991). Single individuals tend to be more mobile, making homeownership less attractive. Elderly widowed singles, on the other hand, have very high ownership rates, underscoring the importance of including both age and family type in the model.

Occupation   Although income is an important determinant of homeownership, other economic variables such as credit and job history and wealth are also crucial (Jones 1989; Munnell et al. 1992). Unfortunately, most of these variables are not directly measurable from the census. Occupation, although not ideal, is a useful proxy. Those employed in managerial/professional positions are expected to have higher homeownership rates than those in nonprofessional occupations. Those household heads not in the labor force and under age 62 (presumably not retired) are expected to have the lowest rates.

Model 1 of this study regresses TENURE on a series of socioeconomic and demographic variables as well as a set of dummies defining nativity, race/ethnicity, and year of entry for immigrants. Table 12.2 presents regression results in terms of odds ratios and t-statistics. Coefficients are presented in appendix 12.C-1.

As indicated in table 12.2, the majority of variables behaved as expected and are statistically significant at the 95 percent confidence level. The odds ratios of age and income are greater than 1 and are highly significant. Compared to single-person households, married couples are much more likely to be homeowners, while other household types are only slightly more likely to own. Households with heads working in professional/managerial occupations are 26 percent

Table 12.2 LOGISTIC REGRESSIONS ON TENURE: MODEL 1

Independent Variable	Households (excluding Puerto Ricans)		Households (including Puerto Ricans)	
	Odds Ratio	t-Statistic	Odds Ratio	t-Statistic
Age	1.1703	56.83	1.1659	56.05
Age squared	0.9988	−42.39	0.9989	−41.30
Household income ($1,000s)	1.0246	73.46	1.0250	75.35
Area median home value ($1,000s)	0.9957	−28.08	0.9959	−27.42
Household Type Dummies				
Married-couple household	3.3396	56.16	3.2868	55.87
Other household	1.0904	4.11	1.0778	3.59
Occupation Dummies				
Professional-level occupation	1.2562	12.88	1.2700	13.60
Not in labor force, under age 62	0.8985	−2.48	0.8098	−5.14
Not in labor force, over age 61	1.2828	8.78	1.2772	8.70
Race/Ethnicity/Immigrant Dummies				
Native-born black	0.3178	−49.57	0.3220	−49.02
Native-born Hispanic	0.3955	−15.70	0.3987	−15.54
Native-born Asian	1.3717	1.64	1.3694	1.64
Native-born other	0.5748	−3.80	0.5811	−3.73
Entered before 1965	0.9497	−1.61	0.7409	−10.58
Entered 1965–69	0.4858	−13.93	0.4107	−19.18
Entered 1970–79	0.4517	−22.20	0.4170	−25.84
Entered 1980–90	0.1581	−50.97	0.1538	−53.21
R^2	0.25		0.25	
−2 Log likelihood	−65,035		−66,657	
Chi-square	42,560 with 17 DF (p = .0005)		44,595 with 17 DF (p = .0005)	
Sample size	141,248		144,091	

Source: Author's calculations from 1990 New Jersey PUMS 5 percent file.
Notes: Sample includes all households except those born in U.S. territories and outlying areas or born abroad of American parents. Analysis performed on unweighted data; for coefficients, see appendix 12.C-1.

more likely to own than are those with heads in nonprofessional occupations, whereas those not in the labor force and over age 61 are 28 percent more likely to own. Understandably, those not in the labor force and under age 62 are less likely to own. Perhaps surprisingly, the house value of owned homes in the household's area had relatively little effect on the probability of ownership, although the effect was negative, as expected, and significant.

In this analysis of the effect of nativity, race/ethnicity, and immigrant year of entry, native-born non-Hispanic whites form the omitted variable. Compared to this base group, native-born blacks had less than one-third the probability of owning, while native Hispanics were two-fifths as likely to own (see table 12.2). Native Asians, on the other hand, were 37 percent more likely to own than were native whites, even after controlling for income and occupation.

Among immigrants, those who entered the United States before 1965 were just slightly less likely to own than were native-born whites, although the difference was not statistically significant at the 95 percent confidence level (see table 12.2). Immigrants who entered between 1965 and 1969 were half as likely to own as were native-born whites, even after controlling for socioeconomic and demographic variables. Immigrants who entered during the 1980s were only about one-sixth as likely to own as native-born whites.

The right-hand panel of table 12.2 repeats the analysis, this time including Puerto Ricans. The primary differences appear in the year-of-entry variables. Inclusion of those born in Puerto Rico causes the odds of owning to decrease for each of the entry cohorts, especially for those who entered before 1965. Hence, Puerto Ricans are shown to have a dampening effect on overall immigrant homeownership.

Even controlling for age, occupation, income, and so on, immigrants who have been in the United States for 10 or more years still achieve higher ownership rates than do native-born blacks and Hispanics. Although an in-depth comparison of the effect of race on the homeownership rates of immigrants and the native born is beyond the scope of this study, my preliminary analysis suggests that foreign-born blacks and Hispanics are more likely to own than are native-born blacks and Hispanics (excluding those born in Puerto Rico), after controlling for economic and demographic characteristics. However, this difference is not statistically significant even at the 90 percent confidence level.

Figure 12.1 illustrated that immigrants from different countries have achieved different levels of homeownership, despite having similar period-of-entry profiles. Table 12.3 examines a subset of New Jersey

Table 12.3 LOGISTIC REGRESSIONS ON TENURE: MODEL 2

Independent Variable	Households (excluding Puerto Ricans)		Households (including Puerto Ricans)	
	Odds Ratio	t-Statistic	Odds Ratio	t-Statistic
Age	1.0976	9.17	1.1075	11.03
Age squared	0.9993	−7.58	0.9992	−9.20
Household income ($1,000s)	1.0266	21.84	1.0278	25.38
Area median home value ($1,000s)	0.9971	−4.19	0.9953	−8.00
Noncitizen	0.6531	−6.78	0.6408	−7.22
Household Type Dummies				
Married-couple household	2.5659	10.58	2.5639	11.37
Other household	1.0043	0.05	1.0245	0.29
Occupation Dummies				
Professional-level occupation	1.0918	1.20	1.1477	2.05
Not in labor force, under age 62	1.0279	0.16	0.6308	−3.84
Not in labor force, over age 61	1.0753	0.66	1.1338	1.24
Year-of-Entry Dummies				
Entered 1965–69	0.7539	−3.06	0.7190	−4.39
Entered 1970–79	0.6208	−5.43	0.6146	−6.71
Entered 1980–90	0.2221	−14.90	0.2310	−17.04

Place-of-Birth Dummies

Philippines	0.7505	-2.22	0.7321	-2.41
Colombia	0.2665	-9.50	0.2777	-9.23
Dominican Republic	0.2636	-9.38	0.2757	-9.09
Cuba	0.2391	-12.39	0.2521	-12.05
Puerto Rico	N.A.	N.A.	0.2046	-14.22
Portugal	0.8022	-1.72	0.8272	-1.49
Italy	1.8421	5.05	1.9818	5.74
Germany	1.3679	2.44	1.4380	2.88
Poland	1.1404	1.07	1.2012	1.50
United Kingdom	1.0286	0.22	1.0637	0.49
R^2	0.303		0.326	
-2 Log likelihood	-4.643		-5.981	
Chi-square	4,029 with 22 DF (p = .0005)		5,794 with 23 DF (p = .0005)	
Sample size	10,108		12,951	

Source: Author's calculations from 1990 New Jersey PUMS 5 percent file.
Notes: Sample includes all households from top 10 immigrant groups and Puerto Ricans only. Analysis performed on unweighted data; for coefficients, see appendix 12.E-1.

households—only those immigrants from the 10 largest groups and Puerto Ricans—in terms of the effects of place of birth after controlling for period of entry. Results of this second model are presented in terms of odds ratios and *t*-statistics; coefficients are presented in appendix 12.E-1.

Once again, most of the socioeconomic/demographic variables behaved as expected, although *t*-statistics are lower than in the previous model, partially owing to the much smaller sample size (see table 12.3). Age, income, and married-couple status are all positively related to homeownership and are significant. Area median home value once again has a small negative, yet significant, effect. The occupational dummies behaved quite differently than in the first analysis. No category shows a significant difference at the 95 percent confidence level from employment in a nonprofessional occupation. Surprisingly, those not in the labor force and under age 62 are more likely to own than are those employed in nonprofessional occupations.

For immigrants, the year-of-entry variables behaved as expected (table 12.3). "Entered before 1965" forms the omitted category in this case. The more recent the entry cohort, the lower the probability of owning and the more statistically significant the difference from the ownership rate of those who entered before 1965. This model includes an additional dummy variable indicating whether the household head is a noncitizen of the United States. One might expect that the choice not to become a citizen may indicate a lack of long-term attachment or commitment to remaining in the United States, which should decrease the probability of becoming a homebuyer. Indeed, noncitizens in this analysis are shown to be only 65 percent as likely to be owners as are citizens.

Focusing on immigrant place of birth, immigrants from Latin American countries are shown to generally have lower odds of being owners than those from Asian and European countries (see table 12.3). Immigrants from India form the omitted category. Those from Puerto Rico, Cuba, Colombia, and the Dominican Republic each have only 20–30 percent of the ownership probability of Indians. Each of these differences is statistically significant at the 95 percent confidence level. Immigrants from the Philippines and Portugal have 75–80 percent of the probability of Indians to be owners. Those from Germany and Italy have significantly higher odds of being owners than do Indians, while those from Poland and the United Kingdom have higher odds as well, but are not significant at the 95 percent confidence level.

DECOMPOSITION OF HOMEOWNERSHIP VARIATION

This analysis has shown that immigrants of various entry cohorts and nationalities achieve differing homeownership rates, even after controlling for a set of economic and demographic variables. I next asked, "To what extent do the ownership rates of immigrants and native minorities differ from those of a baseline group, in this case native-born whites, and to what degree are these differences due to economic and demographic endowments as opposed to differences in behavior or preferences?" I could then calculate the potential number of additional owners in each group that would be formed if the group's homeownership rate matched that of native-born whites with similar characteristics.

The importance of this analysis is underscored by survey data suggesting that immigrants strongly desire to own a home. If, in fact, they do not own at the same rate as similarly endowed native-born whites, despite their preferences, this may be because of factors such as lack of information about the buying process or discrimination, factors that could be addressed through policy. A recent Fannie Mae survey reported that 35 percent of immigrants stated that "not knowing how to get started" was a barrier to owning, as compared to 25 percent of all adults. Similarly, 22 percent of immigrants stated that "discrimination and other social barriers" are a problem, compared to just 12 percent of all adults (Fannie Mae 1995).

In the third model, following the work of Bourassa (1993), I first regressed TENURE on a set of economic and demographic variables for a baseline group of native-born non-Hispanic whites (table 12.4). The coefficients from this equation were then used to predict hypothetical ownership rates for each immigrant and minority group. This hypothetical rate was the one that these groups would be expected to obtain if they owned at the same rates as native-born whites with similar characteristics. In table 12.5, column (1) shows the actual group homeownership rates whereas column (2) shows the hypothetical rates. Column (3) presents the difference between the actual ownership rate for native-born whites and the actual rate for each group. This difference can be decomposed into two parts. The endowment portion, in column (4), is defined as the difference between the hypothetical rate for each group and the actual rate for native whites. The residual or behavioral effect, in column (5), is defined as the difference between the actual homeownership rate for each group and

Table 12.4 LOGISTIC REGRESSIONS ON TENURE: MODEL 3

Independent Variable	Coefficient	t-Statistic
Age	0.1706	52.62
Agesq	− 0.0013	− 40.14
Household income ($1,000s)	0.0232	59.31
Area median home value ($1,000s)	− 0.0045	− 25.72
Household Type Dummies		
Married-couple household	1.2520	51.17
Other household	0.0772	3.23
Occupation Dummies		
Professional-level occupation	0.1873	9.16
Not in labor force, <62	− 0.0074	− 0.01
Not in labor force, 62 +	0.2915	8.92
Constant	− 4.8230	− 58.52
R²	0.20	
− 2 Log likelihood	147,511	
Chi-square	24,174 with 9 DF (p = .00005)	
Sample size	107,034	

Note: Sample includes native-born non-Hispanic white households only.

its hypothetical rate. Although I term this difference a "behavioral" effect, it includes any residual effects of endowments that are not included in the model. It is important to also recognize that this effect represents more than just preferences about homeownership, but can include behavioral effects caused by discrimination and lack of information as well as other factors.

A positive endowment factor (column [4] in table 12.5) indicates that the group has a set of endowments (age, income, etc.) that is more favorable to ownership than do native-born whites. Groups with this characteristic include immigrants who entered before 1970, as well as Indians, Filipinos, Portuguese, and Italians.

A positive residual or behavioral factor (column [5] in table 12.5) indicates that the group chooses to or is able to achieve a higher homeownership rate than do native-born whites who share similar economic and demographic characteristics. Native-born Asians, as well as immigrants from Germany and Italy, share this characteristic.

Long-term immigrants as a whole have endowments that make them more likely to own than native-born whites. Although a more detailed decomposition of the endowments is not presented here, age is of major significance. More recent immigrants are less favorably endowed. Similarly, long-term immigrants behave almost exactly the same as similarly endowed native-born whites, whereas new immigrants are much less likely to own than native whites who share similar socioeconomic characteristics.

Among immigrants by place of birth, behavioral factors strongly outweigh the importance of endowment factors. New immigrants, even those with positive endowment factors (the Indians and Filipinos) own at substantially lower rates than do similarly endowed native whites. Recent Latin American immigrants fare poorly in both the endowment and behavioral areas. The Cubans and Puerto Ricans, who share similar year-of-entry profiles, pose an interesting comparison. Although the negative endowment effect is small for Cubans and large for Puerto Ricans, both groups have large negative behavioral effects. As mentioned, long-term immigrants have small endowment effects, but vary somewhat in their behaviors. Italians and Germans are more likely to own than are similarly endowed native whites, whereas Poles and those from the United Kingdom are somewhat less likely to own (see table 12.5).

As noted, the behavioral effect reflects both differences in behavior and preferences between immigrants and native-born whites, as well as the residual effects of variables not specified in the model. Although age, occupation, and income may, to some degree, proxy the effects of wealth, credit, and job history, the importance of these omitted variables is probably not fully accounted for by the model. Many studies have established the importance of wealth in achieving homeownership (Joint Center for Housing Studies 1993; Jones 1989; Struyk 1976). The accumulation of funds for down-payment and closing costs often poses a higher barrier to homeownership for young households than do income requirements. For immigrants, who may have spent much of their savings on the journey to the United States and on necessities (and who in certain areas of New Jersey are faced with high rents), saving this amount can take considerable time. Many immigrants have attempted to address the problem of accumulating savings by living in crowded conditions (to reduce the per capita rent) and by pooling their resources in family or multifamily bank accounts (Leigh 1995).

The job and credit history necessary to obtain a mortgage may also be more difficult to establish for immigrants, particularly recent immigrants. Some financial institutions have adopted flexible requirements for dealing with immigrants, such as accepting letters of reference from utility, cable, and trash removal companies to establish credit and looking more favorably on workers who work consistently but change jobs frequently to "move up the ladder" (Adams 1995). A lack of knowledge about mortgage markets and local communities

Table 12.5 DECOMPOSITION OF HOMEOWNERSHIP INTO ENDOWMENT AND RESIDUAL EFFECTS

| | Ownership Rates (%) | | | Decomposition (in Percentage Points) | | Potential Homeowner Analysis | | |
	(1) Actual Homeownership Rate	(2) Hypothetical Homeownership Rate	(3) Native White Rate Minus Actual Group Rate	(4) Endowment	(5) Behavioral	(6) Number of Households (thousands)	(7) Number of Homeowners (thousands)	(8) Potential Number of New Homeowners (thousands)
Native-Born								
White	72.7					1,975	1,435	
Black	38.2	60.8	34.5	-11.9	-22.6	291	111	66
Asian	72.2	66.7	0.5	-6.0	5.5	4	3	0
Hispanic	35.1	51.7	37.6	-21.0	-16.7	38	13	6
Other	56.8	64.3	15.9	-8.4	-7.4	4	2	0
Year of Immigrant Entry								
Before 1965	74.2	75.2	-1.6	2.5	-0.9	145	108	1
1965–69	62.0	74.5	10.7	1.8	-12.5	46	29	6
1970–79	56.7	71.4	16.0	-1.3	-14.7	95	54	14
1980–90	25.7	59.7	47.0	-13.0	-34.0	112	29	38

Place of Birth

Place of Birth								
India	60.6	76.4	12.1	3.7	− 15.8	19	12	3
Philippines	57.7	75.1	15.0	2.4	− 17.4	13	7	2
Colombia	25.3	60.4	47.4	− 12.3	− 35.2	13	3	5
Dominican Republic	23.9	59.7	48.8	− 13.0	− 35.8	12	3	4
Cuba	38.9	71.3	33.8	− 1.4	− 32.4	28	11	9
Puerto Rico	28.5	59.6	44.2	− 13.1	− 31.0	61	17	19
Portugal	55.3	73.3	17.4	0.6	− 18.0	13	7	2
Italy	81.4	75.1	− 8.8	2.4	6.4	36	29	0
Germany	78.5	72.6	− 5.8	− 0.1	5.9	23	18	0
Poland	66.3	70.9	6.4	− 1.8	− 4.6	20	13	1
United Kingdom	66.0	71.8	6.7	− 0.9	− 5.8	16	11	1

Source: Author's calculations of 1990 New Jersey PUMS 5 percent file.
Note: Year-of-entry groups exclude those born in Puerto Rico.

may also present barriers to ownership. Mortgage instruments are unknown in many foreign countries; homes are often built on a cash basis or through short-term loans with large balloon payments. Although more and more lenders, including some in New Jersey, are producing documents and holding homebuying seminars in foreign languages, learning to understand and trust the mortgage process still takes time (Adams 1995).

Racial discrimination is another potential factor that may account for behavioral differences or homeownership outcomes between some immigrants and native-born whites. Data available through the Home Mortgage Disclosure Act, analyzed by the Federal Reserve Bank of Boston (Munnell et al. 1992), revealed that lenders are more likely to deny mortgage loans to black applicants than they are to whites, even after controlling for a wide spectrum of job, credit, income, and asset variables. If lenders have different perceptions of immigrants' creditworthiness, based purely on their race, racial discrimination may be influencing the different outcomes for different nationality groups.

Yet another important consideration in explaining variation in homeownership is the effect of differences in housing stock characteristics in the locations where immigrant groups live. This analysis has shown a small, statistically significant negative effect of the area median housing price on homeownership. The availability of owner-occupied, as opposed to rental, housing may also play a role. Immigrants from Cuba, the Dominican Republic, Colombia, Puerto Rico, and the Philippines are most highly concentrated in Hudson County, a county in which only one-third of the housing stock is owner occupied. Although it is true that immigrants could move to areas with more owner-occupied stock, it may be quite difficult to leave the strong social and kin networks of ethnic enclaves.

The third panel of table 12.5 presents an analysis of potential homeowners and includes the number of total households, as well as owner households, and the number of additional owner households that would exist if each group achieved its hypothetical ownership rate. Given immigrants' stated desire for homeownership, this potential number gives a possible target for the number of additional owners that could be fostered through homebuyer counseling, addressing problems of discrimination, and tailoring real estate and mortgage services to immigrant needs. A comparison of the number of potential new owners to the number of existing owners shows that there is much work to be done. Although older immigrants have largely reached their homeownership potential, 1980s immigrants have more potential owners than current owners. Remember, these differences

are net of endowment effects. Puerto Ricans, Colombians, Dominicans, and Cubans have the largest potential owner-to-actual-owner
ratios.

In light of substantial homeownership potential of immigrants, it
is important not to forget the sizable potential of native-born blacks.
Attainment of their potential ownership rates would add more New
Jersey homeowners than would the attainment of potential ownership
of all immigrants combined.

HOMEOWNERSHIP PROGRESS OF 1970s IMMIGRANTS

The cross-sectional analysis presented thus far suggests that the longer
an immigrant household resides in the United States, the more it
"catches up" to the homeownership rates of similarly endowed
native-born whites. However, significant research, particularly that of
Borjas (1994), has pointed out the danger of drawing conclusions
about immigrant progress through the use of cross-sectional data.
Differences in the "quality" of immigrant cohorts, rather than actual
progress of any particular cohort, may explain apparent changes in
homeownership within an age group when using cross-sectional data.
For instance, long-term immigrants may have arrived in the United
States with greater educational, monetary, or skill endowments than
do current immigrants. These endowments, rather than the immigrants' length of residency in the United States, may underlie their
homeownership progress. Tracing specific age cohorts over time controls for the distinct characteristics of different entry cohorts and allows for more reliable assessment of immigrant progress. The 1980
and 1990 Decennial Census PUMS data sets allow one to trace the
homeownership progress of particular age cohorts. Although this type
of analysis is more suited to national-level data (where it is much less
affected by immigrants moving into and out of the area over time), it
is illustrative at the state level.[6]

Figures 12.2 and 12.3 plot cohort transitions in homeownership
from 1980 to 1990 for native-born whites and blacks and for Asian
and Latin American/Caribbean immigrants who entered the United
States during the 1970s (underlying data are presented in table 12.6).
Unfortunately, small sample sizes for individual immigrant nationality groups in the 1980 Census make it very difficult to show meaningful trends for immigrants on a more detailed level.

Figure 12.2 HOMEOWNERSHIP PROGRESS OF NATIVE-BORN
              COHORTS: 1980–90

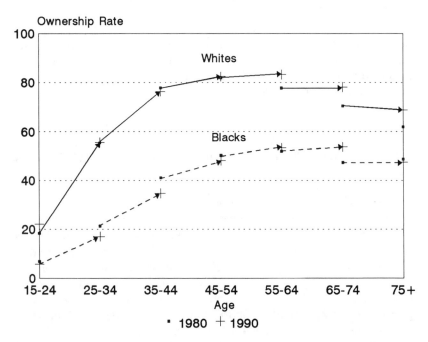

The slope of a cohort trajectory in figures 12.2 and 12.3 represents the increase or decrease in homeownership rates as the cohort ages 10 years from 1980 to 1990. For native-born whites, steep increases are observed in ownership through ages 35–44, followed by a leveling off in middle age and then a decrease in later years (figure 12.2). The vertical distance between the 1980 and 1990 points for any particular age group shows that young to middle-aged whites of similar ages had similar homeownership rates in both 1980 and 1990. Native-born whites aged 55 and over in 1990 had higher ownership rates than did their same aged forebears in 1980.

Native-born black trajectories (figure 12.2) reveal a somewhat different pattern. First, blacks start at and remain at significantly lower ownership rates than do whites at each age group. Second, the upward slope for young blacks is noticeably less steep than for young whites, showing slower relative progress. Interestingly, ownership rates among older blacks appear to drop off more moderately than do those

Figure 12.3 HOMEOWNERSHIP PROGRESS OF IMMIGRANT COHORTS: 1980–90

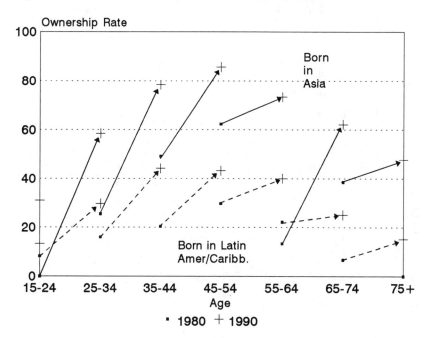

Age

∎ 1980 + 1990

for older whites. Most important, though, the ownership rates for young blacks in 1990 were noticeably lower than for the same age group in 1980. Today's young native-born blacks in New Jersey are increasingly renters compared to young blacks in 1980.

Among 1970s immigrants, homeownership rates for the Asian-born generally start at levels between those of native-born whites and blacks but show remarkable progress as cohorts age (figure 12.3). In fact, the ownership rate for the Asian-born cohort aged 25–34 in 1980 tripled as it aged 10 years. The upward slope of ownership progress moderates for older age groups (except for the 55–64 age group in 1980, which is probably affected by small sample size), but does not become negative, as with older native whites. On the other hand, 1970s immigrants from Latin America and the Caribbean generally start at much lower homeownership levels than do Asians and, among the younger age groups, have somewhat flatter ownership trajectories. However, their trajectories are notably steeper than are those of native

Table 12.6 HOMEOWNERSHIP PROGRESS OF NATIVE-BORN BLACKS AND 1970s IMMIGRANTS RELATIVE TO SAME-AGED NATIVE-BORN WHITES

Native-Born Blacks

Age in 1980	1980			1990			1980 to 1990
	Native White Ownership Rate (%)	Native Black Ownership Rate (%)	Ratio of Black/White Rates	Native White Ownership Rate (%)	Native Black Ownership Rate (%)	Ratio of Black/White Rates	Percent Change in Ratios[a]
15–24	18.3	6.9	37.7	22.1	5.8	26.2	−18.9
25–34	55.4	21.3	38.4	55.6	17.0	30.6	18.1
35–44	77.9	41.1	52.8	76.4	34.7	45.4	10.5
45–54	81.9	50.2	61.3	82.5	48.1	58.3	4.4
55–64	77.8	51.9	66.7	83.3	53.3	64.0	2.9
65–74	70.5	47.3	67.1	78.2	53.7	68.7	2.7
75+	62.0	48.7	78.5	68.8	47.4	68.9	

Asian Immigrants

Age in 1980	1980			1990			1980 to 1990
	Native White Ownership Rate (%)	Asian Immigrant Ownership Rate (%)	Ratio of Asian/White Rates	Native White Ownership Rate (%)	Asian Immigrant Ownership Rate (%)	Ratio of Asian/White Rates	Percent Change in Ratios[a]
15–24	18.3	N.A.	N.A.	22.1	N.A.	N.A.	N.A.
25–34	55.4	25.5	46.0	55.6	58.5	105.2	122.9
35–44	77.9	49.1	63.0	76.4	78.4	102.6	64.8
45–54	81.9	62.4	76.2	82.5	85.7	103.9	15.7
55–64	77.8	13.3	17.1	83.3	73.4	88.1	365.3
65–74	70.5	38.5	54.6	78.2	62.2	79.5	
75+	62.0	N.A.	N.A.	68.8	N.A.	N.A.	N.A.

Latin American/Caribbean Immigrants

	1980			1990			1980 to 1990
Age in 1980	Native White Ownership Rate (%)	Latin American/ Caribbean Ownership Rate (%)	Ratio of Latin American/ White Rates	Native White Ownership Rate (%)	Latin American/ Caribbean Ownership Rate (%)	Ratio of Latin American/ White Rates	Percent Change in Ratios[a]
15–24	18.3	8.2	44.8	22.1	13.3	60.2	19.2
25–34	55.4	16.0	28.9	55.6	29.7	53.4	99.9
35–44	77.9	20.3	26.1	76.4	44.1	57.7	100.9
45–54	81.9	29.8	36.4	82.5	43.2	52.4	100.9
55–64	77.8	22.2	28.5	83.3	40.0	48.0	32.0
65–74	70.5	6.7	9.5	78.2	25.1	32.1	12.5
75+	62.0	N.A.	N.A.	68.8	N.A.	N.A.	N.A.

Source: Author's analysis of 1980 and 1990 Censuses, New Jersey PUMS 5 percent file.

Note: Data for older immigrants should be interpreted with care owing to small sample sizes.

a. Percent change in ratios is from age group specified in 1980 to age group 10 years older in 1990.

whites or blacks. Like Asians, homeownership rates within cohorts continue to rise even among older age groups.

These cohort data allow one to evaluate the homeownership progress of different groups relative to same-aged native-born whites. Table 12.6 shows the ratio of the homeownership rates for each group (native blacks, 1970s immigrants from Asia, and 1970s immigrants from Latin America/Caribbean) to those of the same-aged native-born white cohort. These ratios are presented for both 1980 and 1990 and allow one to trace the progress of cohorts as they age 10 years. The last column of the table presents the percentage change in the ratios from 1980 to 1990, as the cohorts age 10 years. For example, in 1980, native-born blacks aged 25 to 34 had 38.4 percent of the homeownership rate of same-aged native whites. In 1990, this same cohort of native blacks (now aged 35 to 44) had 45.4 percent of the homeownership rate of native whites, an increase in the ratios of 18.1 percent. By comparison, Asian-born 1970s immigrants aged 25 to 34 had 46 percent of the ownership rates of same-aged native whites. By 1990, this cohort had 102.6 percent of the rate of same-aged native whites, an increase in the ratios of 122.9 percent.

In general, 1970s Asian immigrants attained higher homeownership rates within 10 years of entering the United States than did 1970s immigrants from Latin America and the Caribbean. Within 20 years of entry, young to middle-aged Asian immigrants actually surpassed the homeownership rates of same-aged native whites. Data for older immigrant age groups should be interpreted with care owing to small sample sizes (most immigrants enter the United States when they are fairly young). Young to middle-aged 1970s immigrants from Latin America and the Caribbean attained only 20–30 percent of same-aged native white ownership rates within 10 years of entry. Within 20 years, however, they achieved 50–60 percent of the ownership rates of native whites. Whereas they do not attain the levels of their Asian counterparts, they show remarkable progress, with some age groups cutting the disparity between themselves and their native white counterparts by half.

Asian immigrants quickly outstrip the homeownership progress of native-born blacks, as do Latin American immigrants in some age groups (see table 12.6). Even those Latin American immigrants who do not attain the ownership levels of native blacks show more rapid percentage increases over the 1980s than do blacks. The success of immigrants relative to native-born blacks in achieving homeownership, as well as in other spheres, is a significant area of research in itself. These differences may underlie some of the tensions between these communities. In terms of housing policy, it is important not to focus on the potential of promoting immigrant homeownership to the detriment of promoting ownership among native minorities. Both populations clearly have untapped homeownership capacity.

CHARACTERISTICS OF OWNED UNITS

Although this chapter has focused on attainment of homeownership, it is important to note that not all owned homes have similar characteristics. Table 12.7 contrasts the owned homes of immigrant groups (categorized by entry cohort) by year built, unit type, and house value.[7] It also presents median household income. Not surprisingly, the lowest-income groups tend to live in the oldest stock. Approximately half of Dominicans, Colombians, Cubans, Puerto Ricans, and Portuguese live in units built before 1950. Indians and Filipinos, the wealthier of the recent immigrants, live in the newest stock. Almost 40 percent of Indian owners live in units built during the 1980s. Thirty to 40 percent of long-term immigrants uniformly live in pre-1950 housing, and the rest are fairly evenly distributed over the next few decades. Of course, these data provide just a glimpse of the housing occupied by immigrants in 1990. Long-term immigrants may have occupied new housing at the time of their arrival, much as the Asian Indians do, and simply aged in place.

Single-family detached dwellings are clearly the predominant dwelling type for both long-term immigrants as well as wealthier new immigrants (table 12.7). Two distinct patterns of ownership are found among long-term immigrants. The great majority of units owned by Germans and those from the United Kingdom are single-family detached dwellings. Italians and Poles, on the other hand, have a somewhat lower rate of single-family ownership (65 percent) and are much more likely to own units in two- to four-unit structures. The probability of owning a home in a two- to four-unit structure is substantial for several immigrant groups. Half of all owned units occupied by Portuguese and Dominicans are in such structures, but all groups except Indians, Filipinos, Germans, and those from the United Kingdom have at least 20 percent of their owner households in such structures. In contrast, only 6 percent of native whites live in two- to four-unit structures.

The value of owned units is generally correlated with the income of the owners. Recent Indian and Filipino immigrants have the highest

Table 12.7 CHARACTERISTICS OF IMMIGRANT OWNER-OCCUPIED HOUSING STOCK: 1990 (PERCENT DISTRIBUTION)

Place of Birth	Median Household Income ($)	Year Unit Built					Unit Type					House Value		
		1980–90	1970–79	1960–69	1950–59	Before 1950	Single-family Detached	Single-family Attached	2–4 Units	5+ Units	Mobiles and Other	Less than $100,000	$100,000–$199,999	$200,000 and Over
India	54,708	38.6	17.4	14.4	14.3	15.3	75.7	12.2	6.2	5.6	0.3	6.7	45.7	48.1
Philippines	57,149	26.6	13.2	15.8	17.3	27.1	71.3	10.2	11.6	4.2	2.6	11.3	50.0	39.1
Colombia	34,000	11.3	9.9	15.0	15.9	47.9	53.1	9.3	27.5	5.7	4.2	14.1	60.9	25.0
Dominican Republic	28,913	11.5	11.5	11.6	9.9	55.5	29.2	6.0	54.8	4.9	5.2	12.4	57.3	30.4
Cuba	32,500	9.3	8.8	12.1	13.7	56.2	48.3	6.5	38.5	4.2	2.5	7.4	48.5	44.2
Puerto Rico	24,000	8.7	9.1	12.5	15.1	54.5	54.1	15.9	23.9	4.4	1.8	38.5	44.8	16.7
Portugal	29,339	10.8	7.8	12.5	13.7	55.2	41.9	4.2	48.8	3.6	1.5	7.9	56.9	35.2
Italy	35,000	12.3	12.8	17.6	18.8	38.4	65.9	6.3	24.5	1.9	1.6	14.1	46.2	39.7
Germany	36,770	10.8	17.0	21.0	20.5	30.6	82.0	6.8	5.9	3.9	1.5	21.0	43.0	36.0
Poland	31,000	9.5	13.6	19.3	18.6	39.0	64.2	6.7	24.5	3.5	1.0	17.7	47.5	34.9
United Kingdom	37,150	13.5	17.4	15.7	18.6	34.8	77.3	9.3	6.2	4.0	3.4	20.3	46.2	33.5

Source: Tabulations of the 1990 Census, New Jersey PUMS 5 percent file, by Joint Center for Housing Studies, Harvard University.

Note: Percentages may not sum to 100 due to rounding.

valued housing, followed by the longer-term immigrants and then the more recent, Latin American, immigrant groups (see table 12.7). While Italians have a somewhat higher percentage than Filipinos of houses valued over $200,000, they have a higher percentage of very low-valued houses as well (14.1 percent vs. 11.3 percent under $100,000). Median-value data (not shown here) show Italians to have lower median values than Filipinos. Puerto Ricans and Cubans, with similar period-of-entry profiles, differ dramatically in the value of their homes. Close to 40 percent of Puerto Rican owners have houses valued at less than $100,000, as compared to only 7 percent of Cubans. Meanwhile, 44 percent of Cuban owners have homes valued at $200,000 and over, whereas only 17 percent of Puerto Ricans have homes valued at such prices.

IMMIGRANT HOMEOWNERSHIP PROGRESS AT THE NATIONAL LEVEL

An axiom in the study of housing policy is that all housing markets are local, reflecting the fixed nature of housing stock. Certainly, the level of homeownership and the ease of attaining it differ across market areas according to housing price as a percentage of income, type of housing stock available, the cost and quality of rental alternatives, and, in the case of minorities, presence of discrimination. However, the experience of New Jersey's immigrants in attaining homeownership does reflect, to a large degree, immigrant experience in the nation as whole. Although the countries of origin for immigrants in New Jersey differ from those of the aggregate U.S. immigrant population, New Jersey immigrants' variety of experience is reflective of experience at the national level and is suggestive of differences between immigrants from Asian and Latin American countries.

As in New Jersey, immigrants nationally improve their homeownership rates relative to same-aged, native-born, white cohorts the longer they remain in the United States (Joint Center for Housing Studies 1994). For example, 1970s immigrants aged 25 to 34 in 1980 achieved just 24.2 percent of the ownership rates of same-aged native whites. By 1990, this same group had attained 76.1 percent of the native white rate.

Nationally, immigrants from different countries vary greatly in the ownership rates attained within 10 years of entry (see figure 12.4). Although the major countries of origin differ from those in New Jersey,

Figure 12.4 HOMEOWNERSHIP RATES FOR YOUNG IMMIGRANTS (NATIONAL)

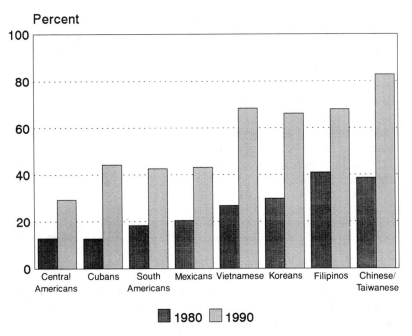

Source: Author's calculations of 1980 and 1990 PUMS 1 percent files.
Note: Data refer to 1970s immigrants who were aged 25–34 in 1980 and 35–44 in 1990.

overall patterns are similar. First, young immigrants from Latin American regions—in this case, Central and South Americans, Cubans, and Mexicans—initially achieve lower ownership rates than do those from Asian areas. However, all immigrants improve their rates substantially as they age 10 years. Asian immigrants attain the highest ownership rates. In the case of those from China and Taiwan, they surpass levels of their same-aged, native-white counterparts (82.8 percent versus 72.1 percent, respectively). Those from Latin American countries attain lower levels of ownership but make exceptional progress, doubling or tripling their initial levels.

After controlling for a series of economic characteristics, immigrants from Asian countries have higher hypothetical or potential ownership rates than do those from Latin American countries, and they actually come closer to attaining these potential rates. Table 12.8 shows actual and hypothetical 1990 homeownership rates for immigrants who entered the United States during the 1970s for major im-

Table 12.8 ACTUAL AND HYPOTHETICAL OWNERSHIP RATES FOR
MAJOR IMMIGRANT GROUPS: 1990 NATIONAL LEVEL

Area of Origin	Actual Rate (%)	Hypothetical Rate (%)	Percentage of Hypothetical Rate Achieved
Central America	27.0	61.9	43.6
Caribbean	33.6	61.4	54.7
Mexico	38.8	60.6	64.0
Cuba	48.8	71.7	68.1
Vietnam	58.4	67.0	87.2
Philippines	65.9	75.7	87.1
China/Taiwan	68.1	76.8	88.7
India	76.8	81.3	94.5

Source: Author's calculations of 1990 PUMS 1 percent sample for the United States.
Note: Data are for immigrants who entered the United States from 1970 to 1979.

migrant groups at the national level. The hypothetical rates are the
rates that immigrants would achieve if they owned at the same rates
as native whites with similar economic and demographic characteristics. The table also shows the percentage of the potential rate actually achieved. Those from Asian countries, particularly India,
China/Taiwan, and the Philippines, have higher potential rates, reflecting higher incomes, ages, and other characteristics favorable to
homeownership. Those immigrants from Latin American countries
and the Caribbean, while having lower hypothetical ownership rates,
also lag further behind in achieving them than do Asian immigrants.
In other words, as in New Jersey, those immigrants achieve a smaller
proportion of the ownership rates of similarly endowed native whites.

In sum, the immigant experience in New Jersey, although not directly transferable to the national level, does illustrate many of the
same patterns of homeownership attainment. At the aggregate level,
young immigrants increase their ownership rates relative to same-
aged native-white cohorts the longer they remain in the United States.
Immigrants from different countries initially attain varying degrees of
ownership, but all make substantial progress over time. The difference
in homeownership achievement between those from Latin American
and Asian countries, even after controlling for a host of demographic
and economic characteristics, deserves further attention.

CONCLUSION

The heterogeneity of the immigrant experience is reflected by their
varied success in attaining homeownership in New Jersey, as well as

by the differing characteristics of the homes they purchase. Those immigrants, mostly European, who entered the United States before 1965 have largely attained the American Dream of owning their own home, at least to a degree similar to their native-born counterparts. More recent immigrants have been less successful thus far, but certain nationalities within this group have done well indeed. Why these nationalities have flourished in the homebuying market while others have lagged goes beyond simple explanations of income, occupation, age, or family type. Further research is necessary to explore the effects of differential asset accumulation, credit and job history, knowledge of the mortgage market and the community, preferences for homeownership, as well as the possibility of discrimination in lending. Tracing age cohorts over time reveals that, whereas Asian-born immigrants start out at higher levels of homeownership and progress at higher rates than do those born in Latin America and the Caribbean, all the major immigrant groups in New Jersey make substantial progress toward homeownership the longer they reside in the state.

The importance of homeownership in providing a stable economic base for a household is difficult to overestimate. Ownership is clearly not feasible for all households, but it is reasonable to expect that immigrants should be able to own their own homes at the same rate as native whites with similar economic and demographic characteristics. In many areas throughout the country, lenders, community development organizations, and major actors in the mortgage market, such as Fannie Mae, are realizing the potential of immigrant ownership and are tailoring products and services to make it a reality. Generations of immigrants have used homeownership to establish a secure economic foothold in the United States. Helping new immigrants to likewise achieve homeownership will benefit not only them and their children but their communities as well.

Notes

I am grateful for the comments of participants at the "Conference on Impacts of Immigration to New Jersey" (at Princeton University, May 18–19, 1995), particularly those of Thomas J. Espenshade, and I thank Beth Martin for research assistance.

1. Although persons born in Puerto Rico are U.S. citizens and are classified by the census as "native born," their experience of assimilation is similar to that of the foreign born. For the purposes of this study, they are classified as immigrants. However, most

analyses are presented both with and without Puerto Ricans included so that readers who wish to examine only the strictly defined "foreign born" may do so.

2. "Whites," "blacks," "Asians," and "Indians" all refer to non-Hispanic members of these racial categories, unless otherwise specified.

3. An immigrant household is defined as one *headed* by a foreign-born or Puerto Rican-born individual. Excluded from analysis are those born abroad of American parents and those born in U.S. territories or outlying areas, except for Puerto Rico.

4. Excluding those born in Puerto Rico, immigrants headed 399,000 households, or 14.7 percent of all households and 12.3 percent of owner households.

5. The large proportion of Portuguese who entered after 1958 is due in part to the Azorean refugee acts implemented after volcanic eruptions and ensuing earthquakes on the island of Faial in 1957. These special nonquota visas given to the Portuguese significantly increased their immigration beyond their annual quota of 440 (Thernstrom 1980: 818).

6. This analysis assumes that all immigrant groups with similar predispositions to be owners or renters face the same incentives to move out of or into New Jersey. In other words, Asians predisposed to be renters are not more likely to move out of New Jersey than are other immigrant renters; and Asian owners are not more likely to move into New Jersey than are other immigrant owners.

7. Value is self-reported.

References

Adams, John. 1995. "A Surge of Newcomers to the U.S. Deserves Special Examination as to their Housing and Credit Capabilities." Testimony at the Housing Roundtable Conference. San Antonio, January 19.

Borjas, George J. 1994. "The Economics of Immigration." *Journal of Economic Literature* 32 (December): 1667–1717.

Bourassa, Steven C. 1993. *Immigration and Housing Tenure Choice in Australia.* Canberra: Australian National University.

Canada Mortgage and Housing Corporation, Research Division. 1994. *Immigrant Housing Choices, 1986,* prepared by Clayton Research Associated Ltd. Ottawa, Ontario: Canada Mortgage and Housing Corporation.

Census Bureau. *See* U.S. Bureau of the Census.

Easterlin, Richard A., David Ward, William S. Bernard, and Reed Ueeda. 1982. "Settlement Patterns and Spatial Distribution." In *Dimensions of Ethnicity,* edited by Stephan Thernstrom (35–74). Cambridge, Mass.: Belknap Press of Harvard University Press.

Fannie Mae. 1995. *Fannie Mae National Housing Survey: 1995. Immigrants, Homeownership, and the American Dream.* Washington, D.C.: Author.

Joint Center for Housing Studies, Harvard University. 1993. *The State of the Nation's Housing: 1993*. Cambridge, Mass.: Author.

————. 1994. *The State of the Nation's Housing*. Cambridge, Mass.: Author.

Jones, Lawrence. 1989. "Current Wealth and Tenure Choice." *Journal of the American Real Estate and Urban Economics Association* 17(1): 17–40.

Lapham, Susan J. 1992. *1990 Ethnic Profiles for States*. Washington, D.C.: U.S. Bureau of the Census, Population Division.

Leigh, Susan. 1995. "A Surge of Newcomers to the U.S. Deserves Special Examination as to Their Housing and Credit Capabilities." Testimony at the Housing Roundtable Conference. San Antonio, January 19.

Linneman, Peter, and Susan Wachter. 1989. "The Impacts of Borrowing Constraints on Homeownership." *Journal of the American Real Estate and Urban Economics Association* 17: 389–402.

Masnick, George S., John R. Pitkin, and John Brennan. 1990. "Cohort Housing Trends in a Local Housing Market: The Case of Southern California." In *Housing Demography*, edited by Dowell Myers. Madison, Wis.: University of Wisconsin Press.

McArdle, Nancy, and Kelly Mikelson. 1994. *The New Immigrants: Demographic and Housing Characteristics*. Joint Center for Housing Studies Working Paper W94-1. Cambridge, Mass.: Harvard University, Joint Center for Housing Studies.

Moore, Dora J. 1991. "Forecasting the Probability of Homeownership: A Cross-Sectional Regression Analysis." *Journal of Housing Research* (Fannie Mae, Office of Policy Research, Washington, D.C.) 2(2): 125–43.

Munnell, Alicia H., Lynne E. Browne, James McEneaney, and Geoffrey M. B. Tootell. 1992. "Mortgage Lending in Boston: Interpreting the HMDA Data." Working Paper 92-7. Boston: Federal Reserve Bank of Boston.

Myers, Dowell. 1993. "Upward Mobility and the Filtering Process." *Journal of Planning Education and Research* 2: 101–12.

————. 1995. "Immigration Cohorts and Residential Overcrowding: A Double Cohort Method for Estimating Improvement Over Time in Southern California." Paper presented at the annual meeting of the Population Association of America, San Francisco, April 20, 1995.

Passel, Jeffrey, and Barry Edmonston. 1992. "Immigration and Race: Recent Trends in Immigration to the United States." Urban Institute Working Paper PRIP-UI-22. Washington, D.C.: Urban Institute, May.

Pindyck, Robert S., and Daniel L. Rubenfeld. 1981. *Econometric Models and Economic Forecasts*. New York: McGraw Hill.

Struyk, Raymond J. 1976. *Urban Homeownership*. Lexington, Mass.: Lexington Books.

Thernstrom, Stephan, ed. 1980. *Harvard Encyclopedia of American Ethnic Groups*. Cambridge, Mass.: Belknap Press of Harvard University Press.

U.S. Bureau of the Census. 1933. *Census of Population, 1930: Special Report on Foreign-Born White Families by Country of Birth of Head*. Washington, D.C.: Author.

————. 1983a. *Census of Population and Housing, 1980: Public Use Microdata Samples, A Sample, New Jersey*. Washington, D.C.: Author.

————. 1983b. *Census of Population and Housing, 1980: Public Use Microdata Samples, B Sample, United States*. Washington, D.C.: Author.

————. 1983c. *Census of Population and Housing, 1980: Public Use Microdata Samples, Technical Documentation*. Washington, D.C.: Author.

————. 1992a. *Census of Population and Housing, 1990: Public Use Microdata Samples, United States*. Washington, D.C.: Author.

————. 1992b. *Census of Population and Housing, 1990: Public Use Microdata Samples, U.S. Technical Documentation*. Washington, D.C.: Author.

————. 1993a. *Census of Population and Housing Summary Tape File 3C*. CD90-3C-1. Washington, D.C.: Author, May.

————. 1993b. *Census of Population: The Foreign-Born Population in the United States*. CP-3-1. Washington, D.C.: Author, July.

Ward, David. 1971. *Cities and Immigrants: A Geography of Change in Nineteenth-Century America*. New York: Oxford University Press.

Appendix 12.A-1 MAJOR NEW JERSEY IMMIGRANT GROUPS BY
PLACE OF BIRTH AND ENTRY COHORT (PERCENTAGE DISTRIBUTION)

Place	Total	Period of Entry			
of Birth	Households	1980–90	1970–79	1965–69	Before 1965
India	18,901	51.1	35.4	9.3	4.2
Philippines	13,161	43.3	38.3	13.6	4.9
Colombia	13,485	44.0	32.9	16.2	6.9
Dominican Republic	12,133	41.7	34.5	14.3	9.5
Portugal	13,436	31.1	41.2	13.4	14.3
Cuba	28,358	17.6	22.2	27.6	32.7
Puerto Rico	60,738	20.2	19.7	16.4	43.7
Poland	20,156	18.9	11.7	7.9	61.6
United Kingdom	16,439	16.5	10.9	6.7	65.9
Italy	36,154	3.0	11.4	12.2	73.5
Germany	22,715	4.5	4.9	5.0	85.6

Source: Tabulations of 1990 Census, New Jersey PUMS 5 percent file, by Joint Center for Housing Studies, Harvard University.

Appendix 12.B-1 SAMPLE MEANS AND CORRELATION OF
INDEPENDENT VARIABLES WITH TENURE: MODEL 1

Variable	Mean	Correlation Coefficient
TENURE	0.6997	
Age	50.19	0.187
Agesq	2803.4	0.148
Income ($1,000s)	51.095	0.289
Median area house value ($1,000s)	163.3	0.023
Household Type Dummies		
Married-couple household	0.5973	0.323
Single person[a]	0.138	−0.142
Other household	0.2647	−0.248
Occupation Dummies		
Professional/managerial occupation	0.2744	0.106
Nonprofessional occupation[a]	0.5438	−0.086
Not in labor force, under age 62	0.0248	−0.074
Not in labor force, over age 61	0.1569	0.018
Race/Ethnicity/Immigrant Dummies		
Native white[a]	0.7578	0.213
Native black	0.0878	−0.178
Native Asian	0.0015	0.005
Native Hispanic	0.0124	−0.075
Native other	0.0018	−0.011
Immigrant/entered before 1965	0.0528	0.037
Immigrant/entered 1965–69	0.0161	−0.011
Immigrant/entered 1970–79	0.0331	−0.036
Immigrant/entered 1980–90	0.0368	−0.017

Source: Author's analysis of 1990 New Jersey PUMS 5 percent file.
Notes: Sample includes all households, except those with heads born in Puerto Rico and other U.S. territories, and those born abroad of American parents.
a. Omitted categorical variable.

Appendix 12.C-1 LOGISTIC REGRESSIONS ON TENURE: MODEL 1

Independent Variables	Households (excluding Puerto Ricans)		Households (including Puerto Ricans)	
	Coefficient	t-Statistic	Coefficient	t-Statistic
Age	0.1572	56.83	0.1535	56.05
Age square	-0.0012	-42.39	-0.0011	-41.30
Household income ($1,000s)	0.0243	73.46	0.0247	75.35
Area median home value ($1,000s)	-0.0043	-28.08	-0.0041	-27.42
Household Type Dummies				
Married-couple household	1.2059	56.16	1.1899	55.87
Other household	0.0865	4.11	0.0749	3.59
Occupation Dummies				
Professional-level occupation	0.2281	12.88	0.2390	13.60
Not in labor force, under age 62	-0.1070	-2.48	-0.2109	-5.14
Not in labor force, over age 61	0.2490	8.78	0.2446	8.70
Race/Ethnicity/Immigrant Dummies				
Native-born Black	-1.1464	-49.57	-1.1333	-49.02
Native-born Hispanic	-0.9275	-15.70	-0.9197	-15.54
Native-born Asian	0.3160	1.64	0.3143	1.64
Native-born other	-0.5537	-3.80	-0.5429	-3.73
Entered before 1965	-0.0516	-1.61	-0.2999	-10.58
Entered 1965–69	-0.7220	-13.93	-0.8899	-19.18
Entered 1970–79	-0.7946	-22.20	-0.8746	-25.84
Entered 1980–90	-1.8446	-50.97	-1.8724	-53.21
R^2	0.25		0.25	
-2 Log likelihood	-65,035		-66,657	
Chi-square	42,560 with 17 DF (p = .0005)		44,595 with 17 DF (p = .0005)	
Sample size	141,248		144,091	

Source: Author's calculations of 1990 New Jersey PUMS 5 percent file.
Notes: Sample includes all households, except those born in U.S. territories and outlying areas or born abroad of American parents. Analysis performed on unweighted data.

Appendix 12.D-1 SAMPLE MEANS AND CORRELATION OF INDEPENDENT
VARIABLES WITH TENURE: MODEL 2

Variable	Mean	Correlation Coefficient
TENURE	0.5617	
Age	50.07	0.2343
Agesq	2792.32	0.2018
Income ($1,000s)	43.821	0.3421
Noncitizen	0.281	−0.1411
Median area house value ($1,000s)	167.17	0.0861
Household Type Dummies		
Married-couple household	0.6220	0.2693
Single person[a]	0.1036	−0.0510
Other household	0.2744	−0.2579
Occupation Dummies		
Professional/managerial occupation	0.1946	0.1566
Nonprofessional occupation[a]	0.6015	−0.0928
Not in labor force, under age 62	0.0557	0.0633
Not in labor force, over age 61	0.1482	−0.1704
Year-of-Entry Dummies		
Entered before 1965[a]	0.4485	0.2641
Entered 1965–69	0.1369	−0.0054
Entered 1970–79	0.2071	−0.0202
Entered 1980–90	0.2075	−0.2991
Place-of-Birth Dummies		
Puerto Rico	0.2195	−0.2620
Cuba	0.1062	−0.1058
India[a]	0.0730	0.0498
Germany	0.0981	0.1526
Colombia	0.0489	−0.1303
Poland	0.0808	0.0751
Philippines	0.0520	0.0269
Dominican Republic	0.0435	−0.1310
Portugal	0.0529	0.0189
United Kingdom	0.0706	0.0818
Italy	0.1546	0.2378

Source: Author's analysis of 1990 New Jersey PUMS 5 percent file.
Note: Sample includes households from top 10 immigrant groups and Puerto Ricans only.
a. Omitted categorical variable.

Appendix 12.E-1 LOGISTIC REGRESSIONS ON TENURE: MODEL 2

Independent Variables	Households (excluding Puerto Ricans)		Households (including Puerto Ricans)	
	Coefficient	t-Statistic	Coefficient	t-Statistic
Age	0.0931	9.17	0.1021	11.03
Age square	-0.0007	-7.58	-0.0008	-9.20
Household income ($1,000s)	0.0262	21.84	0.0275	25.38
Area median home value ($1,000s)	-0.0029	-4.19	-0.0047	-8.00
Noncitizen	-0.4261	-6.78	-0.4451	-7.22
Household Type Dummies				
Married-couple household	0.9423	10.58	0.9415	11.37
Other household	0.0043	0.05	0.0242	0.29
Occupation Dummies				
Professional-level occupation	0.0879	1.20	0.1377	2.05
Not in labor force, under age 62	0.0275	0.16	-0.4607	-3.84
Not in labor force, over age 61	0.0726	0.66	0.1256	1.24
Year-of-Entry Dummies				
Entered 1965–69	-0.2825	-3.06	-0.3300	-4.39
Entered 1970–79	-0.4768	-5.43	-0.4867	-6.71
Entered 1980–90	-1.5047	-14.90	-1.4653	-17.04
				(continued)

Appendix 12.E-1 LOGISTIC REGRESSIONS ON TENURE: MODEL 2 (continued)

Independent Variables	Households (excluding Puerto Ricans)		Households (including Puerto Ricans)	
	Coefficient	t-Statistic	Coefficient	t-Statistic
Place-of-Birth Dummies				
Philippines	-0.2870	-2.22	-0.3119	-2.41
Colombia	-1.3225	-9.50	-1.2812	-9.23
Dominican Republic	-1.3332	-9.38	-1.2885	-9.09
Cuba	-1.4310	-12.39	-1.3779	-12.05
Puerto Rico	N.A.	N.A.	-1.5864	-14.22
Portugal	-0.2204	-1.72	-0.1897	-1.49
Italy	0.6109	5.05	0.6840	5.74
Germany	0.3133	2.44	0.3632	2.88
Poland	0.1314	1.07	0.1834	1.50
United Kingdom	0.0282	0.22	0.0618	0.49
R^2	0.303		0.326	
-2 Log likelihood	-4,643		-5,981	
Chi-square	4,029 with 22 DF ($p = .0005$)		5,794 with 23 DF ($p = .0005$)	
Sample size	10,108		12,951	

Source: Author's calculations of 1990 New Jersey PUMS 5 percent file.
Notes: Sample includes all households from top 10 immigrant groups and Puerto Rico only. Analysis performed on unweighted data.

Chapter Thirteen

SEGREGATION BY ETHNICITY AND IMMIGRANT STATUS IN NEW JERSEY

Michael J. White and Afaf Omer

Residential patterns tell us about social life. There is a well-known maxim in sociology, first attributed to the sociologist and journalist of the Chicago School Robert Park, that "spatial distance reflects social distance." Patterns of population distribution, redistribution, and residential segregation provide windows on the social structure of American society. This chapter draws on that tradition in discussing residential segregation among immigrants and ethnic groups in the state of New Jersey, a suitable setting for the task (Espenshade 1994; see also Western and Kelly, chapter 2, this volume).

Segregation measurement provides key insights into urban residential patterns from readily available observational data, such as the decennial census. Theoretical and empirical studies of segregation remain a major window on ethnic and racial relations (Bean and Tienda 1987; Farley and Frey 1994; Massey and Denton 1993; Massey and Mullan 1984).

It is widely recognized that segregation indexes only summarize the outcome of several related processes, including discrimination, self-selection, and segregation incidental to compositional processes. So why, then, measure residential segregation? We can offer several reasons. First, this cumulative outcome is of interest in itself, for it is the combination of these processes that ultimately separates groups in American society. Second, as the preceding maxim notes, spatial distance is of intrinsic interest: who one chooses or permits as neighbors provides a great deal of information about intergroup tolerance in society. Third, housing (and hence residential patterns) provides one of the most intimate domains in which public policy regarding civil rights intervenes. Furthermore, this involvement is asymmetrical: although outright discrimination is forbidden, voluntary movement away from neighbors one does not desire (e.g., "white flight") receives no direct intervention. (By contrast, no policy intervenes to regulate the more intimate domains of friendship choice or intermarriage.) Residential patterns, therefore, become a key way in which to view the net results of policy, immigration patterns, and intergroup accommodation in an environment highly relevant to the average urban dweller.

As the previous chapters in this book have demonstrated, New Jersey is a state from which we can gain particularly useful insights. It has received immigrants for many years, and thus has a stock of immigrant groups who arrived before the major changes in immigration law that occurred with the Immigration and Nationality Act Amendments of 1965, in addition to a flow of newer immigrants who arrived during the 1980s. Equally important for the present analysis, New Jersey has a wide array of residential environments across which persons have sorted themselves. The large, older, industrial urban areas (Newark, Paterson, Camden) are complemented by low-density service growth poles (the Route 287 corridor; the Princeton-Trenton office parks) and a considerable amount of suburban territory of all vintages. Intervention in the housing sphere has been (since the 1960s) driven by federal housing policy rather than state-level activity. In this sense, New Jersey's housing, from large-scale publicly constructed units to the sprawl that accompanies investment in highway infrastructure, is a reflection of the evolution of the American pattern of urban housing policy.

There is one arena of policy related to housing (and hence to residential patterns) in which New Jersey may be unique. Through the action of an active state judiciary, New Jersey embarked upon a policy to limit (or even reverse) income-segregating activities of localities, particularly "snob-zoning." In what became known as the *Mt. Laurel* decision (which itself evolved over time), municipalities in this home rule state were required to accept their fair share of low-income housing or to provide transfer payments to other municipalities containing higher fractions of low- and moderate-income residents (Burchell 1983). Even though the original *Mt. Laurel* decision was itself far-reaching, subsequent revisions in the courts and in the New Jersey Legislature appear to have weakened it considerably. Even though the decision garnered considerable national attention, its ultimate impact appears to have been minimal. To our knowledge, very little "Mt. Laurel" housing was built, and so the opportunities to realize the spatial redistribution implied by the original court decision remained unrealized.

This chapter has two broad objectives. The first objective is to analyze the degree of residential segregation of immigrants and ethnic groups in New Jersey. We calculate segregation indexes for persons by nativity, year of immigration, and ethnic group, drawing on tabulations of the census. Despite the substantial tradition of work on *racial and ethnic* segregation, there is little direct analysis of *immigrant* segregation. By studying the segregation of the foreign born and taking into account period of arrival, we hope to break new ground in demonstrating the link between immigration and ethnicity in producing the neighborhood patterns we see today in New Jersey and in the United States generally.

The second objective of this chapter is more conceptual. We want to use the increasing diversity of American society—seen especially in New Jersey—to question our thinking about the analysis of residential assimilation. The challenges that arise in developing a comprehensive statistical assessment of segregation by nativity and ethnicity lend focus to this question. Our analysis may help to shed light on current debate about the meaning of ethnicity, itself a concept that has evolved through U.S. history (White and Sassler 1995; Wright 1994).

IMMIGRATION AND ETHNICITY

Immigration and ethnicity are closely intertwined. Immigration brings to the host society new members whose physiognomy may make them easily distinguishable from the host society. The religion, kinship and family patterns, and occupational skills of these immigrants may further differentiate them. Of course, language differences offer the most telling source of "differentness." But how much does all this differentness matter? National myths about the historical experience of immigrants tell us that despite distinct appearance and language, immigrants themselves have adapted and assimilated into the wide society—the very phrase "melting pot" conveys this notion. Nevertheless, individual groups have experienced different rates of assimilation, and to be sure, have been accepted to quite varying degrees by American society. Limited historical information about the spatial manifestation of these ethnic differences exists, but work with historical census materials suggests that the "new" groups of 1910 were quite highly isolated in urban space (White et al. 1994). The different initial conditions and the subsequent experience of immigrant groups begs the question of how the assimilation process fared for each.

Ethnic identity arises from a dynamic interplay between hosts and new arrivals. Ethnic classification contains elements of both self-identification and "other-identification." By other-identification is meant identity recognized (and attributed) by the host society as well. These identities can be welcome or forced. Just as one may actively articulate an Italian-American heritage, the remaining society helps develop and reify that category. The notion of American Indian as an ethnic minority is the result of a long history of interaction between the indigenous population and those who followed the first European settlement.

For many Americans of African descent, the experience of slavery and subsequent race relations in the United States served to amalgamate various African origins and ethnicities. Although the U.S. Census of 1890 included the categories of mulatto, quadroon, and octoroon (White and Sassler 1995), the system of racial apartheid in the United States clung to the "one-drop rule," holding that any African ancestry served to classify an American as Negro or black (Wright 1994). Experience in the host country can spur the evolution of ethnic identity, such as leading regional origins (Sicily) to become subsumed under a wider geographic entity (Italy). Furthermore, residence in a plural society produces the opportunity for an individual to choose among several ethnic categories for his or her stated identity. Scholars working in the area of historical demography (again with census materials) struggle to work across country of birth, parentage, and language to classify persons (Watkins 1994).

The 1990 Census materials on which this discussion relies are a product of that process. The definition of race and ethnicity has evolved considerably in the United States (White and Sassler 1995). Both the 1980 and 1990 Censuses elected to ask persons their self-identified "ancestry," and virtually no editing of the responses was done, save to remove responses in religious categories or to limit the number of classifications when many are given. These censuses provide several routes to the measurement and identification of "ethnicity." Distinct questions (each with several response categories) were asked with reference to race, Spanish origin, ancestry, place of birth, and language. Each of these variables, then, offers a different "dimension" of ethnicity. In theory, a person could occupy any category on each of these variables. Classification as a Chinese (race)-Cuban (Spanish origin)-Filipino (ancestry) individual is possible. (Particular options for language and place of birth could make the combination even less probable.) In everyday life, however, people on the street do not think in census terms. We suggest, rather, that individuals think in the vernacular of ethnicity as a single dimension, but one in which a person may claim multiple heritages or responses. Our approach tries to incorporate this aspect of U.S. social life.

Intermarriage (or miscegenation) complicates the ethnicity picture even more. Even if people consistently identified a label for themselves, the intermingling of the population across ethnic lines creates further diversity and difficulties in measurement, even as it produces the melting pot that America is purported to be. Through intermarriage, people gather multiple heritages. Two considerations are important. One is obvious: rates of intermarriage vary significantly across ethnic group (and sometimes by gender within ethnic group). The second consideration may be less obvious: as individuals' line of ancestry becomes complicated, there is a tendency toward selective reporting. This is aggravated by the fact that most social science survey instruments (including the census) only allows for one or a few responses to the question about ancestry. Thus, some ethnic heritages tend to be favored (or at least more frequently reported) than others. These responses vary by time. For example, the 1980–90 growth in the American Indian population was too large to be accounted for by natural increase and is attributable partly to increased self-identification (Eschbach 1993; Passel 1996).

This chapter also incorporates the concept of ethnic *vintage*, giving it a quantitative turn. It has been common in the immigration and ethnicity literature to speak of "old" and "new" groups. More recently, observers have spoken of "new, new groups" or the "fourth wave" (Muller and Espenshade 1985). Despite the inevitable pitfalls of doing so, we attempt to calculate a measure that will indicate how "old" a group is. Besides the advantage of avoiding fumbling over terminology such as "new, new," the vintage concept can be introduced into statistical studies of immigrant adapation, as described in the next section.

DATA AND METHODS

Data

Our analysis is based entirely on 1990 Census data. More specifically, it is drawn from Summary Tape File 3A (STF3A), which includes tabulations for geographic areas for the subject categories of race, Spanish origin, year of immigration, and ancestry. Each of these tabulations taps a facet of "ethnicity," especially in that immigration is a chief mechanism for generating population diversity. Each of these four variables—indeed, every category within each variable—is a possible source of a segregation statistic. Clearly, one task is to condense this information into a coherent story about ethnic residential segregation.

We chose to measure segregation on the basis of the distribution of persons across neighborhoods in New Jersey. To do so we used (from STF3A) census *tract* data. (In this respect, our approach parallels the work of Stevens and Garrett in the concluding chapter of this volume.) Tracts are small, relatively compact areas into which urban areas are divided for statistical purposes. For all intents, they are the closest demographic and statistical approximation to "neighborhood" (White 1987). Most tracts contain between 3,000 and 6,000 persons. They are quite useful for segregation statistics and have been used regularly by other researchers in the past.

Census tracts in most states are delineated only for metropolitan areas. By 1990 all territory in New Jersey was within a metropolitan area. Thus, for many of our calculations we have elected to develop a *statewide* segregation index value. This approach treats the entire state as a residential environment. This is unconventional, but it has the advantages of (1) not maintaining artificial barriers between metropolitan areas that are part of the same conurbation, and (2) allowing us to measure *exactly* how unevenly groups are dispersed *throughout* the state, combining both within and between metropolitan area segregation.

Dissimilarity

For each calculation and interpretation, we chose to use the index of dissimilarity—the workhorse of segregation measurement for many decades. Even though White (1986), in a methodological review, argues that the index of dissimilarity is an inferior measure, the same study also shows that the measure gives results equivalent to other measures. In fact, some discussion still exists about the best way(s) to measure segregation, and many researchers are routinely calculating multiple indexes; however, for our purposes the index of dissimilarity is sufficient. It is calculated as:

$$D = \frac{1}{2} \sum_{i=1}^{N} \left| \frac{P_{1i}}{P_1} - \frac{P_{2i}}{P_2} \right|, \tag{13.1}$$

where P_1 and P_2 indicate the overall (metropolitanwide or statewide) populations of groups 1 and 2. The values indexed by i in the numerator correspond to the group populations in the tracts. The sum is over all tracts in the metropolitan area or the state, as appropriate.

The index of dissimilarity, D, has one very attractive feature. Its value is intuitively meaningful: D is the proportion of one group that would have to relocate to produce an even (unsegregated) distribution. Values of D range from zero to 1 (100 percent). For example, in a region with 10 percent immigrants in the population, a value of D of 50 percent would mean that half the immigrants would have to relocate so that *every* neighborhood would have 10 percent immigrants in it. The calculation of D is limited to the comparison of two groups only. In many cases we calculate it for membership in a group of interest versus all others.

Vintage

For each country of origin, we can calculate from statistics tabulated by the U.S. Immigration and Naturalization Service the average year of arrival of immigrants. More precisely, we calculate the median year of arrival (to the nearest five-year point) from these statistics. The year is the date by which half of the immigrants recorded from that origin had arrived in the United States.

Such a procedure has pitfalls, of course. It omits undocumented migrants, whether contemporary (such as Mexicans) or from an earlier point in time (Canadians). It also fixes national origins to a set of historical countries maintained by the Immigration and Naturalization Service. Nevertheless, as our analysis demonstrates, this measure serves as a reasonable proxy for immigrant or ethnic group vintage.

SEGREGATION OF FOREIGN BORN IN NEW JERSEY, 1990

Most social scientists and the general public draw on a model of residential assimilation in which new arrivals to an area are clustered (i.e., residentially segregated). Rarely, however, are segregation statistics calculated directly by nativity (United States, not United States) or year of immigration. Rather, inferences are made from the segregation patterns exhibited by various ethnic minorities. This study calculates immigrant segregation directly.

Table 13.1 presents values of D for immigrants for the several metropolitan areas of New Jersey. The value of D therefore represents the segregation of the foreign born from U.S. natives. For reference we include some corresponding D values for New Jersey metropolitan areas for the segregation of blacks, Hispanics, and Asians. These figures are taken from work at the U.S. Bureau of the Census (Harrison and Weinberg 1992), which used non-Hispanic whites (Anglos) as the comparison group in all three cases.

By conventional standards, the segregation of the foreign born is modest. Only in the most dense, urban territory of Jersey City and Newark do we find that over 30 percent of immigrants would have to change neighborhoods to produce an even distribution (see table 13.1). Segregation of each of the three major ethnic groups exceeds that of the foreign born, usually by a considerable margin. Hispanics, a group containing many immigrants, are far more segregated than immigrants generally.[1] This more modest level of segregation is consistent with work done for 1980 on a national sample of cities (White 1986). In that study, segregation of the foreign born exhibited an average D value of 29 in 21 U.S. metropolitan areas. The Newark metropolitan area had a nativity segregation score of 28 in 1980, slightly below the level we found in these 1990 data. In general, 1990 segregation of the

Table 13.1 INDEX OF DISSIMILARITY FOR NEW JERSEY METROPOLITAN AREAS: WHOLE OR NEW JERSEY PART, 1990

Metropolitan Area (or New Jersey Part)	Foreign Born	Black	Spanish-Origin	Asian
Atlantic City	.280	.643	.518	.426
Bergen-Passaic	.244	.768	.588	.344
Jersey City	.334	.660	.429	.419
Middlesex-Somerset-Hunterdon	.230	.543	.499	.361
Monmouth-Ocean	.201	.658	.343	
Newark	.317	.822	.667	.296
Philadelphia	.239	.771	.626	.432
Trenton	.215	.681	.545	.370
Vineland-Mil-Brid	.178	.406	.457	
U.S. average		.643	.429	.430

Notes: Dissimilarity for foreign born is for New Jersey sections of metropolitan areas only. Dissimilarity for blacks, Spanish-origin, and Asians is for all metropolitan territories; indexes are from Harrison and Weinberg (1992). U.S. average values are from Farley and Frey (1994). Nonmetropolitan statistics were not calculated by Harrison and Weinberg. Asian dissimilarity was not calculated for metropolitan areas with very small total Asian populations.

foreign born falls below levels exhibited by racial and Spanish-origin groups.

Another comparative perspective is provided by the 1990 segregation statistics in the final row of table 13.1. These numbers are taken from a recent article by Farley and Frey (1994), in which they reviewed the determinants of segregation level for major ethnic groups in U.S. metropolitan areas with substantial concentrations of each ethnic group. As shown in the table, the New Jersey metropolitan areas are generally more segregated than the national average: African Americans in almost all of the state's metropolitan areas are more segregated than the national average; and the same can be said of persons of Spanish origin. Asians, by contrast, appear to be a little less segregated in New Jersey than elsewhere in the United States, although the population numbers are small enough that we do not present figures for two New Jersey metropolitan areas, and Farley and Frey used a sample of only 66 metropolitan areas.

Although New Jersey cities exhibit more Latino and African American segregation than the United States as a whole, we posit a couple of reasons why this would be expected. First, New Jersey cities are larger, older, declining more in population, or growing more slowly than the national average. Such cities have higher segregation levels than smaller fast-growing metropolises of the South and West, as Farley and Frey (1994) have shown. The New Jersey Latino population has a higher fraction of Puerto Rican and Dominican-origin persons, two groups that tend to be more segregated than other Latinos.

Overall, New Jersey does resemble the nation in the broad aspects of ethnic segregation for these three major classifications. First, African Americans are found to be more segregated than Latinos or Asians. Second, the larger, older urbanized areas *within* New Jersey (i.e., the Newark Metropolitan Statistical Area [MSA]; the New Jersey portion of the Philadelphia MSA; the Bergen-Passaic MSA) exhibit greater segregation for blacks and Latinos.

We found that immigrant segregation is less pronounced than that of the three broad ethnic groups also appearing in table 13.1; however, this is partly an artifact of a "second-generation effect." Persons of all generations are still classified by race, Spanish origin, and ancestry. U.S.-born children of immigrants are natives, however, no matter how much the household behavior appears to be that of immigrants. Thus, childbearing in the United States will tend to reduce apparent segregation because of this "second-generation effect." In other words, the co-residence of foreign-born parents and native-born children in the same household tends to reduce the amount of spatial segregation between native and foreign individuals. When census data are aggregated across all age groups, this effect exerts more influence.

Table 13.2 further explores the second-generation effect. Using the entire state as the reference, we calculated (1) immigrant–native segregation, (2) immigrant–native segregation for adults only, and (3) immigrant–native segregation for children only. Interestingly, the adults are no more segregated than immigrants as a whole. Foreign-born children (born outside the United States and immigrants by 1990) are substantially segregated from native-born children. Thus, the higher segregation of child immigrants compensates for the lower segregation of immigrant parents from their second-generation children.

This difference no doubt arises from variation in adult–child ratios at the household level. These ratios are in turn linked to higher fertility among immigrants than natives. A plausible explanation for this lies in recency of immigration. Very recent immigrants (who came with children) would be more likely to have immigrant children residing at home. Immigrants who arrived some time ago would be more likely to have native-born children or to have children who had aged into adulthood and/or moved out of the home. This phenomenon warrants further study, as obvious differences would emerge across different national origin groups and for ethnic groups of differing age distributions. The implications are potentially significant, since the segregation statistic suggests that foreign-born children may be more isolated in society than one might imagine based on the distribution by nativity alone.

SEGREGATION BY YEAR OF ARRIVAL

The standard model of assimilation argues that as time passes, immigrants adapt and the host society accommodates. Thus, over time

Table 13.2 SEGREGATION BY NATIVITY AND AGE: NEW JERSEY

Dissimilarity for:	D
Natives (total) versus foreign born (total)	0.36
Native adults over 17 years of age versus foreign-born adults over 18 years of age	0.35
Native children under 18 years of age versus foreign-born children under 18 years of age	0.50

we would expect any group to experience residential assimilation and its level of segregation to decline. If this model holds, and holds equivalently for succeeding waves (cohorts) of immigrants, we would expect groups with a longer residence in the United States to be less segregated. Cross-sectional analyses are always a bit risky in this regard. If successive waves of immigrants encounter varying U.S. experiences, then cross-sectional data (such as we have for 1990 only) could produce an apparent, but spurious, longitudinal relationship. We do know, however, that in other analyses, length of residence has been positively associated with residential integration (Duncan and Lieberson 1959; White et al. 1993).

We calculated segregation indexes (versus the native born) for the 10 period-of-arrival categories tabulated in the 1990 Census. These results are pooled for the state of New Jersey and are presented in table 13.3. These index values demonstrate clearly that experience in the United States is associated with residential mingling with the native born. To further explore this result, we estimated a regression equation predicting the segregation index from number of years in the United States. To obtain the latter, we assigned a value on the basis of (usually) the midpoint of the interval. We also added a dummy variable term for whether the arrival period predates 1965, the year in which revision in the U.S. immigration law purportedly ushered in a sea change in the kinds and origins of immigrants being received by the United States.

The estimated equation (with t-statistics below) is:

$$\hat{D} = 0.1065 + 0.0047 \ (Year) - 0.030 \ (Pre\text{-}1965). \tag{13.2}$$
$$(1.172) \quad (4.168) \quad\quad (-0.878)$$

Table 13.3 SEGREGATION BY YEAR OF ARRIVAL: NEW JERSEY

Dissimilarity for:	D
Arrived 1987–90	0.52
Arrived 1985–87	0.53
Arrived 1982–85	0.50
Arrived 1980–81	0.52
Arrived 1975–79	0.44
Arrived 1970–74	0.44
Arrived 1965–69	0.43
Arrived 1960–64	0.38
Arrived 1950–59	0.30
Arrived before 1950	0.32

The coefficient on *Year* is statistically significant at $p < 0.01$. The coefficient on the *Pre-1965* dummy variable is not significant. The plot of segregation score by year is graphed in figure 13.1, with the regression line (after dropping the dummy variable for *Pre-1965*) superimposed. The fit ($R^2 = .92$) is remarkably good.

It still remains to be seen how much of this apparently strong relationship is due to the second-generation effect.[2] It does suggest, however, that the notion of persistent, constricted areas of arrival to which successive waves of immigrants come is an unlikely description of the pattern. If the conventional immigrant settlement model were to hold strictly, those who arrived over 40 years ago should be quite segregated, since their children would have aged out of their households and new immigrants would have replaced some of their neighbors.

Other recent work has challenged the conventional immigrant settlement model. Using 1990 Census data for Southern California, Allen and Turner (1996) examined the residential patterns of recently ar-

Figure 13.1 SEGREGATION OF IMMIGRANTS BY YEAR OF ARRIVAL: NEW JERSEY, 1990

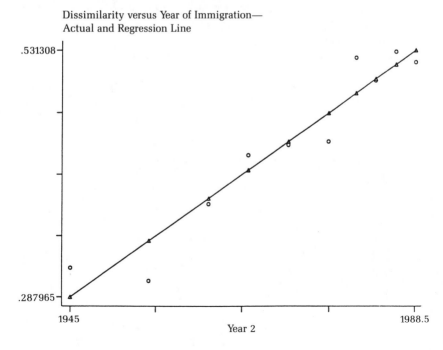

rived immigrants. They found that recent immigrants to Los Angeles do not necessarily reside in the areas of highest immigrant concentration. These results recommend a reexamination of the model of first settlement in concentrated zones followed by gradual dispersal within and across generations.

SEGREGATION BY ETHNICITY AND VINTAGE

A question about ancestry is asked of all persons who receive the "long form" version of the census. Considerable ink has been spilled setting down the caveats for the analysis of ancestry questions from the U.S. Census. Our discussion earlier hinted at some of the difficulties of definition, which are equally applicable to measures of race and Spanish origin. Ancestry appears to be a more malleable concept than nativity, race, or Spanish origin, and is not as consistently reported by census or survey respondents. Moreover, the way that ancestry is coded and tabulated in the census allows for multiple ancestries to be recorded.

The confusion may be an authentic contrast to an artificially rigid and exclusive set of categories used for race. Of course, the introduction of the ancestry question itself was a response in part to a demand that "white ethnics," principally persons of European stock, be given a distinct recording mechanism in the census. Previous census-taking practice was one of "administrative assimilation," since the identification of ethnicity via a person's own and parents' nativity would fail by the third generation.

To analyze ethnicity, we combined information from questions on race, Spanish origin, and ancestry. From the detailed race tabulations in STF3A, we identified blacks and several Asian ethnicities as distinct groups. Detailed Spanish-origin tabulations offered several more Latino ethnic groups. Finally, we identified several additional (mostly) European-origin groups based on assignments from single and multiple ancestry. For those who reported multiple ancestries, we distributed them proportionately across categories. For ease of comparison, we limited our analysis to the 25 most populous groups, defined as follows.

Each of these groups has at least about 20 persons per census tract, with each tract averaging about 4,000 persons in the state of New Jersey (and for tracts nationally as well). The most populous ethnic groups in New Jersey are those of German, black, Irish, Italian, English, and Puerto Rican descent. Latino groups in this analysis include Cuban-, Dominican-, and Colombian-origin persons. Major Asian ethnic subpopulations in New Jersey include Asian Indian, Chinese, and Filipino. It should be remembered that, although we attempted to define mutually exclusive ethnic groups by this procedure, the very format of the census—explicit response categories for Asian and Spanish origin questions; open-ended responses for ancestries—may have influenced the relative frequency of responses.

For each of these groups we calculated the index of dissimilarity versus all persons not in that group. Thus, we looked at Cuban to non-Cuban dissimilarity and Italian to non-Italian dissimilarity. Such a calculation gives a summary of the residential experience of ethnic groups; for those with low levels of segregation (low values of D), the measure does not reveal the identities of other groups with which the particular group is residentially intermingled.

Table 13.4 presents the segregation levels exhibited by these 25 ethnic groups. Again the results were pooled across all tracts in New Jersey. The segregation statistics reveal Dominicans to be the most segregated. Some 78 percent of Dominicans would have to change neighborhoods throughout the state to produce an even distribution. Colombian and Cuban-origin persons also have segregation levels near 70 percent. Puerto Ricans, the one remaining Spanish-origin group, follow closely with the segregation value of 60 percent. The high level of Puerto Rican segregation is noteworthy since this population is the largest of the New Jersey Spanish-origin groups, has a long history of moving to the region, and is represented in many of its metropolitan areas. Analysis of 1980 Census data indicated that segregation by race *within* the Spanish-origin population is nearly as high as racial segregation overall (White 1986). The pattern may still hold.

The segregation of major Asian groups in New Jersey is also appreciable. Koreans, Filipinos, Chinese, and Asian Indians all exhibit dissimilarity values between 60 percent and 67 percent (see table 13.4). We noted that the groups classified on the basis of race or Spanish origin in the census comprised 9 of the 10 most segregated groups. French-Canadians are the one highly segregated European-stock group.

Several groups fall into what might be classified as the midrange of segregation, at about 0.35 to 0.56 (see table 13.4). These include persons of Russian[3] descent and persons whose origins are in Scandinavia or Southern and Eastern Europe. Comparatively low levels of segregation are exhibited by persons of Irish, German, English, and

Table 13.4 INDEX OF DISSIMILARITY (RANKED) FOR 25 MOST POPULOUS
ETHNIC GROUPS: NEW JERSEY

Ethnic Group	Dissimilarity	Vintage	Residual
Dominican	0.78	1985	0.12
Cuban	0.70	1975	0.07
Colombian	0.69	1985	0.03
Black	0.69		
Korean	0.67	1985	0.01
Filipino	0.62	1985	−0.04
French Canadian	0.62	1925	0.09
Chinese	0.60	1975	−0.03
Puerto Rican	0.60		
Asian Indian	0.60	1985	−0.06
Russian	0.56	1905	0.08
Norwegian	0.54	1905	0.06
Greek	0.52	1915	0.02
Slovak	0.50	1925	−0.03
Hungarian	0.47	1925	−0.01
Italian	0.47	1925	−0.01
Swedish	0.45	1895	−0.01
Polish	0.41	1925	−0.11
Dutch	0.40	1915	−0.10
French	0.37	1820	0.07
Scots-Irish	0.36	1820	0.06
Scottish	0.32	1820	0.02
German	0.32	1885	−0.12
English	0.31	1820	0.01
Irish	0.26	1865	−0.14

Scottish (including Scots-Irish) ancestry. Since the ancestry question (and our reclassification) removes the second-generation effect to some degree, this ethnic pattern is noteworthy.

The conventional vintage model of immigrant and ethnic settlement would predict that those groups with more residential experience in the United States would be the least segregated. We performed a simple, direct test of this using information on ethnic vintage. For each of these groups (blacks and Puerto Ricans excepted), we calculated from Immigration and Naturalization Service statistics the *median* year of arrival for the group. Thus, the vintage of the group is that year marking the point (between 1820 and 1990) at which half the immigrant arrivals had taken place and half were yet to come. The value of the vintage for each group is also contained in table 13.4. Thus, we found that the Irish have a vintage of 1865, whereas Cubans have a vintage of 1975, reflecting their much more recent arrival to the United States during the Castro era.

We regressed dissimilarity on vintage for the 23 groups for whom we could develop vintage information. We estimated the regression equation as:

$$\hat{D} = -3.665 + 0.0021767 \, (Vintage).$$
$$(-7.024) \quad (7.990) \tag{13.3}$$

Vintage is a powerful predictor of segregation. For these 23 groups, the adjusted R^2 statistic is 0.74. As an illustration, consider a comparison between a group entering (the median immigrant) in 1900 versus another group whose vintage is 1980. The 80-year span predicts a 0.18 increment in dissimilarity, a gap approximately equivalent to the difference we have stated characterizes moderate versus high.

Still, these results from table 13.4 only partly support the vintage model. Within the European stock group, it is true that some of the "old" immigrant groups (German, Irish, English) exhibit very low levels of segregation, but other older groups, including those of Scandinavian origin and especially African Americans, trace their arrival to previous centuries and do not fall in order of expectation. To more precisely gauge the accuracy of the vintage model, the final column of table 13.4 presents residuals from the regression equation. Positive values indicate that the group is *more* segregated than one would expect on the basis of its vintage; negative values indicate the converse.

We found that the residuals are quite small for several groups, in accord with the fairly good fit of this simple model and its adjusted R-squared of 74 percent. The discrepancies are worth noting. Irish and German ancestry individuals are less segregated than vintage would predict; the same can be said of New Jersey Polish and Dutch ancestry individuals. Russians (including some Jews) and French Canadians are more segregated than vintage would predict.[4] The model notably underpredicts the three most segregated groups, Dominicans, Cubans, and Colombians. We also found that none of the four Asian-origin groups was substantially underpredicted; Asian Indians in New Jersey live in more intermingled residential settings than one would expect on the basis of their very recent average arrival to the United States.

Two groups were not included in the regression equation, but we can still gather some insights regarding their experience. Puerto Rican–origin individuals do not (at least predominantly) come to the United States as immigrants, and therefore, no median year of arrival can be calculated. Still, we know that substantial movement from the mainland to the New York/New Jersey region began in the earlier part of the 20th century and accelerated particularly in the 1950s. The level of segregation exhibited by Puerto Ricans in New Jersey is consistent with a vintage of about 1960, which is perhaps an underprediction as well.

For African Americans, the long period of enslavement and the discriminatory conditions that followed emancipation make the notion of vintage meaningless. Some social scientists do, however, cite the Great Migration in the early 20th century as marking the transition from a rural agrarian and southern life to an urban setting in the North. Sometimes the analogy is carried further to intentional migration. In any case, the dissimilarity statistics we have for New Jersey blacks are consistent with a vintage of the year 2000. Clearly blacks, like Dominicans and Cubans, are much more segregated than one would predict on the basis of their long history of residence in the United States. To say that African Americans have not yet arrived is only a bitterly ironic turn of phrase for what these calculations have shown.

Despite the notable exceptions, the simple vintage calculation does show that for many groups of European, Latin, and Asian heritage, the vintage model offers some empirically verified description of the path of residential integration with time in the United States. Race, however, would seem to operate beyond vintage. Latino groups that have appreciable African heritage are very highly segregated, consistent with White's (1986) finding of substantial racial segregation within the Hispanic population. Unfortunately, such aggregate tabulations as STF3A do not allow one to further break down each group's segregation by timing of arrival or generation, but the indication is that vintage, although important, cannot explain all of the variation we observe.

CONCLUSION: SEGREGATION IN NEW JERSEY AND NATION

This chapter has provided an overview of the level of segregation in New Jersey experienced by a variety of ethnic and immigrant groups. First, we found that time in the United States is clearly related to residential assimilation with the native population. We warn that the second-generation effect may modify the strong time trend observed in figure 13.1, but our other results suggest that controlling for this effect will not remove the relationship.

Second, these results indicate that residential assimilation of immigrants is occurring within a broader environment of ethnic segregation. Vintage matters, but the ordering of ethnic group segregation does not exactly match vintage. Groups may intermingle with the native born after living some time in the United States, but these natives are not themselves a random admixture of the polyglot that is New Jersey or the United States.

The results also suggest avenues for further research. On a technical dimension, further investigation of the magnitude of the second-generation effect would be worthwhile. Given that legions of segregation statistics have been calculated on the basis of country of birth and parentage, such a correction could help scholars compare indexes from earlier points in the 20th century and more recent statistics. Also, direct tabulation of unidimensional ethnic identity by neighborhood (tract) would be welcome, and would avoid the indirect methods we have had to employ here.

The premise of this research is that residential patterns reveal much about social patterns that apply in the wider society, whether that of the state of New Jersey or the nation as a whole. The (once-again) increasing diversity of the United States argues for rethinking several conventional notions of ethnic residential patterns in the United States. The dichotomy of black–white segregation, a framework that guided research, vernacular thought, and policy for years, is becoming woefully out of date. We say this recognizing also that our results point to the continuing salience of ethnicity and physiognomy in determining residential outcomes. Public opinion trends indicate an increasing tolerance of blacks and other minorities by whites,[5] but the debate over California's Proposition 187 suggests that this movement may be limited in scope or extent. Furthermore, our results and other recent work suggest that the age-old model of distinctly segregated and centralized areas of first-immigrant settlement may not be quite accurate for the contemporary period. A framework that recognizes ethnic pluralism, group vintage, and demographic composition will go far toward understanding how groups adapt in the American mosaic.

Notes

Support for this research was provided, in part, by a grant from the National Science Foundation on "Metropolitan Restructuring, Neighborhood Change, and Concentrated

Poverty." We thank Thomas J. Espenshade and other participants at the "Conference on Impacts of Immigration to New Jersey" (at Princeton University, May 18–19, 1995) for comments on this research.

1. Puerto Rican migrants are not counted as immigrants.

2. Unfortunately, we cannot separate year of arrival by age. In White's other research, arrival time is not nearly so consistently associated with segregation (White 1992; White et al. 1993).

3. Some researchers take Russian ancestry to proxy the segregation pattern of the Jewish population.

4. The French-Candian discrepancy is undoubtedly larger, since a great deal of unrecorded movement between Quebec and the United States occurred prior to 1925.

5. The national trend among whites is in the direction of greater racial tolerance according to three indicators (school integration, willingness to vote for a black presidential candidate, and racial intermarriage), as reported by Schuman, Steeh, and Bobo in their book, *Racial Attitudes in America* (1985). We have no comparable time trend of survey responses for opinions about Asian, Latinos, and other groups, nor of attitudes held by these minority group members about whites.

References

Alba, R., and J. Logan. 1991. "Variations on Two Themes: Racial and Ethnic Patterns in the Attainment of Suburban Residence." *Demography* 28(August): 431–53.

Allen, J., and E. Turner. 1996. "Spatial Patterns of Immigrant Assimilation." *Professional Geographer* 48(May): 140–55.

Bean, F. D., and M. Tienda. 1987. *The Hispanic Population of the United States.* New York: Russell Sage Foundation.

Burchell, Robert W. 1983. *Mount Laurel II: Challenge and Delivery of Low-Cost Housing.* New Brunswick, N.J.: Center for Urban Policy Research, Rutgers University.

Duncan, O. D., and S. Lieberson. 1959. "Ethnic Segregation and Assimilation." *American Journal of Sociology* 64: 364–74.

Eschbach, K. 1993. "Changing Identification among American Indians and Alaska Natives." *Demography* 30: 635–52.

Espenshade, T., ed. 1994. *A Stone's Throw from Ellis Island.* New York: Lanham.

Farley, R., and W. Frey. 1994. "Changes in the Segregation of Whites from Blacks during the 1980s: Small Steps toward a more Integrated Society." *American Sociological Review* 59(February): 23–45.

Harrison, R., and D. Weinberg. 1992. "Segregation in U.S. Metropolitan Areas, 1990." Paper presented to the meetings of the Population Association of America, April.

Lieberson, S. 1963. *Ethnic Patterns in American Cities.* New York: Free Press.

Logan, J., and R. Alba. 1993. "Locational Returns to Human Capital: Minority Access to Suburban Community Resources." *Demography* 30(May): 243–68.

Massey, D., and N. Denton. 1993. *American Apartheid: Segregation and the Making of the Underclass.* Cambridge, Mass.: Harvard University Press.

Massey, D., and B. Mullan. 1984. "Processes of Hispanic and Black Spatial Assimilation." *American Journal of Sociology* 89: 836–73.

Muller, T., and T. Espenshade. 1985. *The Fourth Wave.* Washington, D.C.: Urban Institute Press.

Passel, J. 1996. "The Growing American Indian Population, 1960–90: Beyond Demography." Washington, D.C.: Urban Institute.

Schuman, Howard, Charlotte Steeh, and Lawrence Bobo. 1985. *Racial Attitudes in America.* Cambridge, Mass.: Harvard University Press.

Taeuber, K., and I. Taeuber. 1964. *Negroes in Cities.* Chicago: Aldine.

Watkins, S. C., ed. 1994. *After Ellis Island.* New York: Russell Sage Foundation.

White, M. 1986. "Segregation and Diversity Indexes in Population Distribution." *Population Index* (Summer): 198–221.

————. 1987. *American Neighborhoods and Residential Differentiation.* New York: Russell Sage Foundation.

————. 1992. "Immigrants, Cities, and Equal Opportunity." *Urban Labor Markets and Job Opportunity,* edited by G.E. Peterson and W. Vroman (283–308). Washington, D.C.: Urban Institute Press.

White, M., and S. Sassler. 1995. "Ethnic Definitions, Social Mobility, and Residential Segregation in the United States." In *Population, Ethnicity, Nation-Building,* edited by C. Goldscheider (267–97). Boulder, Colo.: Westview Press.

White, M., A. Biddlecom, and S. Guo. 1993. "Immigration, Naturalization, and Residential Assimilation among Asian Americans in 1980." *Social Forces* 72(September): 93–117.

White, M., R. Dymowski, and S. Wang. 1994. "Ethnic Neighbors and Ethnic Myths." In *After Ellis Island,* edited by S. Watkins. New York: Russell Sage Foundation.

Wright, L. 1994. "One Drop of Blood." *New Yorker,* July 25: 46–55.

Chapter Fourteen

MIGRANTS AND THE LINGUISTIC ECOLOGY OF NEW JERSEY, 1990

Gillian Stevens and Nancy Garrett

The general effect of the continuous sifting and sorting of [a] population . . .
is to produce a patchwork of local areas differentiated from one another by
cultural, racial, or linguistic peculiarities.

McKenzie, On Human Ecology

In 1990, 15 million of the 19.6 million immigrants in the United States, or 79 percent, reported speaking a non-English language at home, and 9.2 million, or 47 percent of all immigrants, reported that they do not speak English "very well." Among the 4 million recent immigrants who entered the United States during 1985–90, 88 percent reported speaking a non-English language and over 70 percent reported that they did not speak English "very well" (U.S. Bureau of the Census 1993b). Because of historically high rates of language shift from non-English languages to English (Lieberson and Curry 1971), immigration is the single most important source of potential non-English-language speakers in the United States. The extent to which immigrants continue to speak their non-English language therefore largely accounts for the continuing presence of non-English languages in the United States and shapes the setting for transmission of the language to the next generation. The extent to which immigrants become proficient in English is also one of the best predictors of immigrants' social and economic adaptation to the larger American society. Immigrants who do not speak English, for example, can suffer severe occupational and economic penalties (e.g., Stolzenberg 1990).

To survive in a setting dominated by a majority language, minority languages must be used by potential speakers in a variety of social contexts (Fishman 1985). However, minority-language speakers can only continue to use their minority language in public contexts if they live close to each other. The geographic concentration of immigrants in non-English-language communities thus allows the continued use of a minority language and so has implications for the current and future representation of minority languages in the United States. Furthermore, because residence in non-English-language communities can support minority language use, and by inference undercut opportunities and motivations for learning English, residence in a non-English-language community can influence processes of adaptation and assimilation among immigrants.

This chapter investigates the extent to which immigrants and recent migrants from Puerto Rico are clustered into various types of non-English-language communities in New Jersey in 1990 and describes some of the socioeconomic characteristics of those communities. First, we discuss the theoretical processes involved in the formation and persistence of minority-language communities and present hypotheses about the demographic and socioeconomic attributes of these communities. We then test the hypotheses using aggregate-level data for New Jersey from the 1990 U.S. Census.

The focus on New Jersey is opportune because it is one of six major immigrant states in the United States and contains a significant percentage of the country's immigrant population (see table 14.1). Like

Table 14.1 NUMBERS (IN 1,000s) OF IMMIGRANTS AND NON-ENGLISH-LANGUAGE SPEAKERS IN SIX MAJOR IMMIGRANT STATES: 1990

State	Total Population	Total Foreign Born	Non-English Speakers			
			Total Non-English Speakers	Number Speaking Spanish	Number Speaking API Language	Number Speaking "Other" Language
New York	17,990	2,878	3,909	1,849	460	1,600
			100.0%	47.3%	11.8%	40.9%
New Jersey	7,730	1,005	1,406	621	154	631
			100.1%	44.2%	11.0%	44.9%
Illinois	11,430	914	1,499	728	167	604
			100.0%	48.6%	11.1%	40.3%
Florida	12,938	1,682	2,098	1,448	86	564
			100.0%	69.0%	4.1%	26.9%
Texas	16,987	1,529	3,970	3,443	107	420
			100.0%	86.7%	2.7%	10.6%
California	29,760	6,458	8,619	6,119	1,906	594
			100.0%	71.0%	22.1%	6.9%
Total: above	96,835	14,466	21,501	14,208	2,880	4,413
			100.0%	66.1%	13.4%	20.5%
Total: U.S.	248,710	19,897	31,845	17,345	4,472	10,028
			100.0%	54.5%	14.0%	31.5%

Source: U.S. Bureau of the Census (1993a).

New York and Illinois, New Jersey also contains significant concentrations of immigrants from each of the three major language groupings—Spanish, Asian and Pacific Island (API), and "Other" (a category that includes mostly European languages)—and so allows for easy comparisons of the characteristics of these communities and immigrants across these groupings.

Our results show that in New Jersey, immigrants, particularly recent immigrants, migrants from Puerto Rico, and people who are not fluent in English, are likely to live in large non-English-language communities. The results of our analysis thus suggest that many non-English communities form because of in-migration and that they begin to dissipate as the flow of new arrivals slows and as non-English speakers shift to the use of English. The results of further analysis suggest that the socioeconomic disadvantages of non-English-language communities are most apparent in neighborhoods containing large numbers of Spanish speakers. We conclude with a discussion of how these findings may apply to immigrants and to non-English-language communities in the other major immigrant states in the United States.

ASSIMILATION OF IMMIGRANTS AND LANGUAGE COMMUNITIES

The classic model of immigrant assimilation, formulated from observation of the large cohorts of mostly European immigrants arriving around the turn of the century, focuses on the adaptation and incorporation of individual immigrants and their children into the larger American society and its social institutions. Because minority languages are such a strong symbol of cultural uniqueness and because proficiency in English has been a requirement for full participation in American society and its social institutions, the classic model of assimilation views the shift from minority languages to English as necessary, rapid, and ubiquitous. However, unlike earlier European immigrants, the new immigrants that have arrived since the late 1960s and that are slated to continue to arrive in large numbers in the foreseeable future come from a limited number of countries and are highly geographically concentrated in a handful of states. In 1990, for example, 73 percent of all immigrants and 68 percent of all minority-language speakers in the United States lived in only six states: New York, New Jersey, Illinois, Florida, Texas, and California (see table

14.1), and each of these states now contains large foreign-language and cultural communities (Frey 1995).

The nature of the new immigration has led researchers to question the applicability of the classic assimilation model. Portes and Zhou (1993) have argued, for example, that there are at least three different paths to assimilation: acculturation and parallel integration into the white middle class; permanent poverty and assimilation into the underclass; and rapid economic advancement associated with the deliberate preservation of the immigrant community's values and solidarity. Portes and Zhou have emphasized the importance of the resources associated with membership in a co-ethnic community for immigrants' economic success. Massey (1995) has also stressed the diversity of outcomes by noting the increasing fragmentation within ethnic groups along the lines of generation, class, ancestry, and identity.

We focus here on the possible roles of minority-language communities in the linguistic, social, and economic adaptation of immigrants. Minority languages are one of the strongest indicators of ethnic and cultural ancestry (Fishman 1985), and the use of a minority language is a prominent signal of agreement with an immigrant community's traditional values. Communities defined through the use of a minority language are thus likely to be more culturally cohesive and distinctive than those defined by ethnic descent alone and are consequently a likely source of the cultural attributes and resources that aid economic advancement. The presence of non-English-language communities can also provide a haven for immigrants who wish to use a minority language for reasons of cultural identification and continuity, and can ease daily life for the many non-English-language speakers who are not fluent in English. The spatial concentration of non-English-language speakers may support the survival of non-English languages in an English-dominated society by providing numerous opportunities for the use of minority languages in social settings outside the household (e.g., Portes and Stepick 1993). Non-English-language communities thus help maintain minority languages (Angle 1981; Garrett and Stevens 1996; Stevens 1992), and, by extension, help maintain cultural distinctiveness.

On the other hand, non-English-language communities may foster continued reliance on the non-English language and so undercut the immediate need for the acquisition of English-language skills among the immigrants who live within them. Non-English-language communities may thus trap some immigrants in a milieu linked to poverty and the underclass by supporting minority-language usage and, by inference, discouraging the acquisition of fluency in English. Furthermore, because poor English skills are associated with poor job prospects and earnings (Borjas and Tienda 1994), the geographic clustering of non-English speakers can concentrate the effects of inequality in areas that are less equipped to deal with the special needs of poorer or marginal populations (Massey et al. 1991). Language communities may thus be either a boon or a tax on the social and economic mobility of immigrants, and the outcome that predominates may vary according to the ethnolinguistic group.

Non-English-Language Communities

This analysis considers a non-English-language community to have two defining features: size and a geographic location. We consider "geographic location" to be determined by residence in a geographically defined neighborhood. We consider "size" to be determined by the number of non-English-language speakers living within the neighborhood. We therefore assume that a non-English-language community consists of a large number of non-English speakers living in a geographically defined neighborhood. These two features produce a potential for social interaction and communication in a non-English language in various social institutions located in the neighborhood.

Massey (1985) has argued that the geographic concentration of immigrants in ethnic communities is fed by immigrants' social networks and initial residential preferences, whereas spatial dispersion or assimilation is driven by processes of acculturation and socioeconomic mobility. Like ethnic communities, language communities form and change as a result of two opposing spatial forces: concentration and dispersion. The concentration of minority-language speakers into specific neighborhoods is strongly affected by the history and scale of migration, since the use of non-English languages in the United States is much more common among immigrants than among native-born Americans. The formation of non-English-language communities is also determined by the neighborhood destinations selected by migrants. The dispersion of non-English-language communities, on the other hand, occurs through out-migration and language shift. Non-English-language communities can disappear if the non-English speakers move elsewhere; they may also disappear if their residents shift to the use of English.

The processes that create and dissolve non-English-language communities are dynamic. Our analysis relies on cross-sectional data that cannot directly measure the dynamics of these processes. However, our theoretical framework about how these processes lead to the formation and disappearance of non-English-language communities leads to specific predictions about what these communities will look like at a given point in time. The following paragraphs outline these hypotheses and discuss the rationales underlying them.

Hypothesis One: Most non-English-language speakers live in neighborhoods containing large non-English-language communities.

There are several reasons for expecting most non-English-language speakers, both native born and foreign born, to live in non-English-language communities, including the effects of community context on the languages used by community residents and processes of residential choice. First, people who are fluent in a non-English language may not have the opportunity to use that language with others if they live in a neighborhood context that contains only English speakers. Those who live in a non-English-language community, on the other hand, have the opportunity to use a minority language in contexts outside of the home (Garrett and Stevens 1996). Second, people who are fluent in a non-English language may be more likely to know of non-English-language communities, and may choose to live in one in order to use the language, to live near family members who are also likely to be fluent in a non-English language, or to live in an ethnic community. We expect the processes of residential choice to be particularly pertinent for non-English-language speakers who are foreign born. Immigrants' knowledge of residential alternatives may be limited by English-language skills, and their choices may be more influenced by family and social networks.

Hypothesis Two: Most migrants live in non-English-language communities. This relationship is particularly strong for recent immigrants and recent arrivals from Puerto Rico.

Unfortunately, data constraints mean that we are unable to determine whether immigrants speak a non-English language or speak only English. However, we expect non-English-language communities to contain large numbers of immigrants because the use of non-English languages is much more common among immigrants than among the native born (U.S. Bureau of the Census 1993b). Furthermore, new migrants do not spread themselves evenly across neighborhoods. Many immigrants select or are channeled to first destinations on the basis of knowledge or advice from family members and friends. Thus, ethnolinguistic communities often form because of social and family networks among migrants (Boyd 1989). Once institutionalized, these communities may become magnets for migrants not tapped into such networks.

Secondary migration—geographic mobility after arrival in the United States—is, however, pervasive (Neumann and Tienda 1994). Migrants who are initially attracted to a large non-English community may move away from the community and/or shift to the use of English as they adjust to life in the United States. Thus, the larger non-English-language communities are likely to contain higher proportions of recent migrants who have not yet had the opportunity or inclination to seek alternative places to live.

Hypothesis Three: Non-English-language speakers who are not fluent in English are particularly likely to be concentrated in non-English-language communities.

In 1990, over two-thirds of the most recent immigrants (who entered the United States between 1987 and 1990) reported not speaking English "very well" (U.S. Bureau of the Census 1993b). Large non-English-language communities may be particularly attractive for migrants lacking English skills, for several reasons. First, such communities promise an opportunity to acclimate to the United States in a local context that downplays difficulties with the English language. Furthermore, social networks transmit information via a language. If migrants lack facility in English before arrival, any prior information about the United States and appropriate destinations must originate from or be transmitted via a non-English-language speaker, someone who is likely to know about extant non-English-language communities. Analyses based on U.S. 1980 Census data confirm this supposition: migrants lacking English-language skills are more likely to locate in a non-English-language community than those who are fluent in English (Jasso and Rosenzweig 1990).

Secondary migration may also act to concentrate minority-language speakers who are not proficient in English. Geographic mobility is often a result of socioeconomic mobility because individuals may invest added economic resources in residential amenities such as better housing in suburbs, better schooling, and freedom from crime (e.g., Alba et al. 1994). It can also be difficult for people who are not fluent in English to learn about residential alternatives. For example, as mentioned earlier in this volume, Mei Cheng, an immigrant who traveled halfway across the world to live and work in New York City, stated: "I know that a woman like myself, . . . not speaking English, cannot go beyond Chinatown" (Zhou 1992: 158). Kritz and Nogle's (1994) larger-scale study suggests that migrants who are proficient in English are more mobile than those lacking proficiency in English (although it is unclear whether the migrants moved to another non-English-language community or to an English-language community). In general, non-English-language communities may be particularly prone to losing residents who are or who become proficient in English, while retaining those with limited English skills.

Hypothesis Four: Neighborhoods containing larger non-English-language communities are socioeconomically disadvantaged compared to neighborhoods containing smaller non-English-language communities.

Neighborhoods containing larger non-English-language communities are probably disadvantaged relative to other neighborhoods because of the nativity and language characteristics of their residents, language shift, the effects of context on residents' economic attainments, and processes of selective geographic mobility and community succession.

Many residents in large non-English-language communities may be immigrants still suffering the socioeconomic and economic upheavals associated with adjustment to a new society. Non-English-language communities can contain sizable cores of residents who are not proficient in English—and individuals with low levels of English proficiency are apt to have low socioeconomic and economic attainments. Because processes of language shift are tied to socioeconomic and economic mobility (e.g., Stolzenberg 1990), neighborhoods containing shrinking non-English-language communities may be more affluent than those containing larger communities.

Although evidence here is more mixed, residence within a non-English-language community may be costly with respect to various social outcomes, such as earnings. Jasso and Rosenzweig (1990) have shown, for example, that Hispanic residents living in Spanish-language communities receive lower wages, net of their own English proficiency, than those living in areas with fewer Spanish-speaking residents. Living in a non-English-language community may thus have costs even for fluent English speakers.

Geographic mobility may drain communities of their economically more successful residents. Non-English speakers moving out of language communities may also be shifting to the use of English, so that their new neighborhoods do not experience the in-migration of economically successful non-English-language speakers. Poorer areas may also become primary destinations for new non-English-speaking arrivals, particularly as occurred in periods such as the 1980s that were characterized by heavy immigration. Existing language communities may be unable to absorb all the new arrivals, who may therefore "spill over" into neighboring areas or into new areas linked through transportation networks to those already established. Because many new migrants lack the resources to move to wealthy areas, the poorer areas may be the only feasible locations for the development of new language communities.

On the other hand, some minority-language communities may be more successful than others. Smith (1995) has pointed out that many of New York's neighborhoods have been transformed and economically revitalized by the heavy influx of Asian immigration since the late 1960s; in addition, Portes and Zhou (1993) have shown that the deliberate preservation of an immigrant community's values and solidarity is related to economic success for some groups.

Hypothesis Five: The demographic and socioeconomic characteristics of non-English-language communities and their neighborhoods vary according to the specific languages spoken.

In much of our analysis, data constraints force us to classify non-English-language speakers by whether they speak Spanish; an Asian or Pacific Island language such as Chinese, Japanese, or Tagalog; or some other language such as Arabic or a European language. Speakers of the Spanish language, an API language, or some other language differ in the probability that they are native born versus foreign born. Proportionately more speakers of European languages are native born because the major European immigration streams peaked around the turn of the century. In contrast, relatively more of the Spanish and API language speakers are foreign born or migrants from Puerto Rico. The timing of migration and levels of proficiency in English prior to arrival in the United States also differ between foreign-born Spanish, API, and other language speakers. Because English is an official language in some Asian countries (e.g., India), immigrants from Asian countries are more likely to know English when they arrive in the United States than are migrants from Spanish-speaking countries (Stevens 1994).

We therefore expect that the concentration of recent migrants and of non-fluent English speakers in language communities will vary by major language grouping. For example, we expect API language and Spanish speakers to be more concentrated in larger non-English-language communities than speakers of other minority languages, because API and Spanish speakers are more likely to be foreign born and less likely to be fluent in English. We also expect Spanish speakers to be more concentrated in larger non-English-language communities than API language speakers because immigrants from Spanish-speaking countries are less likely to be fluent in English than immigrants from Asian language countries.

In addition, we expect the socioeconomic characteristics of non-English-language communities to differ according to whether the community is composed of speakers of Spanish, API languages, or other minority languages. In the United States, the use of non-English languages is strongly connected to ethnicity and minority status—which in turn are strongly connected to social and economic outcomes and residential characteristics (e.g., Massey and Denton 1993). A large percentage of the Puerto Rican Spanish-speaking population in New Jersey is black, whereas most speakers of European languages are white. Furthermore, analyses of residential segregation show that Asians are more highly segregated from blacks than are Hispanics (Massey and Denton 1992). We therefore expect that processes of ethnic and racial discrimination will have a two-pronged impact on the socioeconomic characteristics of non-English-language communities. First, individuals who speak Spanish or an API language may face added impediments in economic and socioeconomic achievements because the use of Spanish or an Asian language is such a strong marker of race and ethnicity. Second, processes of discrimination and prejudice may restrict the residential choices of Spanish speakers and so channel them into poorer communities (cf. Massey and Denton 1987).

DATA

In 1990, the U.S. Census asked a sample of the population about whether respondents spoke a non-English language at home. If the answer was "yes," then the respondent was asked the name of the non-English language. Respondents who reported speaking a non-English language were also asked whether they spoke English "very well," "well," "not well," or "not at all."

But do the non-English-language speakers live in non-English-language communities? The census question concerned the usage of a non-English language *at home*. Respondents could therefore be using a non-English language with household members rather than with other members of a non-English-language community. Because individual-level data from the U.S. Census contain very limited information on respondents' residential or community characteristics, our analysis relies heavily on the U.S. Census Summary Tape Files (STF3), which contain detailed geographically based information, to describe the linguistic, demographic, and socioeconomic characteristics of neighborhoods and their residents.

The aggregate-level data files from the U.S. Census contain geographically based information at varying levels of discrimination, such as counties, places, tracts, and blocks. We decided to use tracts as our main geographic unit. Census tracts, or as White (1987) referred to them, "statistical neighborhoods," are relatively constant in size, with an average population of 4,000, and are thus small enough to provide the potential for social interaction between tract residents. Most important, tract boundaries were originally constructed to include as homogeneous a population as possible. Our analysis therefore used the census tract to operationalize the concept of a neighborhood, and so uses the terms *tract* and *neighborhood* interchangeably.

The STF3 files yield aggregate information about the residents of each tract, such as the total number of non-English speakers and the number of immigrants; or distributional information such as the median income of the tract population. The major cost of using the STF3 files is the inability to further cross-classify the information. It is, for example, impossible to tabulate the number of non-English-language speakers who are immigrants. A minor cost is the fact that the STF3 files aggregated the two lowest response categories on the item on English-language proficiency. This analysis therefore classifies respondents as not proficient in English if they reported that they speak English "not well" or "not at all."

In New Jersey, there were 1,840 census tracts in 1990 containing 100 or more people.[1] Most contained between 2,000 and 8,000 people, with an average of about 4,000. We focused on three major language groupings: Spanish, Asian and Pacific Island languages, and "other" languages because the STF3 files contain information on proficiency in English for only these three major groupings.

NON-ENGLISH-LANGUAGE COMMUNITIES IN NEW JERSEY

In 1990, almost 20 percent of New Jersey's population over the age of five years—close to 1.5 million people—reported speaking a non-English language at home. Figure 14.1 shows the numbers of non-

Figure 14.1 NUMBERS OF NON-ENGLISH-LANGUAGE SPEAKERS AND
OF IMMIGRANTS IN NEW JERSEY BY COUNTY: 1990

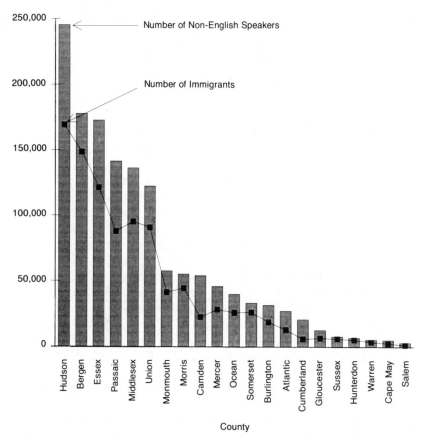

Source: U.S. Bureau of the Census (1992).

English speakers arrayed by county. In Hudson County alone, almost
a quarter of a million people—44 percent of the county's population—
reported speaking a non-English language. Five additional counties
in northeastern New Jersey—Bergen, Essex, Passaic, Middlesex, and
Union—each contained well over 100,000 non-English-language
speakers. In tiny Cape May, on the other hand, only about 5,500 people, or about 6 percent of the county's population, reported speaking
a non-English language (U.S. Bureau of the Census 1992). Figure 14.1
also overlays the numbers of immigrants in each county to show the

close relationship between the numbers of non-English speakers and the numbers of immigrants in each county.

Table 14.2 shows the numbers of non-English language speakers over five years of age classified by the language that they speak. Of the 1.4 million non-English speakers living in New Jersey in 1990, over 620,000 speak Spanish, about 150,000 speak an Asian and Pacific Island language, and about 630,000 speak some "other" language (most of which are European languages). Many of the specific non-English languages are spoken by large numbers of people. Besides Spanish, which is by far the most common non-English language used by New Jersey residents, Chinese, Korean, Tagalog, French, German, Italian, Portuguese, and Polish are each spoken by more than 30,000 New Jersey residents.

The speakers of the various non-English languages are not, however, spread proportionately across the state. Many of them are concentrated in a handful of counties. Bergen County, for example, contains the largest numbers of speakers of six different languages: Japanese, Korean, German, Greek, Italian, and Polish. One-quarter of all Spanish speakers in New Jersey live in Hudson County, and one-quarter of all

Table 14.2 NUMBERS OF NON-ENGLISH-LANGUAGE SPEAKERS AND COUNTIES
WITH LARGEST COMMUNITIES OF SPEAKERS IN NEW JERSEY: 1990

Non-English Language	Number of Speakers Over Age of 5	County Containing Largest Number of Speakers (number in parentheses)
Spanish or Spanish Creole	621,416	Hudson (164,064)
Asian and Pacific Island Languages	153,671	Bergen (38,512)
Chinese	47,334	Middlesex (9,187)
Japanese	14,272	Bergen (9,025)
Korean	30,712	Bergen (13,491)
Tagalog	38,107	Hudson (10,690)
Vietnamese	4,892	Middlesex (820)
Unspecified API language	18,354	Bergen (4,002)
Other	631,061	Bergen (97,002)
Arabic	24,384	Hudson (5,372)
French or French Creole	52,351	Essex (13,840)
German	56,877	Bergen (9,335)
Greek	28,080	Bergen (7,502)
Italian	154,160	Bergen (27,158)
Portuguese or Portuguese Creole	55,285	Essex (22,696)
Polish	69,145	Bergen (10,963)
Unspecified Other	190,779	Middlesex (32,182)
Total	1,406,148	Hudson (245,367)

Source: U.S. Bureau of the Census (1993a).

Asian-language speakers live in Bergen County. Essex County contains the largest county-specific numbers of French and Portuguese speakers.

Figures 14.2, 14.3, and 14.4 show the distribution of Spanish-language speakers, speakers of an Asian or Pacific Island language, and speakers of some "other" language across census tracts in New Jersey. The maps are scaled similarly, with darker shades showing greater numbers of speakers in the neighborhood. Keeping in mind that the census tracts contain roughly the same numbers of residents (about 4,000 each), the maps show that people who speak Spanish, an API language, or some other language tend to live in specific neighborhoods. Many Spanish speakers, for example, live in neighborhoods in northeastern New Jersey in Hudson, Passaic, and Union counties (figure 14.2)—although the high population density of these counties and of the neighborhoods within them means that the individual tracts are small in area and thus difficult to distinguish. Asian-language speakers tend to be concentrated in neighborhoods in Bergen and Camden counties (see figure 14.3). Speakers of "other" minority languages, which are mostly European languages, tend to be more spread out. There are numerous neighborhoods in Passaic, Bergen, Union, Camden, and Ocean counties containing 1,000 or more "other" language speakers (figure 14.4).

Table 14.3 classifies each neighborhood according to the absolute size of its embedded non-English-language community. The precise criteria used to categorize the tracts are to some extent arbitrary—although varying the criteria did little to change our main conclusions. We called a neighborhood "English only" if it contained fewer than 100 non-English-language speakers and "non-English" if it contained more. We called a non-English tract "small non-English" if it contained between 100 and 499 non-English speakers, and "large non-English" if it contained between 500 and 999 non-English speakers. Finally, we considered a tract to have a "very large" non-English-language community if it contained 1,000 or more non-English speakers.

Table 14.4 demonstrates that a majority of non-English speakers live in neighborhoods containing "large" or "very large" non-English communities—although the size of the majority varies across the three major language groupings. For example, only about 11 percent of Spanish speakers live in tracts with "small" non-English-language populations as compared to about 15 percent of the API language speakers and 20 percent of "other" language speakers. Around 18 percent of Spanish speakers and one-third of API and "other" lan-

Figure 14.2 NUMBER OF PERSONS SPEAKING SPANISH
AT HOME IN NEW JERSEY, BY CENSUS TRACT: 1990

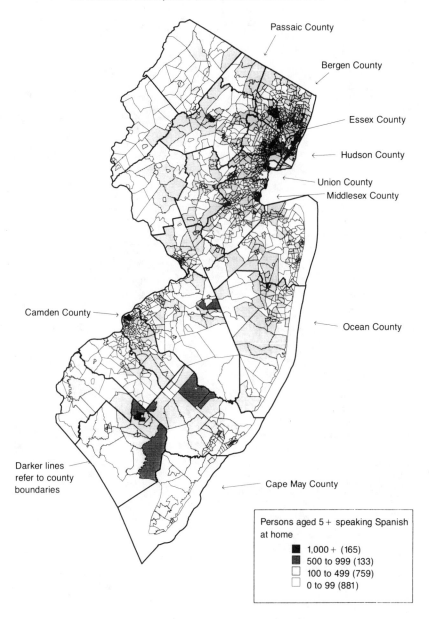

Passaic County

Bergen County

Essex County

Hudson County

Union County
Middlesex County

Camden County

Ocean County

Darker lines
refer to county
boundaries

Cape May County

Persons aged 5 + speaking Spanish
at home

■ 1,000 + (165)
▨ 500 to 999 (133)
☐ 100 to 499 (759)
☐ 0 to 99 (881)

Figure 14.3 NUMBER OF PERSONS SPEAKING ASIAN OR PACIFIC ISLAND
LANGUAGE AT HOME IN NEW JERSEY, BY CENSUS TRACT: 1990

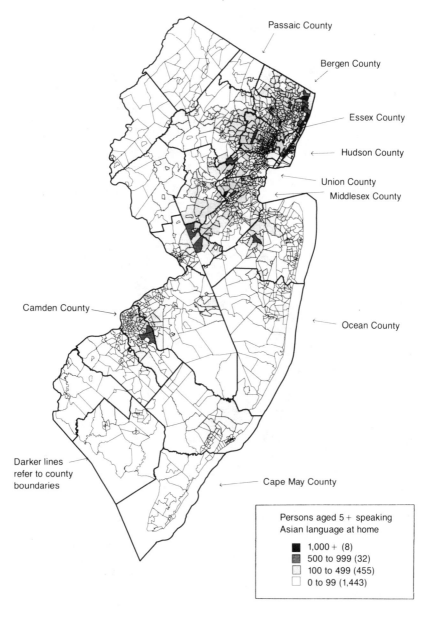

Passaic County

Bergen County

Essex County

Hudson County

Union County
Middlesex County

Camden County

Ocean County

Darker lines
refer to county
boundaries

Cape May County

Persons aged 5 + speaking
Asian language at home

■ 1,000 + (8)
▨ 500 to 999 (32)
▫ 100 to 499 (455)
□ 0 to 99 (1,443)

Figure 14.4 NUMBER OF PERSONS SPEAKING OTHER LANGUAGE
AT HOME IN NEW JERSEY, BY CENSUS TRACT: 1990

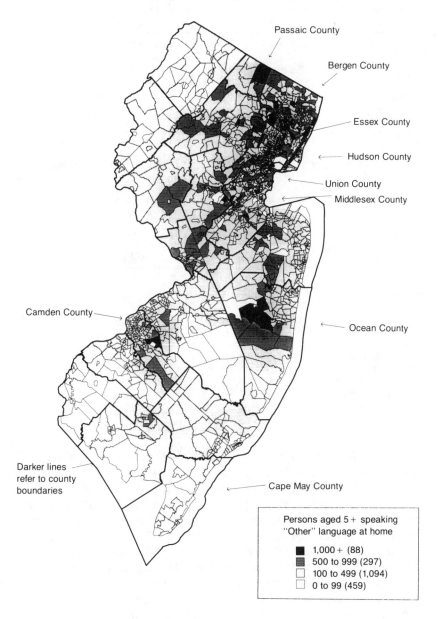

Passaic County

Bergen County

Essex County

Hudson County

Union County

Middlesex County

Camden County

Ocean County

Darker lines
refer to county
boundaries

Cape May County

Persons aged 5 + speaking
"Other" language at home

■ 1,000 + (88)
▨ 500 to 999 (297)
☐ 100 to 499 (1,094)
☐ 0 to 99 (459)

Table 14.3 CLASSIFICATION OF TRACTS BY SIZE OF POTENTIAL
NON-ENGLISH-LANGUAGE COMMUNITY

Size of Non-English-Language Community	Number of Non-English-Language Speakers Living in Tract
English Only	Fewer than 100 non-English-language speakers
Non-English	100 or more non-English-language speakers
Small	Between 100 and 499 non-English-language speakers inclusive
Large	Between 500 and 999 non-English-language speakers inclusive
Very large	1,000 or more non-English-language speakers

Table 14.4 PERCENTAGES OF NON-ENGLISH-LANGUAGE SPEAKERS LIVING IN
EACH TYPE OF TRACT IN NEW JERSEY BY MAJOR LANGUAGE
GROUPING

	Percentage of People Speaking:			
Type of Tract	Any Non-English Language	Spanish	Asian or Pacific Island Language (API)	Other Minority Language
English Only	0.6	0.5	0.3	0.8
Non-English				
Small	15.4	10.9	14.8	20.1
Large	25.6	17.8	34.7	31.0
Very large	58.4	70.9	50.1	48.1
Total Percentage	100.0	100.1	99.9	100.0
Total Number of Speakers	1,405,827	621,324	153,615	630,888

Notes: See table 14.3 for definitions of tract types. The total numbers of speakers are slightly less than the totals presented in table 14.2 because non-English-language speakers living in tracts of 100 or fewer people are omitted. Column percentages do not always add to 100 because of rounding error.

guage speakers are found in neighborhoods containing between 500 and 999 non-English-language speakers. Well over two-thirds (about 71 percent) of Spanish speakers live in neighborhoods with 1,000 or more non-English-language speakers, whereas only about half of API and "other" language speakers live in neighborhoods containing "very large" non-English communities.

Unfortunately, the STF3 files do not provide cross-classifications of language use by nativity. However, figure 14.1 suggests a large fraction of the non-English-language speakers are foreign born.[2] Are immigrants also likely to live in neighborhoods containing non-English-language communities? As we predicted, almost all of the immigrants are found in neighborhoods containing "large" or "very large" non-

English populations (see table 14.5). Processes of geographic mobility and language shift predict, however, that relatively few of the earlier arrivals would live in the "large" non-English-language population tracts in 1990. This is the case, although the major distinction is between immigrants who entered the United States before 1980 and those who entered in 1980 or after. About 18 percent of immigrants entering the country before 1980 live in tracts with "small" non-English-language populations, whereas only about 12 percent of the immigrants entering the country after 1980 live in neighborhoods containing "small" non-English-language tracts. Conversely, almost two-thirds of immigrants entering the country after 1980 live in "very large" non-English-language tracts, whereas only about 52 percent of those entering before 1980 live in neighborhoods containing very large non-English-language tracts.

Table 14.6 shows the percentages of non-English-language speakers who are not fluent in English (i.e., speak English "not well" or "not at all") by major language grouping and by type of tract. As a whole, over one-quarter of Spanish speakers are not fluent in English, whereas only about 18 percent of API language speakers and 13 percent of the "other" language speakers are not fluent in English. The differences between the percentages of Spanish, API, and "other" language speakers who are not fluent in English reflect, in part, the fact that relatively more of those speaking a European language are native born and so are very likely to be fluent in English. In addition, more immigrants from an Asian language country are fluent in English at time of entry into the United States than immigrants from a Spanish language country.

Table 14.5 DISTRIBUTION OF NEW JERSEY IMMIGRANTS ACROSS TYPE OF TRACT AND YEAR OF ENTRY

Type of Tract	Foreign Born and Migrated			In Puerto Rico in 1985
	Before 1980	1980–84	1985–90	
English Only	0.7	0.4	0.4	0.4
Non-English				
Small	18.3	11.5	10.8	12.7
Large	29.3	24.3	23.5	16.6
Very large	51.6	63.8	65.3	70.3
Total Percentage	99.9	100.0	100.0	100.0
Total Number of Migrants	581,874	166,338	218,136	21,624

Table 14.6 PERCENTAGES OF NON-ENGLISH-LANGUAGE SPEAKERS NOT FLUENT IN ENGLISH, BY MAJOR LANGUAGE GROUPING AND TYPE OF TRACT

| Type of Tract | Percentage of Speakers in Major Language Grouping Not Fluent in English | | | |
	Total: All Non-English Languages	Spanish	Asian or Pacific Island Language (API)	Other Non-English Language
English Only	10.8	16.2	14.2	7.5
Non-English				
Small	11.9	16.8	13.5	8.9
Large	14.8	21.1	17.4	10.4
Very large	24.2	30.3	19.1	16.6
Total Percentage Not Fluent	19.8	27.1	17.7	13.1
Total Number of Speakers	1,405,827	621,324	153,615	630,888

Note: "Not fluent in English" refers to non-English-language speakers reporting that they speak English "not at all" or "not well."

Within each major language grouping, the percentage of speakers who are not fluent in English varies by the size of the non-English-language community. In general, neighborhoods containing larger non-English-language communities also contain higher proportions of non-English-language speakers who are not fluent in English. This tendency is particularly marked for Spanish speakers. Whereas only 17 percent of Spanish speakers living in neighborhoods with "small" non-English-language communities are not fluent in English, over 30 percent of the Spanish speakers living in neighborhoods containing "very large" non-English-language communities are not fluent in English (see table 14.6).

Table 14.7 investigates the socioeconomic characteristics of neighborhoods in New Jersey using correlations between the nativity and language characteristics of the neighborhood populations and three indicators of the affluence and stability of neighborhoods: the percentage of the neighborhood population living below the poverty line, the median income of the area's population, and the percentage of the neighborhood population owning rather than renting their homes. All but five of the correlations are statistically significant.

The first panel of table 14.7 shows the correlations between the three socioeconomic indicators and the percentages of the neighborhood population that are foreign born, that migrated before 1980, that migrated during 1980–84, that migrated during 1985–89, and that migrated from Puerto Rico after 1985. Neighborhoods with large proportions of migrants, particularly recent migrants, are clearly

Table 14.7 CORRELATIONS BETWEEN NEIGHBORHOOD-SPECIFIC DEMOGRAPHIC
AND SOCIOECONOMIC CHARACTERISTICS

Characteristic of Neighborhood Population	Percentage Living in Poverty	Median Income	Percentage Owning Homes
Percentage Foreign Born	.165	−.154	−.441
Percentage migrating before 1980	.016ˆ	−.029ˆ	−.270
Percentage migrating 1980–84	.285	−.259	−.527
Percentage migrating 1985–89	.259	−.224	−.508
Percentage in Puerto Rico in 1985	.413	−.301	−.347
Percentage Non-English Speakers	.383	−.320	−.547
Percentage API	−.121	.219	−.019ˆ
Percentage Other	−.080	−.019ˆ	−.167
Percentage Spanish	.513	−.412	−.568
Percentage Speakers Not Fluent in English	.411	−.358	−.532
Percentage API—not fluent	−.067	.105	−.051
Percentage Other—not fluent	.078	−.152	−.245
Percentage Spanish—not fluent	.458	−.370	−.513
Size of Language Community (N of tracts in parentheses)			
Very large versus all others (N = 1,840)	.206	−.187	−.337
Large versus all smaller (N = 1,403)	−.072	.101	−.049ˆ
Small versus English only (N = 897)	−.098	.181	.109

Note: See text for description of nested dichotomous variables contrasting neighborhoods by size of non-English-language community.
ˆp > .05

disadvantaged relative to communities with smaller proportions of migrants. Table 14.7 shows that levels of poverty are strongly and consistently positively correlated, median incomes are negatively correlated, and the percentages of the population living in owned versus rented housing are negatively correlated, with the percentages of neighborhood residents who are recent immigrants or recent migrants from Puerto Rico.

Our hypothesis that neighborhoods containing larger non-English-language communities will be poorer than other neighborhoods, however, is true only for those containing large Spanish-language communities. The second panel in table 14.7 shows the correlations between the socioeconomic outcomes and the percentages of the neighborhood populations who speak an API language, an "other" language, or the Spanish language, respectively. The neighborhood-specific percentage of Spanish speakers is always related to negative outcomes on the socioeconomic variables, whereas the neighborhood percentages of API or "other" speakers are either positively related or not related to positive socioeconomic outcomes. Thus, it appears that the relationships between the higher percentages of migrants and negative socioeconomic outcomes noted in the first panel of table 14.7 are a product of the fact that such a large proportion of immigrants and of recent Puerto Rican migrants are Spanish speakers.

The third panel in table 14.7 shows the correlation between lack of fluency in English and the three socioeconomic indicators. Overall, the higher the overall proportion of the tract population that is not fluent in English, the higher the level of poverty, the lower the median income, and the lower the percentage of the population living in owned versus rented housing. Again, however, there is marked variation across major language groups. The associations between the percentages of the population that are not fluent in English and negative outcomes on socioeconomic variables are particularly apparent for Spanish speakers. The correlations are weaker, and sometimes the signs even reversed, for API and "other" speakers.

This variation across major language groups, which suggests that Spanish speakers tend to live in tracts with lower socioeconomic attributes than do other non-English-language speakers, could be attributable to the fact that speakers of Spanish, an API language, and some "other" minority language tend to live in different types of non-English-language communities. Spanish speakers, for example, are more likely to be found in neighborhoods with very large non-English communities (see table 14.4).

The bottom panel of table 14.7 shows the zero-order relationships between the socioeconomic indicators and three nested dichotomous variables contrasting the four types of neighborhoods. The first dichotomous variable contrasts neighborhoods containing "very large" non-English-language communities (i.e., those containing 1,000 or more non-English-language speakers) and neighborhoods containing fewer than 1,000 non-English-language speakers. The second dichotomous variable contrasts neighborhoods containing a "large" non-English-language community (i.e., those containing between 500 and 999 non-English-language speakers) and all neighborhoods containing fewer than 500 non-English-language speakers. The third dichotomous variable contrasts neighborhoods containing between 100 and 499 speakers and those containing fewer than 100 non-English-language speakers.

The correlations between the three socioeconomic indicators and the three nested dichotomous variables show that the relationships between the size of the non-English-language community and the three socioeconomic indicators concern only the distinction between neighborhoods containing "very large" non-English-language communities (i.e., over 1,000 non-English-language speakers) and all others. The correlations showing the relationships between the three socioeconomic indicators and whether the neighborhood contains a "large" versus a smaller non-English-language community, or whether the neighborhood contains a "small" non-English-language community versus being English only, are either insignificant or in the opposite direction than predicted (see table 14.7).

On the whole, the zero-order correlations in table 14.7 suggest that neighborhoods containing Spanish-language communities are significantly disadvantaged in terms of poverty levels, median income, and levels of home ownership. This finding reflects in part the fact that Spanish speakers are more likely to be immigrants than speakers of other non-English languages, and are more likely to have limited English skills. It may also reflect the fact that Spanish speakers are more likely to live in neighborhoods containing very large non-English-language communities than speakers of other minority languages.

It is important to recognize, however, that ethnic and racial discrimination may also be responsible for these results. The socioeconomic obstacles faced by black communities have been well documented. Of the three language groups we examine, Spanish speakers, particularly those of Puerto Rican ancestry, are those most likely to be black and to live in neighborhoods with non-Hispanic blacks. Furthermore, in metropolitan New York, black-Hispanic neighborhoods tend to be poorer than all-black neighborhoods (Alba et al. 1995). The disadvantages that we see accruing to neighborhoods containing large Spanish-speaking communities probably reflect a complex interaction between language characteristics, race and ethnicity, and processes of discrimination.

SUMMARY AND CONCLUSION

Data from the 1990 U.S. Census show that about 20 percent of the New Jersey population, over 1.4 million people, speak a non-English language at home. This chapter's description of the linguistic ecology of New Jersey first showed that the majority of non-English-language speakers live in the northeastern counties of Hudson, Bergen, Essex, Passaic, Middlesex, and Union. Because people use languages to communicate with others, we then focused on the extent to which non-

English-language speakers are concentrated in local neighborhoods and are thus able to use minority languages in social and public contexts outside the home. We argued that non-English-language communities form and are maintained through processes of in-migration and residential choice, and are dissolved through secondary migration and language shift. We used tract-level data to show that the majority of non-English-language speakers in New Jersey live in neighborhoods containing large or very large non-English-language communities. Although data constraints did not allow the cross-classification of neighborhood residents' language characteristics by nativity, we demonstrated that immigrants from abroad and recent migrants from Puerto Rico are likely to live in neighborhoods containing large or very large non-English communities and that this tendency was strongest for the more recent arrivals. We also found that the percentage of non-English-language speakers who are not fluent in English climbs as the size of the neighborhood's non-English-language community rises.

Because the use of non-English languages and lack of fluency in English are strongly associated with negative socioeconomic outcomes, we expected that neighborhoods containing large percentages of non-English-language speakers and large percentages of people not fluent in English would be socioeconomically disadvantaged. This appears to be the case—but only when considering Spanish speakers. People who speak an Asian or Pacific Island language or some other minority language do not live disproportionately in disadvantaged neighborhoods.

These results have several implications. The new sustained waves of immigration from Spanish-language and Asian-language countries are transforming the American landscape. Recent research on the assimilation of immigrants suggests that there are several paths of adaptation to the American context (Portes and Zhou 1993); our results suggest that these different paths may traverse minority-language communities in complex ways. First, the strong link between migrant flows and language communities suggests that continuing in-migration may be a necessary condition for the continued vitality of language communities in an English-dominated society. The evidence presented in this analysis implies that communities containing earlier-arriving migrants are in the midst of transforming from non-English to English-only communities. Second, the concentration of non-English-language speakers and of people who are not fluent in English in socioeconomically disadvantaged neighborhoods may impede the social and economic adaptation of some of the nation's newest arrivals. Disadvantaged neighborhoods may lack the resources to provide special services such as English-language training or bilingual school programs. In New Jersey, for example, less-affluent districts have larger proportions of immigrant students with limited proficiency in English and fewer resources to deal with the students' needs for special language programs (see Villegas and Young, chapter 7, this volume).

Third, our results hint at a complex set of relationships between language, race and ethnicity, socioeconomic attainments, and the sorting of populations into neighborhoods. Spanish speakers in New Jersey, for example, are more likely to be black than are speakers of other minority languages. They may therefore suffer more from active discrimination that restricts their residential choices and impedes their social and economic attainments. The fact that speakers of an Asian and Pacific Island language do not live disproportionately in disadvantaged neighborhoods, even if they are not fluent in English, suggests that the Asian-language communities may be providing effective resources for their group members.

Our analysis raises many issues, such as the degree to which these findings in New Jersey are generalizable to other settings, the dynamics underlying how language communities form and change, and the reasons for the relative disadvantages suffered by Spanish-language communities. It is important to keep in mind, for example, that the nature of language communities in other parts of the country may differ from those in New Jersey. In Texas, for example, communities with large proportions of third- and higher-generation Americans may be retaining and using the Spanish language with little need of input from current immigration. The ethnic composition of Spanish-language communities, whether of predominantly Mexican, Cuban, Puerto Rican, or some other Hispanic ancestry, also varies strongly across regions and may be implicated in the social and economic standing of the communities. Puerto Ricans are a dominant Hispanic group in the northeastern states of New Jersey and New York, for example, whereas Mexicans constitute 90 percent of all Hispanics in Texas (U.S. Bureau of the Census 1993a). Similarly, the relative proportions of Spanish, Asian and Pacific Island language, and "other" language speakers vary across the major immigrant states. The relatively large concentration of Asian- or Pacific-Island-language speakers in California relative to New Jersey means that the nature of these language communities in California may differ significantly from those in New Jersey. For example, these communities may be relatively small in New Jersey but quite large in California.

The answers to these and further questions demand more investigation. Our results do suggest, however, that the paths of assimilation followed by immigrants and by their descendants are neither linear nor uniform, and that studies of immigrant assimilation should consider the ways in which minority languages and minority-language communities condition and determine the social and economic contexts in which new immigrants live.

Notes

We thank Dawn Owens and James F. Klein for research assistance, Thomas J. Espenshade and C. Gray Swicegood for helpful comments during the preparation of this manuscript, and the University of Illinois Research Board for research support.

1. Ninety-eight tracts contained fewer than 100 people and of these, 52 tracts contained zero people.

2. Correlations between the language characteristics of tract populations (e.g., percentage speaking a non-English language and percentage not fluent in English) and the percentages of the tract population that are foreign born or lived in Puerto Rico in 1985 are all large and statistically significant.

References

Alba, Richard D., John R. Logan, and Paul E. Bellair. 1994. "Living with Crime: The Implications of Racial/Ethnic Differences in Suburban Location." *Social Forces* 73: 395–434.

Alba, Richard D., Nancy Denton, Shu-yin Leung, and John R. Logan. 1995. "Neighborhood Change under Conditions of Mass Immigration: The New York City Region, 1970–1990." *Social Forces* 29: 625–56.

Angle, John. 1981. "The Ecology of Language Maintenance: Data from Nine U.S. Metropolitan Areas." *Urban Affairs Quarterly* 17: 219–31.

Borjas, George J., and Marta Tienda. 1994. "The Employment and Wages of Legalized Immigrants." *International Migration Review* 27: 260–85.

Boyd, Monica. 1989. "Family and Personal Networks in International Migration: Recent Developments and New Agendas." *International Migration Review* 23: 638–66.

Fishman, Joshua A. 1985. *The Rise and Fall of the Ethnic Revival: Perspectives on Language and Ethnicity*. New York: Mouton.

Frey, William. 1995. "The New Geography of Population Shifts." In *State of the Union. America in the 1990s*. Vol. 2 of *Social Trends*, edited by Reynolds Farley (271–336). New York: Russell Sage Foundation.

Garrett, Nancy, and Gillian Stevens. 1996. "The Effect of Metropolitan Context on the Use of Spanish among Hispanic Americans." Paper presented at the Annual Meetings of the Population Association of America, New Orleans, May.

Jasso, Guillermina, and Mark R. Rosenzweig. 1990. *The New Chosen People: Immigrants to the United States*. New York: Russell Sage Foundation.

Kasinitz, Philip. 1992. *Caribbean New York. Black Immigrants and the Politics of Race*. Ithaca, N.Y.: Cornell University Press.

Kritz, Mary M., and June M. Nogle. 1994. "Nativity Concentration and Internal Migration among the Foreign Born." *Demography* 31: 509–24.

Lieberson, Stanley, and Timothy J. Curry. 1971. "Language Shift in the United States: Some Demographic Clues." *International Migration Review* 5: 125–37.

Massey, Douglas S. 1985. "Ethnic Residential Segregation: A Theoretical Synthesis and Empirical Review." *Sociology and Social Research* 69: 315–60.

————. 1995. "The New Immigration and Ethnicity in the United States." *Population and Development Review* 21: 631–52.

Massey, Douglas S., and Nancy A. Denton. 1987. "Trends in the Residential Segregation of Blacks, Hispanics, and Asians: 1970–1980." *American Sociological Review* 52: 802–25.

————. 1992. "Residential Segregation of Asian Groups in United States Metropolitan Areas." *Sociology and Social Research* 76: 170–77.

————. 1993. *American Apartheid. Segregation and the Making of the Underclass*. Cambridge, Mass.: Harvard University Press.

Massey, Douglas S., Andrew B. Gross, and Mitchell L. Eggers. 1991. "Segregation, the Concentration of Poverty, and the Life Chances of Individuals." *Social Science Research* 20: 397–420.

McKenzie, Roderick D. 1968 [1921]. *On Human Ecology*. Chicago: University of Chicago Press.

Neumann, Kristin, and Marta Tienda. 1994. "The Settlement and Secondary Migration Patterns of Legalized Immigrants: Insights from Administrative Records." In *Immigration and Ethnicity: The Integration of America's Newest Arrivals*, edited by Barry Edmonston and Jeffrey Passel (187–226). Washington, D.C.: Urban Institute Press.

Portes, Alejandro, and Alex Stepick. 1993. *City on the Edge*. Berkeley: University of California Press.

Portes, Alejandro, and Min Zhou. 1993. "The New Second Generation: Segmented Assimilation and Its Variants." *Annals of the American Academy of Political and Social Science* 530: 74–96.

Smith, Christopher J. 1995. "Asian New York: The Geography and Politics of Diversity." *International Migration Review* 29: 59–84.

Stevens, Gillian. 1992. "The Social and Demographic Context of Non-English Language Use in the United States." *American Sociological Review* 57: 171–85.

―――――. 1994. "Immigration, Emigration, Language Acquisition, and the English Language Proficiency of Immigrants in the U.S." In *Immigration and Ethnicity: The Integration of America's Newest Arrivals*, edited by Barry Edmonston and Jeffrey Passel (163–86). Washington, D.C.: Urban Institute Press.

Stolzenberg, Ross M. 1990. "Ethnicity, Geography, and Occupations of U.S. Hispanic Men." *American Sociological Review* 55: 143–54.

U.S. Bureau of the Census. 1992. *1990 Census of Population and Housing. Summary Social, Economic, and Housing Characteristics, New Jersey*. Washington, D.C.: U.S. Government Printing Office.

―――――. 1993a. *Census of Population and Housing, 1990, United States: Summary Tape File 3*. Machine-readable data file. Washington, D.C.: Author (producer); distributed by Inter-university Consortium for Political and Social Research, Ann Arbor, Mich., 1994.

―――――. 1993b. *1990 Census of Population and Housing. Summary Social, Economic, and Housing Characteristics*. Washington, D.C.: Author.

White, Michael J. 1987. *American Neighborhoods and Residential Differentiation*. New York: Russell Sage Foundation.

Zhou, Min. 1992. *Chinatown: The Socioeconomic Potential of an Urban Enclave*. Philadelphia: Temple University Press.

ABOUT THE EDITOR

Thomas J. Espenshade is professor of sociology and a faculty associate of the Office of Population Research at Princeton University. He was formerly senior research associate and director of the Program in Demographic Studies at the Urban Institute. He is the author of *Investing in Children: New Estimates of Parental Expenditures* (Urban Institute Press, 1984) and coauthor of *The Fourth Wave: California's Newest Immigrants* (Urban Institute Press, 1985). Dr. Espenshade is a member of the Panel on Demographic and Economic Impacts of Immigration, National Research Council, of the Academic Advisory Board for The New Immigrant Survey at the RAND Corporation, and of the Social Science Research Council's Postdoctoral Awards Committee for the Program on International Migration. His research interests include patterns of undocumented migration to the United States, the fiscal impacts of new immigrants, and attitudes toward U.S. immigration. He is presently directing a study on the contributions of immigrants to the science and engineering work force in the United States.

ABOUT THE CONTRIBUTORS

Kristin F. Butcher is an assistant professor of economics at Boston College. She has published papers on the economic effect of immigration on the wages of the native born (with David Card) and on the labor market outcomes of black immigrants to the United States. Her current interests include investigating whether immigration affects crime rates and/or institutionalization rates in the United States (with Anne Piehl) and researching the extent to which the increase in inequality in the United States wage distribution adversely affects immigrants' labor market outcomes (with John DiNardo).

Rebecca L. Clark, a senior research associate at the Population Studies Center of the Urban Institute, is researching illegal aliens in the federal, state, and local criminal justice systems and how welfare reform will affect immigrants. She has done several studies on the costs of immigrants, most notably "The Fiscal Impacts of Undocumented Aliens: Selected Estimates for Seven States" (with Jeffrey S. Passel, Wendy N. Zimmermann, and Michael Fix), a report commissioned by the Office of Management and Budget.

Louis DeSipio is an assistant professor of political science at the University of Illinois at Urbana-Champaign. He is the author of *Counting on the Latino Vote: Latinos as a New Electorate* (Charlottesville, Va.: University Press of Virginia, 1996). His research examines the political incorporation of new immigrant populations in the United States as well as U.S. ethnic politics.

Nancy Garrett is a doctoral student at the University of Illinois at Urbana-Champaign. She is currently writing a dissertation on the effect of social context on language shift and language maintenance among second-generation Latina/o children.

Deborah L. Garvey is Lecturer in the Woodrow Wilson School of Public and International Affairs and a doctoral candidate in the Department of Economics at Princeton University. Her current research focuses on the public finance aspects of school finance, with a particular emphasis on the impact of court mandates on school district expenditures. Her other work on contemporary immigration to New Jersey includes a socioeconomic profile of immigrants to the state in "A Stone's Throw from Ellis Island: Economic Implications of Immigration to New Jersey."

Erin Kelly is a Ph.D. candidate in sociology at Princeton University. Her dissertation examines work/family policies, including family leave, flexible scheduling, and childcare assistance, in American firms. She is interested in gender and social change in states, families, and organizations.

Genevieve M. Kenney is a senior research associate in the Health Policy Center at the Urban Institute, where she has been working for over ten years. She recently completed a comprehensive study on the effects of expanding Medicaid coverage for pregnant women and is now directing the Urban Institute's New Federalism Survey.

Nancy McArdle is a research analyst at the Joint Center for Housing Studies of Harvard University. She is currently researching patterns of population, employment, and construction decentralization. In addition to prior work on the housing characteristics of immigrants, she is a coauthor of the annual "State of the Nation's Housing" report.

Afaf Omer is an assistant professor of sociology at the University of North Carolina at Asheville. Previously she served as a postdoctoral fellow at the Population Studies and Training Center at Brown University. She has also taught at the University of Michigan and at the University of Gezeira, Sudan. Her other research issues include the impact of social change and development on gender systems.

Deanna Pagnini is an assistant professor of sociology and public affairs at Princeton University. Her work focuses on reproductive behavior in the United States. She is currently analyzing the effects of changes in abortion policy on pregnancy outcomes and is also examining how individual and contextual factors affect birth outcomes.

Anne Morrison Piehl is an assistant professor of public policy at Harvard University's John F. Kennedy School of Government. She writes in the fields of criminal justice and labor economics. She has written several papers (with Kristin Butcher) on the relationship between immigration and crime. Piehl is currently researching the connection between labor market outcomes and criminal activity.

Nancy E. Reichman is a research associate at the Office of Population Research at Princeton University and a faculty research fellow in the Health Economics Program of the National Bureau of Economic Research. She is involved in a number of projects analyzing infant health in New Jersey. Her ongoing research includes analyses of the effects of maternal age on birth outcomes, variations in birth outcomes among large cities in New Jersey, and the effects of prenatal WIC participation on hospital costs.

Gillian Stevens is an associate professor at the University of Toronto and University of Illinois at Urbana-Champaign. She is currently investigating the impact of context on second-language acquisition among immigrants in Canada and the United States and has written several articles on patterns of language use and language acquisition among first- and second-generation Americans.

Ana María Villegas is a professor in the College of Education at Montclair State University, where she teaches courses in culturally relevant pedagogy. Dr. Villegas specializes in issues related to the education of linguistically and culturally different students. Her publications include articles on teaching and learning in a multicultural society and a widely disseminated handbook that offers strategies for helping immigrant students to succeed in U.S. schools.

Bruce Western is an assistant professor in the Sociology Department at Princeton University. He previously studied the development of labor unions in Western Europe and North America. He is now examining the impact of unions on labor markets under the current conditions of economic globalization and structural change.

Michael J. White is a professor of sociology at Brown University, where he is also a faculty associate of the Population Studies and Training Center. During 1995–96 he was a visiting scholar at the

Urban Institute, in Washington, D.C., where he conducted research on patterns of immigration in the labor market and in schools. He has written articles on immigrant-native differentials in school dropout rates; the effect of immigration policy on the flow of undocumented migration to the United States; and numerous publications on the subject of residential patterns of American ethnic groups.

John W. Young is an associate professor of educational statistics and measurement in the Graduate School of Education at Rutgers University. A psychometrician by training, his principal line of research is on the validity of college admissions tests. Prior to his appointment at Rutgers, he was a researcher at the Educational Testing Service.

Wendy N. Zimmermann is a research associate at the Urban Institute. She has conducted extensive research on U.S. immigration and immigrant policy and is currently examining the impact of recent welfare reform legislation on immigrants. Her recent publications include "Immigrant Families and Public Policy: A Deepening Divide" (with Michael Fix) in *International Migration and Family Change*, edited by Alan Bloom, and "The Fiscal Impacts of Undocumented Aliens: Selected Estimates for Seven States" (with Rebecca Clark, Jeffrey Passel, and Michael Fix).